Vermeer

ANDREW GRAHAM-DIXON

Vermeer
A Life Lost and Found

W. W. Norton & Company
Independent Publishers Since 1923

Copyright © 2025 by Andrew Graham-Dixon

First published in Great Britain in 2025 by Allen Lane,
an imprint of the Penguin Random House group of companies

All rights reserved
Printed in the United States of America
First American Edition

For information about permission to reproduce selections from this book, write to
Permissions, W. W. Norton & Company, Inc., 500 Fifth Avenue, New York, NY 10110

For information about special discounts for bulk purchases,
please contact W. W. Norton Special Sales
at specialsales@wwnorton.com or 800-233-4830

Manufacturing by Versa Press

ISBN 978-1-324-12411-5

W. W. Norton & Company, Inc., 500 Fifth Avenue, New York, NY 10110
www.wwnorton.com

W. W. Norton & Company Ltd., 15 Carlisle Street, London W1D 3BS

Authorized EU representative: EAS, Mustamäe tee 50, 10621 Tallinn, Estonia

1 2 3 4 5 6 7 8 9 0

To my kind and brave father, Anthony. You once said I was an advocate, like you. I hope this book proves you right.

Hatred is increased by being reciprocated,
and can on the other hand be destroyed by love.
Baruch Spinoza, *Ethics*

Contents

List of Illustrations	xi
Maps	xix
Family Trees	xxv
Preface and Acknowledgements	xxxiii
Prologue	1
Part One: The Inheritance, 1560–1632	17
Part Two: Childhood, Education, Marriage, 1632–57	79
Part Three: The Invisible Church, 1657–72	163
Part Four: Disaster, Death, Legacy, 1672–5	293
Appendices	329
Notes	335
Index	361

List of Illustrations

All paintings are by Johannes Vermeer, unless otherwise stated. Images of the works are reproduced by kind permission of the current owners or custodians, unless otherwise noted in italics.

Endpapers

Front: Abraham Goos, *Comitatus Hollandia*, 1630. Hand-coloured engraved map of Holland, published by Claes Jansz Visscher. *Universitätsbibliothek, Bern.*

Rear: Joan Blaeu, *Delfi Batavorum vernacule Delft*, 1649. Hand-coloured engraved plan of the city of Delft. *Geography and Map Division, Library of Congress, Washington, D.C.*

Colour Plates

1. *Diana and her Companions*, c. 1653. Oil on canvas. 98.5 x 105 cm. Mauritshuis, The Hague.
2. *The Procuress*, 1656. Oil on canvas. 143 x 130 cm. Gemäldegalerie Alte Meister, Dresden. *Photo: Bridgeman Images.*
3. *Christ in the House of Martha and Mary*, c. 1654. Oil on canvas. 160 x 142 cm. National Gallery of Scotland, Edinburgh. *Photo: © National Galleries of Scotland / Bridgeman Images*
4. Andrea Vaccaro, *The Death of St Joseph*, c. 1645–50. Oil on canvas. 211.5 cm x 158 cm. Museo di Capodimonte, Naples. *Photo: Scala, Florence, courtesy of the Ministero Beni e Att. Culturali e del Turismo.*

LIST OF ILLUSTRATIONS

5. *St Praxedis*, 1655. Oil on canvas. 101.6 x 82.6 cm. Kufu Company Inc., on long-term loan to the National Museum of Western Art, Tokyo. *Photo: Christie's/Bridgeman Images.*
6. Felice Ficherelli, *St Praxedis*, c. 1645–50. Oil on canvas. 115cm x 90 cm. Private collection. *Photo: Piemags/Alamy.*
7. *Officer with a Laughing Girl*, c. 1658. Oil on canvas. 50.5 x 46 cm. The Frick Collection, New York. Henry Clay Frick Bequest. *Photo: © The Frick Collection*
8. *A Maid Asleep*, c. 1658. Oil on canvas. 87.6 x 76.5 cm. The Metropolitan Museum of Art, New York. Bequest of Benjamin Altman, 1913.
9. Gerard ter Borch, *Self-portrait*, 1668. Oil on canvas, 62.7 x 43.7 cm. Mauritshuis, The Hague.
10. Gerard ter Borch, *Man on Horseback*, c. 1634–5. Oil on panel. 54.9 x 41 cm. Museum of Fine Arts, Boston. Juliana Cheney Edwards Collection. *Photo: © 2025 Museum of Fine Arts, Boston. All rights reserved / Bridgeman Images.*
11. Caspar Luyken, *The Explosion of the Gunpowder Tower in Delft in 1654*, 1698. Etching published by Pieter van der Aa, Leiden. Rijksmuseum, Amsterdam.
12. Egbert van der Poel, *A View of Delft after the Explosion*, 1654. Oil on wood. 36.2 x 49.5 cm. The National Gallery, London. Bequeathed by John Henderson, 1879. *Photo: © The National Gallery, London.*
13. Cornelis Cornelisz van Haarlem, *The Massacre of the Innocents*, 1590. Central panel of a triptych. Oil on canvas, 268 x 257 cm. Frans Halsmuseum, Haarlem. *Photo: © NPL – DeA Picture Library / M. Carrieri / Bridgeman Images.*
14. Gerard ter Borch, *The Ratification of the Treaty of Münster*, 1648. Oil on copper. 45.4 x 58.5 cm. Rijksmuseum, Amsterdam, on loan from the National Gallery, London. Presented by Sir Richard Wallace, 1871. *Photo: Rijksmuseum.*
15. Willem Duyster, *The Marauders*, c. 1635. Musée du Louvre, Paris. Oil on wood. 37 x 50 cm. *Photo: RMN-Grand Palais / Adrien Didierjean / Dist. Foto SCALA, Florence.*
16. *Girl Reading a Letter at an Open Window*, c. 1656–7 (pre-restoration). Oil on canvas. 83 x 64.5 cm. Gemäldegalerie Alte Meister, Dresden. *© Staatliche Kunstsammlungen Dresden / Bridgeman Images.*

LIST OF ILLUSTRATIONS

17. *Girl Reading a Letter at an Open Window*, c. 1656–7 (post-restoration). Oil on canvas. 83 x 64.5 cm. Gemäldegalerie Alte Meister, Dresden. © *Staatliche Kunstsammlungen Dresden / Bridgeman Images.*
18. *Woman in Blue Reading a Letter*, c. 1664. Oil on canvas. 46.5 x 39 cm. Rijksmuseum, Amsterdam.
19. *The Glass of Wine*, c. 1659–60. Oil on canvas. 65 x 77 cm. Staatliche Museen Preußischer Kulturbesitz, Gemäldegalerie, Berlin. *Photo: Scala, Florence / bpk, Bildagentur für Kunst, Kultur und Geschichte, Berlin.*
20. *Young Woman with a Wine Glass*, c. 1659–60. Oil on canvas. 67 x 78 cm. Herzog Anton Ulrich-Museum, Brauschweig. *Photo: Scala, Florence / bpk, Bildagentur für Kunst, Kultur und Geschichte, Berlin*
21. *The Music Lesson*, c. 1661–2. Oil on canvas. 73.3 x 64.5 cm. The Royal Collection Trust. © His Majesty King Charles III, 2025. *Photo: Bridgeman Images*
22. *The Concert*, c. 1661–2. Oil on canvas. 72.5 x 64.7 cm. Isabella Stewart Gardner Museum, Boston, MA. Stolen in 1990. *Photo: Photo © Isabella Stewart Gardner Museum / Bridgeman Images.*
23. Cornelius Boel, *Inconcvssa Fide (Unshakeable Faith)*. Illustration from Otto van Veen, *Amorum Emblemata*, Antwerp, 1608, p. 55.
24. Dirck van Baburen, *The Procuress*, 1622. Oil on canvas. 101.6 x 107.6 cm. Museum of Fine Arts, Boston, MA. M. Theresa B. Hopkins Fund. *Photo:* © 2025 *Museum of Fine Arts, Boston. All rights reserved/Bridgeman Images.*
25. Gerard ter Borch, *An Officer Writing a Letter, with a Trumpeter*, c. 1658. Oil on canvas. 56.8 × 43.8 cm. Philadelphia Museum of Art, Philadelphia, PA. The William L. Elkins Collection, 1924.
26. Gerard Houckgeest, *Interior of the Oude Kerk in Delft*, 1654. Oil on panel. 48.7 x 40.2 cm. Rijksmuseum, Amsterdam.
27. *Young Woman with a Water Pitcher*, c. 1662. Oil on canvas. 45.7 x 40.6 cm. The Metropolitan Museum of Art, New York. Marquand Collection, Gift of Henry G. Marquand, 1889.
28. *The Milkmaid*, c. 1659. Oil on canvas. 45.5 x 41 cm. Rijksmuseum, Amsterdam.
29. *Woman with a Balance*, c. 1659. Oil on canvas. 42.5 x 38 cm. National Gallery of Art, Washington, DC. Widener Collection.

LIST OF ILLUSTRATIONS

30. *A Lady Writing*, c. 1665–7. Oil on canvas. 45 x 39.9 cm. National Gallery of Art, Washington, DC. Gift of Harry Waldron Havemeyer and Horace Havemeyer, Jr., in memory of their father, Horace Havemeyer.
31. *Woman with a Pearl Necklace*, c. 1665–7. Oil on canvas. 55 x 45 cm. Staatliche Museen Preußischer Kulturbesitz, Gemäldegalerie, Berlin. *Photo: Scala, Florence / bpk, Bildagentur für Kunst, Kultur und Geschichte, Berlin.*
32. *Girl with a Pearl Earring*, c. 1667–8. Oil on canvas. 46.5 x 40 cm. Mauritshuis, The Hague.
33. *Study of a Young Woman*, c. 1667–8. Oil on canvas. 44.5 x 40 cm. Metropolitan Museum of Art, New York. Gift of Mr and Mrs Charles Wrightsman, in memory of Theodore Rousseau Jr, 1979.
34. *Girl with a Red Hat*, c. 1668. Oil on panel. 23.2 x 18.1 cm. National Gallery of Art, Washington, DC. Andrew W. Mellon Collection.
35. *The Lacemaker*, c. 1670–71. Oil on canvas (attached to panel). 24.5 x 21 cm. Musée du Louvre, Paris. *Photo: RMN-Grand Palais /Dist. Photo SCALA, Florence*
36. *The Guitar Player*, c. 1670. Oil on canvas. 53 x 46.3 cm. Kenwood House. English Heritage, Trustees of the Iveagh Bequest, London. *Photo: © Historic England/Bridgeman Images.*
37. *A Young Woman Standing at a Virginal*, c. 1670. Oil on canvas. 51.7 x 45.2 cm. The National Gallery, London. *Photo: © The National Gallery, London.*
38. *The Love Letter*, c. 1672–5. Oil on canvas. 44 x 38.5 cm. Rijksmuseum, Amsterdam.
39. *Mistress and Maid*, c. 1668. Oil on canvas. 90.2 x 78.7 cm. Frick Collection, New York. Henry Clay Frick Bequest.
40. *View of Delft*, c. 1665. Oil on canvas. 98.5 x 117.5 cm. Mauritshuis, The Hague.
41. *The Little Street*, c. 1660. Oil on canvas. 54.3 x 44 cm. Rijksmuseum, Amsterdam
42. Modern photograph of the site of the house/hidden church, Delft. *Photo: Edwin Raap/Rijksdienst voor het Cultureel Erfgoed.*
43. Modern photograph of the hidden Remonstrant church, Delft. *Photo: © Andrew Graham-Dixon.*

LIST OF ILLUSTRATIONS

44. *The Little Street* (detail), c. 1660. As above.
45. Godfried Schalcken, *Pieter Teding van Berkhout*, 1674. Oil on copper. 13.3 x 11.1 cm. Private collection. *Photo: RKD/Netherlands Institute for Art History*
46. Godfried Schalcken, *Elisabeth Ruysch*, 1675. Oil on copper. 13.3 x 11.1 cm. Private collection. *Photo: RKD/Netherlands Institute for Art History*
47. Pieter van der Werff, *Adrian Paets*, 1668. Oil on canvas. 82 x 68 cm. Rijksmuseum, Amsterdam.
48. Anon. (Dutch or German school), *Baruch Spinoza*, c. 1675–1750. Oil on canvas. 74.0 × 59.8 cm. Herzog August Bibliothek Wolfenbüttel.
49. *The Astronomer*, 1668. Oil on canvas. 50 x 45 cm. Musée du Louvre, Paris. *Photo: RMN-Grand Palais / Franck Raux/ Dist. Photo SCALA, Florence.*
50. *The Geographer*, 1669. Oil on canvas. 51.6 x 45.4 cm. Städelsches Kunstinstitut, Städel Museum, Frankfurt am Main.
51. *Allegory of the Catholic Faith*, c. 1670–72. Oil on canvas. 114.3 x 88.9 cm. Metropolitan Museum of Art, New York. The Friedsam Collection, Bequest of Michael Friedsam, 1931.
52. *The Art of Painting*, c. 1670–72. Oil on canvas. 120 x 100 cm. Kunsthistorisches Museum, Vienna. *Photo: Bridgeman Images.*
53. *Lady Writing a Letter with Her Maid*, c. 1672–5. Oil on canvas. 72.2 x 59.5 cm. National Gallery of Ireland, Dublin. Presented by Sir Alfred and Lady Beit, 1987. *Photo: Bridgeman Images.*
54. *Woman with a Lute*, c. 1662–5. Oil on canvas. 51.4 x 45.7 cm. Metropolitan Museum, New York. Bequest of Collis P. Huntington, 1900 (25.110.24).
55. *Young Woman Seated at a Virginal*, c. 1675. Oil on canvas. 51.5 × 45.5 cm. The National Gallery, London. Salting Bequest, 1910. © *The National Gallery, London*

Black and White Illustrations

p. 24. Jan Luyken, *The Cruel Massacre of Naarden by the Spanish in 1572*, 1679. Etching. Amsterdam Museum, Amsterdam.
p. 26. Anon., *Executions of Haarlem Residents by the Spanish on the*

LIST OF ILLUSTRATIONS

Grote Markt in front of the Town Hall in Haarlem after the Surrender of the City on 13 July 1573, 1782–4. Etching. Rijksmuseum, Amsterdam.

p. 29. Frans Hogenberg, *The 'Spanish Fury' in Antwerp: Atrocities of the Spanish Soldiers on 5 November 1576*, 1576–8. Etching. Rijksmuseum, Amsterdam.

p. 40. Anon., *Jacobus Arminius*, 1650–74. Engraving. Museum Catharijneconvent, Utrecht.

p. 50. Anon., *The Beheading of Oldenbarnevelt in The Hague on 13 May 1619*, 1619. Engraving. Rijksmuseum, Amsterdam.

p. 65. Anon. (Northern Netherlandish school), after François Schillemans, *The Opening of the National Synod in Dordrecht on 13 November 1618*, 1618–19. Engraving. Rijksmuseum, Amsterdam.

p. 72. Salomon Savery after Casper Casteleyn, *Camphuysen Surrounded by Allegorical Personifications of Faith, Hope and Love*, 1635–65. Engraving. Rijksmuseum, Amsterdam.

p. 89. Gerrit Lamberts, *The Guild of St Luke on the Voldersgracht seen from the Oude Manhuissteeg*, 1820. Drawing. Delft City Archives.

p. 97. Anon. (Northern Netherlandish school), *The Siege of Sas-van-Gent by Frederik Hendrik in 1644*, 1662–4. Etching. Rijksmuseum, Amsterdam.

p. 103. Jacques Callot, *La Pendaison (The Hanging)*, plate 11 from *Les Misères et les Malheurs de la Guerre (The Miseries and Misfortunes of War)*, 1633. Etching; first or second state of three. Metropolitan Museum of Art, New York. Bequest of Edwin De T. Bechtel, 1957.

p. 111. Romeyn de Hooghe, after Johannes de Vouw, *A View of the Statue of Erasmus on the Grotemarkt in Rotterdam*, 1694–5. Etching with engraving. Rijksmuseum, Amsterdam.

p. 115. Detail of a register with the names of Johannes Vermeer, Pieter de Hooch and Carel Fabritius, from *Twee Meesterboeken van het St Lucasgilde te Delft (The Book of Masters of St Luke's Guild)*, 1613–1715. Koninklijke Bibliotheek, Nationale bibliotheek van Nederland, The Hague, KW 75 C 6, part 2, p.3r.

p. 154. Frans van Mieris the Elder, *The Charlatan* (detail), c. 1653–5. Oil on panel. 45 x 36 cm. Galeria della Uffizi, Florence. *Photo:*

LIST OF ILLUSTRATIONS

Scala, Florence – courtesy of the Ministero Beni e Att. Culturali e del Turismo.

p. 175. Egbert van Heemskerck, *L'Assemblée des Couacres (The Quaker Assembly)*, c. 1680. Engraving. Bibliothèque nationale de France, département Estampes et photographie, Paris (RESERVE QB-201 (76)-FOL). *Photo: BnF.*

p. 180. Pierre Tanjé after Louis Fabritius Dubourg, *Lord's Supper in a Collegiant Church in Rijnsburg*, c. 1735. Illustration from J. F. Bernard, *Ceremonies et Coutumes Religieuses de Tous les Peuples du Monde*, Amsterdam, 1736. Rijksmuseum, Amsterdam.

p. 187 Rembrandt (Rembrandt van Rijn), *Cornelis Claesz Anslo*, 1641. Etching; second of five states. Metropolitan Museum of Art, New York. Gift of Felix M. Warburg and his family, 1941 (41.1.51)

p. 196. Balthasar Bernards, after Louis Fabricius Dubourg, *A Baptism at the 'Grote Huis', Rijnsburg*, 1736. Etching with engraving and drypoint. Rijksmuseum, Amsterdam.

p. 244. Abraham Rademaker, *Interior of Remonstrant Church, Delft*, c. 1700. Drawing. Cultural Heritage Agency of the Netherlands.

p. 302. Coenraet Decker, *View of the Muiderslot and the city of Muiden*, 1660–85. Etching. Rijksmuseum, Amsterdam.

p. 305. Anon. (German School) after Romeyn de Hooghe, *The Shameful Execution of the de Witt Brothers*, 1672–99. Etching with engraving. Rijksmuseum, Amsterdam.

p. 308. Romeyn de Hooghe, illustration of French atrocities against Dutch villagers, from Abraham de Wicquefort, *Advis fidelle aux veritables Hollandois*, 1673. Koninklijke Bibliotheek, Nationale bibliotheek van Nederland, The Hague.

p. 329. Act of Ownership for 106 Oude Delft, with Pieter Claesz van Ruijven's signature: Gemeentearchief, Delft, akte 2268, folio 923r1 (waarbrief 01001). The document is undated.

p. 331. Matthijs Pool, *A trekschuit at the Inn and Peacock Garden on the Nieuweramstel*, 1700–1725. Etching. Noord-hollands Archief, Haarlem.

Maps

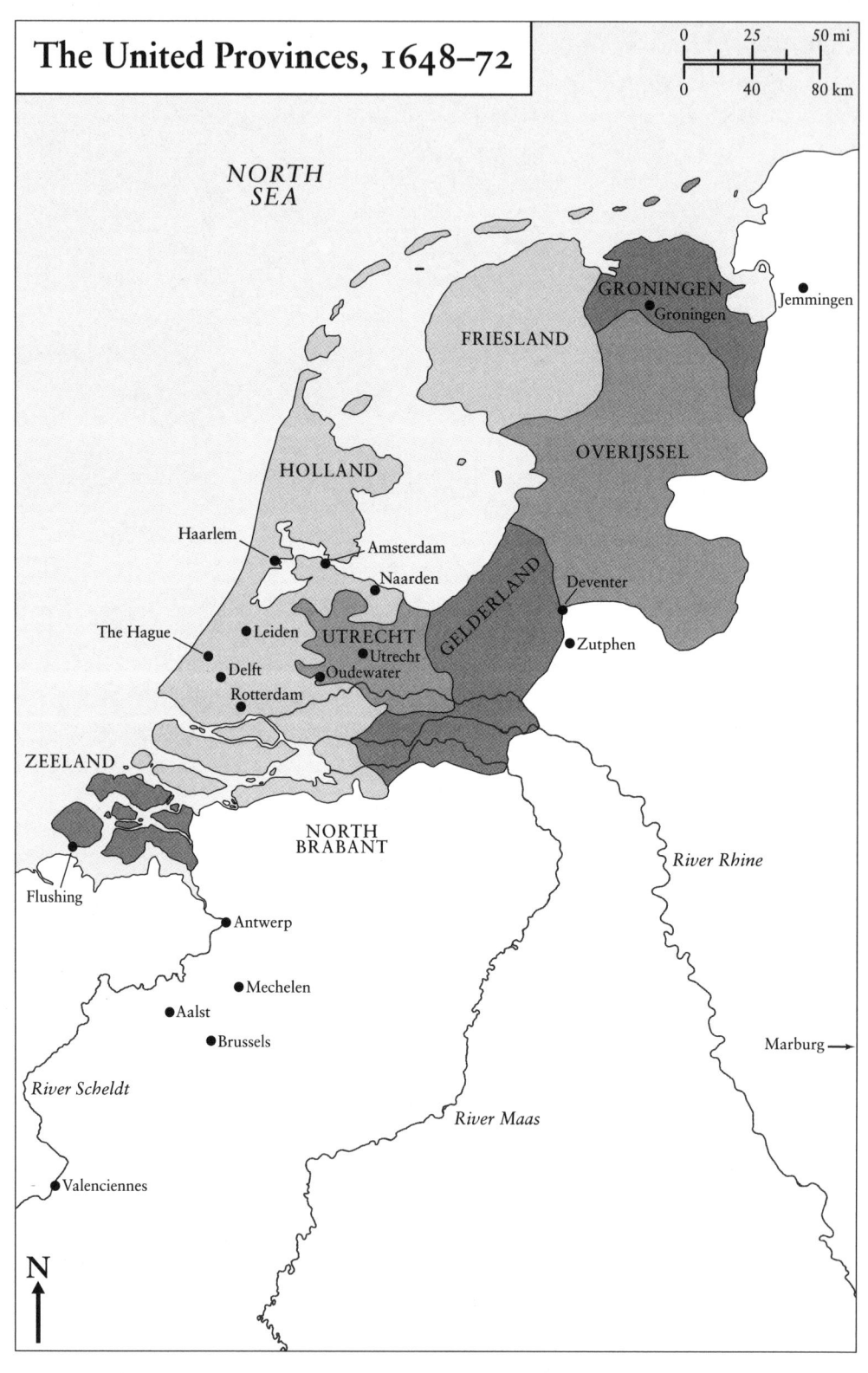

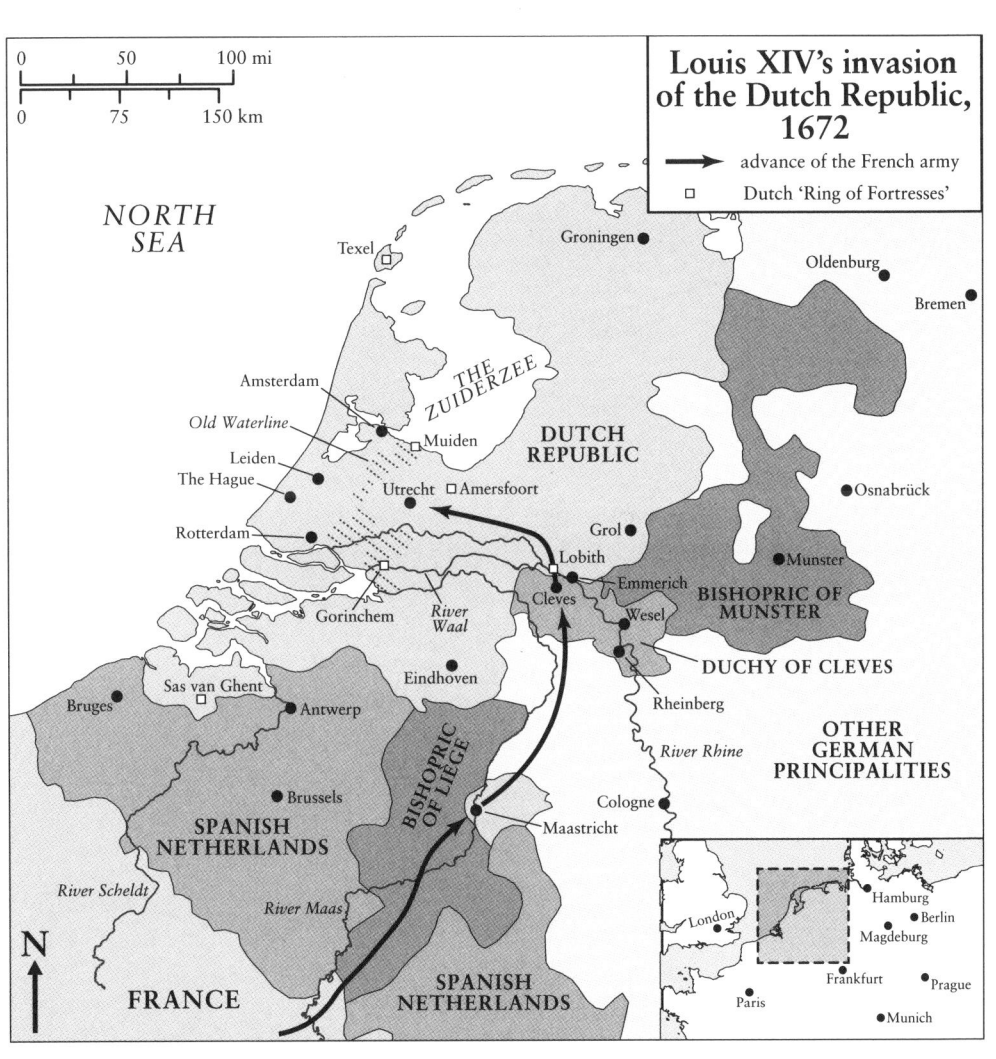

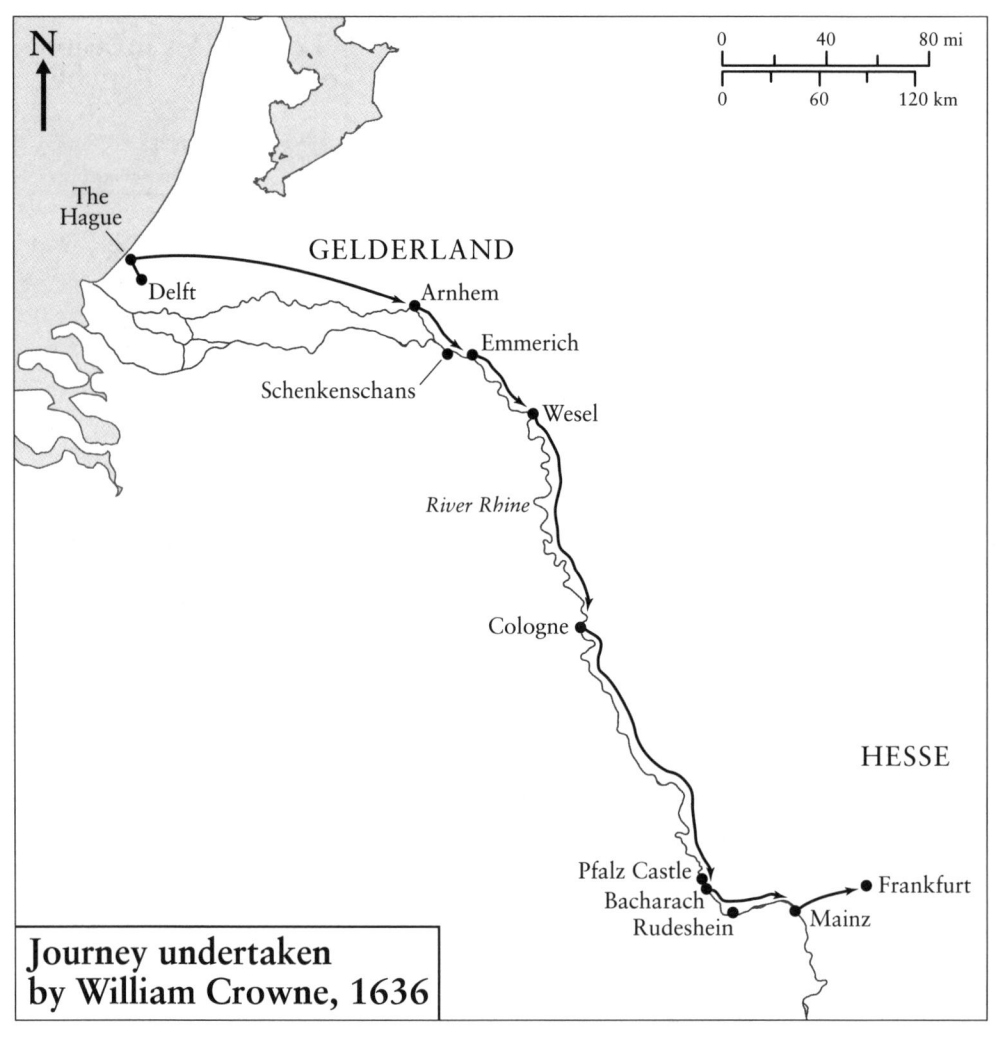

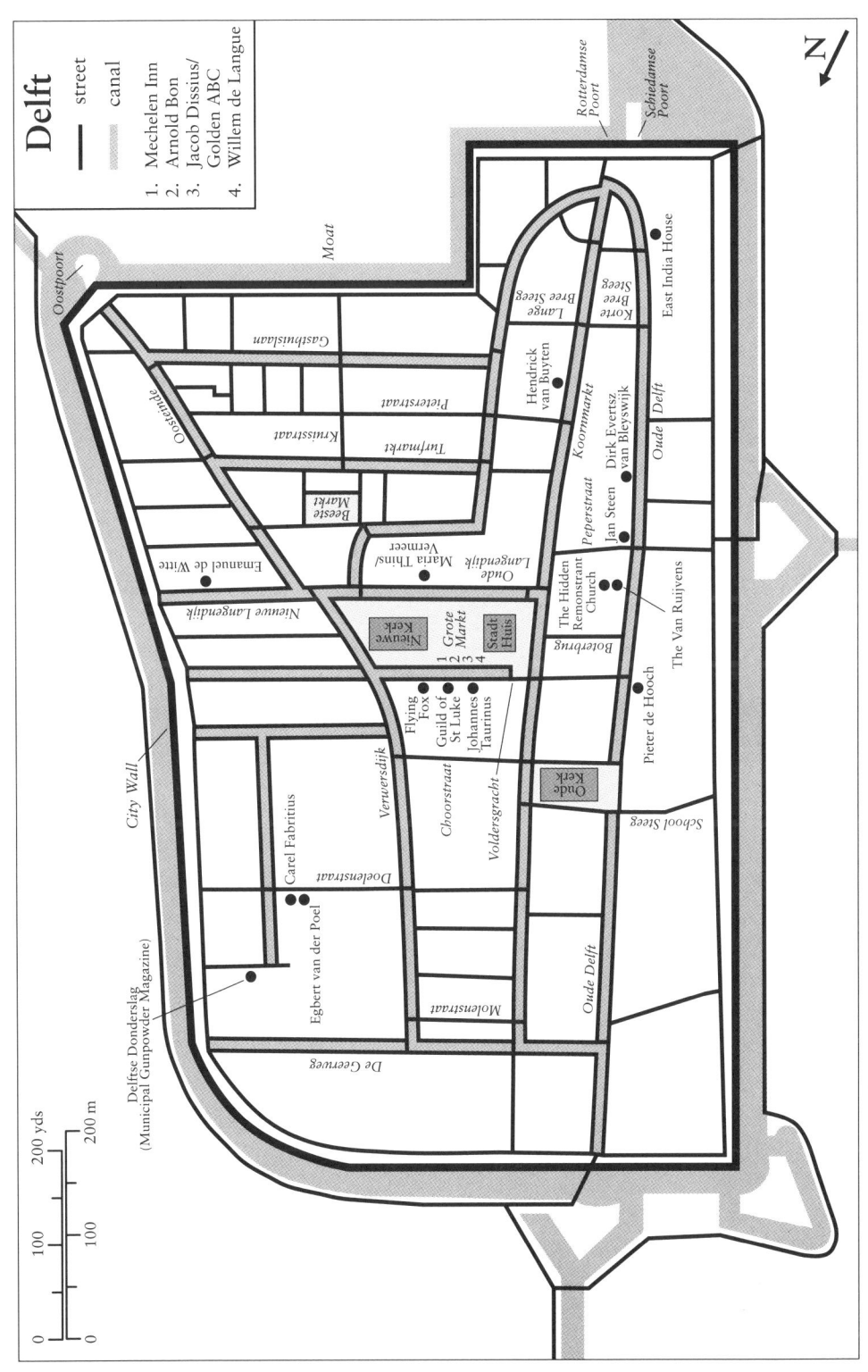

Family Trees

The Family of Johannes Vermeer

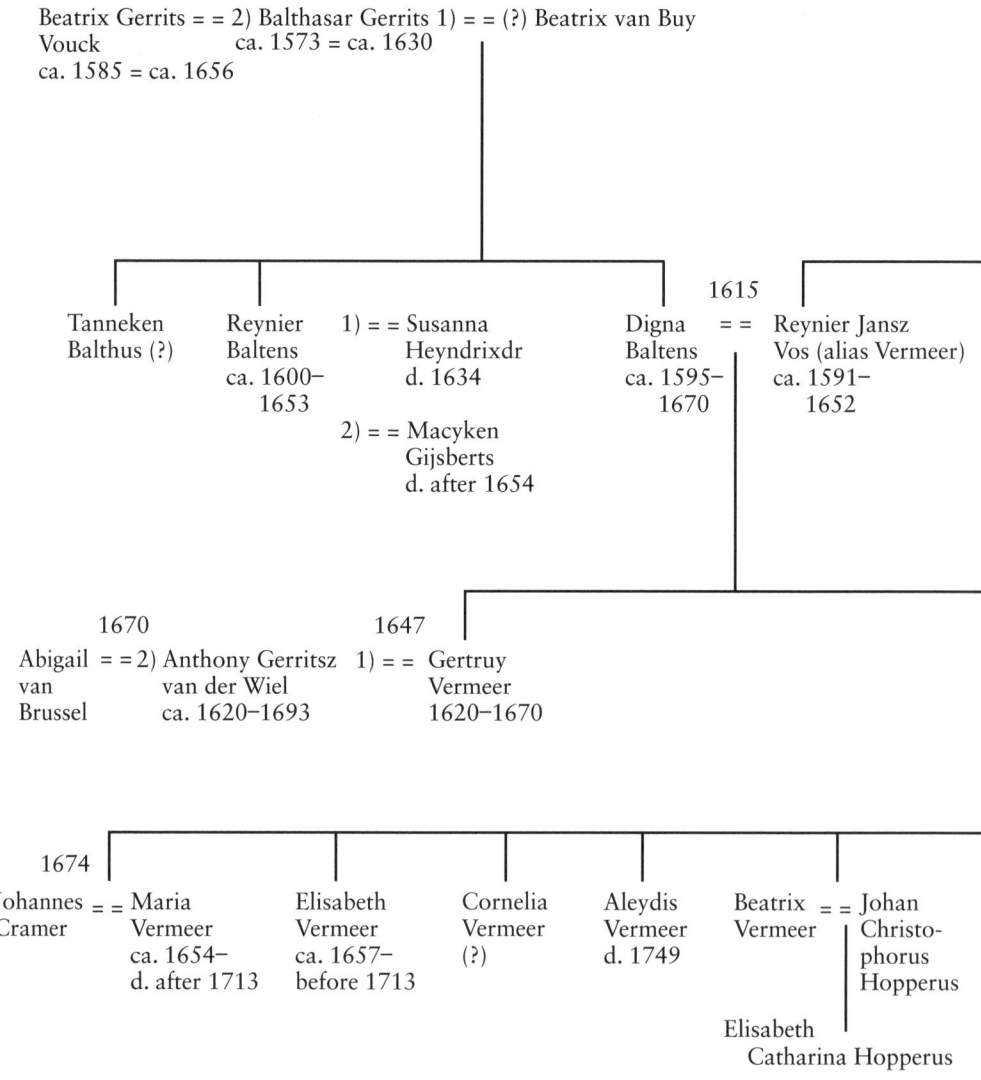

Note: This chart omits the children of Vermeer's uncles and aunts.

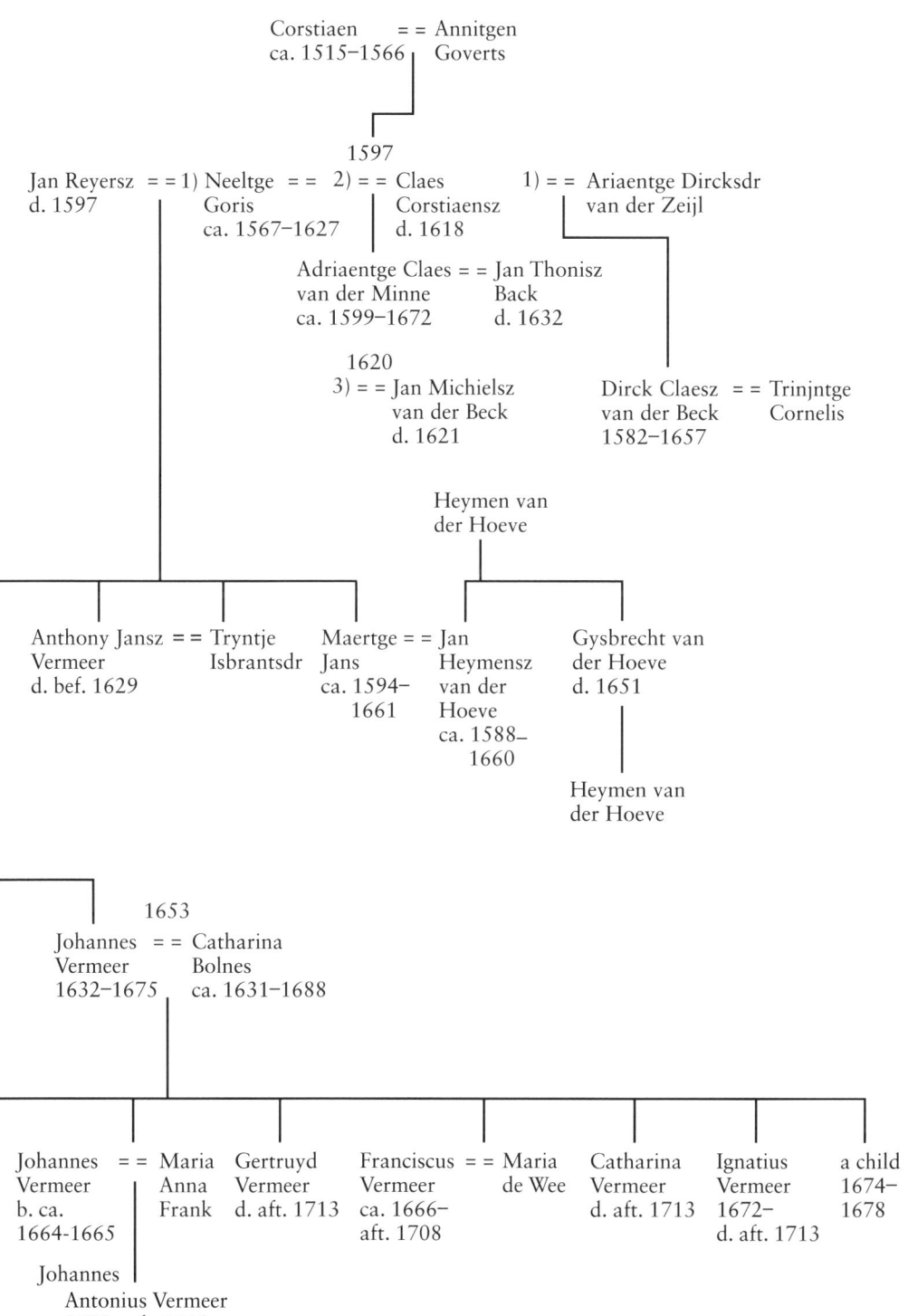

The Family of Catharina Bolnes

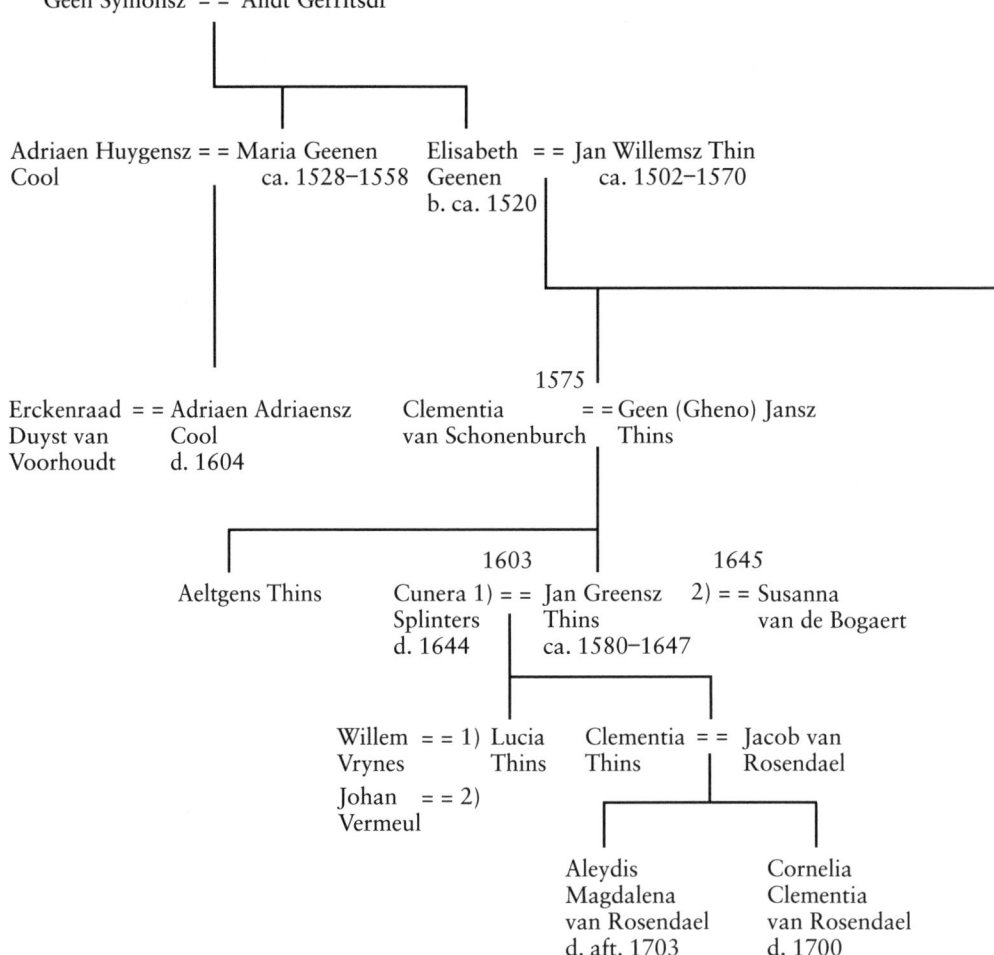

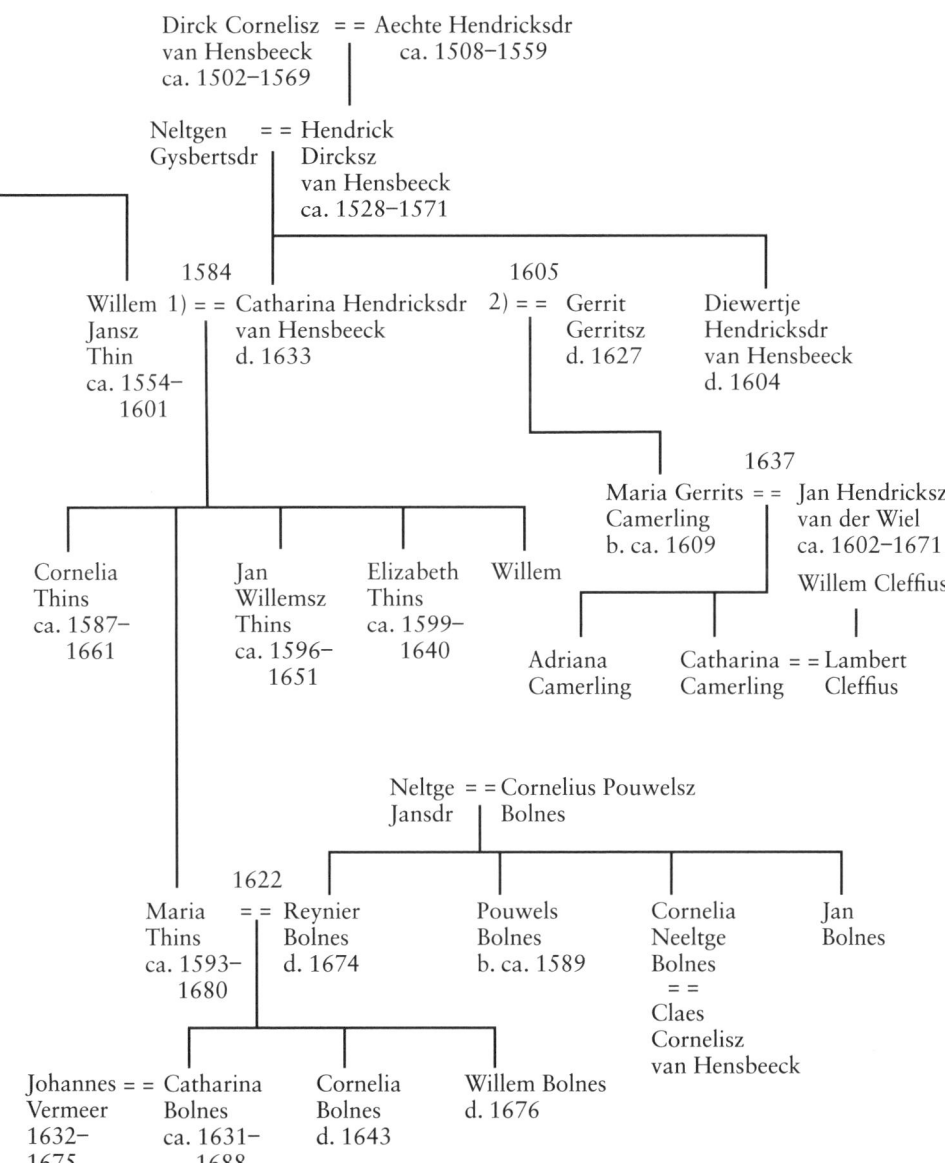

The Family of Pieter Claesz van Ruijven

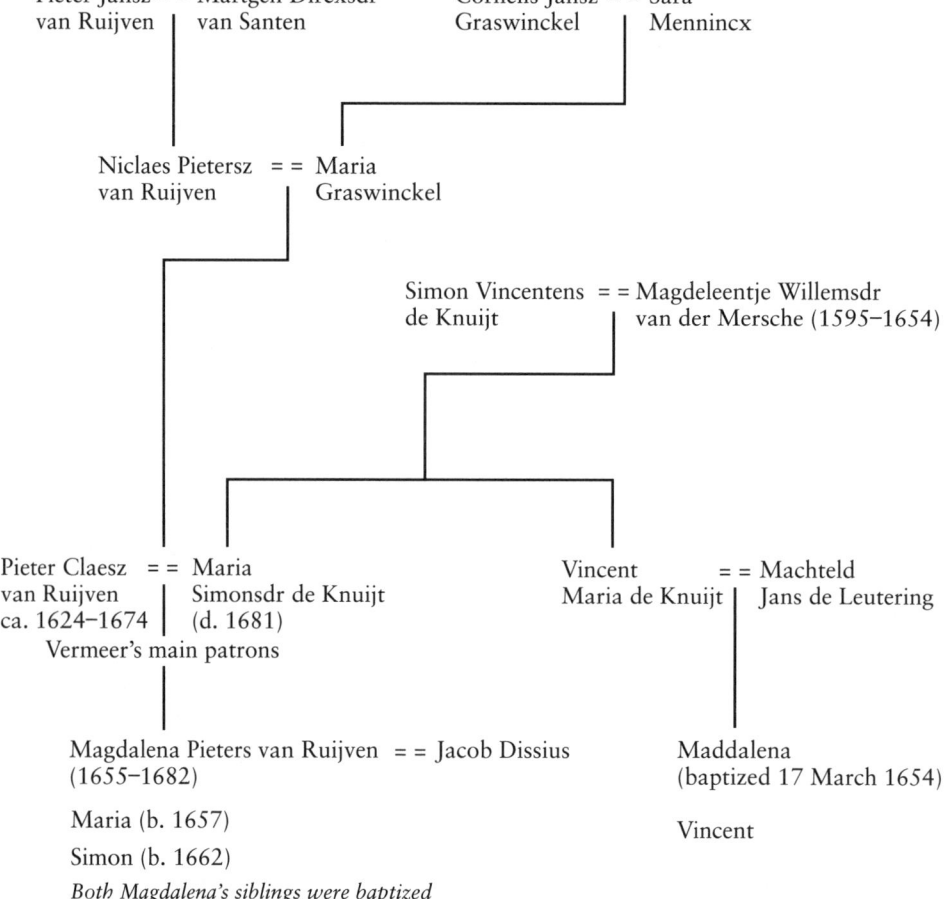

The Family of Adrian Paets

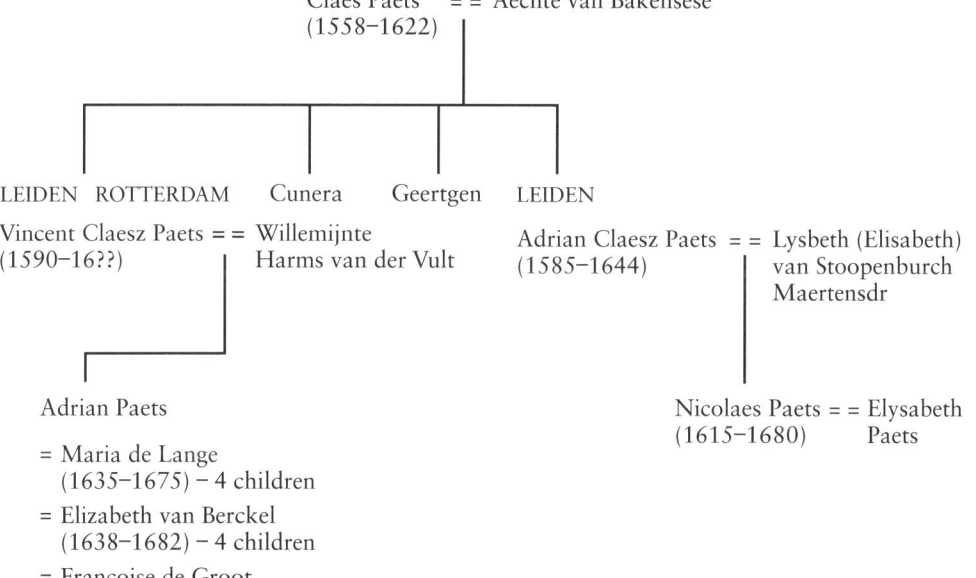

The Paets van Santhorst cousins, and the Van Berkhouts

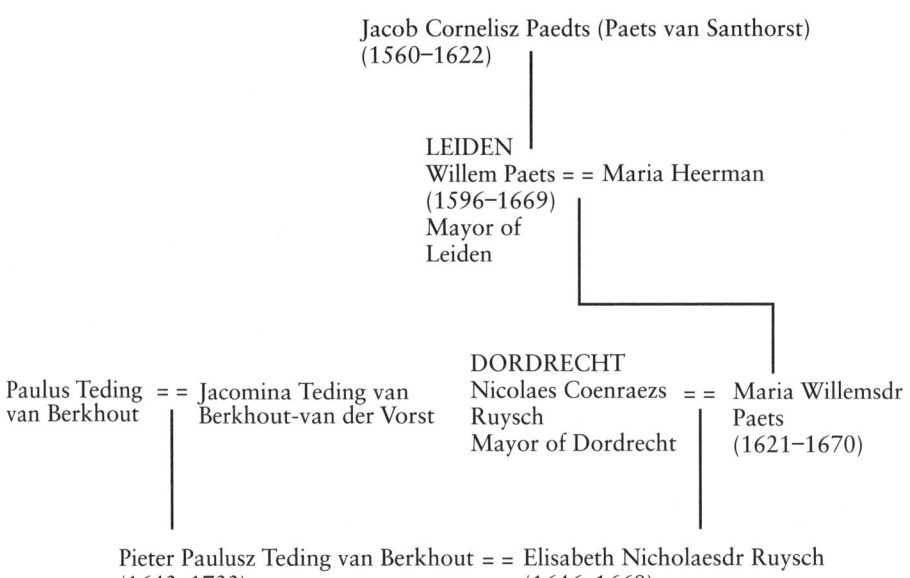

Preface and Acknowledgements

The origins of this book lie in two conversations that took place a long time ago, and a decade apart. In early 1990 I had lunch with Lawrence Gowing, who was kind enough during his later years to show an interest in a young art critic with much to learn. On that particular day he was filled with enthusiasm for a new book that he had just read and reviewed: *Vermeer and His Milieu: A Web of Social History*, by the economist and art historian John Michael Montias. He told me that it contained a remarkable trove of newly discovered archival information about the enigmatic Johannes Vermeer, a painter close to his heart. Lawrence described Montias's book as a kind of Pandora's box, containing numerous revelations and promising yet more to anyone prepared to follow the lines of enquiry that it had opened up. 'Vermeer has always been mysterious; one might like him to become a little less so.' I sensed that his words were meant as a challenge.

Some ten years later I spent a day with John Michael Montias at his home in New Haven, Connecticut. I was making a documentary about Vermeer, for which he had generously agreed to be interviewed. Off camera, he said he was disappointed that so little use had been made of his work by art historians. He had hoped for more to have been discovered about Vermeer's principal patrons, whose existence he had been the first to reveal. His own days of archival research were over, but, had they not been, that was where he would have focused his attention. I noted what he said but did not act upon it because I was busy with other projects. A few years later, when he passed away, I resolved to look into Vermeer more deeply as soon as I had time.

That did not happen until 2017, when I embarked on a systematic re-evaluation of the existing archival evidence on Vermeer and his circle.

Montias's *Vermeer and His Milieu* contains nearly all the important documents, most of which had been discovered by him, alongside a number found by his predecessors. A few other documents have turned up in the years since his death. I was not entirely sure what I was hoping to find in this mass of material, but after four or five years of sifting through it I realized that something startling had emerged from Pandora's box: previously unseen connections linking much of what is already known about Vermeer. This quickly led to one breakthrough after another. The box seemed to be well and truly open. It was then that I decided I had enough to write this book.

The account of Vermeer that follows is largely and perhaps disconcertingly new. Because I have been fortunate enough to make a number of fresh discoveries about the painter and those close to him, it has been possible to reveal more about his life and work than was previously known. Much of this information may be unfamiliar, even to those well acquainted with the copious existing literature on the artist.

I hope the result is an enriched understanding of Vermeer's personality, and of the beliefs and emotions that drove him to create his pictures. Seeing him in a new way has also entailed placing him in a fresh perspective. I have written at some length about the wars through which he lived and the fierce religious conflicts in which he may have participated, and for good reason. Once Vermeer's place in history is properly understood, it becomes clear that he was one of a chosen few who built the values on which a tolerant and liberal civilization, our own even, might be based. This is a side of Vermeer that has been lost from view, although I believe that those who have truly loved his work have often sensed its presence.

Montias's tip was a good one. Many of the new finds presented here concern Vermeer's patrons. Information of this kind inevitably changes how we think about an artist's work to some degree. But in the case of Vermeer its effect is both transformative and surprising. That is because it contains the key to a wide range of meanings long hidden within his paintings, yet clear as day once seen. When I started work on this book, I never anticipated the way in which my research would eventually lead me to challenge most if not all of my own preconceptions about his pictures, including even what *kind* of pictures they are. But that is what has happened. In almost no case does my account of a given picture match up with anything previously written about it. This does not reflect any vigorous striving for originality on my part. It is simply the consequence of having to reconceive Vermeer's work on the basis of what I have stumbled upon. I hope the effect will be stimulating, at the least.

I have been helped to write this book by a great many people, but foremost I would like to thank my loyal editor and publisher, Stuart Proffitt. Stuart commissioned the book more than twenty years ago, at a time when neither of us had much idea of how it would turn out. His steadfast patience and support for this voyage of discovery, through thick and thin, have meant the world to me.

Eleo Gordon, brought in by Stuart to help edit the book even as it was being written, offered sound and welcome advice, as well as much encouragement when it was sorely needed. Richard Mason copyedited the final text with forbearance, good humour and a beady eye. Picture researcher Cecilia Mackay made many helpful suggestions, especially for the contextual illustrations. Thanks to her the book is more vivid and approachable than it might otherwise have been. Richard Duguid and Sandra Fuller oversaw the production process, more extended than expected, with exceptional care and sensitivity. Vartika Rastogi has coordinated the efforts of the various cooks in the kitchen with enthusiasm, energy and grace. My agent, Georgina Capel, has provided wise guidance throughout, as she has now for decades.

Numerous friends and colleagues in the Netherlands have generously given of their time. Where appropriate they are credited in the footnotes, but several must also be mentioned here. Taco Dibbits, director of the Rijksmuseum, has been talking Vermeer with me for more than thirty years, off camera and on. He and his team, including Elles Kamphuis and Hendrikje Crebolder, allowed me the extraordinary privilege of more or less unlimited access to the extensive exhibition of Vermeer's work staged by the Rijksmuseum in 2023, just as I was concluding my research for this book. During more than twenty visits to that exhibition, I was able to refine my thinking about many of Vermeer's most compelling pictures. I am deeply grateful to everyone involved for allowing me this rare opportunity to study the artist's works at first hand, in depth, over such a protracted period of time. It was an unforgettable experience.

PREFACE AND ACKNOWLEDGEMENTS

I am also grateful to Gregor Weber, former Head of the Department of Fine Arts at the Rijksmuseum and a lead curator of the Vermeer exhibition. In conversation he kindly shared some of the fruits of his own research into Vermeer, offering valuable insights in particular into the Catholic milieu of Vermeer's mother-in-law. My own conclusions about the painter's religious affiliations vary greatly from those of Gregor, but life would be dull indeed without space for difference. The cheerful toleration of opposing views has long been part of the fabric of Dutch intellectual life, and is one of the principal themes of this book.

While lecturing at the Mauritshuis in 2019, I came to know Jane Choy-Thurlow, who was kind enough to take an interest in my work on Vermeer and helped to unearth a number of letters that shed light on the life of his one important patron in Rotterdam. Those letters were a thread I needed when I was in the heart of the labyrinth. I am very glad to have met Jane when I did.

Another important encounter at the Mauritshuis took place many years earlier, in the late 1990s, when I visited the museum with my friend and colleague Roger Parsons. We were making a television documentary about Vermeer and were lucky enough to be granted an interview with the conservator Jørgen Wadum about *Girl with a Pearl Earring* and the *View of Delft*. He had just cleaned both pictures and shared innumerable insights about the way in which they had been painted, which greatly deepened my understanding of Vermeer's methods. I am also grateful to the conservator Ari Wallaerts, who shared the results of his research into the composition of *St Praxedis*, concerning pigment analysis in particular, confirming that it is indeed an autograph painting by Vermeer.

My long-time researcher Eugénie Aperghis-van Nispen tot Sevenaer investigated the family trees of numerous individuals in Vermeer's circle of friends and patrons, as well as finding out a great deal about the treatment of the mentally ill in seventeenth-century Delft, among other things. It was Eugénie who called my attention to the presence of Hendrik Doedijns in the household of Vermeer's last patron, Postmaster Van Swoll: a small but important detail. She also organized two extremely helpful trips, to the Netherlands and Germany, arranging for me to meet numerous people with knowledge of the subjects that interested me. I have been exceptionally lucky to have had Eugénie as an ally for so many years.

PREFACE AND ACKNOWLEDGEMENTS

Friso Lammertse and Pieter Roelofs were kind enough to meet me, at the Boymans van Beuningen Museum and Rijksmuseum respectively, and share their own ideas about aspects of Vermeer's practice. In Dresden, I was given the warmest welcome by curator Uta Neidhardt and conservator Christoph Schölzel, who shared with me their remarkable discovery of the painting-within-a-painting that had lurked for so many years beneath the surface of Vermeer's *Girl Reading a Letter at an Open Window*. Their find and its implications gave a tremendous impetus to my own work, encouraging me to continue in a direction that would eventually lead to a great many other discoveries.

I have also benefited immeasurably from conversations with a great many experts on Dutch religion. In Amsterdam, Henk Leegte, pastor of the Mennonite Church of Amsterdam, and Piet Visser, religious historian, taught me a great deal about Dutch nonconformist Christianity in general and the Mennonites in particular. In Rotterdam, I had the remarkable good fortune to meet Tjaard Barnard, preacher at the Remonstrant church there. During the course of a few hours and many coffees, Tjaard shed much light on the Remonstrant movement and the place of Jacobus Arminius within it. Shortly afterwards the unfailingly helpful chief administrator of the Remonstrant Church, Kitty Havinga, persuaded a member of her own Rotterdam congregation to help me track down a particular group of documents concerning Vermeer and his friends in the Delft archive. Not only did my new Remonstrant assistant, Titus van Hille, give me many days and hours of his time entirely gratis, but he did so while welcoming a family of refugees into his home in Rotterdam: Remonstrants are clearly as generous now as they were in Vermeer's time. Titus went on to do tremendous detective work on my behalf, uncovering the previously unknown and extremely significant location of the house in Delft where Vermeer's main patrons lived: a golden piece of data which confirmed my strong suspicions about the painter's religious milieu. I cannot thank Titus enough.

Bas van der Wulp, who knows the Delft archives as well as anyone, has patiently fielded my queries about Vermeer off and on for a great many years. He was kind enough to meet me and share his thoughts about his own most recent discovery, namely a burial record describing the painter's funeral arrangements, which dispelled the myth that

PREFACE AND ACKNOWLEDGEMENTS

Vermeer died in poverty. He had also helped me, many years previously, to understand the temperament of Vermeer's troubled and probably deranged brother-in-law Willem. The distinguished archival researcher Jaap van der Veen was also kind enough to meet me and share his expertise on the vanished world of the seventeenth century. We talked about the wealth of Vermeer's mother-in-law, Maria Thins, which I had rather underestimated up to that point. We also discussed Pieter Claesz van Ruijven's closeness to Vermeer, confirmed by Jaap's discovery of their signatures side by side on a document of 1672, and he helpfully impressed upon me the importance of understanding seventeenth-century Dutch naming traditions.

Albert Vossepoel, an expert on Spinoza, met me at the Spinozahuis in Rijnsburg, where we explored the philosopher's views on love and his close links to the Collegiants. Adam Boreel's biographer Francesco Quatrini kindly gave me a tutorial on the Collegiant movement and the role played within it by Adrian Paets.

Bettiena Drukker volunteered to decipher Johannes Taurinus's *Reflections on the Parable of the Samaritan Woman*, a text which only survives in its first edition: no easy task given the devilishly difficult Gothic font in which it is set. Having rendered it into readable Dutch, Bettiena also helped to translate a number of key passages, and all at a time when she was extremely busy with her own projects.

Paul Abels, who is immensely knowledgeable about the religious life of Delft (and Gouda) in the seventeenth century, kindly agreed to cast a critical eye over the entire book in manuscript. His comments, observations and objections made for numerous improvements to the original text, and I am deeply grateful to him for his help.

In New York, Peter Carey has been a constant inspiration. More or less as soon as I had completed my previous book, on Caravaggio, Peter insisted that I prioritize Vermeer forthwith, even drafting a mock agreement on the napkin of a New York restaurant and then insisting that I sign it. Obligations incurred under such circumstances have to be honoured.

Closer to home, in Sussex, my sister Elizabeth kindly read a number of passages in manuscript and gave her valuable opinions on matters of theology, in particular. My friends Neil Gonzalez and Christian Birmingham have each in their different ways given me hope and encouragement. Nick Gosset has set me straight many times. Carol Reed, as ever, has done what she can.

I must also thank Dr Kees Kaldenbach, with whom I have sporadically corresponded about Vermeer over many years. I also owe a debt of gratitude to Jonathan Janson, whom I have never met, but whose website, 'Essential Vermeer', has been a mine of helpful information since its inception more than twenty years ago.

Thanks also to Mrs. F. Cossee-De Wijs, retired senior archivist of the Gemeentearchief Delft, who kindly helped with the translation and interpretation of certain key documents touching on the Van Ruijven family home.

My assistant Kate Adams has been a perfect pillar of strength and has done extraordinary things to make this book possible. I remember in particular a gruelling four-week stint during which she managed not only to elicit its entire narrative structure from me, but also to transcribe it into a five-metre flow chart running much the length of my office, which then became the touchstone for everything I wrote. Had she not gone to such lengths I would surely never have completed my text in time for it to be published when it needed to be. Kate has also obtained numerous hard-to-find books and documents and has helped frequently with translation. She has phoned people who needed to be phoned and found pictures that needed to be found, more times than I can say. Unlike me, she is the epitome of calm under pressure, and I cannot thank her enough.

In conclusion, I must thank my older son, Arthur, who applied his own keen advocate's mind to the final draft of the manuscript, pointing out numerous errors, inaccuracies and unnecessary ambiguities while providing elegant solutions in almost every case. I must also thank my younger son, Vincent, for putting up with me on the many (very many) occasions on which I, as he put it, 'Vermeered' him. The Vermeering is all done for now.

Finally, my deepest debt of all is to my dear wife, the messenger. She saw it, just by looking at the pictures.

Prologue

THE SPHINX OF DELFT

The painter Johannes Vermeer died in December 1675 at the age of forty-three. Most of his works were dispersed some twenty years later, and within a generation his name had been forgotten. People lucky enough to own his pictures would continue to cherish them, but with little or no knowledge about their creator. When those pictures changed hands they would often be passed off by unscrupulous dealers as the work of more well-known Dutch masters, such as Pieter de Hooch, Frans van Mieris and even Rembrandt. Fake signatures were added. Vermeer was being written out of history with each transaction, becoming more and more of a nobody.

But in the mid-nineteenth century that changed. Vermeer was rediscovered, his name rightfully reattached to the pictures he had made. Since then his popularity has increased, to the extent that he has become one of the best-loved painters in the world. But while his work has grown ever more popular with the passing of time, it has also proved stubbornly resistant to interpretation. Despite the vast amount of writing on Vermeer, the most important questions about him remain unanswered. Why did he create his paintings? What did they mean to their creator, and to those for whom they were painted? This book provides answers to those questions, partly on the basis of documentary evidence, much of which has escaped notice until now.

Anyone wishing to uncover the truth about Vermeer needs to bear in mind how unusual he was. Unlike the Dutch genre painters of his time, with whom he has been routinely compared, he made pictures that are uniquely introverted and conspicuously lacking in any overt ambition to amuse or entertain. While his paintings radiate a deep sense of ethical conviction, they cannot be boiled down to a series of moral platitudes. The people we see in them are invariably thoughtful, though that is really an understatement: truer to say that they are rapt, caught up in a profoundly inward state of meditation, *lost* in thought. They are mostly women: shown reading or writing, playing music, pouring milk, making lace, or simply looking out at us. They are framed with such solemnity that we are left in no doubt about the importance, to them, of whatever it is that they are contemplating.

Vermeer had a rare gift for painting light, and the play of light. He was one of the first purely tonal painters in the history of Western art: that is to say, one of the first to describe forms purely through gradations of light and shade, without recourse to line. A number of writers have argued that he created his paintings with the aid of a camera obscura, namely a darkened box or room, pierced by a small aperture, through which an image of the outside world is projected onto a surface within. While Vermeer's understanding of light was probably enhanced by seeing the images produced by such a device, there is no evidence that he used one in his studio practice. In any event, to draw analogies between Vermeer's art and this precursor of photography is misleading. His pictures may give the illusion of depicting fragments of the real world, but they are premeditated and artfully composed. If they consistently represent anything, it is an idealized version of reality. And, while the light in them might resemble the light of nature, what they are showing us is really another kind of light, not easily caught in a camera: the indwelling light of the soul, the light of hope and love.

Théophile Thoré, the French art critic and connoisseur who rediscovered Vermeer in the mid-nineteenth century, was fascinated and mystified by him in equal measure. Having encountered a number of the painter's works during his travels in Holland, in particular the *View of Delft* and *The Milkmaid,* Thoré found that nothing could erase their 'indelible memory' from his mind. He wondered why their creator was so little known: 'Jan Van der Meer of Delft! The astounding painter! But, after Rembrandt and Frans Hals, is this van der Meer, then, one of the foremost masters of the entire Dutch School? How was it that one knew nothing of an artist who equals, if he does not surpass, Pieter de Hooch and [Gabriel] Metsu?'[1]

Thoré also noted Vermeer's absence from the existing literature on Dutch painting, and the surprisingly small number of his works on public display: 'his name was missing from the biographies and histories of painting; his works were missing from the museums and private collections.' But he could no more explain these puzzles than he could fathom what he felt to be the mysteries of the paintings themselves. His sense of baffled wonder was implicit in the nickname he gave to Vermeer: 'The Sphinx of Delft'.

Like many subsequent students of Vermeer, Thoré regarded the painter as an enigma. The artist was unusual in many respects, not least in being singularly unproductive. He was active as a painter for less than two decades, during which time he created surprisingly few pictures. Only some thirty-six or so survive in total, but even if we account for a few that have gone missing it seems there were never many more. By contrast Rembrandt painted well over 300 oil paintings, as most likely did Frans Hals, allowing for some losses. Even a *fijnschilder* ('fine painter') with an extremely slow and exacting method, such as Gerrit Dou, painted well over 200 pictures during the course of his life. Vermeer died young, but even so the meagreness of his output is striking. Whereas the pictures of Hals, Rembrandt and Dou were known all over Holland during their own lifetimes, his were virtually unknown outside Delft.

He seems to have been driven neither by fame nor money. But he was driven by something, by some deep feeling or belief, or he could not have painted in the way that he did. His pictures are haunting and extraordinary and in many respects quite unlike any other pictures painted before or since. They depict the world, but seem as though they are not entirely of this world. They are representations, but have the power of revelation. Many people have fallen under their spell, and have wondered what secrets they might hold.

Johannes Vermeer's internal life is uncharted territory. What kind of a man was he? What did he believe? What were his political opinions? What was his religious outlook? How might his personality and attitudes have been shaped by the many wars and struggles – the Thirty Years War, the Eighty Years War, the Dutch fight for independence, the French invasion of the Netherlands in the 'Year of Disaster', 1672 – that took place during his lifetime? Solving some of those mysteries might help us to answer the questions about his work and its meanings with which we began.

That said, the case of Vermeer presents significant challenges. There is, for example, no extant transcript of anything that he actually said: not a single recorded statement. This paucity of information reflects the fact that he probably led a largely peaceable and law-abiding life. The most revealing evidence about the behaviour of seventeenth-century people preserved in archives tends to take the form of criminal proceedings, church discipline or reports of disturbances. Nothing of that kind has been discovered in relation to Vermeer. But that is not to say that we have nothing to go on.

Over the past half-century a mass of highly revealing new information has been uncovered concerning Vermeer's extended family, and that of his wife, Catharina Bolnes. Documents have also been found touching on his contacts with other artists and, crucially, his contacts with his patrons. Few of these documents shed light on Vermeer's personality, but they reveal a great deal about the networks within which he moved and therefore give us clues to his probable allegiances and values. Seventeenth-century Holland was fought over by highly vocal, contesting factions that tended to be polarized in their positions. So to know where a man stood on one issue – war versus peace, for example, or religious tolerance versus intolerance – was often to know much else about him besides.

Like all documents, those concerning Vermeer and the people around him need to be placed in the broader context of history. In this case that means above all the history of those wars and religious conflicts that arose as a consequence of the Reformation, that great divide within Western Christianity opened up by Martin Luther in 1517 with his 'Ninety-Five Theses', in which he protested against the authority of the Pope and the Church of Rome, and corruption within it, and in so doing founded an alternative 'Protestant' form of Christianity. The resulting schism between Catholic and Protestant produced many smaller splits, as the Protestants themselves divided into Calvinists, Lutherans, Mennonites and others. As a result of all this, for a century and more, Europe would be torn apart by religious warfare, often waged on the battlefield of the Low Countries.

The shadow of war loomed large in the collective memory of

Vermeer's generation, as it had in that of his parents and grandparents. If we reckon properly with this hard legacy it becomes possible to see the painter more precisely than before in the Dutch society of his time, at a period of great political, intellectual and religious ferment. That in turn can lead to a richer sense of what his paintings might be about, of the beliefs they might enshrine and the hopes they might embody.

THE GOLDEN ABC

Not every story begins at the beginning. This one begins six years after the death of Johannes Vermeer, with the death of someone else: a woman who had known him called Magdalena.

Magdalena Pieters van Ruijven died on 16 June 1682 in the house that she had shared with her husband, a printer and publisher named Jacob Dissius, on the Great Market Square (Grote Markt) in Delft. She was young at the time of her death, only twenty-seven. She had married just two years earlier and had probably intended to start a family. Magdalena's strong feelings for Jacob are indicated by an effusive phrase in her last will and testament, in which she refers to 'her beloved husband Jacob Abrahamsz Dissius'.[2]

Magdalena was better off than Jacob, which made them an unusual couple in Delft at that time. Unusual, but not exceptional: it was not unheard of for a lady to marry for love rather than money in seventeenth-century Holland, where women enjoyed considerably more independence than elsewhere in Europe. Magdalena was the only surviving child of Pieter Claesz van Ruijven, who was heir to a fortune made in the brewing business, and Maria de Knuijt, who was from a solidly wealthy family in Delft and had considerable assets of her own.[3] Magdalena's father had died in 1674, her mother in 1681, so Magdalena had inherited their money and property by the time of her own death. Part of their legacy to her was a collection of paintings, mostly acquired during Magdalena's own childhood and adolescence. She still had them when she died.

Jacob, by contrast, had little in the way of worldly goods. His savings amounted to a life annuity yielding 100 guilders a year, which was not enough to support a single person, let alone a married couple. His only tangible asset was the home in which he and Magdalena lived, which was also a small publishing house, originally set up by his father Abraham (and most likely given to Jacob to tip the scales of the new husband and wife's fortunes back slightly in his favour). Its name, indicated by a sign on the front of their home, was The Golden ABC (*Het Gulden ABC*). It is a mark of just how little money Jacob was able to lay his hands on, in the immediate aftermath of Magdalena's death, that he had to borrow 400 guilders from his father to pay her funeral expenses.[4] That he was forced to do so suggests that his wife's death may have been sudden and unforeseen. That he borrowed so much indicates that the funeral must have been a grand affair, with numerous pallbearers and (as was sometimes the custom) the donation of a sizeable sum to the local charity chamber.

The Delft City Archives still preserve a notarial inventory of all the goods, movable and unmovable, bequeathed to her husband by Magdalena Pieters van Ruijven.[5] The list of unmovable assets shows that Jacob Dissius would have had no difficulty repaying debts incurred as a result of her funeral. His late wife's legacy included numerous interest-bearing obligations as well as the annual rental income from a sizeable house in the Voorstraet, a street in the heart of Delft. It also included 'the domain of Spalant', namely twenty-one and a half *morgen* of land near the village of Kethel, close to Schiedam. The *morgen* was an old northern European measure derived from the German word for morning, which denoted the amount of land a single ox under plough could till between dawn and noon on any given day; so this was a sizeable holding, and well placed, lying about eight miles to the south of Delft in a fertile triangle of meadowland between The Hague, Rotterdam and the Hook of Holland. The domain carried a title with it, allowing Jacob Dissius, son of a printer, to style himself henceforth 'Lord of Spalant' (whether he did so or not is unknown). Its value was 16,000 guilders: a large amount of money.

All this would be of merely passing interest to anyone concerned with Johannes Vermeer were it not for the other list included in the inventory of Magdalena's assets: that of her movable goods, compiled by a notary's clerk during a visit to the home of the deceased one spring day in 1683. What did he find as he passed under the sign of

PROLOGUE

The Golden ABC and crossed the threshold into the house? He listed an unsurprising miscellany of Magdalena's personal possessions, including various items of clothing, a chest of drawers containing musical instruments, and 'a little coffer containing three diamond rings'. Greater treasures by far were all around him, hanging on the walls. Whether he knew it or not, the notary's clerk had stumbled on one of the wonders of the seventeenth-century world: an art collection the like of which had never been seen before and would never be seen again.

Here is his inventory:

In the front room

> 8 paintings by Vermeer
> 3 ditto by the same, in boxes
> a seascape by Porcellis
> a landscape

In the back room

> 4 paintings by Vermeer
> 2 paintings of churches
> 2 *tronien* [a *tronie* was a kind of portrait in which the person shown was depicted in character or displaying a particular emotion]
> 2 night scenes
> 1 landscape
> 1 with houses

In the kitchen

> a painting by Vermeer
> 2 *tronien*
> a night scene
> 2 landscapes
> a little church
> a painter (presumably a self-portrait by an artist)

In the basement room

>   2 paintings by Vermeer
>   a landscape
>   a church

Besides the above items there still follow

>   2 paintings by Vermeer
>   2 landscapes

This list, which was discovered and published by John Michael Montias over thirty years ago, has provoked little response from Vermeer scholars: there are few mentions of it in the existing literature on the artist. Yet it is one of the most extraordinary documents concerning the painter, indeed in the whole history of art.

Imagine stepping from the bustle of the Great Market Square in Delft, away from the rumbling of carriages, the din of workshops, the cries of quacks and pedlars and merchants hawking every kind of merchandise – 'Fine brandy!' 'Fresh herrings, sweet as sugar!' 'Bread rolls, cakes, rye and barley!' – and suddenly entering Vermeer's painted world of stilled and silent contemplation.

Magdalena's collection, now become Jacob's, contained not only pictures by Vermeer: besides the twenty by his hand, twenty-one others are listed. But the notary's clerk did not trouble to name the artists responsible for them, other than in one instance, that of the marine painting by Jan Porcellis, which was hung together with an anonymous landscape beside those eleven Vermeers in the front room. No doubt the clerk took his lead from Magdalena's widower, who must have been his guide through the house.

All this was not just out of the ordinary. It was unique. Many remarkable private art collections were formed in the Dutch Republic during the seventeenth century, but such collections were invariably larger and more eclectic than that housed within The Golden ABC. None was built around the work of a single painter. Magdalena's parents had moreover owned most of Vermeer's paintings. The twenty pictures in her death inventory amount to nearly two-thirds of his known production.

PROLOGUE

The collection was not only unique in its nature but unique in the way it was cherished and preserved. As long as it remained within the family of its original owners, it was never broken up or diminished by part sales. For reasons that remain unclear, following Magdalena's death Jacob was obliged to share her estate with his father, Abraham: a ruling to that effect was made by the commissioners of the High Court of Holland on 18 July 1684. As a result six of Vermeer's paintings became the property of Dissius the elder.[6] It is not known whether Abraham Dissius ever took physical possession of those six pictures, or was merely content with nominal ownership of them. But Jacob got them back from his father, either by purchase or inheritance, and kept them at The Golden ABC, together with the others, for the rest of his life. At the time of his death in 1695 he had ensured that the collection was still intact. Only then was it dispersed.

Documentary evidence shows that Vermeer began working for the Van Ruijven family in about 1657, when he was in his mid-twenties. For the next thirteen years he painted almost all his pictures for that family, and afterwards more or less gave up painting altogether. His relationship to his patrons was like none other that we know of in his time, just as his paintings are unlike any other Dutch pictures of the period. It is reasonable to assume that this is not a coincidence.

There is another aspect to the mystery of Vermeer: namely his place in art history, or rather his lack of one until the mid-nineteenth century. No other Old Master as highly regarded as he is today was ever forgotten for as long. This would surely never have been the case had he not painted nearly all of his pictures for one family, and had that family not kept them so close. For some forty years, unless a person happened to know Pieter Claesz van Ruijven or Maria de Knuijt, Magdalena Pieters van Ruijven or Jacob Dissius, it would have been difficult to know much about the work of Johannes Vermeer. So no wonder he was never as famous as Rembrandt, Hals, Gerard Dou, Frans van Mieris or Albert Cuyp; no wonder that his name was left out of the biographies of Dutch artists compiled in the seventeenth and eighteenth centuries; and no wonder that Théophile Thoré, who rescued Vermeer from obscurity, described him as a man risen without trace. The pattern had been set early: for most of his life, and for two decades afterwards, his art had been kept out of public view, apparently with his willing cooperation.

Yet Vermeer was not entirely unknown to his contemporaries. His work was praised in a poem, written and published in Delft in his lifetime. He was twice elected headman of the Guild of St Luke, the painter's guild in Delft, so he must have played an active role in its administration. He was clearly respected by his fellow painters in the town where he lived. For all the hiddenness of his work, it is plain that some people held his pictures in high regard. All this is confirmed by an event that took place in 1696, some twenty-one years after his death.

A few months after Jacob Dissius died, in 1695, his paintings were sold at auction. The sale took place not in Delft but in Amsterdam, the hub of the seventeenth-century Dutch art market. The auctioneer must have known that there were at least a few collectors with enough interest in the elusive Vermeer to bid at such a sale. He must have hoped that competition for the paintings would be all the keener because none of them had been offered to the market before. He was probably not disappointed. The bids achieved were good if not spectacular: more than 200 guilders for the top lot, and even the cheapest Vermeer fetched a respectable 30 guilders or so.

The original wording of the auction advertisement, a handbill distributed in Amsterdam in April 1696, alerted potential bidders to the forthcoming sale of 'excellent artful paintings, among them 21 pieces extraordinarily vigorously and delightfully painted by the late J. Vermeer of Delft, representing several compositions, being the best he ever made'.[7] This shows that the Dissius collection was put on the market as *the* collection of paintings by Vermeer, in which his finest works were to be found.

The notary's clerk who had visited The Golden ABC back in 1683 merely enumerated the paintings by Vermeer on the walls of the house without describing them in any way. (He also listed one fewer than the twenty-one that subsequently appeared at auction.) The catalogue of the Amsterdam sale, which took place on 16 May 1696, is invaluable because it identifies each and every one of the late Jacob Dissius's pictures by Vermeer. The titles given to the pictures by the auctioneer were in most cases not the same as those in use today (nor do they reflect Vermeer's own titles: if such ever existed, they are unknown now, with one exception). But the lot descriptions are sufficiently precise to be matched, quite exactly, to known paintings by the artist. Remarkably, nearly all of the works sold more than three centuries ago in Amsterdam have survived to the present. So not only can the collection be reconstructed with a high degree of certainty: most of the pictures once in it can still be seen.

So what were they, and where are they now?

> *A Maid Asleep* (Metropolitan Museum, New York)
> *Officer with a Laughing Girl* (Frick Collection, New York)
> *The Milkmaid* (Rijksmuseum, Amsterdam)
> *Woman with a Balance* (National Gallery of Art, Washington)
> *The Little Street* (Rijksmuseum, Amsterdam)
> *The Concert* (formerly in the Isabella Stewart Gardner Museum, Boston: stolen in 1990, still unrecovered)
> *The Music Lesson* (The Royal Collection, throughout Great Britain)
> Possibly *A Young Woman Interrupted at Music* (Frick Collection, New York)
> *View of Delft* (Mauritshuis, The Hague)
> *Woman with a Pearl Necklace* (Gemäldegalerie, Berlin)
> *A Lady Writing* (National Gallery of Art, Washington)
> *Girl with a Pearl Earring* (Mauritshuis, The Hague)
> Probably *Study of a Young Woman* (Metropolitan Museum, New York)
> Another similar portrait of a young woman (whereabouts unknown since 1696, presumed lost; see pp. 267–8)
> *Mistress and Maid* (Frick Collection, New York)
> *The Lacemaker* (Louvre, Paris)
> *The Guitar Player* (Kenwood House, London)
> *A Young Woman Standing at a Virginal* (National Gallery, London)

In addition to these eighteen pictures, the auction contained three others, referred to in the 1696 sale catalogue as follows:

> 'A picture in which a gentleman is washing his hands in a see-through room with sculptures, artful and rare'
> 'A view of a house standing in Delft'

> 'The portrait of Vermeer in a room with various accessories uncommonly beautifully painted by him'

The first of these has never been heard of since and is presumed lost. The second is also lost. The third can plausibly be identified with Vermeer's only extant self-portrait, *The Art of Painting*, in the Kunsthistorisches Museum in Vienna. If the 'portrait of Vermeer in a room' was indeed that painting then it was the odd one out in the Van Ruijven's family collection, in that unlike all the others it would have been purchased after the artist's death. We know that Vermeer kept *The Art of Painting* until the end of his life, when it was inherited by his widow, Catharina, then sold against her wishes by the administrator of Vermeer's estate. If it was bought at that time by a member of the Van Ruijven family, that person would have to have been either Magdalena or her mother, Maria de Knuijt, since the father of the family, Pieter Claesz van Ruijven, was by then no longer alive. But it is also possible that the 'portrait of Vermeer in a room' listed in the Dissius sale has simply disappeared, in which case it may have been a secondary version of *The Art of Painting*, done in addition to the one he kept for himself, or a different painting altogether. Unless another self-portrait by Vermeer turns up, we will never know which of these three hypotheses is the truth.

However that may be, the Dissius collection that went to auction in 1696 contained twenty-one paintings by Vermeer, compared to the twenty such paintings listed by the notary's clerk in the collection bequeathed to Jacob by Magdalena in 1683. There are two possible explanations for this small discrepancy: either Jacob Dissius bought another Vermeer between 1683 and 1695, the year of his death, or the notary's clerk who visited The Golden ABC in 1683 failed to identify one or other of the pictures in the house *as* a Vermeer. The latter seems more probable: looking through the list of unattributed pictures in the inventory, either the picture 'with houses' or one of the two *tronien* (all in the back room) could actually have been a Vermeer.

Not only did the collection amount to roughly two-thirds of Vermeer's total production as an artist, it contained almost all of the pictures on which his modern reputation rests: the pictures in which Vermeer seems most distinctively and uniquely *himself*, the heart and

PROLOGUE

soul of his work. The auctioneer's claim to be selling 'the best' of Vermeer was no exaggeration.

Another way to grasp the status of the Van Ruijven family's collection is to consider the known pictures by Vermeer that were *not* once part of it. There are seventeen such pictures, remarkably few of which might be described as classic Vermeers.

Four of them are early works, painted on themes drawn from mythology or the Bible: *Diana and Her Companions* (Mauritshuis, The Hague), *St Praxedis* (Private collection, Japan), *Christ in the House of Martha and Mary* (National Galleries of Scotland, Edinburgh), and *The Procuress* (Gemäldegalerie, Dresden), which despite its modern title may actually illustrate the parable of the Prodigal Son.

Then there is a pair of uncharacteristically obvious genre paintings in which women are drinking wine while being courted, namely *Young Woman with a Wine Glass* (Herzog Anton Ulrich Museum, Braunschweig) and *The Glass of Wine* (Gemäldegalerie, Berlin). Both were seemingly commissioned by the same family, to judge by the identical coat of arms that appears in a stained-glass window in each picture. To these may be added *The Love Letter* (Rijksmuseum, Amsterdam), another rare example of a picture by Vermeer that follows the storytelling conventions of Dutch genre painting in a straightforward way. It is not known for whom Vermeer painted it.

The Astronomer (Louvre, Paris) and *The Geographer* (Städel Museum, Frankfurt), which were commissioned from Vermeer by a director of the Dutch East India Company, are characterizations of the spirit of scientific enquiry with no counterparts elsewhere in Vermeer's work. *Allegory of the Catholic Faith* (Metropolitan Museum, New York) was commissioned by a wealthy burgher of Amsterdam, and is plainly an unusual painting in the context of the rest of Vermeer's work.

So most of the pictures by Vermeer that were *not* in the Dissius sale share one characteristic: they seem untypical. They are certainly not the pictures that would be at the top of the loan list for any museum seeking to organize an exhibition of the painter's work.

This leaves a handful of what we might call the most Vermeer-like Vermeers not painted for the Van Ruijven family. Those pictures are:

Girl Reading a Letter at an Open Window (Gemäldegalerie, Dresden)

Woman in Blue Reading a Letter (Rijksmuseum, Amsterdam)
Young Woman with a Water Pitcher (Metropolitan Museum, New York)
Woman with a Lute (Metropolitan Museum, New York)
Lady Writing a Letter with Her Maid (National Gallery of Ireland, Dublin)
Girl with a Red Hat (National Gallery of Art, Washington)
Young Woman Seated at a Virginal (National Gallery, London)

To these some might add the *Girl with a Flute* (National Gallery of Art, Washington), but the attribution of this picture to Vermeer is not entirely secure.

It is hard to identify the people for whom these variously becalmed and contemplative pictures were created, because their early ownership is undocumented. One of them, the *Young Woman with a Water Pitcher*, was almost certainly acquired from Vermeer by a baker named Hendrick van Buyten. Others, perhaps most of them, were probably painted by Vermeer either for himself or for his wife, Catharina. We know that he kept a number of his own pictures, because Catharina owned several at the time of his death, including the *Lady Writing a Letter with Her Maid* and (probably) the *Woman with a Lute*.

What can be concluded from all this? With few exceptions, Vermeer created his most distinctive and memorable pictures for the Van Ruijven family. Anybody investigating the mysteries of the painter must therefore take a keen interest in that family. Who were they? What drew Vermeer to them, and them to him? What was the nature of their relationship, and how might it have affected his work? One more question should be added. Why were three of those paintings in 'the front room' of The Golden ABC said to be 'in boxes'? Was the notary's clerk merely referring to rectangular crates for storage, or did he mean something else?

None of these questions can be answered without a proper understanding of the patterns of thought and belief that animated Vermeer and those for whom he painted his pictures. Context is everything. The painter's story, together with the long-lost meanings and messages embedded in his work, are inextricably linked with the story of the Dutch Republic itself: its birth, rise and fall.

PART ONE

The Inheritance, 1560–1632

REPUBLIC OF REFUGEES

Owen Feltham, a patriotic Englishman with a gift for comic prose, spent three weeks touring the Low Countries in 1648. He enjoyed poking fun at the Dutch and their homeland, describing the Netherlands as 'The great Bog of Europe ... the buttock of the World, full of veines and bloud, but no bones in't.' Inhospitably damp, perpetually sodden, it was to his mind the wettest of wet places: 'There is not such another marsh in the world that's flat. They are a universal quagmire: epitomiz'd, *A green cheese in a pickle*. There is in them an *aequilibrium* of mud and water ... They are the ingredients of a black-pudding ... Even their dwelling is a miracle: They live lower than the fishes, in the very lap of the floods, and encircled in their watery arms.'[1]

Why would anyone choose such a place as home? Feltham, who was no fool, knew the answer. The Dutch had no choice but to live where they did. Their land, hemmed in by river and sea, was their safe haven. It enabled them to trade with the world while remaining protected from their enemies, in particular the mighty Spanish, against whom they had rebelled to form their breakaway state. Feltham, who was writing for an audience of Englishmen keen to discover how the Dutch had come from nowhere to dominate world trade, summed all this up in a single paragraph. The keys to their success were: 'their strength in shipping, the open sea, their many fortified Towns and the country, by reason of its lowness and irrigation, becoming unpassable for an army when the Winter approaches. Otherwise it is hardly possible that so small a parcel of Mankind should brave the most potent

Monarch in Christendom, who ... hath now a command so wide that out of his Dominions the Sun can neither rise nor set.'[2]

The Dutch Republic was the unplanned result of a bitter and bloody war, marked by numerous atrocities, most of which were motivated by religious intolerance or outright sectarian hatred. The trouble had begun in the 1550s, when the Spanish Habsburg monarchy ruled the entire Low Countries, from Brussels in the south to Groningen in the north. During that decade King Philip II of Spain imposed swingeing new taxes on his subjects in the Netherlands, while attempting to turn back the tide of the Reformation by persecuting Lutherans, Calvinists and any other Protestants daring to dissent from the Church of Rome. A staunch Catholic, he regarded such people as heretics, polluting his realm with their presence. He also took steps to centralize the local institutions of power, threatening to diminish the fiercely guarded liberties granted to towns such as Antwerp by their earlier rulers the Dukes of Burgundy.

The result of his actions was increasingly open rebellion against Spanish rule. In 1566 several hundred members of the lesser nobility solicited Philip II's appointed regent, his half-sister Margaret of Parma, to repeal the existing laws against heresy. She acceded to the request without asking Philip for his approval, unleashing a wave of Protestant enthusiasm. People long used to worshipping in private suddenly revealed their true beliefs. Militant Calvinist 'hedge-preachers' spoke to large congregations in the open air, provoking popular demonstrations that culminated in orgiastic episodes of iconoclasm: sackings of church, chapel or monastery collectively remembered as the *Beeldenstorm*, or Iconoclastic Fury.

Such spectacular outbreaks of violence against shrines and stained glass, statues and paintings, confirmed something that Philip already knew. The Catholic Church had become fatally weak in the Low Countries, making it all but impossible to stem the tide of those leaving it to find other ways to God. Just a few years earlier he had said as much to the Pope, when pleading with him to increase to fourteen the pathetically small number of four bishoprics offering Catholic pastoral care to one of the most densely populated regions of Europe: 'I cannot see how our religion can be maintained in these states.'[3]

Philip set out to maintain it nonetheless. Stung into action by the

Beeldenstorm, which amounted to open defiance of his government, he retracted his half-sister's repeal of the heresy laws and unleashed a Fury of his own. In 1567 he sent an army of 10,000 Spanish and Neapolitan troops marching northwards across Europe to crush his opponents in the Netherlands. At the head of this Army of Flanders he placed the Duke of Alva, a battle-hardened veteran who had fought in the military campaigns of Philip's father, Charles V. Alva was a short-tempered hardliner determined to root out heresy wherever he found it. On his arrival in the Low Countries, having promised his king a flood of gold from 'this northern Indies', he imposed a number of new taxes, which would be universally resisted, and set up a body that he called the Council of Troubles – and which the people of the Netherlands soon christened 'the Council of Blood'. Staffed by 170 inquisitors, its function was to seek out anyone suspected of heretical beliefs. Nearly 10,000 people would be investigated, of whom almost 1,000 were executed. Death sentences were passed 'without regard to sex, age or condition'; in other words, no exceptions were made for women, children or the elderly.

The Duke of Alva also ordered the construction of citadels directly above a number of larger towns, to cow them into submission. These heavily fortified garrisons were built at Valenciennes, Flushing and Groningen, but the most impressive was the citadel at Antwerp, erected by the military architect Francesco Paciotto of Urbino, in just four months, on the east bank of the River Scheldt and immediately above the city. To ensure that its purpose was lost on nobody, Alva erected at its centre a monumental statue of himself trampling Dutch rebels underfoot, cast from the bronze of cannon captured in his defeat of rebel forces at the Battle of Jemmingen (July 1568). This had been no glorious victory but a grim massacre, with 7,000 rebels left dead at the cost of around only 50 Spanish casualties. The city of Antwerp was even obliged to pay for the casting of the statue, which was dedicated 'To the Duke of Alva ... who extirpated sedition, reduced rebellion, restored religion, secured justice and established peace.'[4]

The duke's shock tactics cost thousands of people their lives and displaced many thousands more from their homes. Most Netherlandish nobles were forced into exile, including their eventual leader William I, Prince of Orange, who at first planned rebellion from his family castle in Dillenburg in the German state of Hesse.[5] Altogether some 60,000 men and women fled the country during the early years of the Duke of Alva's tyranny, most settling in England or Germany. But ultimately his arrogance and cruelty only strengthened the resolve of those determined to resist Spanish rule, creating a mood of simmering fury that finally boiled over in 1572. A ragtag army of recent converts to Calvinism, led by a small number of refugee nobles, captured the fortified seaport of Brielle, west of Rotterdam, and committed an atrocity of their own, rounding up and executing nineteen Catholic priests. Emboldened by their actions the rebel leader William of Orange appealed for more widespread resistance, rousing most of the northern Netherlands to open revolt. William was no Protestant radical, but he was fiercely opposed to Spanish tyranny and appalled by the actions of the Army of Flanders.

The Duke of Alva responded with brutal reprisals intended to extinguish the spirit of the rebels once and for all. Because of the intensely urbanized nature of society in the Low Countries, his campaign would be waged almost exclusively against people clustered together in towns and cities, during which the same dire pattern of events would be repeated: siege then surrender, followed by unspeakable atrocities carried out on a civilian population trapped within its own walls.

The terrors began at the southern city of Mechelen on 2 October 1572. The town had pledged allegiance to William of Orange a month before, opening its gates to his lieutenant Bernard van Merode, who had brought with him a garrison of 300 infantry and 5,000 cavalrymen. But when the Duke of Alva marched on Mechelen, Merode and his men made themselves scarce, leaving the town to fend for itself. A delegation of priests and citizens was sent out to placate the duke and his army, which they attempted to do by singing penitential psalms and promising unswerving fealty. They were ignored, as Alva decided instead to allow his men 'a little refreshment'. Even before the psalm-singing had finished the soldiers were inside the city. They would spend the following three days and nights pillaging the town, abusing and murdering its inhabitants. According to one traumatized eyewitness, Jean Richardot, every memory of those events was itself like an open wound: 'One could say much more about it if the horror of it did not make one's hair stand on end – not at recounting it, but just at remembering it.'⁶ The duke's report on the sack to his master Philip II consisted of a single phrase: 'not a nail was left in the wall'.

After Mechelen, the Duke of Alva focused his attention on the northern Netherlands, where resistance to Spain was at its strongest. On 14 November 1572 his son Don Fadrique entered the town of Zutphen, in Gelderland. He was met with little resistance but nonetheless ordered the entire garrison there to be executed, then turned his soldiers loose on the townspeople. Count Nieuwenaar, a stalwart of the Dutch Revolt, recorded that the city experienced a 'great wail of agony'. No further details are known because no other reports exist, a fact in itself ominous. It seems probable that more or less the entire population of Zutphen, amounting to some 7,500 men, women and children, were killed by the occupying troops.

From Zutphen, Don Fadrique continued on his murderous way to Naarden in Holland, just a few miles south-east of Amsterdam, arriving on 2 December. Within a day or two the townspeople were all dead, slaughtered by his soldiers. Some women and children briefly escaped the carnage by fleeing into the frozen fields beyond the city walls, but their tracks were visible in the snow and they were soon hunted down. Following the massacre, the Duke of Alva sent another of his terse reports to the King of Spain: 'not a mother's son escaped'.⁷

The massacres at Zutphen and Naarden changed the course of the Dutch Revolt, although not in the way that Alva and his Spanish overlords had envisaged. The campaigns were intended as exemplary acts of terror that would destroy the morale of the rebels and bring them to heel. The tactic had worked at Mechelen, but that was in the southern Netherlands, where support for the Revolt was by no means universal, and where the nature of the terrain stacked the odds against the rebel forces: the heartland provinces of Brabant and Flanders were open country, where the Spanish superiority in regular troops was almost impossible to overcome. In the Protestant northern Netherlands the situation was different. This was the place to which many of the most determined rebels had fled from the south, following their leader William of Orange, who proclaimed that he had decided 'to make my grave there'.⁸ Spurred on by his example, most of the nobility and patriciate had already shown their commitment to the rebel cause by late 1572: they had purged their civic government

Massacre of citizens at Naarden, December 1572. According to the eyewitness account of a local schoolmaster, the men of the town were made to assemble in the parish church, where they were ambushed and murdered while their wives prepared food to greet the Spanish invaders. This was merely a grim prelude to the killing of the entire population.

of Spanish supporters, pillaged Catholic churches and taken over monastic buildings for secular use. The mass murder of the citizens of two small northern towns did not demoralize them. On the contrary, it galvanized them, sharpening their awareness that now there really could be no turning back. Alva had reminded them of just how high the stakes were – failure meant death – but they were already all in. Besides, they had a trump card: the watery geography of the lowest of the Low Countries.

Dutch nationhood has its origins in the rebels' decision to retreat northwards and make their base in the seaward provinces of Holland and Zeeland. It was in the natural redoubt shaped by the geography of this region that they took refuge during the greatest crisis of the Revolt, in 1572–3. As a contemporary Italian observer, Cardinal Bentivoglio, observed, 'It is almost impossible to enter either of those provinces by force: because not only the chief places, but even the commonest towns are environed either by the sea, rivers or lakes, or by earth, than which there can be none more low, nor more miry.'[9]

In the words of an old Netherlandish proverb, 'God made the world, but the Dutch made Holland.' Much of the land they called home was reclaimed from the sea, the result of a contest between man and nature going back centuries and involving the creation of huge dykes of sand and rubble, the digging of hundreds of miles of canals and the drainage of thousands of acres of polder. Having shaped their environment so profoundly, they understood well how to defend it. With the forces of the Duke of Alva and Spain ranged against them, they used their expertise in water management and hydraulic engineering to repel any prospective invasion, creating a system of barriers and fortifications that included river forts and block-houses, areas of marshy wasteland and lakes that could be suddenly undammed to inundate advancing enemy troops. It was a strategy designed to cramp the movements of any conventional field army, and to sap their morale. Transporting equipment was a nightmare, as wagons loaded with cannon and shot were liable to sink and stick in muddy soil. Simply getting into position was a struggle when every key point of access was squeezed to a narrow, watery channel. Even the Duke of Alva's resolve was tested by such conditions: he complained that he had never been 'put to more trouble than in waging war against the rebels in the province of Holland, land of dykes, ponds and difficult passages'.[10]

By the winter of 1572, having doused the fires of rebellion in the southern Netherlands, Alva set out to subdue the troublesome northern provinces. He laid siege to the city of Haarlem with an army of some 18,000 men, expecting an easy victory. The statistics were on his side: the city's garrison numbered less than 2,000, while the entire population of the town amounted to just 11,500. But they put up such fierce resistance that any hope of a quick capitulation soon evaporated. The besieging Spanish army dug trenches, enabling them to advance on the V-shaped outwork that was the main defence of the town. It took them over a month in freezing winter weather, but when they finally scaled the fortifications they discovered that the citizens had pulled down several rows of houses immediately within the

VERMEER

Following the siege of Haarlem, in July 1573, the entire garrison was put to death in a single day, many bodies left to swing from the gibbet for weeks afterwards. This spectacle of death and retribution was staged on a platform erected in the Great Market Square, with the town hall and the famous cathedral of Saint Bavo as backdrop.

walls, creating new barricades from the rubble. The Spanish brought in coalminers from Liège to dig out the stubborn Haarlemmers, who promptly dug back, laying explosives and collapsing the besiegers' tunnels on top of them. As time passed, Spanish casualties ran into the thousands, caused as much by the persistent freezing damp as by the actions of an enemy held captive like a trapped animal.

Eventually, some seven months into the siege, cut off from supplies and without hope of relief, the starving townspeople surrendered. The Duke of Alva's son Don Fadrique entered the town on 14 July 1573, rounding up the entire garrison and those deemed to be the leading rebels among the townspeople. What followed was a bloodbath: the public execution of some 2,000 men. The first several hundred were beheaded, until the executioners could no longer raise their swords. The rest were tied back to back and thrown into the River Spaarne to drown. Those who survived this, many of them women and children, were subjected to a further orgy of looting, pillage, rape and assault.

Haarlem's fate seemed like the dire fulfilment of a prophecy made in a rebel song written in 1568, at the start of the Revolt, in which the Duke of Alva was compared to Herod:

> You come to these Netherlands
> As Herod, angry and fierce:
> To hang, murder and burn,
> To decapitate all with haste.
> So you will be disgraced with Babylon
> For all the innocent blood.[11]

Despite the fall of the town to Alva's men, the siege marked a turn in the tide of war. Its long duration and extreme difficulty brought home the scale of the problem facing Spanish forces in the northern Netherlands, where Haarlem was only one of many heavily fortified towns, defended by a people so fanatically committed to their cause that they were prepared to die for it.

After Haarlem, the Duke of Alva laid siege to Leiden in October 1573. He calculated that, if Leiden fell, then so too would Delft and The Hague, but resistance in Leiden was equally stout. Part way through the siege, finally worn out by the obduracy of the rebels and the persistence of his gout, Alva asked to be relieved of his command. He tartly advised his successor, Don Luis de Requesens, that 'every city in the Netherlands should be burned to the ground, except for a few to serve as garrisons and fortresses'.[12]

That was easier said than done: after five months of attritional siege warfare Requesens was obliged to lift the blockade of Leiden to counter a rebel incursion into the eastern Netherlands. When he returned to besiege the town once again, in May 1574, the surrounding countryside had been tactically inundated. In the words of a later Spanish historian of the conflict, 'The waters flowed ... among the trees and farmhouses, and a multitude of boats made their way through the drowned woods. It was like the ancient Roman theatres, where forest scenes gave way to wonderful inundations, on which whole fleets did battle.'[13] There was no garrison at Leiden, only the town's civic militia or home guard, known as the *schutters* (or shooters), but the people held firm nonetheless, encouraged by messages borne by carrier pigeons sent from Delft, where William of Orange had set up camp with 15,000 troops. At the eleventh hour, when there was nothing left for the townspeople to eat but cats, dogs and rats, William broke through the blockade with a flotilla of flatboats. The Spanish were forced to raise the siege.

The secretary to Governor Requesens was one of the first to realize that the Spanish campaign in the northern Netherlands was doomed to failure: 'The quantity of rebel towns and districts is so great that they embrace almost all of Holland and Zeeland . . . Indeed, if several towns decide to hold out, we shall never be able to take them. We who are on the spot can see all this with our own eyes, but the people at the Court of Spain have a dim and distant view . . .'[14] As expected, the order came from Madrid to push on regardless. A last desperate attempt to penetrate the northern heartlands of the Revolt was made in 1575, but although the Spanish army advanced deep into enemy territory it could gain no foothold. The town of Oudewater was sacked, resulting in another massacre, but it was a pyrrhic victory, stiffening rebel resolve and reinforcing the popular Dutch perception of Spanish soldiers as devils in human form.

Within a year the entire northern Netherlands was lost to Spain. Within a decade the Low Countries had been divided in two, a partition that would eventually result in a Roman Catholic southern state and an independent Protestant north known as the United Provinces, although not before a great deal more blood had been shed. The increasingly mutinous Spanish army, which was not merely underpaid but often unpaid for years on end, alienated the populations both north and south with their frequent brutalities. In an age of atrocities, the worst atrocity of all was the Sack of Antwerp in November 1576, when a 3,000-strong troop of Spanish soldiers mutinied against their commanding officers and ran amok in what was then Europe's richest city. Disillusioned by many months of siege warfare in low-lying Zeeland, and without pay for over a year, they marched south, first brutally sacking the Flemish town of Aalst before heading for Antwerp. They occupied the Duke of Alva's proud citadel, then descended on the city like wolves, storming its fortifications with such reckless bravery that Cardinal Bentivoglio was moved to comment, 'Never has disobedience been seen which produced greater obedience.'¹⁵ Having smashed a way into the city, they poured into its streets beneath a banner with Christ on the cross on one side and the Madonna on the other. They destroyed more than a thousand houses and burned down the town hall, repository of the city's ancient privileges, looting and murdering at every twist and turn of their rampage. Some 8,000 civilians died during the three days and nights that the horror lasted.

The Sack of Antwerp marked a turning point in the course of the Revolt. Revulsion against the Spanish was so widespread in its aftermath that the rebels were even able to establish a number of strongholds in the southern Netherlands. These included Brussels and Antwerp itself, where the Duke of Alva's citadel was levelled to the ground and the bronze monument to his hubris broken into pieces. But over the longer

Mutinous soldiers of the Army of Flanders run amok in Antwerp as the town hall goes up in flames: one of many depictions of Spanish atrocities produced by the printmaker Frans Hogenberg (1535–90), who moved to London and eventually settled in Cologne after having been exiled from Antwerp in 1568 by the Duke of Alva for his rebel sympathies.

term the rebels could not hold these gains in southern territory. Spain's new general in the Netherlands, Alessandro Farnese, Duke of Parma, retook Antwerp in August 1585, having already subdued Brussels. He thereby brought the lands under Habsburg control northwards to a line that would eventually be recognized by the treaties signed in 1648, at the end of the Eighty Years War, forming the permanent legal border between the Spanish Netherlands and the United Provinces. Essentially the same line defines the northern border of Belgium today.

The Spanish could not press home their advantage after the retaking of Antwerp. In 1588 Philip II tried to conquer England by linking a fleet from Spain with an army in the Netherlands. But his Armada was defeated and scattered to the oceans, which dealt a crippling blow to Spanish military power. Thereafter the Spanish had little choice but to concentrate on consolidating their power in the southern Netherlands, leaving the rebels in control of their watery northern redoubt above the deltas of the Rhine and Maas.

So it was that the Spanish Netherlands became a stronghold of the Catholic Counter-Reformation, while the United Provinces gradually took shape as a new political state, unlike any other in northern Europe. In 1590 a long-standing internal debate was resolved when it was decided that the rebels would no longer look for a monarch to act as their supreme head of state. They ruled that their own States-General, formed of delegates from the seven provinces of the northern Netherlands, possessed absolute sovereignty. These United Provinces became known as the Dutch Republic, although it was a highly decentralized one, with many powers reserved to each separate province and even each town.[16]

The Dutch Republic acted as a beacon to the traumatized Protestant peoples of the southern Netherlands during the years that followed the retaking of Antwerp. People travelled north to escape religious persecution but they were also drawn by the economic ambition of the Republic, which was determined to eclipse the old trading centres of Brabant and Flanders. Antwerp had once been the greatest commodity market of the Low Countries, but immediately after its recapture by the Spanish, in 1585, Dutch rebels blocked the River Scheldt and cut the city off from the sea. Amsterdam, the best-protected port in Holland, attracted the lion's share of displaced trade. Already a vibrant hub of shipping and distribution, it would rapidly become Europe's greatest trading forum in the first age of truly global commerce. From logs of pine felled in the Baltic states to spices sourced in the countries of the New World, more or less everything anyone might want to buy was stocked in the warehouses of Amsterdam. The city became a centre for banking, where credit and insurance could easily be arranged, while its commodity market was a permanent hive of activity. Meanwhile Antwerp's famous Bourse, once the lender of first resort to kings and emperors, was closed without fanfare and turned into a library.

The contrast between the two cities could hardly have been more extreme, illustrating in microcosm the rise of the north and the decline of the south. During the second half of the sixteenth century the population of Amsterdam trebled, rising from 30,000 to 90,000. Meanwhile that of Antwerp plummeted.[17] Just before the sack of 1576 it stood at 92,000, falling to 55,000 just after the Spanish retaking of the town in 1585, then down again to fewer than 40,000 by the end of the century. Sir Dudley Carleton, British ambassador to The Hague from 1616 to 1624, visited Antwerp and Amsterdam in close succession and was deeply impressed by the disparity between them. Antwerp was splendid but empty, whereas Amsterdam was seething with people but looked like a building site: 'there was a town without people, and here a people as it were without a town'. But Amsterdam's masses would be housed soon enough, such was the speed at which the city was rising: 'Their new town goeth up apace, which they make account will be finished and filled within two years.'[18]

Equally striking were the differences in rural life north and south of the line separating the Spanish and the Dutch Netherlands. Amsterdam was surrounded by fertile and productive farmland, and also by the Zaan industrial belt, where hundreds of commercial windmills and watermills produced a proliferating range of consumer goods. By contrast much of the countryside of Brabant and Flanders resembled the scene of a nightmare. By the century's end the entire region was little more than a war-torn wasteland, ravaged for years on end by the renegade troops of the perennially mutinous Spanish army. The fields were untilled and unsown, the dykes broken and the polders either flooded or dry as dust. There were no cattle and the farms lay in ruins because all the farmers and their families had either been murdered or had run away. Packs of wolves roamed the countryside, by day as well as night.

No wonder then that in the years after 1585 a great tide of humanity swept northwards, forsaking the Spanish Netherlands with all its terrors for the new world of the Dutch Republic. It was the largest displacement of population in the history of early modern Europe. Altogether more than 150,000 men and women emigrated, the majority settling in the towns of Holland and Zeeland. They made new homes and hoped to find work, as well as peace, in places such as Amsterdam, Leiden, Zierikzee, Groningen – and Delft.

It is among this swarm of refugees that the ancestors of Johannes Vermeer first come into view. The earliest known document about the painter's family is a notarial deposition of 11 January 1597 recording the presence in Delft, on that date, of his paternal grandfather, a tailor called Jan Reyerszoon: Jan, the son of Reyer. In those days ordinary working people had no surnames, men and women alike being identified by their father's Christian names. Jan's wife, Vermeer's paternal grandmother, was named Cornelia Gorisdochter (daughter of Gregory), which she abbreviated to Neeltge Goris. The fact that Jan was identified as a tailor is indicative of the couple's probable origins in the Spanish Netherlands. For centuries Flanders had been one of the centres of the European textile trade. Thousands of Flemish tailors, dyers, drapers and cloth merchants emigrated to the Dutch Republic during the exodus of the 1580s and 1590s. Jan and Neeltge had a son, Reynier, who was Vermeer's father. He was born in Delft in 1591, so it seems probable that the couple had arrived from the south just a year or two earlier than that.

Vermeer's forebears on his mother's side were immigrants from Antwerp. His maternal grandfather, Balthasar Gerrits, was born there in 1573. The painter's mother, Digna Baltens (daughter of Balthasar), was born in the same city around 1595. Balthasar and his wife, Beatrix van Buy, Vermeer's maternal grandmother, must have decided to leave their homeland not long afterwards. They emigrated north towards the end of the 1590s, when Digna was three or four years old. They were living in the province of Holland by 1600. A son, Reynier Baltens, was born to them in that year, in the city of Amsterdam.

These people were among the founders of the Dutch state, which was in large measure a republic of refugees. Their stories, which differed in detail but not in essentials, would be passed down the generations. Vermeer's grandfather Balthasar was old enough to have been present in Antwerp when the city was looted in 1576, its town hall burned and thousands of its inhabitants tortured and murdered. He was only three years old at the time, and there is no record of what happened to him or the rest of his family during those days and nights. But it cannot have been anything good. His daughter Digna would have been told the stories of mayhem and murder. She would have told them in turn to her son, Johannes Vermeer, future painter of peaceful rooms flooded with light.

Such stories were repeated in other families. Vermeer's older contemporary P. C. Hooft, a noted Dutch poet and historian, recorded hearing bloody tales of the Sack of Antwerp from his wife's grandmother. She, like Balthasar, lived through it all and survived to tell her nearest and dearest about the members of her family who had been robbed, beaten and tortured.[19] Inspired by her still smouldering sense of outrage at the atrocities committed, Hooft managed to acquire a small fragment from the statue of the infamous Duke of Alva that had once dominated the citadel at Antwerp: a thumb, made of bronze, which he used as a paperweight. Hooft's friend Joost van Vondel, the most celebrated playwright of the Dutch seventeenth century, wrote a short poem inspired by it:

> Your hand, Hooft, now plays with Alva's thumb
> But were he still in power
> His hand would have played with your head
> As with a ball in a game.
> How brittle and fragile tyranny is!
> Once you, Alva, had the nation under your thumb
> Now your thumb only inspires this poem.[20]

The people of the Dutch Republic shared a troubled history, one that would long rouse them to anger, regret and jubilant pride. But united as they were by the experiences of loss and exile, and the presence of a powerful enemy just beyond their borders, they were by no means unified. A new state required new rules and a new way forward, but during the early years of the Republic there was no consensus on how this was to be achieved. When the parents of Johannes Vermeer met and decided to marry, in Amsterdam in 1615, the Dutch Republic was so deeply divided as to be on the brink of civil war. At the root of it all lay a bitter dispute about religion. A proper understanding of both the nature of that dispute and the side Vermeer's parents took in it will be key to grasping the milieu that would eventually shape him and his art.

THE UNITED PROVINCES, DIVIDED

The Dutch Republic was unlike any other political state of its time, save perhaps Venice. But it was not a democracy. It was a federation of medieval oligarchies, each one representing a different city or region, with all sharing sovereignty. So, for example, the municipal government of a town such as Amsterdam was not made up of delegates elected by the people to represent their interests but instead composed of men known as regents, who were drawn from a self-perpetuating caste of ruling families. Every local government in the United Provinces was formed in the same way. The regents represented the upper crust of the Dutch bourgeoisie, many of them coming from merchant or manufacturing backgrounds. Not for nothing has the Dutch Republic been nicknamed 'a dictatorship of the upper middle-class'.[21]

During its formative years the Republic was blessed with an inspired leader, Johan van Oldenbarnevelt, who had taken the reins of power by 1590 and would hold them for nearly thirty years. With great diplomatic skill, he overcame the provinces' mutual suspicions to create a highly efficient federal state run from The Hague. Oldenbarnevelt held high office in the government and legal administration of Holland, so most of the key political decisions made by his administration reflected the will of Holland's regents. Because Holland was by far the richest and most powerful member of the seven United Provinces, the regents of its partner provinces were for the most part content to follow its lead. They also recognized the pragmatic need for someone to play the part of political leader. After all, the country was still at war with Spain, and would remain so for the best part of fifty years. Oldenbarnevelt's formal title was Grand Pensionary of Holland, but he was in effect prime minister of the fledgling Republic.

The exigencies of war added another layer of complexity to the Dutch political system. It had become customary for each member province to appoint a Stadtholder, or military commander, from the House of Orange, thus preserving a trace element of monarchy in a republican state. Oldenbarnevelt took the view that such important responsibilities were best consolidated under the command of a single individual. He succeeded in having his own preferred candidate, Prince Maurice of Nassau, second son of William of Orange, elected as Stadtholder in all but one of the United Provinces. Until their relationship soured, they proved to be a formidable partnership.

As supreme military commander of the Dutch Republic, Prince Maurice was a resounding success. He assembled a large army of reliable troops, subjected them to new codes of discipline, organized them into the tactical unit of the battalion, and paid them well and on time. Working with leading Dutch engineers such as Simon Stevin, he mastered the techniques of siege warfare developed by the Spanish and went on the counter-offensive. Between 1590 and 1604 Maurice captured swathes of Spanish-controlled territory in the Dutch provinces of Gelderland, Overijssel, Drenthe, Groningen and north Brabant, including forty-three towns and fifty-five fortresses. By doing so he took control of the entire network of strongholds and fortifications created for Spain, at huge cost, by the Duke of Parma as the basis of a future landward invasion of the Republic. By the end of Maurice's campaign it had become a common saying that 'the fence of the Netherlands is closed'.

The tides of war would continue to ebb and flow. In 1605–6 the offensives of a new Spanish commander, Ambrogio Spinola, reminded the Dutch that they could not afford to relax their guard. Thereafter the conflict became a stalemate, as the Spanish grudgingly resigned themselves to consolidating their power in the south and the Dutch focused on making their defences as impregnable as possible in the north. A large standing army was maintained, at times numbering almost 10 per cent of the entire population, and mostly stationed in garrison towns on the periphery of the Republic.

This entailed a huge and constant flow of money from the centre of the state – Amsterdam and the other great trading towns – to its vulnerable edge. But the merchants who bankrolled the Dutch military machine could hardly begrudge the burden of taxation it placed upon them: without the military efforts involved in securing the Republic's territory, the Dutch economic miracle could never have taken place. Immediately after the fall of Antwerp, many of that city's elite merchants and entrepreneurs had emigrated to German towns such as Hamburg, Bremen or Cologne; but by the end of the 1590s, convinced that the United Provinces were secure from military threat, the majority had settled in Amsterdam, bringing with them not only their capital but their skills and contacts.

By 1609, when the Twelve Years Truce was signed between the Spanish and the Dutch, it might be thought that all was well in the new Republic. Oldenbarnevelt's politics were those of the archetypal wise merchant, liberal and inclusive but with an eye for the bottom line. Under his leadership, which reflected the values of the regent class as a whole, the Netherlands was renowned throughout Europe for its unparalleled religious tolerance. Anyone settling there could hope to exercise their religion, so long as they did so in private, without persecution. This applied not only to people of every Christian denomination but also to Jews, who were demonized elsewhere. So it was that Sephardic Jews made unwelcome in Portugal and Spain flooded to Amsterdam during the first half of the sixteenth century, bringing with them their trading expertise and network of contacts in the New World. Religious discrimination would persist well into the mid-seventeenth century, meaning that Catholics for example were treated as second-class citizens in many towns, having to pay for their freedom to worship in barns or hidden churches. But, in the context of European society as a whole, the Dutch Republic was a beacon of tolerance.

To Oldenbarnevelt and his allies in the regent assemblies of the Republic, the acceptance of diverse religious opinions and practices was a cornerstone of the new state, and one of the primary causes of its prosperity. But they faced strong opposition from the leaders of the dominant Protestant Church in the Dutch Republic, namely the Reformed Church of the Calvinists. Theirs was the only Church privileged by the state, and the only Church in which public worship was permitted by law. But that was not enough for the more hard-line Calvinist preachers. They wanted religion to be more tightly regulated and envisaged a society that would itself be ordered according to religious codes of belief: a theocracy, from which anyone failing to embrace their idea of orthodoxy would be ruthlessly purged. The argument between the Calvinists and their opponents would divide the young Dutch nation for decades, causing bloodshed and unrest but also giving rise to vigorous new movements in theology, politics, philosophy and even painting.

The leaders of the Reformed Church dreamed of establishing a monopoly of recognized religion in the Dutch Republic, such as existed in most other western European countries. Their model was not so much Catholic France or Spain as Protestant England, where dissent from the doctrines of the state Church was tantamount to treason and punished accordingly: judicial murder, preceded by prolonged torture, those found guilty being burned at the stake or hanged, drawn and quartered. But constraining faith in such a way would prove all but impossible in the United Provinces, for reasons to do largely with history.

By 1600, only about 10 per cent of the Dutch population were members of the Reformed Church, meaning those who not only attended weekly service but also made confession and submitted to the discipline of their local Calvinist consistory. That figure can be doubled or even trebled if those attending church without actually becoming members are added: such people were known as *liefhebbers*, or well-wishers. But even so, the fact remains that far fewer than half of Dutch people were regular worshippers in the state-privileged Church. The rest of the Christian population followed many different paths and practices, reflecting every shade of dissenting belief spawned by the Reformation. There were Lutherans but also Mennonites, the followers of Menno Simons, who believed in adult baptism, marking commitment to the idea that every individual must act as if they were their own church, undergoing a personal reformation, beginning a new life modelled on that of Christ himself. There were followers of the spiritualist Sebastian Franck, for whom 'God is an utterable sigh, lying in the depths of the heart'. In the exasperated words of Reinier Donteclock, a Reformed minister in Delft, 'this Dutch land is as full of religious sects as the summer is full of mosquitoes.'[22]

This fragmentation of evangelical belief was a result of the peculiarly troubled history of the Reformation in the Low Countries. Fierce persecution of Protestants by the Spanish Habsburgs going back to the 1560s had included measures such as the setting up of a local Inquisition. People disenchanted with the Catholic Church had had no option, given the risks, but to continue attending regular Mass while keeping their real opinions to themselves. There was a name for such conscientious dissemblers: Nicodemites. In such circumstances it is hardly surprising that so many Netherlanders should have been drawn to discreet or private forms of Protestant rebellion.[23] John Calvin condemned such people as 'Libertines'. In truth the Dutch Republic was full of Libertines, who would never be easily persuaded that the Calvinist Reformed Church held the only keys to salvation. Having acquired the habit of spiritual independence, the Dutch would not easily surrender it.

Most Dutch regents practised a mild, tolerant and distinctly undogmatic form of Protestant Christianity. They had no objection to the existence of a single public Church. Some of them were members of it. But they were determined to restrict its powers. The more extreme Calvinists wanted control over publishing, bookselling and education, and demanded that the private right to worship of all non-Calvinists be rescinded. This was anathema to the moderate, wise merchant mentality. At the heart of the dispute lay two mutually exclusive conceptions of the Dutch Revolt itself. The hard-line Calvinists saw it as a struggle to establish a homeland for all who cleaved to the one true faith, namely theirs. The moderate regents saw it as a fight for freedom, everyone's freedom, from tyranny and repression. They believed that the state should have control of the Church, not the other way round.

This clash of attitudes led to open conflict, especially when the Calvinist consistories tried to clamp down on those whom they regarded as heretics. One such freethinking dissenter to come to their notice was an unfortunate textile worker in Amsterdam named Goosen Michielsz Vogelsangh, who denied not only the doctrines of God's omnipresence and the Trinity but even publicly doubted the divinity of Jesus Christ. The Calvinist authorities persuaded the Amsterdam magistracy that the man represented a threat and he was taken into custody, leaving his wife with five children to care for and no means of support. One of the leading Amsterdam regents, Burgomaster Hooft – father of P. C. Hooft, owner of Alva's thumb – was infuriated by what he regarded as a pernicious violation of the freedom of conscience. He made a public statement in response to Vogelsangh's imprisonment, which reveals the gulf separating the two sides in what was to become an irreparably rancorous argument.[24]

According to Burgomaster Hooft, the war against Spain had been fought to secure 'shelter for liberty but not an unbounded power for invading others'. Surely no government in the Dutch Republic could justify the use of force in matters of conscience, after so many years of persecution by Papists. Besides, any attempt to impose religious conformity was bound to be a losing battle: theirs was a land filled with sects reflecting every shade of Christian belief. Hooft's own wife was a Mennonite, he added, but he was hardly going to divorce her on account of that. It was completely unreasonable to think that in the mere twenty-five years that had passed since the formation of the Dutch state so many people of such widely differing opinions could be united within a single Church. He ended by rebuking the zealous Calvinists for failing to grasp the temper of 'our Hollanders, for we are wont to search the Scripture for ourselves'. The best way forward was the old Dutch way: live and let live.

Hooft made his speech in October 1597. Eventually the magistracy took his side and Vogelsangh was released. But the divisions exposed by the incident were not easily healed. Such was the depth of the divide that within a decade it had spawned a new terminology. On the one hand there were the *preciezen*, or precisionists, sticklers for absolute adherence to Church doctrine; on the other there were the *rekkelijken*, literally the looser, or more broad-minded, members of the Church. The argument between them soon became a larger struggle over the future of the nation. During these formative years of the Dutch Republic that argument would be fought out, essentially, over the ideas of one man. His name was Jacobus Arminius. He was one of the great moral and intellectual rebels of the early seventeenth century and also, it will be seen, a powerful influence on the life of Johannes Vermeer, from start to end.

ARMINIUS AND HIS OPPONENTS

The most formidable opponent of strict Calvinism was all the more repugnant to the *preciezen* because he emerged from within their own ranks. He was born Jacob Harmensz, son of Harmen, in 1560 in the small town of Oudewater, a typically Dutch oblong of human settlement strategically placed on a bend in the River Ijssel. His father, a maker of arms and armour, died shortly before Jacob's birth. At that time the town was under Spanish control and the official faith was Roman Catholicism, but the new ideas of the Reformation were spreading fast. A local priest with Protestant sympathies named Theodore Aemilius took the young Jacob under his wing, acting *in loco parentis* with the consent of the boy's mother, who had many other children to care for. Aemelius taught young Jacob Latin and Greek and probably encouraged him to reinvent himself as Jacobus Arminius, marking his vocation as a minister. It was the custom in the Low Countries for men of the Church to adopt fashionably humanist latinized names.

In his early teens Arminius moved with his adoptive father to Utrecht, where he studied at the *Hieronymusschool*, or St Jerome School. This was one of a number of schools that had sprung up

Jacobus Arminius, founding father of the Remonstrant movement and an inspiration to the Collegiants.

across the northern Netherlands more than a century before, under the impetus of a spiritual movement known as the *Devotio Moderna*, intended to galvanize popular devotion to Christ by promoting education for all. Adherents of the movement, whose leader was Geert Groote from Deventer, were known as the Brethren of the Common Life, and although they pre-dated the Reformation of Luther and Calvin they also prefigured it in many ways. They encouraged every man and woman to read the Bible and dared to suggest that the truly enlightened individual, who acted on Christ's example, had little need of the rites and rituals of formal religious observance.

'The man who knows how to walk the road of the inward life, and set little store by things outside of himself, has no need of special places, or set times, to perform his exercises of piety,' wrote Thomas à Kempis in the most widely read text of the movement, a devotional handbook entitled *The Imitation of Christ*. At Utrecht's St Jerome School, Arminius was exposed to such ideas. The Sermon on the Mount became his Bible within the Bible, and he would spend much of his life attempting to follow its instructions, caring for the poor and the sick, practising love not hate, turning the other cheek. He had a motto on the seal that he used to close letters: 'A good conscience is paradise'.

When Arminius was fourteen years old his protector died and he came into the care of another learned benefactor, a mathematician and linguist at the University of Marburg named Rudolphus Snellius, who took him to study at the university where he taught, enrolling him in the early summer of 1575. Two weeks later, news arrived from the front line of the war with Spain. Arminius's native town of Oudewater, which had taken the side of the rebels, had been sacked by Spanish soldiers. Every single member of his large extended family had perished in the resulting massacre: his mother, his brothers and sisters, his aunts and uncles, his grandparents, all had died. According to the later account of a friend, after two weeks of 'weeping and lamentation, almost without intermission', Arminius walked from Marburg to Oudewater to see the burnt-out ruins of the town and confirm the fate of his family. Then he walked back: a dismal pilgrimage of over 500 miles.

Somehow he managed to continue his studies. In 1576, aged seventeen, he enrolled at the brand-new Protestant University of Leiden, founded by William of Orange in a town specifically chosen for its heroic resistance to a Spanish siege. Supporters of the Revolt liked to repeat an adage popular with the republican humanists of Renaissance Italy: 'Every tyrant hates an educated population'; so for the Dutch rebels there could be no better rebuke to the tyranny of Philip II than to erect a university exactly where he had hoped to secure the defeat of their republic. According to its charter, the new university was to reverse 'that setback to needed education of the youth of Holland and Zeeland which the war had caused ... and the lack of good education in those lands, whereby all morality, knowledge and learning have gone to nothing'.[25]

Its opening ceremony was a spectacular riposte to the Baroque theatricals beloved of Europe's absolute monarchs, whose court artists regularly devised street pageants involving all kinds of allegorical bric-a-brac – triumphal arches made of wood and paper and such like – to proclaim the god-like powers of The Great Ruler. The procession inaugurating Leiden University turned all that on its head by proclaiming, instead, the power of God's own truth to liberate and enlighten mankind. Mounted cavalry escorted a single woman, dressed in robes of purest white, riding in a chariot with four attendants. She was Holy Scripture, they were the Four Evangelists. Behind them came four more figures who symbolized the four faculties of Theology, Law, Medicine and the Arts. They travelled from town hall to university, proceeding through a series of triumphal arches that can only have underlined the event's perfect inversion of the norms of Baroque propaganda: this was the triumph of no king or emperor, but of sacred education, the antithesis of despotism.

Arminius was only the twelfth student to be enrolled in Leiden University. By all accounts he was an exemplary one, being marked out for a bright future by the leaders of the Reformed Church. In 1581 he went from Leiden to Geneva, the crucible of the Calvinist Reformation, where he studied directly under Theodore Beza, John Calvin's leading acolyte. Beza was notably ruthless when it came to sharpening Calvin's views on salvation. Calvin had favoured the doctrine of predestination, according to which the fate of every human being had been decreed by God, but he had chosen not to spell out its full implications. Beza pushed that same doctrine to its logical extreme.

According to his formulation, even before Creation God had devised a great plan in which every single human being was irrevocably marked out as damned or saved. This plan was unalterable, non-negotiable and immune to human agency. If someone had been preordained to salvation then no matter what they did in this life they would, at the End of Days, ascend to heaven. If someone had been preordained to damnation there was nothing they could do to save themselves.

Arminius found Beza's teachings morally repugnant. From Geneva he was called to Amsterdam to become a minister in the Reformed Church, and duly ordained in 1588. It was not long afterwards that the depth of his unease with orthodox Calvinism became apparent. The occasion was a dispute within the Church caused by the irritant polemics of a self-taught theologian and confirmed Libertine named Dirck Volckertz Coornhert, who had raised serious objections to the doctrine of predestination. Arminius was called upon to compose a systematic refutation of Coornhert's arguments. He would not find it easy.

According to Coornhert, if the Calvinists were right and the fate of every soul were fixed forever, then repentance would be pointless and redemption impossible. But stories such as the parable of the Prodigal Son, the sinner who mended his ways, taught the exact opposite: 'this thy brother ... was lost, and now is found'. Coornhert branded Calvinism a murderously intolerant creed, citing the order given by Calvin himself for the execution of a presumed heretic named Michael Servetus in Geneva in 1553.

Charged with defending Calvinist orthodoxy against such withering attacks, Arminius faltered. His difficulty was that he agreed with his opponent. From the early 1590s he began sharing his doubts with his congregation in Amsterdam. This caused controversy throughout the city, and consternation among the elders of the Reformed Church. But the more Arminius thought about the doctrine at the heart of the matter, the more convinced he became that it was not just a mistake but a spiritual contagion, a pox of the spirit.

In 1602 Amsterdam suffered an outbreak of actual plague, which killed 10,000 people. Arminius tended to the sick for months. Many members of the Reformed Church, faced with the prospect of imminent death, took to strong drink or fell into other forms of debauchery. When challenged by Arminius they said that anyone predestined for salvation would know it from a feeling of unshakeable confidence, or *fiducia*. Because they felt *fiducia*, they believed they would be saved no matter what. On the other hand, Arminius encountered people who had led utterly blameless lives yet believed they were going to hell. A theology producing such results, he concluded, must be the work of the devil.

A year later, in 1603, he was appointed to a professorship in the Faculty of Theology at Leiden University. His enemies in the ranks of the *preciezen* publicized his supposedly scandalous opinions in the hope of having him condemned as a blasphemer. But the regents of the free Dutch Republic, men such as P. C. Hooft, made sure that every attempt to bring him to book was blocked by the civil magistrates. Arminius also had many friends within the Reformed Church itself: those who had their doubts about predestination, as he did, or who simply felt it should never have been made an article of faith. Thanks to their influence not only did he remain in post as Professor of Theology at Leiden, but in 1605 he was elected *Rector Magnificus*, chief officer of the entire university, the period of tenure being exactly a year. Increasingly debilitated by incurable tuberculosis, he decided that his parting shot should be a message of hope.

When Arminius stepped down as rector, in February 1606, he marked the moment by delivering an oration that distilled a lifetime's reflections on the horrors of war and the evils of religious intolerance: *On Reconciling Religious Dissension among Christians*. Republished and plagiarized many times throughout the seventeenth century, it was a speech that would have far-reaching consequences. Arminius's passionate arguments in favour of universal tolerance, freedom of religion and freedom of conscience would be widely disseminated by later generations of his followers, reaching far beyond the confines of the Dutch Republic.

He began his plea for toleration by comparing religious discord to a festering gangrene that had gradually spread through the body of Christendom since the start of the Reformation. The infection had been worsened by 'worldly minded rulers' who used it to involve 'their subjects in enmities, dissensions and wars, in which they had themselves engaged for other reasons'. No war is ever good, but a religious war is worse than any other, 'on account of every one considering his adversary as the most infectious and pestilent fellow in the whole Christian world, a public incendiary, a murderer of souls'.[26] Because of such heightened feelings, wars inspired by religion inevitably led to atrocities, ranging from the murder of an entire town's population to attempted genocide, as the events of recent European history proved: 'let us look at what has occurred within the period of our recollection and that of our fathers, in Spain, Portugal, France, England and the Low Countries . . .'

The list is significant, because it shows that Arminius meant to attack all forms of religious discrimination, not merely that between different types of Christian. Alluding as he did to the expulsion of the Arabs from Spain and the Sephardim from Portugal, Arminius drew the net of unacceptable intolerance wide, encompassing not only Catholic persecution of Muslims and Jews but also Protestant persecution of Catholics (in England) and vice-versa (in the Low Countries and France). No matter what the circumstances, faith should never be compelled and freedom of conscience should always be respected. Had not Christ himself approached a woman from Samaria to offer her the 'living water' of salvation, despite her protestation that 'Jews have no dealings with Samaritans'? If Christ had crossed that sectarian divide, his followers should do the same.

When Arminius made his heartfelt plea for peace, he was not speaking in the abstract. The Dutch Republic was at war with Catholic Spain when he gave his oration and had been for nearly forty years. He was calling for an end to that war and for the beginning of a time of reconciliation during which Catholics and Protestants alike might forget the doctrines dividing them and remember their shared devotion to Christ. Coming from a man whose entire family had been massacred on account of their faith, when he was just fourteen years old, the message carried weight.

Arminius had practical advice on how peace might be achieved. He suggested the setting up of an international body, somewhat like a seventeenth-century forerunner of the United Nations, the difference being that it was the churches of Christendom, rather than the sovereign states of the world, that Arminius wanted to bring together. What he had in mind was 'an orderly and free convention of the parties that differ from one another', a great synod to which all the purest spirits in the Christian world would be invited, regardless of Church or confession: 'men burning with zeal for God and for the salvation of mankind, and inflamed with the love of truth and peace'. Together the delegates would produce a consensus on all the issues that really mattered, namely the core Christian beliefs to which all Christians must subscribe. These need not be many, most being listed by Christ himself in the Sermon on the Mount. On everything else these new universal Christians would agree to differ, allowing brotherly love to prevail. The confessions and catechisms of every existing church would have to be put aside, or at least rewritten.

Arminius ended with a rousing vision of a future where all this would have been achieved. He foresaw a world in which religious discord would be no more, where universal love and harmony would reign and all Christians would be united as true followers of Jesus Christ. Then they would sing as one the words of Psalm 133: 'Behold, how good and how pleasant it is for brethren to dwell together in unity!'

CRISIS AND COUP D'ÉTAT

Arminius possessed the power of persuasion and drew multitudes to his cause. By the end of 1606 he had become the single most controversial individual in the Dutch Republic. He had delivered his oration at a particularly troubled time, when there was increasing friction between the political leader of the state, Johann van Oldenbarnevelt, and its military commander, Prince Maurice. Oldenbarnevelt was for making peace with Catholic Spain, whereas Maurice, as leader of the Republic's army, was predisposed to continue the fight. Because Arminius had spoken so decisively, not only on war and peace but many of the other issues that divided them, their differences crystallized around his name. Soon more or less everyone in the northern Netherlands would be either an 'Arminian' or an 'anti-Arminian'.

To be an Arminian was to be a member of the peace party, unreservedly republican, supportive of trade, and a defender of local and regional autonomy. It was to be tolerant in matters of religion but always to favour Christ's own example over any form of church teaching, as generations of Netherlandish dissenters had done. Arminians were naturally suspicious of the political ambitions of the Calvinist Church and determined to restrict its power, for example insisting that town magistrates rather than church councils had the sole right to appoint ministers.

By contrast, to be anti-Arminian was to be a member of the war party and solidly Calvinistic, to the extent of giving complete autonomy to the state-privileged Church and its ministers. It was to be intolerant of other Christian denominations, especially Catholics, and inflexibly predestinarian. It was to be militaristic, centralist and perhaps even to lean a little in the direction of monarchism.

Arminius himself died in 1609, so he never lived to see the denouement of the conflict that would be played out in his name. In that same year Oldenbarnevelt negotiated a twelve-year truce with Spain, much to the disgust of Prince Maurice. The truce amounted to a recognition that the southern Netherlands were lost forever to Spain, which was too bitter a pill for Maurice to swallow. His sense of betrayal was shared by most strict Dutch Calvinists, usually refugees of southern origin who continued to dream of retaking their homeland. Maurice naturally allied himself with such Calvinist hardliners. Opposing him were the regents, merchants and entrepreneurs, alongside the moderate Arminian Calvinists, all of whom favoured peace and took the side of Oldenbarnevelt. The battle lines were drawn.

On 14 January 1610, less than three months after the death of Arminius, forty-four of his supporters signed a Remonstrance, in which they appealed to the States of Holland to protect them against expulsion from the Reformed Church, while spelling out their disagreements with Calvinist orthodoxy under five headings. In a nutshell, they repudiated Beza's hard doctrine of predestination, asserting in opposition to it that anyone could be saved or fall from grace depending on their own behaviour in this life here on earth. But there was more to the Remonstrance than the signing of a piece of paper. The followers of Arminius saw it as their duty to defend the primacy of Jesus Christ in Christianity and to uphold the simplicity of his moral commandments. Theirs was a religion with a strong sense of mission, forever encouraging its adherents to help the helpless, stop the fighting, stem the blood.

Such was the strength of feeling in the ranks of the strict Calvinists that the Remonstrance could produce only one result: a deep split in the Dutch Reformed Church. Members of the clergy took one side or the other, followed by their congregations. As the schism deepened the combatants acquired new names. The followers of Arminius were now identified as Remonstrants, their orthodox opponents as Counter-Remonstrants.[27]

The Reformed Church proved powerless to resolve the dispute, which had all but paralysed the United Provinces by the middle of the decade. So it became the battleground on which the wily politician Johan van Oldenbarnevelt and the formidable military commander Prince Maurice would fight out their differences. For once in his long career Oldenbarnevelt miscalculated. He believed that the majority of Dutch people shared his own distrust of the Calvinist *preciezen*, whom he dismissed as a puritan fringe. He also believed that most Dutch people yearned, as he did, for a less divisive and more tolerant faith to help unite their infant republic. In truth the Counter-Remonstrants enjoyed a great deal of support, especially among working people living in the larger cities of Holland, and in rural areas in the north and east. Prince Maurice knew this all too well. So while Oldenbarnevelt busied himself winning the propaganda war, recruiting gifted men of letters such as Hugo Grotius to argue the Remonstrant case, Maurice bided his time. Then, in the summer of 1618, he staged a coup d'état. He was confident that the people would not rise against him, and he was proved right. Oldenbarnevelt's supporters were crushed without resistance. Oldenbarnevelt himself was placed under arrest and charged with high treason, along with many of his most prominent allies.

A few months later a national synod of the Reformed Church was called at the port town of Dordrecht, or Dordt, in the western Netherlands. Jacobus Arminius had called for a great synod in his manifesto for tolerance, but this was hardly what he had had in mind. The Synod of Dordt of 1618–19 was no gathering of seekers after truth. It was a show trial. The delegates were ultra-orthodox Calvinists to a man. Some came from as far afield as Switzerland, Germany and England, but the majority were Reformed Dutch divines, determined to enjoy their victory over the rebels in their own midst. There was never any intention that the detested supporters of Arminius would be seated as delegates or involved in the discussions in any way. The Remonstrants were summoned like defendants in court who had already been found guilty, to be reminded of the error of their ways and to learn their fate. Those who persisted in following Arminius would be sentenced to exile, with immediate effect. Those who renounced his teachings would be allowed to return to the fold. The synod concluded by reaffirming all points of Calvinist doctrine challenged by the Remonstrance. Everyone in the world was predestined by God for salvation or damnation. Those chosen to be saved would be saved no matter what, while those chosen to be damned would be damned without exception. There could be no falling from grace, and no rising up to gain it.

The final session of the synod took place on 9 May 1619. Four days later the seventy-one-year-old Johan van Oldenbarnevelt was publicly beheaded in The Hague despite widespread calls for clemency. These two near-simultaneous events signified victory over the double threat posed by the Remonstrants, or Arminians, as many still called them. Their theology had been outlawed, their political movement killed off.

Such at any rate was the message broadcast by Prince Maurice's propagandists and the Dutch Reformed Church in the immediate aftermath of Dordt and the judicial murder of Oldenbarnevelt. It turned out to be wishful thinking. In the long term the Remonstrant movement would recover, to become another of the many sects that multiplied like mosquitoes in the world of the Dutch Republic. Some of its adherents would form a new Protestant denomination on the principles laid down by Arminius, the first actual Remonstrant church being consecrated in Amsterdam in 1630. But, in the short term and until at least 1625, the Remonstrants struggled to come to terms both with their excommunication from the state-privileged Church and the total censorship imposed upon them.

Most, including Arminius's closest friends Johannes Uyttenbogaert and Simon Episcopius, chose exile and a clear conscience. They found refuge in the Generality Lands, a largely Catholic enclave of the United Provinces, and in the southern Netherlands, where they immediately began composing their new confession of faith. A minority recanted and were re-admitted to the Reformed Church, albeit under a cloud of suspicion. Others formed an underground resistance movement, bent mostly on survival, continuing to preach and

The beheading of Johan van Oldenbarnevelt (1547–1619), Grand Pensionary of Holland and the outstanding statesman of the Dutch Republic during its early years. Oldenbarnevelt was a pragmatic politician who preferred diplomacy to war and believed passionately in freedom of conscience and freedom of worship. His public execution, at the age of seventy-one, on the orders of Prince Maurice, raised fears that the Republic was at risk of becoming a tyranny.

teach in the Dutch Republic despite the blanket ban on their activities. They would minister behind closed doors to small groups of diehard Arminians, while keeping on the move to escape detection. They came to be known as the Brotherhood of Remonstrants. There were other brotherhoods (and sisterhoods) besides, some spawned by the Remonstrant example and the ideas of Arminius, but not always in perfect agreement with one another.

What does all this have to do with Johannes Vermeer and the many pictures by his hand once owned by the Van Ruijven family? Despite the relatively slender amount of archival material touching on the painter and his patrons there is a strong body of evidence connecting him, and them, directly to the Remonstrant movement. It includes some documents concerning his father and mother at the time of their meeting and marriage, in Amsterdam in 1615.

REYNIER AND DIGNA AMONG THE REMONSTRANTS

Vermeer's father, Reynier Jansz, was serving an apprenticeship as a caffa-worker in Amsterdam when he met Vermeer's mother, Digna Baltens. Caffa was an expensive silk satin fabric, mixed with wool or cotton, woven into fine patterns to make damask cloth. Reynier's father, Jan, had been a tailor, so Reynier was following a family tradition by going into the textile trade. His future bride, Digna, was living and working in the Amsterdam dyeworks (*'ververijen'*). Hers was a demanding job in the busiest quarter of the busiest town in the Low Countries, known for its bleacheries and soap factories as well as for its forests of creaking windmills, each harnessed to a different machine: mills were used for throwing silk, calendaring cloth and dressing leather, as well as for extracting oil and making gunpowder.[28]

Amsterdam in the second decade of the seventeenth century was a city at the centre of an industrial revolution, powered by wind. Every time it blew, Dutch merchants and manufacturers got richer. As business boomed the population increased, with builders and property developers struggling to keep up with demand for new houses, shop premises, factories. Reynier and Digna were close to the bottom of the city's economic ladder, he an apprentice, she a factory worker, but the entrepreneurial spirit of the place seems to have rubbed off on them. Not only would Vermeer's parents set up home together, but in time they would also start a business together.

The document attesting to their betrothal is dated 27 June 1615.[29] It records that Reynier, the son of Jan, from Delft, twenty-four years of age, having lived four years in Amsterdam, is hereby betrothed to Digna, daughter of Balthasar, aged twenty, from Antwerp, currently living in the '*Verweryen*' (*sic*). Digna was accompanied by her father, who confirmed that she had his consent to marry. Since Reynier was unaccompanied, the clerk noted that he was obliged to provide evidence of his father's consent in writing before the second proclamation of the marriage. The marriage was duly consecrated less than a month later, on 19 July, the ceremony conducted by a Dutch Reformed minister whose identity cannot be confirmed.[30]

This betrothal document has often been taken as proof that Vermeer's mother and father were members of the Reformed Church. But many Dutch people chose to be married or have their children baptized by Reformed ministers simply because they were Christians and the state-privileged Church was the only legally sanctioned public place of worship. In exchange for government support, the Reformed Church had to fulfil the role of a public church, which meant that ministers were obliged to marry or baptize anyone coming to them for that purpose. But only a minority of those doing so were actually members. Membership was not a requirement and it came, besides, with considerable obligations. Members had to make a confession of faith, in effect binding themselves to support and defend the doctrines approved by the Calvinist hierarchy. They also had to submit to Church discipline, which meant acquiescing to close supervision of their behaviour by ministers and elders. Any member committing a crime or misdemeanour would have to make a public confession and apology in front of the church consistory, or in front of the whole church in the case of severe sins, before being allowed once more to attend the Lord's Supper. Many people would not readily comply with these conditions. They might not agree with Calvinist doctrine on every point, or they might simply dislike the religious discipline that membership imposed, with the attendant risk of public humiliation. So it was that members were greatly outnumbered by *liefhebbers*: those who in theory wished the Reformed Church well, were happy to attend on Sundays and listen to the sermons, but preferred not to join.

The marriage of Vermeer's parents was almost certainly the marriage of two such people. It was definitely not the marriage of two committed members of the Reformed Church, whose meticulously kept membership records still survive. The archives of the Reformed Church in Delft, where Reynier and Digna lived from 1616 until their deaths, contain the names of every individual to have made their confession of faith. Nowhere do the names of Reynier Jansz and Digna Baltens appear in these registers. Nor does the name of Reynier appear in the acts of the Delft consistory recording those disciplined for unruly behaviour. Had he been a member of the Reformed Church he would certainly have been called to account for his involvement in a public brawl (known from other sources), that was so violent that one of the combatants died from his injuries.[31]

Vermeer's parents married within the Reformed Church without ever becoming members of it, so they must have been well-wishers. But of what kind? And would they continue to wish it well in the years to come?

In 1615, the year of the couple's betrothal and marriage, the Reformed Church was in a state of chaos: sharply divided between the followers of Arminius and their rigorist Calvinist enemies, between Remonstrant and Counter-Remonstrant. The conflict was at its height, the country at war with itself over the issues involved. No one with links to the Church could avoid taking sides. There are grounds to believe that the parents of Vermeer took the part of the moderates, the pacifists, those who cherished the memory of Arminius. Both Digna and Reynier had close friends and mentors who turn out to have been Remonstrants, and not just members of the rank and file, but significant players: people at the heart of the movement.

In the case of Digna, the trail of clues begins with her address as set down by the Amsterdam clerk recording her betrothal. The dye-works where she lived and worked is known to have been owned by a rich merchant and insurer named Jacques Rombouts I, before passing to his descendants on his death in 1612. The Rombouts family was originally from Digna's own native town of Antwerp, which may explain her presence as a live-in employee in the *ververijen*: it was common for refugees from a particular city to look after their own. Digna may have stayed in touch with members of the Rombouts clan long after she left Amsterdam for Delft. Her son Johannes would be in contact with a member of the same family, as we shall see.[32]

The Rombouts family was well known in Amsterdam for its strong support of Jacobus Arminius, especially during the later and increasingly vexed period of his life. Following his death and the signing by his supporters of the public Remonstrance against the Calvinist position on sin and salvation, they became committed Remonstrants. So close were they to the wellsprings of the Remonstrant movement that one of their number, namely Jacob Rombouts, a son of Jacques Rombouts I, married a daughter of Jacobus Arminius himself.

Jacob's marriage to Gertruyd, the twelfth and last of Arminius's children, took place in Amsterdam on 20 June 1626. The ceremony was conducted in a Reformed Church, but, since there was then as yet no legalized Remonstrant church in Amsterdam, that should not be taken to indicate the couple's allegiances. All it really shows is that they wanted to get married in public. Sure enough, when baptizing their daughter Elizabeth nine years later, in 1635, they took her to the newly consecrated Remonstrant church in Amsterdam.

The after-story of their union, insofar as it can be told from the known documents, is notable for a single striking detail. In 1636 Jacob Rombouts set sail for the other side of the world as an *ondercommis*, or commissary, of the Dutch East India Company. The following year he died, overseas, of causes unknown. Gertruyd Arminius was left with five children to care for, the oldest of whom, a boy, was ten years old at the time. He had been christened Jacob after his father but he also answered to Jacobus, the latinized name of his grandfather, the churchman Jacobus Arminius. The record then goes silent for all of thirty-eight years, at which point the selfsame Jacob or Jacobus Rombouts, by then a merchant approaching fifty years of age, appears in a document identifying him as the husband of one Johanna Kieft and placing him in a house on the Keizersgracht in Amsterdam, next to a soap-making establishment named The Three Mirrors. The document, dated 20 July 1675, records the loan of a considerable amount of money, 1,000 guilders no less, from the merchant and his wife to a painter from Delft named Johannes Vermeer.

This record of debt is Vermeer's last known appearance while still alive in any archival source: he died less than six months later. The wide span in the dates of these documents touching on the relationship between Vermeer's mother, Vermeer himself and the Rombouts clan may itself be meaningful. It suggests that from the time of his mother's betrothal to within a year of his own death a relationship of some kind had persisted between the two families. Might the basis of that relationship have been a shared commitment to the ideals of the Remonstrant movement? The fact that Vermeer's final recorded act was to request (and receive) a large loan from a grandson of that movement's founding father is surely significant.

Vermeer's father, Reynier, also had close links to the Remonstrant movement and its leadership. In his case too those links went back at least as far as the time of the couple's betrothal. It may be remembered that the notary recording that event had reminded Reynier of the requirement that he provide his father's written consent to the marriage. He could not do so, because his father was long dead: Jan the tailor had been buried in Delft's Nieuwe Kerk, or New Church, in 1597. Jan's widow, Neeltge Goris, had remarried, to a tavern keeper and musical entertainer named Claes Corstiaensz, who had brought up Reynier Jansz as his own and contributed 200 guilders towards the cost of his wedding in 1615. Under the circumstances it might have been expected that Reynier would ask his stepfather to provide the marriage affidavit in his father's place. But he did not do so. Instead he approached a preacher of the Reformed Church in his home town of Delft. A note in the margin of the betrothal document confirms that the preacher's attestation was submitted by Reynier in good time for the wedding to take place.[33]

This Reformed *predikant* was evidently Reynier's patron within the Church. This is of more than passing interest because the preacher in question was not just any Reformed minister. He was Johannes Taurinus, a passionate opponent of the Calvinist *preciezen* and the sole member of the Remonstrant faction in Delft during the tumultuous years that preceded its defeat and subsequent humiliation at the Synod of Dordt in 1619. He had close ties to those who would subsequently emerge as leaders of the Remonstrant Church, as well as friends in the splinter groups that formed as soon as the movement was driven underground. If, as seems more than likely, he had influence with Vermeer's father and mother, he can only have pointed them in one direction.

At the time when Johannes Taurinus was signing the attestation for Reynier Jansz in 1615, he and his parishioners were vigorously petitioning the civic government to appoint more *rekkelijke*, or broad-minded preachers. As the only minister in Delft who supported the Remonstrants, Taurinus was trying in vain to turn the tide in their favour. By the start of the following year Remonstrants across the Dutch Republic were waging an increasingly heated war of words with their Counter-Remonstrant enemies.

Johannes Taurinus was not the only member of his family to be involved in the conflict. While he personally mustered support in Delft, his elder brother, Jacobus, was writing pro-Remonstrant pamphlets for distribution in Amsterdam. A gifted satirist, this Jacobus Taurinus became a leading propagandist of their cause. In one rhetorical flourish, he retrospectively recruited the mythical Maid of Holland and the ghost of William of Orange as stalwarts of the Remonstrant movement. In the aftermath of Maurice's coup d'état a warrant was issued for his arrest, and he fled to Brabant.

Johannes Taurinus may not have been as high on the wanted list as his brother Jacobus, but he was a person of interest to the leaders of the new ultra-orthodox regime. Church records reveal that he had a history of agitating against strict Calvinist ministers within the classis of Delft, the governing body of pastors and elders.[34] He was named as an obstinate troublemaker in a booklet written by the secretary of the Synod of Dordt for circulation among its delegates,[35] and less than two weeks before the synod commenced he was suspended from his ministry. He ignored the ban, prevailing on friends in the Delft consistory to allow him to preach in his usual turn on Sunday 4 November 1618. As a result, he was ordered to appear before the Church Council and 'maintain his cause there as well as he could'.[36]

What happened next is intriguing, not least to anyone interested in understanding the religious milieu of Vermeer and his parents. The principal source of information for these events is Gerard Brandt's *History of the Reformation*, which despite its title is no general study of the Reformation but an exhaustive history of (and apology for) the Remonstrant movement, written from the relatively fresh perspective of the 1650s and 1660s by one of its staunchest defenders. According to Brandt, Johannes Taurinus promptly turned traitor to the Remonstrant cause when he appeared before the Delft Church Council. He renounced the teachings of Arminius and apologized for having strayed. A few days later he publicly recanted his Remonstrant beliefs from the pulpit of his own church, before his own congregation. And what did he get for all his trouble and humiliation? The Calvinist consistory 'kept him out of the pulpit ... all they gave him was a small benefice at Maasland, a little village near Delft'.[37] It served the purposes of Brandt's history to turn Taurinus into an exemplary figure of the collaborator who got his just rewards.

All this made for a neat cautionary tale, but further research into the Delft church archives paints a different picture of Johannes Taurinus, family pastor to the parents of Vermeer.[38] While it is true that he publicly recanted his Remonstrant beliefs in 1619, it seems that he may have been acting strategically, so that he could continue to work for the Remonstrant cause. By the mid-1620s he was once more in trouble with the authorities. He had been attempting to negotiate a 'moderation' with the Remonstrants, and was pleading in vain with the elders of the Reformed Church to soften the doctrines of Dordt so that the followers of Arminius might be welcome once more. By the summer of 1627, members of his congregation in Maasland were reporting that he had become increasingly irascible and was introducing into his sermons lengthy attacks on the Delft Church Council. When summoned to account for his behaviour, Taurinus repeatedly failed to appear. He did not even attend the meeting at which he was officially dismissed as a Reformed minister. Three years later, in 1630, Johannes Taurinus reappeared one last time in the reports of the Delft classis. By then he was living as a private citizen, with no church affiliations, but had nonetheless come to their notice by publishing a 'booklet' in which he attacked 'the perseverance of the saints': namely the Calvinist doctrine, detested by Arminius, according to which no member of God's elect can ever fall from grace no matter how they behave.

So Taurinus was no traitor to the Remonstrants, but a moderate and even a would-be moderator: someone who had hoped to heal the wounds of the past from within the state-privileged Church. His recantation had been a pragmatic masquerade. This was a known tactic in the Low Countries: the strategy of the Nicodemite. It had allowed him to continue serving God publicly as a minister while privately preferring the teachings of Arminius to the doctrines of Dordt, and presumably encouraging those close to him to persist in those beliefs themselves.

Given that Johannes Taurinus was part of the Remonstrant resistance in the years after Dordt, it is more than possible that Vermeer's mother and father were part of it too. They certainly had connections to a number of people in the Remonstrant movement. By the early 1630s, when their son, Johannes Vermeer, was conceived and born, Reynier and Digna had long since moved back to Delft and were living on the Voldersgracht, or Fullers' Canal, just off the Great Market Square in Delft. Just a few doors down the canal was the home of none other than Johannes Taurinus and his wife, Margaret van der Meer (no relation).[39] The Remonstrant firebrand and the parents of Delft's most famous painter were living as neighbours.

THE BODY IN THE BARN

This is an opportune moment to recall one of our unanswered questions about Johannes Vermeer. What might he have had in common with his patrons, Pieter Claesz van Ruijven and Maria de Knuijt, the people for whom he would paint almost all of his life's work? The beginnings of an answer may be found during these years of civil conflict, in the histories of their respective families. We have seen that Vermeer's mother and father had close links to people active in the Remonstrant cause during the period immediately before and after the Synod of Dordt. So too did the antecedents of Pieter Claesz van Ruijven.

Not only did the Van Ruijven family know people in the Remonstrant underground, they provided a safe house for them in Delft. This is clear from Gerard Brandt's *History of the Reformation*, which includes a story about a particular incident that took place in Delft at the height of summer in 1621, when 'the times were so bad that a Remonstrant minister was not permitted to live quietly, nor even to die in peace'.[40] During this time of fierce persecution, not only were Remonstrant ministers forbidden to preach but anyone with known Remonstrant sympathies was barred from public office.

Pieter Jansz van Ruijven was the head of the family, father to Niclaes Pietersz and grandfather to Pieter Claesz van Ruijven. He had been a regent of Delft, but having been stripped of his functions and powers by Prince Maurice he was now merely a private citizen, kept under watch by a network of Calvinist scouts. It was at the home of Pieter Jansz van Ruijven on the Voorstraat, next to the family brewery known as The Ox, that a Remonstrant minister had been hiding when calamity struck:

> It happened at Delft that Johannes Spenebovius, who secretly ministered to the Remonstrant church of that town, died suddenly of an

apoplectic fit, on the evening of St Peter and Paul's day, at the house of Heer Peter Joost van Ruven [sic] (formerly one of the Senators of Delft, but turned out upon the late Revolution). Here the family was extremely embarrassed, not knowing what to do with the corpse ... After some deliberation, they put it into a wooden chest, and buried it under a barn, in the backside of the house. But this secret interment was afterwards discovered through the timorousness of a maidservant, who being ordered to fetch something out of the said barn, cried, 'I can't go there, the dead man lies there!' This was accidentally overheard by somebody in the brewer's yard adjoining to this house, and discovered by that person to his sister, who lived with the Scout. Thereupon Ruven was summoned before the Magistrates ... [who] condemned him nevertheless to pay a great fine for having harboured a Minister.

Pieter Jansz van Ruijven was fined the cripplingly large sum of 500 guilders: a townhouse could be bought for less.

His son Niclaes had a stake in The Ox and would inherit the family brewing business. He too was a lifelong Remonstrant, barred from public office but allowed to serve as Master of Delft's Chamber of Charity, which he did from 1623 to 1624.[41] Niclaes' own son Pieter Claesz van Ruijven was born in 1624, when the story of the body in the barn was still fresh in the family memory.

The unfortunate preacher, Johannes Spenebovius (or Speenhovius, as he is more commonly styled), had been a close friend of Jacobus Taurinus, brother to Johannes Taurinus. Delft was a small town and those who had played a part in its Remonstrant resistance were a close-knit circle. Back in the early 1620s Johannes Taurinus and anyone in his orbit would have known the Van Ruijven family, and vice-versa. Each would have considered the other friend not foe. The link between Vermeer and his future patron was forged in these years, before either of them was born.

SECRET AGENTS AND SOLDIERS

During the early part of their married life Reynier and Digna lived in a down-at-heel quarter of Delft, next to the Small Cattle Market where pigs, sheep and bullocks were brought to be slaughtered and sold. In 1620 a daughter was born to them. They named her Gertruy. An inventory of their household goods made three years later reveals that they owned a small collection of pictures. These included two paintings of Old Testament scenes: a *Story of Lot* and a *Sacrifice of Abraham*, the latter illustrating an episode from the Bible that had a particular significance for the refugees clustered in the cities of the United Provinces, reminding them of their own trials of faith and of the sacrifices they had made – including the loss of many Dutch sons – during the struggles of the Revolt.

The little group of paintings in the house also included 'portraits of the prince and princess', namely the future Stadtholder Frederik Hendrik and his wife, as well as a portrait of 'Stadtholder Maurice'.[42] Vermeer's parents were showing their support for the military commanders of the Dutch state, present and future. Arminians or Remonstrants (the terms had become interchangeable by the 1620s) believed that conflicts were best settled through diplomacy, but that did not prevent many of them supporting their own side in the continuing war against Spain.

The Twelve Years Truce came to an end in 1621, followed by a renewal of hostilities. The fighting was not in Holland but far away, in the south and in the east, but the Dutch Republic was once more under siege. Spain had invested heavily in its standing army in the Low Countries, increasing its numbers to some 60,000 troops, deployed in a vast arc to encircle the Dutch Republic from Lingen to Flanders. In response Prince Maurice pursued a cautious strategy, strengthening the chain of fortresses that formed the Dutch defensive cordon, but the States-General were nevertheless obliged to increase their own standing army from 30,000 to 48,000. New taxes to pay for the war effort provoked riots in Delft, The Hague, Amsterdam, Hoorn, Enkhuizen and Haarlem, where the civic militia – the painter Frans Hals among their number – fired on the crowd, killing five.[43]

Vermeer's maternal grandfather, Balthasar Gerrits, and his uncle Reynier Baltens were bit players in the power politics of this volatile time. Sometime in 1619 Digna's father, Balthasar, was recruited by the organizers of a botched undercover operation seemingly intended to enhance the precarious national security of the Republic. He was discovered running a counterfeiters' workshop on the north side of The Hague, where he and his team had allegedly amassed a small fortune in forged coin. Balthasar escaped arrest but his son Reynier, Digna's brother, was subsequently detained as an accomplice. During the ensuing trial it emerged that they were hired hands working for powerful people, including two representatives of George William, the Elector of Brandenburg.

Elector George William was an important ally of the Dutch Republic, a Calvinist and therefore a declared enemy of Spain. He had acquired the Duchy of Cleves by way of a treaty negotiated by his father, Johann Sigismund. Cleves was a natural gateway to the easternmost United Provinces, commanding several crossing points on the lower Rhine that directly approached the weakest section of the Dutch defensive cordon: the route through Cleves was the course of invasion that had been threatened by the Spanish general, Ambrogio Spinola, in 1605–6, causing widespread panic. In 1614 the States of Holland and the States-General of the Republic had loaned Johann Sigismund several hundred thousand guilders to help him acquire Cleves and raise an army of mercenaries to expel the Spanish soldiers who still occupied much of its territory. Elector George William had struggled to repay the loan his father had contracted, much to the concern of Prince Maurice, who worried that in the worst outcome Brandenburg might cede Cleves to the enemy.

It is possible that Maurice himself was behind the counterfeiting plot, the purpose of which may have been to enable his ally to repay his debt with dud coins so convincingly forged they might never be detected by the Dutch treasury. If the bungled plan did not originate with him, it is plausible that he might have given it his blessing. At one point during the trial it was alleged that Maurice would pardon the counterfeiters no matter what, although the testimony paints such a murky picture that the full truth is unlikely to emerge. What is sure is that the two presumed masterminds of the plot, the men with direct links to Brandenburg, were not pardoned but beheaded, in early August 1620. The minnows on the other hand were allowed to escape the net: Digna's father and brother, Balthasar and Reynier, were set free with a caution and nothing more.[44] As a postscript to the episode, some twelve years later and shortly after Balthasar's death, his widow, Beatrix, explained to a committee interviewing her for a job as town midwife that she would have applied for the position earlier had her husband not used her for 'trips and travels in secret services of the Land'.[45] Such an exotic excuse is unlikely to have been a pure fabrication. Was Balthasar a secret agent of some kind?

He and his son Reynier had proven connections to the military. By 1623 both men were in Gorinchem, also known as Gorkum, a fortress town strategically sited on a branch of the Maas, the river separating Holland from Spanish-occupied Brabant. Many troops were deployed there during the years immediately after the end of the Twelve Years Truce. Military engineers were called in to strengthen the fortifications by building new bastions, ravelins and a counterscarp. This type of work may have been something to which the ingenious Balthasar turned his hand during later life. His son Reynier became a qualified military engineer or pioneer, as they were known. During the 1640s this same Reynier, Vermeer's maternal uncle, would be directly employed by Maurice's half-brother and successor, Prince Frederik Hendrik, to produce siege machinery during one of the last military campaigns of the Eighty Years War.

The other Reynier in the family, Digna's husband and Vermeer's father-to-be, had shown solidarity with his brother-in-law during the trial for forgery in 1621, readily giving witness to his good character before a notary in Delft. It was not unusual for men with military connections to get into a spot of trouble with the law: the notarial archives of the time are crowded with the names of soldiers guilty of disturbing the peace in one way or another. Almost a fifth of young men in the Dutch Republic were soldiers or sailors. This heavy military presence, made up mostly of foreign mercenaries, would have been especially evident on the periphery of the Republic, in fortress settlements like Gorkum or Deventer, the largest garrison town of all. But it was also very much a part of life in Delft as Vermeer's parents knew it, indeed throughout the Eighty Years War.

The strategic importance of Delft and its port of Delfshaven had long been recognized. As early as 1572 the States-General of the embryonic Dutch Republic had chosen the city as the site of its central gunpowder store, sequestering a former Catholic chapel at the western edge of the town that became the '*Generaliteits Magazijn*', or General Arsenal. Thirty years later, in 1602, the States of Holland built their own large gunpowder store, the Armamentarium, on the De Geer canal. Soon afterwards the Dutch East India Company opened a branch in Delft, with offices and warehousing opposite the Armamentarium. Not only were troops stationed in the town to guard the vast munitions stores, and oversee the distribution of their contents, but the place was also inundated with enlisted men embarking on ships bound for distant places. Delft was a city crawling with soldiers.

In 1624 Reynier was still trying to make a living from silk-work when the Republic suffered its worst outbreak of plague for a generation. In Amsterdam 11,000 died, and Delft was not far behind: at the height of the epidemic, the notaries responsible for registering deaths were so rushed that their handwriting became all but illegible. Reynier and Digna and their daughter, Gertruy, who had just turned four, could count themselves lucky to survive. But trouble of another kind was just around the corner. In the summer of 1625, as the plague subsided, Reynier and a fellow caffa-worker, together with another man, found themselves accused of assault with intent to cause grievous bodily harm. The case involved a violent dispute between Reynier's little group and one of the many young soldiers temporarily quartered in Delft, a man named Willem van Bylandt. The latter came off worst in the fight, suffering multiple serious injuries. Reynier and the other two assailants initially took flight, but then returned to town, having agreed to pay their victim six Flemish pounds in compensation for his wounds. In exchange Van Bylandt released the three men from all future obligations to him, promising further that should God Almighty restore him to health he would invite them to his house and spend five guilders on a treat for all: a magnanimous gesture, which also suggests that he took some responsibility for provoking the fight in which he had been hurt. In the event, the young soldier died of his injuries in November the same year.

Reynier disappears from the Delft archives for the next three years. In 1629 he re-emerges, but in a different line of business. A number of documents reveal that he was by then an innkeeper, with an establishment on the north side of the Voldersgracht, or Fullers' Canal. Was he prompted to reconsider his life in the aftermath of the soldier's violent death?

The profession of innkeeper was an affront to strict Calvinists, for whom the tavern was a gambling den as well as a breeding ground for alcoholics. But to those with a more relaxed attitude to religious belief, inns felt like home. Innkeepers were obliged to allow their clientele complete freedom of conscience and more or less total freedom of expression, because if they did not people would boycott their establishments. The Dutch went to inns not merely for food and drink but to exchange news, talk politics and argue about religion, with luck in an amicable way, so an innkeeper who excluded people on the grounds of their beliefs could never prosper.

It will be remembered that one of Reynier and Digna's new neighbours on the Voldersgracht was a man they already knew, their former patron in the Delft ministry, Johannes Taurinus. It may be wondered whether he encouraged Vermeer's parents to embark on their new life. What is certain is that these were the years in which Taurinus reshaped his own life, when he gave up his ministry in Maasland, publicly denounced the Reformed Church and wrote a series of reflections in which he attacked various Calvinist doctrines such as the perseverance of the saints.

In the ever turbulent world of Dutch Christianity, the 1620s was a decade of particular turmoil and innovation. As Taurinus and other followers of Arminius urgently thought through the implications of their rebellion against Calvinist dogma, the Remonstrant movement mutated in startlingly unpredictable ways. As a result many of the preconceptions shared by Christians of all persuasions, for centuries and more, were called into doubt.

A CHURCH WITHOUT AUTHORITY

It had never been Arminius's intention to split the Dutch Reformed Church. By arguing for more tolerance from within the Calvinist hierarchy he had hoped to heal dissent between the *preciezen* and those like himself who took a liberal view of the beliefs necessary for salvation and a Christian life well lived. Arminius had encapsulated the republican and libertarian outlook of many Dutch people, but he had never intended to form those people into a revolutionary band of brothers. The Remonstrants became an association by virtue of the Calvinist witch hunt that drove them into exile, or underground. They were reluctant to form another Protestant sect, but felt they had no alternative.

After the Synod of Dordt, the Remonstrant organization was run from Flanders and Brabant by the exiled leaders of the movement. They sent emissaries to the Dutch Republic to coordinate the activities of Remonstrant predicants already hiding there and to swell their numbers. These undercover agents of liberal Dutch Christianity discreetly ministered to loyal congregations who shared their own disenchantment with the Reformed Church. This secret organization of the Remonstrant faithful soon proclaimed itself to be a new

The opening of the Synod of Dordt, 13 November 1618. The synod was convened by the elders of the Dutch Reformed Church with the express purpose of expelling the Remonstrant followers of Jacobus Arminius. Some 'Arminians' merely pretended to toe the line, while staying inwardly true to their beliefs, one such being the only known Remonstrant preacher in Delft: Johannes Taurinus, family preacher to the Vermeer household.

Church, albeit an outlawed one. The event was marked by the publication, in 1621, of Simon Episcopius's *The Remonstrant Confession*, a summary of the movement's beliefs written by its chief spokesman at that time.

It is a text burning with the righteous resentment of a persecuted minority: 'we have been put out of our ministries, separated and violently torn away from our churches ... then ejected from our country and banished forever ...'[46] But, on matters of doctrine, the *Confession* was coolly unrepentant. Episcopius reiterated the Remonstrants' rejection of the Calvinist position on predestination, calling for a return to the freedom and simplicity of the evangelical dawn of Christianity. Like Arminius, the Remonstrants were doctrinal minimalists for whom the entire content of Christianity was distilled to belief in God and belief in the teachings of Jesus: 'we call living and true faith that which necessarily has joined to itself good works and a sincere correction of the whole life, structured upon the commandments of Jesus Christ ...'[47] The message could not have been clearer: pray well, behave well, and you will go to heaven.

The Remonstrant Confession was unlike any previous document of its type, because it did not claim to provide final answers. Episcopius stressed that his text was no more than 'bare expositions of our belief ... formulas which do not define or establish what is held for true or false ... but only make known and testify what Remonstrants believe'.[48] This was the theology of humility taken to an extreme. The Remonstrant Church was unique among Christian churches in claiming no monopoly on truth, and in refusing to condemn those who differed from its opinions. But there was a sting in the tail. What was true of their own Church, the Remonstrants argued, was true of every other. The Catholic Church, the Lutheran Church, the Dutch Reformed, the Church of England: none had any authority to pronounce on the meanings of the Bible, and none could claim to be the one true Church of Christ.

That was not to say such a thing did not exist, because according to the Remonstrants it did. Scattered among the congregations of the world's many churches, sometimes existing outside of any Church, were those men and women who truly believed in Christ. These true Christians, who knew no distinction of sect or dogma, formed the invisible Church: 'This assembly is visible only to God, but invisible to us, since true faith and piety, which lie hidden within the heart, none but God can behold, the only searcher of the hearts and inward parts.'[49] In passages such as this the Remonstrants came close to the spiritualist approach of Sebastian Franck and Dirck Coornhert, who had also believed in the existence of this unseen host of true Christian believers.

Behind *The Remonstrant Confession* lay the utopian vision projected by Arminius. Its aim was not to supplant other confessions but to undermine confessional religion itself, putting an end to sectarian conflict throughout Europe and allowing Christians of all persuasions to unite under the banner of peace and mutual understanding.

CHRISTIANS WITHOUT A CHURCH

Most Remonstrants would have shared the sentiments so carefully worded by Simon Episcopius. But still his text left room for doubt, not so much about the nature of the problem as the choice of solution. If every visible Church with its own confession was an open door to schism, why found yet another new one? Why not embrace the purer idea of the invisible Church, and strive to be part of that instead? Perhaps the time had come to give up on conventional Christian worship and invent something else to put in its place.

One small group of Remonstrants had already come to that conclusion by the time *The Remonstrant Confession* was written. In 1619, following the Synod of Dordt, a Remonstrant preacher named Christian Sopingius was suspended from his ministry at the village of Warmond, outside Leiden. His replacement was an orthodox Calvinist, whom the congregation rejected. They boycotted his sermons and began to hold secret weekly meetings of their own in a private house, during which they prayed, read passages from the Bible out loud and took it in turns to comment on the passages in question, entirely without clerical supervision. Anyone could speak whatever was on their mind, as long as it was spoken with the intention of enlightening others in the room. If no one had anything to say there would be a period of silent prayer.

At first these meetings were no more than an ad hoc substitute for regular Sunday service. The faithful Remonstrants of Warmond were waiting for the Brotherhood to send one of its incognito ministers to lead them once more. But as the wait grew longer they became increasingly comfortable with their new approach. An apparently bereft Remonstrant congregation came to realize that a stratagem chosen by necessity could form the basis for a permanent religious way of life. Theirs was an unplanned revolution, but a revolution nonetheless.

The ringleader was Gijsbert van der Kodde, elder of the village and a self-taught theologian, whose father had been a follower of Arminius and came from a long line of dissenters. Gijsbert had three brothers, Johan, Adrian and Willem, who became his allies in promoting the idea of the leaderless religious gathering. Reading Holy Scripture constantly as they did, they became especially interested in the writings of St Paul. Paul was important to them because he was so early, therefore an authentic voice from the dawn of Christianity. Travelling across the ancient world, to Asia Minor, Greece, Judea and Syria, Paul had nurtured some of the earliest Christian communities, establishing patterns of worship that pre-dated by centuries the practices of any institutional Church. In his epistles, written to instruct the first Christians, the Van der Koddes found descriptions of ancient customs to inspire their own practice. They particularly cherished Paul's exhortations to the early followers of Christ, in which he galvanized them to gather and recite the words of the gospel to one another, to share one another's interpretations of those texts, to teach and encourage one another – without ever a mention of priests or a priesthood.

From Paul's first Epistle to the Corinthians they took their belief that the ability to 'prophesy', a biblical word meaning to explain or elaborate on Scripture, was a gift of the Holy Spirit that every Christian should cultivate:

> desire spiritual gifts ... that ye may prophesy ... he that prophesieth speaketh unto men to edification, and exhortation, and comfort.
> (1 Corinthians 14:1–3)

Later in that same epistle the Van der Koddes discovered a clear directive to hold meetings at which each and every congregant should feel free to speak (or sing) their spiritual beliefs and insights:

> How is it then, brethren? when ye come together, every one of you hath a psalm, hath a doctrine, hath a tongue, hath a revelation, hath an interpretation. Let all things be done unto edifying. (1 Corinthians 14:26)

To the Van der Koddes, such passages proved that priests were unknown in the early communities established by Paul, and therefore unnecessary. By practising 'free prophecy' they and their fellow congregants at Warmond were demonstrating the superfluity of priesthood in the modern world as well. They soon came to think of themselves as pioneers of a new religious movement. But what was it to be called? At first they referred to their meetings as 'Prophets' Assemblies' and to themselves as 'The Prophets'. Later those assemblies came to be called 'Colleges', and those attending 'Collegiants'. That was the name that stuck.

The Remonstrant leadership only became aware of how far things had gone at Warmond in 1620, when one of their novice priests working under the direction of the Brotherhood risked his life to get to the village, only to be informed that his services were not required. Gerard Brandt tells the story in his *History of the Reformation*:

> Gilbert [sic] van der Kodde, hearing of [the novice priest's] arrival, gave him indeed an outward welcome; but . . . he told him, that there was no occasion for his coming into the country with such manifest danger to his person; and that, besides, he brought the people who received and concealed him into the like dangers, without the least necessity . . . Then he gave him an account of the method which had been already used at Warmond; and subjoined, if you would take my advice, it should be to go and learn some good trade.

The Remonstrant leadership then sent in a senior pastor, Paschier de Fijne, to bring the errant sheep of Warmond back into the fold. He later wrote an account of his mission to the village,[50] which paints an incomplete but precious picture of the group's activities:

> They came together to edify one another in the truth and in Godliness, without a preacher. Someone would read a few chapters from the Bible and say a prayer. And then if they could bring messages of admonition, edification and instruction to one another, they would do so. They would do their best, after such knowledge they had of God. Gijsbert

van der Kodde and his brethren had in mind to introduce this way of doing things as a necessary custom in the congregation of God, rejecting the way of preaching ... I have seen them make their prophecies from the evening all the way through to the morning, even until noon. In the meantime there were some among them who were fast asleep.[51]

De Fijne regarded the prophets of Warmond as an eccentric group, although he was grudgingly impressed by their stubborn enthusiasm. When he offered to minister to them, they refused. When he requested a meeting to explain the contrasting views of the Remonstrant leadership on free prophecy, they declined on the grounds that the concept of leadership was essentially unchristian, so for any of them to meet with the leaders of the Remonstrants, any of their representatives, or even one of their priests, would risk corrupting their community. An increasingly frustrated De Fijne proposed a compromise: if they would allow him to minister to them in the usual way, including the preaching of his sermon, he in turn would listen to their prophecies. True to form, they turned him down, saying that preaching could have no place in a Christian gathering. The principle of *'alleensprecken'* – literally, one-person-alone-speaking – was anathema to them. True religion was not a building made by just one bricklayer. Everyone had a part in the work of edification.

De Fijne eventually accepted that the Van der Koddes and their friends would not be persuaded to change their ways.[52] He left Warmond never to return, reluctantly acknowledging the Collegiant movement as a radical new strain of Remonstrantism. In 1621 the Collegiants moved their 'Prophets' Assembly' to Rijnsburg, a village a few miles away, where they continued to hold leaderless meetings at which the principle of free speech was rigorously preserved, and to which all were welcome, the only qualification for attendance being belief in the saving power of Christ.

Despite the initial reservations of their leadership, most Remonstrants soon came to think of the Collegiants as partners in the fight against intolerance, some actively founding Colleges of their own. The Collegiant approach also attracted many Waterlander Mennonites, so named after the watery region in northern Holland that was their heartland, who were doctrinally liberal and determinedly pacifist. But there were Roman Catholics too among the Collegiants, and plenty of Dutch Reformed. There were even a number of Jews. Many continued to go to their own services as well as attending Collegiant meetings. Part of the appeal of the new movement lay in the fact that it was emphatically *not* a Church, nor even strictly speaking an organization, and asked for nothing but good faith from those who entered its circle. During the decades that followed the Collegiant movement grew in size and significance, spreading to many of the principal cities of Holland, where it attracted leading scientists, philosophers and politicians as well as a strong core of working-class men and women drawn by the promise of a space for religious reflection in which their voices might be heard.

None of this might have happened had it not been for the early support given to the Collegiants by the most dynamic and original thinker of the Second Reformation, as it has come to be known, namely the poet, painter and polemicist Dirck Rafaelsz Camphuysen. It was probably Camphuysen who introduced the ideas of the Collegiants to Johannes Taurinus, who subsequently passed them on to Remonstrants in his circle, profoundly influencing the religious climate of Delft during the late 1620s and early 1630s. These are the links in a chain of influence leading to the parents of Vermeer, and ultimately to the painter himself.

THE RELIGION OF CONSCIENCE

Gerard Brandt in his *History of the Reformation* tells us that Camphuysen was the principal evangelist of the Collegiant movement during its early years: 'Among those who joyn'd them, and contributed very much to the increase of their numbers, as well as their credit, was Dirck Camphuysen ... who since then has deserved no small praise among the best Christians, by his ingenious Poems and Paraphrases on the Psalms.'[53] By the 1650s, when those words were most likely written, Camphuysen had become a cult figure among the followers of Jacobus Arminius, conservatives and radicals alike. This was thanks in part to his *Stichtelike Rymen*, a hugely popular book of verse which included a number of variations on the Psalms so admired by Remonstrants

Dirck Rafaelsz Camphuysen (1586–1627) wrote poems, hymns and theological polemics. Advocate for a Christianity without churches, based solely on the teachings of Jesus, he was revered in the freethinking circles to which Vermeer's friends and patrons belonged. He is shown accompanied by Faith, Hope and Love.

and Collegiants alike that they sang them as hymns in their congregations and meetings. One of the best loved was a fugue-like rendering of Arminius's favourite, Psalm 133.[54]

Camphuysen was born in 1586, in the fortress town of Gorkum. Orphaned at a young age, he was brought up by his elder brother and studied painting in the workshop of a local artist. He subsequently enrolled at Leiden University, where it was felt that he was destined for a career in the Church. He began his studies in 1608, just a year before the death of Arminius, when the fierce quarrel between Arminians and their *preciezen* opponents was dominating the university's faculty of theology. Camphuysen took Arminius's side and became close friends with the arch-Remonstrant Jacobus Taurinus, brother to Johannes Taurinus, pastor to Vermeer's parents. Camphuysen took holy orders but his career as a Reformed predicant was cut short by the coup d'état that removed Oldenbarnevelt from power, marking the victory of the hard-line Calvinists over the Arminians. He went into hiding, moving from town to town and preaching in secret at the request of Remonstrant congregations.

Soon after the leaderless meetings began at Warmond, Camphuysen got wind of them and went to investigate. He admired the Collegiants' determination to share one another's thoughts on the New Testament without the intervention of a pastor, and accepted their justification of the practice by reference to the writings of St Paul. He set himself the task of writing what would become in effect the manifesto of their movement.

In 1622 Camphuysen retreated to the sparsely inhabited island of Ameland, north of Friesland, where he wrote his principal treatise, *Vant onbedriegelik oordeel tusschen goede ende quade*, or, *Of Infallible Judgement between Good and Bad Doctrine*: a scathingly brilliant defence of non-confessional religion in which he proposed nothing less than the complete dismantling of institutional Christianity as he and his contemporaries knew it. He was inspired both by the Collegiants' desire to go back to the roots of Christianity and by the spiritualist concept of faith as a personal and interior experience.

Camphuysen was opposed to all confessions and every form of religious organization, especially churches. For him, nothing was *less* Christian than a Church. He saw them as little more than power structures dominated by the power-hungry, therefore implicitly corrupt. To Protestants who argued that this applied only to the Church of Rome, seat of the Pope and origin of the Inquisition, he replied that the leaders of the Protestant churches were themselves just little popes with smaller thrones: 'in sum – it is the same devil'.[55]

Like his Collegiant friends, Camphuysen had an aversion to the principle of *alleenspreken*, the single sermon by the single speaker. No priest had a greater right to interpret Holy Scripture than any other human being. To claim otherwise was to hide Christ's egalitarian message behind an authoritarian lie. Those seeking the cause of sectarian conflict need look no further than the authority figures set up by organized churches, whether *Leeraer*, *Meester*, *Herder* or *Bisschop* (teacher, master, shepherd or bishop).

In politics as in religion Camphuysen was essentially a communist before the invention of Communism. Just as every human soul is created equal by God, he argued, so every human being has an equal right to voice their interpretations of Holy Scripture. Because there can be no exceptions to this rule of equality, men have no priority over women.

The earliest Collegiant meetings were dominated by men, partly it seems out of patriarchal habit. But, once the egalitarian implications of the leaderless gathering had been fully absorbed, women became genuinely equal partners in the movement. In the entire recorded history of Christianity, the seventeenth-century Collegiants were among the rare few to give women equal rights to speak alongside men during worship: at the peak of the movement's popularity roughly 70 per cent of those attending Collegiant meetings were female.[56]

Camphuysen's Christianity was entirely focused on personal morality and behaviour. He reduced religion to private thought and public action, with no space whatsoever allocated to the ceremonies and rituals performed in church. True faith was felt in the heart of each individual, and nowhere else. This rigorously decentred vision of Christendom was regulated by a single principle: the conscience, implanted into every human being by God as an infallible means of judging right from wrong:

> The conscience is like the vicar of God within our hearts; And if, when we scrupulously consult it, and put ourselves to the test according to the Law of Christ, and find then that our conscience does not condemn us, we have the right to believe without hesitation that God has passed a favourable judgement on us.[57]

There was a relentless consistency to Camphuysen's thought. If the heart was the true carrier of authentic faith, and if the conscience was the infallible vicar of God, then the entire caste of priests, specialists in theological knowledge and reasoning, was redundant at a stroke. The primacy of conscience was proof that churches are unnecessary, the corollary of that being a Christianity decoupled from all established power, needing no leadership, no organization, no institution.

Camphuysen distrusted intellectual speculation, but he strongly believed that men and women should exercise their faculty of reason when reading the Bible. Scripture was clear on all questions necessary for salvation. The moral commandments at the heart of Christ's teaching, in passages such as the Sermon on the Mount, were demonstrably rational truths. If everyone obeyed them there would be no conflict. For all his pessimism about the institution of Christian churches, Camphuysen was an optimist. He regarded Original Sin as a myth invented by false priests to control people by shaming them. He believed passionately in the perfectibility of man. What he hoped to see, although not in his own lifetime, was the proliferation, cell by cell, of leaderless gatherings at which individual Christians would help one another, however haltingly, walk into the light.

REFLECTIONS ON THE PARABLE OF THE SAMARITAN WOMAN

Camphuysen died in 1627, at just forty-one years of age, exhausted by a life lived in poverty, much of it on the run. In his last years he associated with the Collegiants at Rijnsburg, by then the centre of their movement. He also spent some months at Delft in 1625, when he was almost certainly in contact with Johannes Taurinus, pastor to Vermeer's parents. One way or another Taurinus came to know about the leaderless gatherings of the Collegiants, and to share Camphuysen's enthusiasm for a Christianity without churches.

During the years when his disenchantment with the Reformed Church boiled over, Taurinus published two volumes of highly personal biblical commentary entitled *Reflections on the Parable of the Samaritan Woman*. The first volume was printed in 1625, the second in 1630, by a publisher named Jan Pietersz Walpot based in the Great Market Square in Delft, possibly in the same premises later known as The Golden ABC. Taurinus's text is, despite its title, a stream-of-consciousness reflection on multiple passages in the Bible. It might almost be an anthology of the open-ended biblical commentaries that Collegiants were wont to share with one another at their meetings. Hardly anyone seems to have read it for hundreds of years.

In his introduction to the first volume, Taurinus referred to his expulsion from the Reformed Church: he was 'putting in writing what I cannot say in the pulpit'.[58] The main thrust of what followed was that Christianity needed to be purified to become a religion of individual believers, reading the Bible for themselves, without interference or doctrinal policing.[59] For Taurinus as for Camphuysen, the outward ceremonies of the Church were meaningless. Faith was experienced internally in the heart, and expressed externally in good deeds.[60]

On the subject of Christian community Taurinus pointedly made no mention of the Reformed Church, nor any other. Instead he recommended his readers to form small groups, to read Holy Scripture together, to encourage one another in the pursuit of Christian virtue, and to bring others into their Christian friendship circles so that they too might participate in mutual edification. He constantly invoked St Paul, quoting in particular his words about 'teaching and admonishing one another' from Colossians 3:16, a text regarded by Collegiants as one of the bedrocks of their movement. He was clearly promoting, in Delft, the spread of small conventicles or cells for prayer, free prophecy and the singing of psalms, on the model of the assemblies at Warmond and Rijnsburg.

Between 1625 and 1630, as he severed his links with the Reformed Church once and for all, Johannes Taurinus was actively and publicly promoting ideas promulgated by the new radical movement that had sprung up within the ranks of the Remonstrants. He was able to do so without fear of persecution because the political climate had changed dramatically in the Dutch Republic during those same years, bringing an end to the harsh intolerance demanded by the Synod of Dordt.

Prince Maurice died in 1625 and was succeeded by Prince Frederik Hendrik, who preferred compromise to confrontation and allowed many leading Remonstrants to return from exile. Within a few years members of the newly established Remonstrant Church would be allowed to worship in private, just like Catholics or Mennonites or any other Christians refusing to join the Reformed Dutch Church. The Remonstrant Church would only ever be home to a small minority of Dutch Christians, but 'Remonstrant' and 'Arminian' became terms freely used to denote anyone thought to be a religious or political liberal.

Such people became markedly more prominent in the public institutions of the Republic after Maurice's death, even though the urban working class remained strongly in favour of the hard-line Calvinists. Frederik Hendrik steered a middle way between these opposing groups, attempting to keep the Counter-Remonstrants happy with the victory they had won within their own Church while at the same time forming an alliance with the increasingly powerful liberal element in the regent class, whose nominations to the town councils of Holland and Utrecht he actively supported. The results of his policy were soon apparent: in

1626, Sir Dudley Carleton noted that 'at Delft ... Arminians are crept into the Magistracie by the nominacion of the burgers'.[61]

The Arminian regents who regained their positions in this way were not inclined to persecute anyone for their beliefs. It was their policy to restrict the powers of the Reformed Church. They believed in the sovereignty of the States assemblies and regarded Maurice's coup as a violation of the Republic's constitutional principles. They disliked the drawn-out war with Spain and longed for an end to it, promoting peace talks at every opportunity and consistently arguing for cuts to the Dutch defence budget. But above all they were for toleration and freedom, not only in the field of religious belief but in the wider sphere of thought, regarding censorship as intellectual tyranny.

Johannes Taurinus was confident in the backing of Delft's new pro-Remonstrant administration. He even dedicated his *Reflections on the Parable of the Samaritan Woman* to two 'Arminians' in the city magistracy, whose names he abbreviated to 'V.Ed.M' and 'A.A.', thanking them all the more 'because they have handed me a certain amount of money to maintain my household'. If we know one thing about Taurinus it is that he was an evangelist. Free from need, free from censorship, free from pastoral duties and supported by a benevolent regime, he presumably spent his remaining years, until his death in 1637, communicating the ideas of the Collegiants to his many friends in Delft, and encouraging them to participate in this radical form of Remonstrant Christianity.

A BOY

When they went into business as innkeepers, Vermeer's mother and father may have resigned themselves to the likelihood that their daughter, Gertruy, would be their only child. She was ten at the time and still had no brothers or sisters. Then, two years later, in the autumn of 1632 a son was born. Digna was thirty-seven when she gave birth. The late coming of this male child was not quite a miracle, but it must have seemed like a blessing.

Digna would have been attended during labour by a midwife, whose duty it was to deliver the baby, wrap him up warmly and present him to his father while making the short speech prescribed by tradition, its sombre tone reflecting the high infant mortality rates of the time: 'Here is your child. May Our Lord grant you much happiness through him, else may He call Him back to Him soon.'[62] It was then customary for the family of the newborn to hang a small placard, made of wood covered with red silk and trimmed with lace, on the door of their house. If the baby were stillborn, the silk over the placard would be black. The placard hung at Reynier and Digna's door was red.

The baby was baptized at the Nieuwe Kerk in Delft, on 31 October 1632, by a minister of the Reformed Church.[63] Not much can be read into that, because there was no other option then available to a family with Remonstrant leanings: Delft's Remonstrant Church would not open until 1638. It does again show that Vermeer's parents were not violently averse to church services and ceremonies, as Camphuysen and some more radical Collegiants were. But many people dissatisfied with the Reformed Church were still happy to get married there, to have their children baptized there and to be buried there: it was part of tradition.[64]

The name chosen for their son by Reynier and Digna was, however, a departure from tradition. It was customary to honour a boy's paternal grandfather by naming the child after him. Reynier's own father had been called Jan, the most common of all male Christian names across the Netherlands. But the new child was christened Johannes, or Joannis, as the name was set down phonetically in the register: a latinate version of Jan hardly ever adopted in working-class families like that of Reynier and Digna. This would normally have indicated a child destined for a classical education or called to serve God. Churchmen proud of their learning, like Jacobus Arminius, often latinized their Christian names; but it was rare for a boy from humble origins to be given such a name from birth.

The only identifiable Johannes in the circle of Vermeer's parents was the charismatic Johannes Taurinus, who had signed as a proxy for Reynier's late father Jan at the time of the couple's betrothal back in 1615. Their choice suggests that they may have followed him on his subsequent journey, from rebellious Remonstrant to pioneering Collegiant, and come to see their neighbour on the Voldersgracht as someone whose example they wanted their own boy to remember.

PART TWO

Childhood, Education, Marriage, 1632–57

THE FLYING FOX

Keeping an inn in the centre of Delft seems to have suited Vermeer's parents. His father was a confident and outgoing man, the more so after his change of job. From the early 1630s and thereafter he appears frequently in the offices of the Delft notaries, taking a hand in the affairs of other people, appearing as witness to their contracts for debt or other obligations.[1] Reynier and Digna liked innkeeping well enough to take on a larger establishment later in life, The Mechelen Inn on the Great Market Square, which they would run together from 1641 until Reynier's death in 1652. It was in and around these busy places, full of talk and news and bustle, that Johannes Vermeer spent his formative years. It was here that he may first have heard about the tolerant religious beliefs of the Remonstrants and the Collegiants.

Reynier named his first inn on the Fullers' Canal after himself, in a punning and playful way: it was called '*De Vliegende Vos*', The Flying Fox. From around 1625, following the new fashion among the Dutch for taking on surnames, Reynier Jansz had taken to calling himself Reynier de Vos. His given name was derived from the French word *renard*, meaning fox, while his new surname was Dutch for the same animal. So from this point in his life until 1641, when he switched to the quite different surname of Vermeer, he wanted people to think of him as a fox twice over: not just cunning, but doubly cunning. That Reynier had fables on his mind when choosing his name seems all the more likely in light of the fact that Aesop's well-known compilation of stories was published in Dutch under the title *Reynaerd de Vos*.

Aesop's tale of the fox and the grapes exists in many versions, the most concise being that of the Roman fabulist Phaedrus:

> Compelled by hunger, a fox tried to reach some grapes high on the vine but could not, although he leaped with all his strength. As he went away, the fox said 'Oh, you aren't even ripe! I don't need sour grapes.'

It is a story about the psychology of self-deception, the moral being that people irrationally disparage that which they cannot attain. The name Vermeer's father gave to his inn proposes a defiant alternative to the sulky defeatism of Aesop's fox. Do not accept your own apparent limitations. If you cannot climb up to the grapes, grow wings and reach them anyway: become a flying fox. There would have been a sign over the door of Reynier's inn, decorated with the arresting image required by its name. The innkeeper may have painted it himself – he had learned to draw when training to be a silk-worker – but, whether he did or not, the idea behind it was his. He was advertising his own optimistic character as well as his ambition to rise above his humble origins and reach for things that his parents and grandparents could never have reached. He was also advertising the quality of his wine: no sour grapes here.

Soon after taking on his new inn and just over a year before the birth of Johannes, Reynier had started another business as well. In October 1631 he registered in Delft's Guild of St Luke as an art dealer, which meant that he was licensed to sell pictures, as well as food and wine, from the premises of The Flying Fox. Anyone employed in the arts or crafts was obliged to apply for membership of the guild, named after St Luke because according to the saint's legend he had painted the first portrait of the Virgin Mary. A forerunner of modern trades unions, the guild protected the interests not only of painters and sculptors but all kinds of other craftsmen, while also overseeing the activities of those trading in their wares. As stated in its regulations, the guild's net was drawn wide enough to include 'everyone earning their living here by the art of painting, be it with fine brushes or otherwise, in oil or watercolours; glassmakers; glass-sellers; faienciers; tapestry-makers; embroiderers; engravers; sculptors working in wood, stone or any other substance; scabbard-makers; art-printers; booksellers; sellers of prints and paintings, of whatever kind they may be'.² Reynier was in no position to flout the rules: The Flying Fox was on the same street and virtually next door to the guild. In due course Reynier's son, Johannes Vermeer, would also become a member.

One of the many consequences of the booming Dutch economy was a rapidly expanding market for Dutch art, which flowered as never before during the four decades of Vermeer's short life. Many of the most celebrated Dutch artists, including Rembrandt, Frans Hals, Pieter De Hooch and the prolific Ruisdael family, were active between 1632 and 1675. Their patrons were regents and rich merchants, and their wives, whose taste was less predictable than that of the kings, queens and aristocrats employing painters in other European countries. This gave Dutch artists scope to experiment and innovate, to explore new ways of painting both the outside world and the inner self. So far as we know, Vermeer's father, Reynier, had no especially famous painters on his books. He most likely sold the work of journeymen artists from Delft to a modest local clientele. Dealing in pictures was a handy sideline for an enterprising innkeeper, who had a constant flow of potential buyers coming through his door.

Reynier probably liked art and artists, and must have shown creative talents of his own to have taken up the skilled craft of damask-weaving. It is probable that he had many friends who were craftsmen or painters by the time he became an innkeeper. Reynier's notary in Delft, Willem de Langue, acted for various members of the city's Guild of St Luke, including the well-known artist Abraham Bloemart. De Langue was also an art collector, so it may have been through him that Reynier came to know some of the painters whose work he would display on the walls of The Flying Fox.³

Reynier and Digna's presumed links with the followers of Jacobus Arminius and their connection with Johannes Taurinus, pioneering initiator of Collegiant meetings in Delft, may also have helped them develop this new side to their business. A number of leading figures in the history of Dutch nonconformist religion had been artists: Dirck Volckerts Coornhert, one of the strongest advocates of non-confessional religion and a powerful influence on Arminius himself, worked as an engraver all his life; Dirck Rafaelsz Camphuysen, advocate of a Christianity without churches, was trained as a painter. Many of the artists whom Vermeer encountered as he was growing up were in sympathy with the tolerant ideals of the Dutch freethinkers and religious rebels. If painters went to a particular place to eat and drink it was probably a place known for openness in matters of religion, politics and most other things.

Reynier's circle of artist friends was extensive enough to include painters from out of town. A document in the records of the Delft notary A. van der Block reveals that in 1631 a still-life painter from The Hague named Jan Baptista van Fornenburgh paid for his son Barend, who had enlisted as a soldier in the Dutch East India Company, to live at The Flying Fox while waiting to set sail from Delfshaven. He was to board the ship *'s-Hertegenbosch*, so named after a recent Dutch victory in the Eighty Years War: the taking by siege in 1629 of a reputedly impregnable fortress on the border of the Republic that had, until then, been Spain's main stronghold in the northern Netherlands. At the request of the boy's father, Reynier sent young Barend off with a barrel of brandy. Despite the auspicious name of the ship, it was an ill-fated foreign adventure. The notary's document reveals that the boy was shot dead on the other side of the world, leaving his father to settle the brandy bill. Van Fornenburgh's pictures from this time, in which single-stem roses and tulips lie scattered on deeply shadowed ledges of chipped stone, have a funereal air.[4]

More than ten years after this episode, by which time Reynier had moved to the larger Mechelen Inn on the Great Market Square, the son of another artist from out of town was recorded in his company and most likely staying in his establishment. A seventeen-year-old cabin boy, he too was in the pay of the Dutch East India Company, but safely home on shore leave: the document recording his presence in Delft with Vermeer's father is a deposition concerning an onboard plot by some of his shipmates to defraud the widow of their captain, who had died at sea, of her rightful inheritance.[5] The cabin boy in question was Reynier Hals, son of Frans Hals of Haarlem, the famous portrait painter.

Artists frequented the two inns run by Reynier, told their friends about them, and sent their sons to stay at them. The society of the Dutch Republic, with its small and compact population, was made up of many such networks. People with similar interests made it their business to know each other, or know about each other. Dutch artists talked to each other a great deal, exchanging not just gossip but information

CHILDHOOD, EDUCATION, MARRIAGE, 1632–57

about techniques, materials and new ways of doing things. They looked at each other's work carefully and incessantly borrowed ideas and compositions from one another. The Flying Fox would have been a place where such talking and looking took place every day. It was a milieu that would shape the lives of Reynier and Digna's children.

Their daughter, Gertruy, would marry a man named Antony van der Wiel, who was a worker in ebony and maker of picture frames; he was both skilful and sought after, to judge by the names in his order book, which included a noted collector from Amsterdam called Maerten Kretzer.

Their son would become a painter.

SCHOOL

Between Vermeer's baptism in 1632 and his betrothal in 1653 stretches an archival void: his name has not been found in any other document that can be dated to his first twenty years of life. He is, however, present by implication in his parents' will, drawn up by notary Willem de Langue on 17 February 1638, when Reynier was forty-seven, Digna forty-three, their daughter, Gertruy, eighteen and their son, Johannes, just five.[6] Husband and wife declared themselves to be of sound mind and body and named one another universal legatees, with one provision: 'the surviving party is beholden to feed, clothe and send to school to learn to read and write their child or children and to teach them a trade. This must all be done until they come of age or to the state of marriage, whereupon each of them should be outfitted and given a marriage feast, all according to the condition of the survivor.'

So Vermeer was to receive an education, no matter what: to be taught to read and write, perhaps more than just that. That he did so can be gleaned from the fluency of his signature on documents and the evidence of his paintings. They include inscriptions and also demonstrate that he was sufficiently familiar with classical mythology to draw on it at least once – in *Diana and Her Companions* – for his subject matter. To judge by Vermeer's own death inventory, drawn up in 1676, he was someone who read books throughout his life. The notary who compiled it described a small storage room that contained bedpans, chairs, a couple of paintings and a *bakermath*, being 'a wicker basket wherein the mother sits and holds her child warm', this last being an ingeniously snug item of furniture, a hybrid of bucket chair and crib, designed to protect infants from the damp and cold of the Dutch climate. It had presumably been used by Vermeer's wife, Catharina, to nurse their children; his mother, Digna, had probably nursed him in one much like it. The little room was clearly used to store bits and pieces, but more than that. It was also where the artist kept part of his library. The notary itemized 'five books in folio' and '25 other of all kinds', all the property of the late Johannes Vermeer, but unfortunately he failed to specify their titles.[7]

Where did the artist go to school? The building immediately next to The Flying Fox on the Voldersgracht was the Old Men's Home, and next to that charitable institution there was a kind of art school or academy for boys run by a painter named Cornelis Damen Rietwijk. He offered basic tuition in reading, writing and mathematics, while mainly teaching his students how to draw, taking them to a fairly advanced level depending on their abilities. Considering the sheer convenience of the school's proximity to The Flying Fox, it seems likely that Johannes would have been a pupil there.[8] By the time he was of school age, six years old or so, his talents might already have shown themselves, in which case a place of learning run by a practising artist would have seemed all the more suitable.

Rietwijk's little academy, with its emphasis on drawing, was a place of practical learning. Some of the boys who went there became professional artists, but many others became carpenters or shipbuilders or workers in one or other of the many branches of the textile trade, where the ability to draw was a necessary condition of employment. Drawing was a key skill too in the defence of the Dutch Republic: essential to the cartographers of the northern Netherlands, renowned throughout Europe for their maps, who surveyed the rivers and their tributaries for the best sites to place the ring of fortresses protecting the state from enemy incursions; essential, too, to military men such as Vermeer's maternal uncle, Reynier Baltens, who was a designer of fortifications and siege machinery. Nonetheless, it was not widely seen as a subject for people with high aspirations. The educational theory of the time classed painting and drawing among the Mechanical

Arts, tainted by association with manual labour. The seven Liberal Arts supposedly formed the proper subjects of study for a gentleman, three of which fell under the categories of language and logic, namely Grammar, Dialectic and Rhetoric, the remaining four treating of science and based on mathematics, namely Arithmetic, Geometry, Astronomy and Music. None of the Liberal Arts were taught by Cornelis Rietwijk, except for a little grammar and maths.

His establishment was nonetheless a stimulating environment for anyone with artistic talent. Rietwijk was not only an artist in his own right, but also the owner of a sizeable art collection. He was a practising Catholic, a fact reflected in the kind of pictures he owned. Inventories taken of his possessions in 1636 and 1660 list some 183 paintings, most of which were *tronien*, the rest being devotional pictures of Christ or Mary or depictions of themes such as the Crucifixion. He also possessed a fairly sizeable library of around 125 titles, including Karel van Mander's *Schilder-boek* – a Netherlandish answer to Giorgio Vasari's *Lives of the Artists* – and a number of emblem books, including the *Amorum emblemata* by Otto van Veen. This last book was certainly known to Vermeer by the time he reached his mid-twenties, because he drew on it for the imagery of one of his most brilliant early pictures, the *Girl Reading a Letter at an Open Window*.[9]

Whatever tuition Vermeer may have received from Cornelis Damen Rietwijk, it is probable that he learned a great deal about painting and drawing at home. The many painters frequenting his parents' inn included a vigorous group of friends who had been to Rome and become members of a loose association of northern émigré artists known as the *Bentvueghels*, or Birds of a Feather. The *Bentvueghels* clustered in the area to the north of Rome, near Santa Maria del Popolo and San Lorenzo in Lucina, a part of town particularly rich in the work of Caravaggio, who became an influence on many of them (as he would, in time, on Vermeer). They were known for giving each other satirical nicknames: the painter of dead game, Jan Baptist Weenix, was known as Rattle, because he had a speech defect, while the unsociable Herman van Swanevelt was The Hermit. Reynier's idea of calling his inn, and by implication himself, The Flying Fox, was possibly influenced by the fondness of the *Bentvueghels* for such sobriquets.

Several of these Birds of a Feather are known to have become clients of Reynier after returning from Italy to the Netherlands. One was Pieter Gronewegen, a painter of Italianized landscapes active in Delft in the 1640s, who went by the nickname of Lion. Another was Reynier van Heuckelom, alias Wolf, who gave up painting to pursue other lines of business, seemingly without success: in 1651 Vermeer's father was chasing him for the not inconsiderable sum of 125 guilders, an unpaid debt for food and drink bought on tick. The painter Leonaert Bramer, not only a client but also a friend to the Vermeer family, had been initiated into the *Bentvueghels* when he was in Rome back in the 1620s. They called him Fidget.

From such well-travelled men Johannes Vermeer is likely to have acquired many of the rudiments of painting. Watching artists draw and listening to artists' tavern conversation must have been an education in itself. As he grew older and more skilful, and as it became clear that he had genuine talent, an element of barter may have been introduced, with various painters teaching him new things in return for food and drink at his father's inn. Even before he was ten or twelve years old, the common age of apprenticeship, Vermeer might have begun to master the art of painting.

NEIGHBOURS

The Mechelen Inn on the Great Market Square, to which Vermeer's family moved in 1641, was one of the principal meeting places in Delft. The building stood on the corner of the Oude Manhuissteg, the Old Men's Alley, which led via a small bridge to the Voldersgracht. The Mechelen was only a stone's throw away from The Flying Fox, but far larger and more prominent. Sandwiched between the town hall and the Nieuwe Kerk, and close to the main markets for meat, fish and vegetables, the Mechelen was busy day and night. Most people in town knew Reynier, Digna, their daughter and their little boy.

Moving to the new inn meant acquiring new neighbours. One in particular would shape the future life of Johannes Vermeer. A search of seventeenth-century house registers and sale deeds in the Delft archives has revealed that a man named Simon Vincenten de Knuijt owned three houses on the north side of the Great Market Square, just

CHILDHOOD, EDUCATION, MARRIAGE, 1632-57

The centre of Delft, depicted a little later than Vermeer's time but still much as he knew it. We are looking down the Old Men's Alley, with the Great Market Square at our backs. The building on the left is The Mechelen Inn, the tavern to which the painter's family moved in 1641. Straight ahead, on the Voldersgracht, is the Guild of St Luke, to which Vermeer and his father belonged. Out of sight but just around the corner to the right, and virtually next door to the guild, was The Flying Fox, the first inn run by Vermeer's parents. Two doors along from that was the school run by Cornelis Damen Rietwijk, which Vermeer probably attended. His family's trusted pastor, the Remonstrant Johannes Taurinus, also lived on the Voldersgracht. Vermeer's was a small world indeed.

west of the Mechelen, including one only a few doors along from the inn itself.[10] It was here that he and his wife, Magdaleentje Willemsdr van der Mersche, brought up their son, Vincent, and their daughter, Maria. Maria de Knuijt was born in 1623, so she would have been eighteen years old when the Vermeer family acquired the inn next door to her home: ten years older than Johannes, and a couple of years younger than his sister, Gertruy.

Maria would reside on the Great Market Square until 1653, the year when she married Pieter Claesz van Ruijven. From 1657 onwards, Johannes Vermeer would paint more or less all of his pictures for Maria and her husband: an arrangement without parallel in the history of art. So at the age of just eight Vermeer was living almost next door to the woman who would eventually own most of his life's work. Even before that he had lived only just around the corner from her, on the Voldersgracht.

We know that Maria de Knuijt would later come to regard Vermeer as almost part of her own family. This much is clear from the terms of her will, in which she made a particular bequest of money to him: the only such bequest from patron to artist known from the whole corpus of seventeenth-century Dutch records.[11] But how they became close in the first place remains a matter of speculation. It seems improbable that Maria would have befriended Johannes when she was in her late teens and he was still a boy of eight or nine. It seems more likely that Maria first became friends with Vermeer's elder sister Gertruy, just a couple of years her senior, and that her relationship with the painter developed subsequently.

There is archival evidence to suggest that Maria de Knuijt and her husband, Pieter Claesz van Ruijven, were close friends not only to Vermeer but also to his sister Gertruy and her husband, the frame-maker Antony van der Wiel. This takes the form of a document dated close to the end of Gertruy's life.[12] At nine o'clock in the evening on 11 February 1670, a notary was called to her and Antony's house on Vlamingstraat in Delft to draft their last will and testament. Digna, the mother of Gertruy and Johannes Vermeer, had died the previous day in that same house, having spent her last few months there. Her body was probably still laid out in one of the back rooms on the ground floor on the evening the notary was called. Now Gertruy herself was mortally ill. She signed her will in a shaky hand, misspelling her name so badly – 'Geertruit Vormeer' – that we cannot be sure that she had all her wits about her. It must have been a painful spectacle, the halting dictation followed by the tremulous signature. It was most likely a long drawn-out spectacle too. The lateness of the hour implies that the notary had been called suddenly, for fear that Gertruy might not make it through the night.

In the event she rallied, but not for long. Within months, she would follow her mother to the grave.

It is safe to assume that only those close to the family would have been invited to witness the signing of the will that evening, as the law required. They would have to have been good friends to be summoned suddenly to the house, after dark and in the depths of winter. Two such witnesses were called upon. One was a man called Arent Pijnacker, who held a mortgage on Mechelen and whose loans to Digna Vermeer had kept the family afloat. The other? Pieter Claesz van Ruijven, husband of Gertruy's childhood neighbour Maria de Knuijt.

Pieter and Maria clearly had a great deal of time for the Vermeer family. Pieter's willingness to help the ailing Gertruy and her husband at such short notice and in such harrowing circumstances is proof of that. He probably took the opportunity to pay his last respects to Digna while he was there that evening: if he was close to her children, the chances are that he had been close to her too. By attending he was also representing his wife. The closeness of the bond between the Van Ruijvens and the Vermeers is all the more remarkable in light of the gulf in wealth and social status separating them. Pieter Claesz van Ruijven was from one of the oldest and richest families in Delft. Maria was even wealthier than him. By contrast the Vermeers were refugees who had scrabbled their way up the social ladder to become innkeepers but would never have much more than a couple of guilders to rub together. In seventeenth-century Delft rich and well-connected people did not, as a general rule, mingle with people much less well off than themselves.

It might be thought that Pieter and Maria's warm feelings for Vermeer's family were a by-product of their admiration for his work as a painter. But that fails to explain why their affection extended beyond him to include his sister and brother-in-law, and quite probably his mother too. There seems to have been some kind of deep affinity between the two families.

One thing the Van Ruijvens seemingly had in common with the Vermeer clan was loyalty to the Remonstrant cause, going all the way back to the troubled time of the 1620s. Pieter Claesz van Ruijven, whose grandfather and father had sheltered at least one ill-fated Remonstrant preacher during the dark days following the Synod of

Dordt, remained a staunch Remonstrant and maintained contacts with both conservative and radical wings of the Remonstrant movement throughout his life.[13] His wife was a member of the Reformed Church, but sufficiently liberal in her religious beliefs to marry a Remonstrant. The links of Vermeer's parents to the dissenting rebel Johannes Taurinus, a Remonstrant with Collegiant affinities, and his mother's links to the Rombouts clan in Amsterdam, make it likely that they too formed part of Delft's Remonstrant minority.

Johannes Taurinus died in 1637. A year later Delft's first Remonstrant church was consecrated. Like all such tolerated alternatives to the Dutch Reformed Church, whether Catholic or Lutheran or Mennonite, such a building was obliged by law to take the form of a *schuilkerk*, or hidden church. On the inside it might be a large and imposing place of worship, but on the outside it was not to resemble anything other than an ordinary house or run-of-the-mill industrial building. No crosses or other signs of the Christian faith might be displayed on the façade, nor could there be any ringing of bells to summon the congregation. In practice everyone in Delft knew exactly where the city's supposedly hidden churches were. It was common knowledge that there was a Catholic church behind the house façades on the Oude Langendijk, and another one nearby, on the Oude Delft. The hidden Remonstrant church was also on the Oude Delft, on the east side of the canal. Converted from an old malt barn, which was what it still appeared to be from the outside, the interior was grand and spacious, with pews and galleries of seating, as in a theatre or auditorium, arranged to face the pulpit. Rebuilt in the late nineteenth century, to the same barn-like model but with art nouveau details, the church still occupies the same spot in Delft as it did in Vermeer's day.

Pieter Claesz van Ruijven and his near relations were close to the Remonstrant Church, spiritually and geographically. The *Huizenprotocol* in the Gemeentearchief Delft, which records house ownership, lists a house called 'The Golden Eagle' on the Oude Delft that certainly belonged to him in the 1660s and early 1670s and had possibly been in his family for years.[14] That house was on the east side of the canal, near the Boterbrug. Study of the pledge data in the archive reveals it to be identical with House 106 on the Oude Delft, which was immediately adjacent to the building that occupied numbers 100–104.¹⁵ That building was the Remonstrant *schuilkerk*, which was set back from the main street frontage at the end of a little alley, as hidden churches often were. (See Appendix 1.) In other words, the house of the Van Ruijvens on the Oude Delft canal was *directly in front of* Delft's Remonstrant church.

This new information raises further questions. Might The Golden Eagle once have been another Van Ruijven brewery, run in tandem with The Ox? Might the malt barn have been part of the Van Ruijven beer business, subsequently gifted away? If so, the Van Ruijvens were more than just proud Remonstrants, they were the prime benefactors of Delft's earliest Remonstrant congregation: the people who gave them their church. The surviving records are too fragmentary to prove or disprove this hypothesis, but what we can say with certainty is that Van Ruijven and his wife were immediate neighbours to Delft's one and only Remonstrant church during the 1660s and early 1670s, when their relationship with Vermeer and his family was at its closest. How this might colour our understanding of his pictures remains to be seen.

Rotterdam, just ten miles to the south-east of Delft, was one of the stronghold cities of the Remonstrants. Roughly a fifth of the city's population attended the hidden Remonstrant church there. Contacts between the followers of Arminius in Rotterdam and Delft would remain close throughout Vermeer's lifetime. During the 1640s, when it is reasonable to suppose that various members of the painter's family grew close to Maria de Knuijt and her future husband Pieter Claesz van Ruijven, the influence of the Collegiant movement spread suddenly and with great rapidity through the Remonstrant congregations of the Dutch Republic, especially those in Rotterdam and Delft.

The seeds had been sown in the 1630s, when groups of Remonstrant rebels in the circle of Johannes Taurinus, possibly including the parents of Vermeer, were spurred on by him to form the first Collegiant cells in Delft. At around the same time in Rotterdam a lay meeting of a similar kind was organized by Samuel Lansbergen, a Remonstrant pastor, and Petrus Cupus, an old friend of Johannes Taurinus and a militant advocate of the universal right to read and freely interpret the Bible.¹⁶ It took place every Friday evening in the new Remonstrant church of Rotterdam and soon attracted the attendance of Frans Joachimsz

Oudaan, who had by then succeeded Gijsbert van der Kodde as the director of the original Collegiant group, founded in Warmond but now based in Rijnsburg. Oudaan introduced the Rotterdam Remonstrants to the radical practices of the Collegiants, in particular the leaderless meeting modelled on the gatherings described in the Epistles of St Paul.

Numerous Collegiant cells were established in Rotterdam during the 1640s and 1650s, some of which have left evidence of their existence in the city's archives. The number of such groups formed either there or in nearby Delft is impossible to establish with certainty because they were part of no established Church and convened secretly in private homes. They neither called attention to their activities nor recorded them, most of the evidence of their sudden increase coming from reports filed to Reformed Church councils by Calvinist spies.[17] The fact that the Calvinists were worried about these Collegiant cells in the first place suggests that participation was by no means limited to Remonstrants, and that members of the Reformed Church also attended such gatherings. In fact we know that many of the new Collegiant groups were actively instigated by members of the Reformed Dutch Church, especially younger female members, among whom there was a rising tide of discontent over the Calvinist hierarchy's conservatism and what was perceived to be a general over-regulation of religious life by the priesthood. Such women particularly disliked the clergy's zealous insistence on instruction by catechism – the learning of set answers to set questions on matters of doctrine – and yearned for a deeper engagement with the actual teachings of Christ. The Collegiant movement offered them exactly that. It was made all the more attractive to such freethinking devout women by its insistence on the equality of men and women, both in the eyes of God and in the rooms where prophecy was to be made.

The intriguing affection shown by Pieter Claesz van Ruijven and Maria de Knuijt for the extended family of Johannes Vermeer over many years may be explained by their collective fellowship in one (or more than one) of these lay Christian gatherings. In the early 1640s Pieter was a Remonstrant, his future wife Maria a freethinking Calvinist, and both were of the right age – late teens, early twenties – to fit the profile of those drawn to experiment with the religious practices of the Collegiants. The same is true of Gertruy, whose parents had been part of the circle of Johannes Taurinus. Being the same age more or less as Maria de Knuijt, she was perhaps a member of the same group as her. As for Reynier and Digna, if they had heeded the advice in Taurinus's *Reflections on the Parable of the Samaritan Woman* they might have been long-standing Collegiants even before moving to The Mechelen Inn. The evidence presented thus far is circumstantial, but there is a great deal of it, all pointing towards the same conclusion: more or less everyone close to Vermeer appears to have had links of one kind or another to the Remonstrants or their radicalized brethren, the Collegiants.

THE LONGEST WAR

At the time of the painter's birth in 1632 the Eighty Years War had entered its final phase. Most of the fighting had been reduced to a contest over the fortresses guarding the Maas-Waal line, the outer perimeter of Dutch defences. The Spanish army, homesick, unpaid and largely forgotten by the court in Madrid, could do little more than put up a show of resistance to the well-drilled troops of Stadtholder Frederik Hendrik. The Dutch lacked the resources, and the will, to push into the southern Netherlands, but they made steady progress to secure their own borders. Fortress after fortress fell to them: Oldenzaal, Grol and, after a siege lasting five months and requiring 28,000 troops, 's-Hertegenbosch. In 1635 the Dutch signed an alliance with France, brokered by Cardinal Richelieu. This prompted the Spanish army under Cardinal-Infante Ferdinand to go on the counter-offensive, taking the strategically vital fortress of Schenkenschans at the division of the Waals and the Lower Rhine. Frederik Hendrik devoted six months to retaking it, which he finally managed after a relentless bombardment. In October 1637 he retook Breda, effectively nullifying the last Spanish threat to the Dutch Netherlands. Ten more years of uneasy stalemate still had to be endured before the two sides would finally make peace with each other.

It was in essence a war of vast siege operations, waged mostly by the Dutch rather than the Spanish, and aimed at capturing strategic military emplacements. Each engagement was tilted heavily in favour of the besieging army by recent innovations in siege strategy and technology, and most ended in the predictable surrender of the defending garrison. The conflict was far more civilized than it had been during the early years of the Dutch Revolt. Surrendering garrisons were allowed to retreat behind their own lines, rather than suffer mass execution. Dutch and Spanish troops fighting over disputed territory spared one another's crops and villages.

The seventeenth century has been remembered as a Golden Age for the Dutch.[18] In some respects it was, but not in all. Thanks to the formidable ambition of Dutch merchants, one of Europe's smallest nations also became its richest, in what seemed like the blink of an eye. Nonetheless, the fact remains that Johannes Vermeer spent the first sixteen years of his life in a country that was at war. Reminders were everywhere around him. Although the conflict was far away from Delft, so less directly threatening than it had been during his grandparents' time, its scale and cost were the same. Vermeer's home town, a vital link in the munitions supply chain, was heavily garrisoned with soldiers throughout his youth and remained so well into the 1650s.

Vermeer's maternal uncle, Reynier Baltens, was an active participant in the later campaigns of Frederik Hendrik.[19] In 1633 he was listed among those responsible for fortifying two trenches dug by Dutch sappers to compromise the moated defence of Rhijnberch, a fort taken and retaken so many times that the Spanish nicknamed it the *puta de la guerra*, the whore of war. By the early 1640s Reynier had been promoted to the position of lieutenant in the engineering corps of the army of the Dutch States-General. In the summer of 1642 he was campaigning in the valleys of the Rhine and the Maas with the States Army, alongside French troops and soldiers from several Protestant principalities of Germany.

In 1645 this same Uncle Reynier played an important part in Frederik Hendrik's last military victory of note, the siege of Sas van Gent in Spanish Flanders. Reynier's task was not a straightforward one. After a team of sappers had tunnelled their way across several hundred yards of sodden ground to the edge of the moat surrounding the fortress, he and his fellow engineers were to lay 'the passage of the ditch', in this case two bridges made of barrels or planks reaching to the ramparts of the fort itself. Once in place, these allowed an advance guard to plant mines or bombs to force entry for the besieging troops. As an extra precaution, Frederik Hendrik instructed

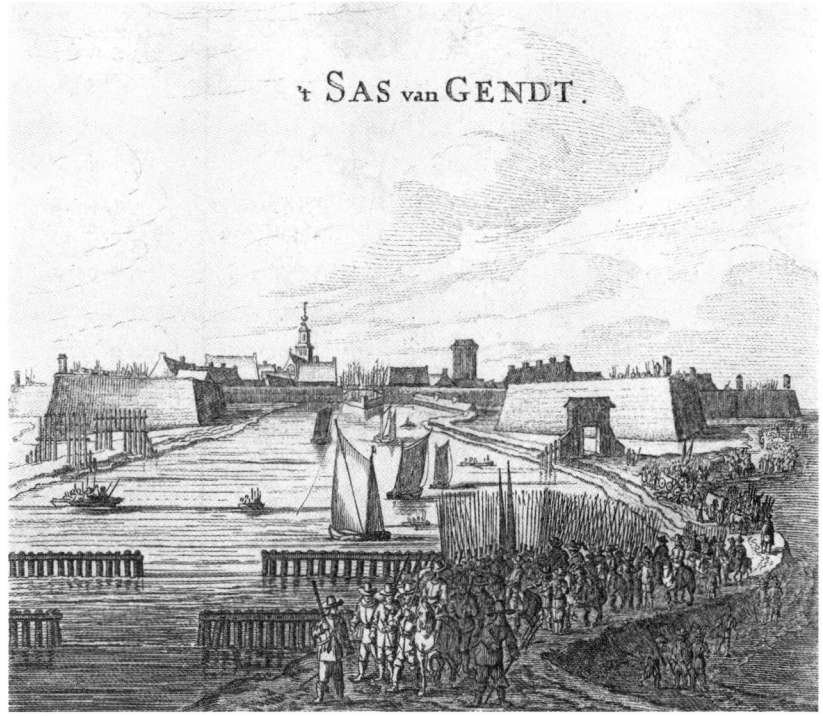

Siege outworks at Sas van Gent in Spanish Flanders, 1644–5. The English military expert Henry Hexham noted that 'such redoubts serve for a retreat to the workmen, if an enemy should make a great sally upon them,' and believed that they tipped the balance greatly in favour of the attackers. Stadholder Frederik Hendrik eventually took Sas van Gent with relative ease, helped by a corps of engineers led by Vermeer's maternal uncle, Reynier Baltens.

his engineers to add low-roofed wooden galleries to each bridge, to shield his men from enemy fire. This dangerous work was carried out at night, but both galleries were washed away by a freak flood tide, upon which Reynier and his comrades worked feverishly to repair the damage. Once the galleries were complete, the Spanish garrison realized they could no longer protect the fort's outer walls and surrendered. Confirmation of a hazardous job well rewarded takes the form of a document, dated 15 March 1645, recording Reynier Baltens's visit to a notary in The Hague to collect the sum of 5,000 guilders owed to him and the rest of his crew for their valiant efforts.

Vermeer's mother, Digna, was close to her brother, helping him out quite a few times when he ran short of money or fell foul of the law. Johannes too kept company with his uncle, to judge by their joint appearance before a Delft notary in April 1653, so he would have known of his exploits at Sas van Gent and would have heard about the ins and outs of siege warfare: the final assault, with all its dangers, preceded by weeks or even months of tunnelling through mud, fortifying redoubts, laying mines.

The war towards its end was less fraught than at its outset, when the entire populations of Dutch towns had been at risk of massacre, but as the collective fear of annihilation receded the older generation became all the more determined that their children should never forget the terrors of the past. Vermeer's mother would have told him about the atrocities committed at Antwerp when his grandfather was just three years old, while he is likely to have learned about many other instances of innocent Netherlanders mass-murdered by bloodthirsty Spaniards, either by word of mouth or from the many popular histories of the Revolt published during his lifetime, in which the Black Legend of Spanish cruelty was repeated and reinforced.

Memories of the dark past were kept alive all over the northern Netherlands, in all kinds of ways.[20] In Naarden, the scene of one of the Duke of Alva's worst atrocities, a painting of the Spanish Fury was commissioned for the town hall, while gable stones were placed at the entrance to the Gasthuiskerk, into which many of the town's inhabitants had been crammed before being murdered, together with an inscription: 'Remember the day that one saw here how Spain against its word plundered the land, burnt this city, killed the citizenry, in the year 1572.' In the town hall of Leiden were preserved two stuffed pigeons, said once to have carried messages from William of Orange to the starving population during the siege of 1574.

In the castle at Breda they displayed a wooden rudder, cherished relic of the fabled peat barge on which Dutch soldiers had smuggled themselves into the town in 1590 before wresting control of it from the Spanish. The barge, a (very Dutch) waterborne version of the Trojan horse, was also remembered in the name of a house in Rotterdam, the *Bredasche Turfschip*, presumably owned by a proud native of Breda. In a similar vein, people from Leiden settling elsewhere might choose to name their new home *Ontstet van Leyden*, 'The Relief of Leyden'. The Mechelen Inn in Delft, where Vermeer spent much of his upbringing, must originally have been christened by defiant refugees from the city of Mechelen, infamously sacked at the outset of the Revolt. The young Vermeer was living in a war memorial, by name if not by nature, which can only have made the pacifism of the Remonstrant movement seem all the more logical and appealing to him.

Just as the town fathers of Naarden commissioned a painting commemorating the massacre that had taken place there, so too did those of Oudewater (and indeed Mechelen). Most striking of all was Haarlem, where the town magistrates repurposed the Prinsenhof, once used to receive the princes of the House of Orange, as a public art gallery: the first in the Dutch Republic, and quite possibly the first anywhere in Europe, although it would be misleading to think of it as a museum in the modern sense because its primary pupose was to commemorate an atrocity. Its principal exhibit was Haarlem's most celebrated painting, as it then was, *The Massacre of the Innocents* by Cornelis Cornelisz van Haarlem, a gruesome masterpiece of Netherlandish mannerism painted in 1590 to honour the thousands of men, women and children tortured and murdered by the Duke of Alva's troops after the siege of Haarlem eighteen years earlier. It was a common trope of Dutch Revolt propaganda to compare Alva to Herod, so everyone looking at Cornelis's monumental picture knew perfectly well that its biblical theme was a pretext for remembering the actual horrors of murder, rape and infanticide visited on a real Dutch town by real Spanish soldiers.

The Prinsenhof collection was open to the public from its inception in the early seventeenth century. It became considerably better known during Vermeer's lifetime, when the Dutch developed the most advanced passenger transport system in Europe, in the form of the *trekschuit* network: a countrywide grid of canals, traversed by horse-drawn barges, run to a strict timetable, that enabled people to get from one town to another quickly, comfortably and cheaply. The first such passenger barge travelled from Amsterdam to Haarlem in 1632. By the time Vermeer was in his teens there were twenty-seven *trekschuits* a day travelling from Delft to Amsterdam, via The Hague, Leiden, Utrecht and Haarlem. Anyone passing through Haarlem was obliged to change boat and make the short walk across town, because the canals stopped at the gates at either end. The pedestrian route from barge to barge took them straight past the Prinsenhof, whose porters were encouraged to invite visitors inside. Vermeer made that journey many times, so he will have known *The Massacre of the Innocents* and taken on board its message, which was both visceral and unambiguous: always remember that this happened here, never forget that it could happen again.

The Dutch Republic was small, more densely populated than anywhere else in Europe and more urbanized: its people were clustered in towns and cities to a degree unknown elsewhere. In other parts of Europe it was possible for people in a particular town or village to remain largely unaware of what was going on beyond the limited sphere of their own daily lives. But the Dutch knew a great deal about what was happening in the world, both within their borders and beyond. The Dutch network of cities, connected by a network of canals, in a country with considerable freedom of speech and little censorship, was also a network of information. Anyone who could read was presented with a daily offering of tracts and pamphlets on the issues of the day. Anyone on the passenger barges was liable to overhear arguments about the price of bread, or the latest rise in taxes to pay for the army. Anyone frequenting an inn or tavern would hear people discussing theology, politics and the progress of the war, or taking different sides in the toleration debate. Vermeer, who actually lived in an inn in the centre of a densely populated town, would have been well informed on all the issues that mattered to a seventeenth-century Dutchman.

During the years of the artist's childhood and adolescence the greatest threat to the Dutch Republic was the threat of war. But, while the atrocities committed by the Duke of Alva and his successors were kept vivid in the memory, there was a growing sense that the worst was over on the home front and that victory, or at least peace, was in sight. The greatest dangers lurked elsewhere. During the 1630s and 1640s the Dutch war against Spain was overshadowed by another, yet more atrocious war, taking place to the east, in 'the German Lands': a war so terrible it seemed to many that Armageddon had come to pass.

CHILDHOOD, EDUCATION, MARRIAGE, 1632–57

THE WORST WAR

On 7 April 1636 Thomas Howard, Earl of Arundel, left England on a diplomatic mission. He was to attend a meeting in Regensburg between the Electors of the Holy Roman Empire, then embroiled in a long and bitter war between Catholics and Protestants, fought out by the Habsburgs and their enemies. It was to be a gruelling journey, not only because of the distances travelled. From Greenwich the earl and his retinue took a barge to Gravesend, then went by coach to Canterbury and on to Margate, where they set sail for Holland on His Majesty's ship *The Happy Entrance*. On the tenth day of their travels they reached Delft, whence they went to The Hague and a meeting with Stadtholder Frederik Hendrik. They then travelled east into Gelderland and via Arnhem to the fortress of Schenkenschans, where the beleaguered Spanish garrison was under heavy bombardment during the last days of the Dutch siege. Here they embarked on a boat and began sailing up the Rhine. They were only just out of the United Provinces, but as soon as they had reached the first few towns and villages along the river it was evident that they had entered another world.

William Crowne, a nineteen-year-old officer of arms in Arundel's retinue, kept a record of the journey. At Wesel, just north-east of Schenkenschans, there was an outbreak of plague so severe that 'they died there of the sicknesse more than thirty a day'. Crowne and his company dared not disembark, even for fresh water. Between Cologne and Frankfurt (a distance of roughly 120 miles) 'all the Townes, Villages, and Castles bee battered, pillaged or burnt, and every place wee lay at on the Rhine on ship-board, we watched, taking every man his turne'. Some villagers fled at their approach, assuming that they were yet another troop of invading soldiers come to steal, pillage and cause havoc. Others, made desperate by hunger, threatened to attack them and steal their provisions.

At the outset young William Crowne had probably planned his journal as a record of memorable experiences, the diary of an English sightseer. The ghost of that original intention is still present in the occasional reference to this or that picturesque detail or landmark, which only makes the rest of his account seem all the more nightmarish:

The first of May being Sunday, and their Whitsunday, we departed, passing by Villages shot downe, and by many pictures of our Saviour and the *Virgin Mary*, set up at the turnings of the water, untill we entered the Land of *Hesse*, where we still viewed pleasant Vines on the Mountaines ... and so to Pfalz Castle, seated in a little Iland in the river, from hence to *Bacharach*, a Towne where we landed, it is seated on the right side of the Rhine, having a Castle on a high Rocke within the walls, and under that a Church. Here the poore people are found dead with grasse in their mouths; from hence by a Village on the same side, in which none but Lepers are ...

... to *Rudesheim*, a Towne on the left side of the *Rhine*, into which I entered, and did see poore people praying where dead bones were in a little old house, and here his Excellencie [Arundel] gave some reliefe to the poore which were almost starved as it appeared by the violence they used to get it from one another ... Then to *Mentz*, a great City seated close by the *Rhine* on the right side against which we cast Anchor and lay on ship-board, for there was nothing in the Towne to relieve us, since it was taken by the King of Sweden, and miserably battered ... here likewise the poor people were almost starved ... and after supper all had reliefe, sent from the Ship ashore, at the sight of which they strove so violently, that some of them fell into the *Rhine* and were like to have drowned ...

These are the sights and sounds that war has left in its trail: images of Christ and the Virgin set up at each bend of the river as prayers for help, unanswered; people dead from starvation with grass in their mouths; villages burned and pillaged; smoke rising from abandoned houses; corpses left to rot in the open; bands of ragged survivors fighting each other for scraps of food. Crowne's diary is a series of descriptions of scenes from hell, written by a man unsure of whether he is awake or dreaming. What makes it all the more harrowing with hindsight is the knowledge that he gives us no more than snapshots of a huge expanse of human misery, reaching out from those few bends in the Rhine to encompass hundreds of thousands of square miles.

The Thirty Years War was a war like no other, bewildering in its extent and astonishing in its devastation. Like the Dutch Revolt it was marked by sieges and sackings, but of such savagery and ferocity as to

Strange fruit: *The Hanging*, from 'The Miseries and Misfortunes of War' by Jacques Callot, a series of prints inspired by the events of the Thirty Years War. This print shows the mass execution of soldiers of fortune found guilty of war crimes, although, as other prints in the same series make clear, the widespread torture and abuse of civilian populations commonly went unpunished. Callot's work inspired Goya's much later and more famous series of prints *The Disasters of War*.

make even the Spanish Furies at Oudewater, Mechelen or Antwerp pale by comparison. When Protestant Magdeburg fell to the army of the Catholic League in the spring of 1631, a year before the birth of Johannes Vermeer, the ensuing conflagration was so fierce that it reduced the town to ashes in a matter of hours. Out of a population of 30,000 only 5,000 survived, the majority of those being women taken captive by plundering soldiers who then treated them with rapacious cruelty. A camp was briefly set up for eighty lost children found in the ruins of the town, but within three weeks all but a handful had died of hunger and disease. To avert the threat of plague Count Tilly, commander of the imperial troops, ordered tens of thousands of bodies to be thrown into the River Elbe. Swollen corpses were snagged in the reeds or caught in the low-hanging branches of trees for many miles downriver, some remaining long after their flesh had been picked clean by carrion, like skeletons accidentally crucified.

For years afterwards the crimes committed by Catholic forces at Magdeburg would be taken as licence for their own by troops fighting on the Protestant side: pleas to give quarter would be met with the sword and the phrase 'Magdeburg quarter'. A pattern had been established: cruelty magnified without mitigation or restraint. The

Thirty Years War itself followed the same pattern, forever expanding with no apparent rhyme or reason, eventually becoming so terrifyingly amorphous that most of its victims had not the faintest idea of why their world was being turned upside down, of why they were being forced from their homes, starved, maimed or murdered.

The origins of the war lay in the Reformation, which had divided the sovereign rulers of the territories of Germany, Austria and Bohemia (now part of the Czech Republic). Some chose to adopt the new Protestant faith whereas others remained Catholic, staying loyal to the Habsburg emperor in Vienna. In 1555 a confessional peace had been negotiated between the Catholic and Lutheran princes of 'the German lands', according to which subjects were bound to follow the same religion as their ruler. It lasted for sixty years but broke down in 1618 when the rebellious aristocracy of Bohemia installed a Protestant ruler in defiance of the Habsburg emperor, Ferdinand II. With military aid from the Pope and the Catholic ruler of Bavaria, Maximilian I, and with financial assistance from Spain, Ferdinand crushed the rebellion. Emboldened by his success, he announced his intention to re-Catholicize each and every one of the Protestant German states of the Holy Roman Empire by force. In response, those European powers most threatened by the tripartite union of Spain, the papacy and the Habsburg emperor took retaliatory action. France made an alliance with the United Provinces, subsequently joined by Sweden. While the Dutch continued to focus on fighting their own battles close to home, the French and the Swedes intervened directly on the side of the German Protestant princes. As a result, what had begun as a local rebellion turned into an all-out war for territorial supremacy, fought over the whole of central Europe.

By the time of Vermeer's birth, that war had spiralled out of control. The main cause was the sheer scale of the armies that had been mobilized with virtually no logistical support. At one stage Count Albrecht von Wallenstein, a Bohemian general raised to supreme military chief by Ferdinand II, commanded an imperial army of more than 160,000 troops. The Swedish field marshal Johan Baner referred to the army under his own command as 'this widespread state'; and it was indeed more numerous than the population of any of the Estates of Sweden. Set adrift on the tides of war, such masses of armed men

1. *Diana and Her Companions*, c. 1653. A muted celebration of female virtue, inspired by classical myth but also evoking Christian symbolism: the furled white cloth at the bottom resembles the dove of the Holy Spirit.

2. *The Procuress*, 1656. This brothel scene may in fact represent the Parable of the Prodigal Son, with Vermeer himself on the far left, 'looking out at us with a grin that fails to convince'.

3 & 4. Vermeer's *Christ in the House of Martha and Mary*, c. 1654 (*above*); Andrea Vaccaro's *The Death of St Joseph*, c. 1645–50 (*left*). Although Vermeer's Christ is shown seated rather than standing, the figure was clearly borrowed from that of Christ in a slightly earlier work by the Neapolitan Vaccaro.

5 & 6. Vermeer's *St Praxedis*, c. 1655 (*above*); Felice Ficherelli's original, c. 1645–50 (*left*). Vermeer's deep familiarity with the art of his Italian contemporaries suggests that he travelled to Italy between 1650 and 1652, shortly after completing his apprenticeship.

7. *Officer with a Laughing Girl*, c. 1658. The first of Vermeer's paintings for the Van Ruijvens, it proclaims the joy of peace, and love. 'The wars are over. The time has come for the soldier to relax his guard and surrender. The time has come for him to be hers.'

8. *A Maid Asleep*, *c.* 1658. The second of Vermeer's paintings for The Golden Eagle, the couple's home on the Oude Delft, may be a portrait of the lady of the house, Maria de Knuijt, in the transports of a mystical vision. 'Has the spirit of the Lord dwelt with her and held communion with her?'

9. Gerard ter Borch, *Self-portrait*, 1668. A well-travelled and cosmopolitan painter, Ter Borch had many supporters among the liberal regents of Amsterdam. He is the most likely candidate for the role of Vermeer's teacher and master.

10. Gerard ter Borch, *Man on Horseback*, c. 1634–5. 'No Dutch painter protested more eloquently against the futility and emptiness of war.'

11. An etching by Caspar Luyken of the Delft Thunderclap of 1654. 'Close to the powder store entire streets were vapourized, while further away the houses were blown to smithereens ... Heads, arms, legs and other body parts were scattered like bits and pieces of broken dolls.'

12. Egbert van der Poel, *A View of Delft after the Explosion*, 1654. Having lost a daughter to the blast, Van der Poel responded by painting this and several other gloomy pictures of the city in ruins. Vermeer was related to him by marriage and doubtless had such images in mind when painting his own, radiant *View of Delft* some eleven years later (Plate 40).

13. Cornelis Cornelisz van Haarlem, *The Massacre of the Innocents*, 1590. Commemorating the many women and children murdered by Spanish troops during the Siege of Haarlem of 1572, this celebrated picture was displayed in the Prinsenhof, one of Europe's first public art galleries, throughout Vermeer's lifetime. 'Its message was unambiguous: always remember that this happened here, never forget that it could happen again.'

14. Gerard ter Borch, *The Ratification of the Treaty of Münster*, 1648. Ter Borch was the only Dutch painter invited to Münster and permitted to depict the signing of the peace treaty that ended the Eighty Years War. If Vermeer were Ter Borch's apprentice, he too may have been a witness to this momentous event.

15. Willem Duyster, *The Marauders*, c. 1635 (detail). Throughout Vermeer's childhood there was a vogue for pictures alluding to the horrors of the Thirty Years War. Here we see a woman begging a group of officers to spare her life, as the soldiers under their command ransack her home.

16. *Girl Reading a Letter at an Open Window*, c. 1656–7 (before restoration).

17. *Girl Reading a Letter at an Open Window, c.* 1656–7 (after restoration). The removal of old overpaint revealed the image of Cupid on the far wall of the room, confirming that this had always been a marriage picture: a celebration of the true love that leads to wedlock. It may have been Vermeer's gift to his own wife, Catharina Bolnes, and therefore a portrait of her.

18. *Woman in Blue Reading a Letter*, c. 1664. This appears to depict the same woman, some years older and heavy with child – perhaps another gift to Catharina, a pair to the earlier picture. Vermeer painted it shortly after she, heavily pregnant, had been assaulted by her deranged brother Willem Bolnes – an ordeal that both mother and baby survived.

19 & 20. *The Glass of Wine*, c. 1659–60 (*above*) and *Young Woman with a Wine Glass*, c. 1659–60 (*right*). These two uncharacteristic and slightly sinister courtship pictures are among the few mature works commissioned by people other than the Van Ruijvens. Vermeer painted them, presumably as a pair, for the Van Nederveens, a Delft family who lived just a few doors away from his principal patrons but seem not to have shared their

deep Christian piety. Animated by moral disapproval rather than religious conviction, they are among Vermeer's very few pure genre paintings and show us the more worldly and satirical artist he might have become had he worked, like most of his contemporaries, for the open market.

21 & 22. *The Music Lesson*, c. 1661–2 (*above*), and *The Concert*, c. 1661–2 (*right*). The titles of these two paintings are modern inventions and best ignored. Vermeer's patrons the Van Ruijvens had strong links with the radical Remonstrants known as

Collegiants, who gathered in each other's homes to worship and make music to the glory of God, without the guidance of priest or pastor. They seem to have hosted such meetings regularly at their house next to the hidden Remonstrant church.

23. Vermeer drew on a breadth of visual imagery, past and present, in creating his pictures. This figure of Cupid, from Otto van Veen's emblem book *Amorum Emblemata* (1608), appears both in his *Girl Reading a Letter at an Open Window* (Plate 17) and *A Maid Asleep* (Plate 8).

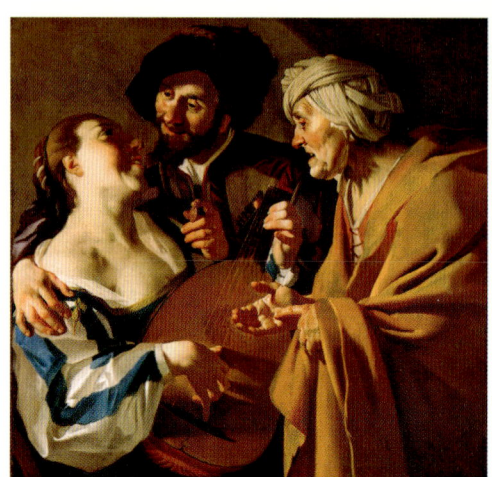

24. Dirck van Baburen's *The Procuress*, 1622, was owned by Vermeer's mother-in-law, Maria Thins, and hung in the house that he and his family shared with her. Vermeer included it, hanging on the wall in deep shadow, directly behind the sunlit female singer in *The Concert* (Plate 22), drawing a stark contrast between profane and sacred music.

25. With *An Officer Writing a Letter, with a Trumpeter*, c. 1658, and earlier works in a similar vein, Gerard ter Borch had invented a new kind of painting in which soldiers became moonstruck lovers. Vermeer, himself a pacifist by inclination and upbringing, was inspired by such pictures to create his own *Officer with a Laughing Girl* (Plate 7).

26. Gerard Houckgeest's *Interior of the Oude Kerk in Delft*, 1654, probably inspired Vermeer's own green curtain, similarly pulled back with a theatrical flourish, in the *Girl Reading a Letter at an Open Window*.

could only feed themselves by theft and plunder, and they could only do that for a short period of time in any given place. So they remained on the move between engagements, gradually stripping each territory they entered of food and any other provisions they could get their hands on, like a plague of locusts. They took the harvests and either killed the farmers or recruited them to their own number, leaving no one to tend to the crops.

In some parts of Germany and what is now the Czech Republic the resulting famines would last more than two hundred years, into the early twentieth century. During the later stages of the war troops on both sides were forced to slow down by the fact that they had already exhausted the territories that were their killing grounds. From the 1640s onwards it was not uncommon for an army to occupy a region from seedtime to harvest, with the soldiers having to sow and reap the grain themselves because the peasantry had been either massacred or displaced. Under such circumstances military manoeuvres were limited to a few weeks at the end of autumn and in early springtime, so major strategic gains became fewer and further between. To underline the utter futility of the conflict, the Treaty of Westphalia that finally ended the Thirty Years War merely confirmed the balance of power that had existed in 1618.

The soldiers who fought out the war behaved the same wherever they were, regardless of the religion or political allegiances of the local inhabitants, which came to matter less and less to those fighting on either side as the conflict dragged on. As people became familiar with its grim pattern, they simply left when the latest troops arrived, abandoning their homes and possessions. Towns dwindled to a tenth of their size, villages emptied. More or less the entire population of central Germany was uprooted, to become a fluctuating throng of refugees. They died in their thousands in the camp at Frankfurt, where there was barely any food and water; they died in the streets at Strasbourg, whose inhabitants grew accustomed to stepping over frozen corpses in the winter months. Some took their chances by returning to their deserted homes, where they risked a repeat of pillage, or worse. The lucky ones made it to the Dutch Republic, where booming business meant that a German fugitive could get a job and a roof over his or her head.

The very idea of having an aim or objective had, by the end, receded more or less completely from the minds of those caught up in the Thirty Years War. It was a conflict that had little to do with causes, noble or otherwise. It had become its own reality, and the trick was to survive it.

The most vivid eyewitness descriptions of the war were written by a man who had served in it, Hans Jakob Christoffel von Grimmelshausen. His autobiographical novel *The Adventures of Simplicius Simplicissimus* tells the story of a boy pressed into years of military service by troops who lay waste to his parents' farm, torturing his father to death in the process. Quite apart from the horrific torments itemized in the book – the cord wound tight around the head until the eyes pop, liquid filth poured into the mouth until the belly is full to bursting (the 'Swedish drink'), thumbs crushed between the hammer and flint of a pistol – its most disturbing passages show how plunder and extortion became little more than tedious routines to soldiers emptied of their humanity by years of conflict.[21]

If William Crowne gives us the world of the war in bleak microcosm, Simplicius reveals the mechanisms by which that world was tortured into existence. A fitting coda to both is the terse and damning summary of Veronica Wedgwood, one of the most eloquent modern chroniclers of the Thirty Years War: 'Morally subversive, economically destructive, socially degrading, confused in its causes, devious in its course, futile in its result, it is the outstanding example in European history of meaningless conflict.'[22]

Reckoning the cost of war on such a scale is not easy. Facts and figures produced at the time are not necessarily reliable but convey the widespread consciousness of irretrievable disaster spawning immeasurable horror. In Bohemia, where the imperial armies of Catholic zealotry had run amok, they believed that five out of every six villages had been destroyed and three-quarters of the population killed. In Germany, the armies of Protestant Sweden alone were held responsible for the destruction of 2,000 castles, 1,500 towns and 18,000 villages. Bavaria claimed the loss of nearly 1,000 villages and the deaths of 80,000 families: men, women and children.

Nineteenth-century historians calculated that roughly two-thirds of the inhabitants of the Holy Roman Empire, or some 15 million people, perished during the course of the war. Modern scholarship favours a lower death toll of around 8 million, but even that reduced figure amounts to some 40 per cent of the population. If the effects of war were to be measured purely on the basis of loss of life, the Thirty Years War was at least six times more destructive than the First World War (6 per cent dead) and eight times more destructive than the Second World War (5 per cent dead). The majority of those who did keep their lives were traumatized out of all recognition by decades of terrifyingly unpredictable violence. If they had by some remote chance escaped torture, mutilation or sexual abuse, they would have seen things to haunt them to the end of their days.

No one survives a war like that without scars. Even just knowing that it was happening would have left an indelible mark on the mind. Many Dutch artists were deeply affected by it and developed new forms of painting to express their sense of horror at what was going on in Germany. The Thirty Years War cast a long shadow over Vermeer's early life, from birth to age sixteen, when it raged with blind intensity. It also stimulated many of the liberal dissenters around whom he grew up to work all the harder to achieve their dream of universal tolerance. Their efforts coalesced to produce the earliest widespread European peace movement, albeit one born out of fear and disgust as much as hope.

BLESSED ARE THE PEACEMAKERS

The people of the Dutch Republic were well aware of the tragedy unfolding in Germany and Bohemia and in some ways benefited from it. From the 1620s onwards thousands of refugees poured over the borders of the United Provinces into Gelderland and Overijssel, many of them soldiers together with their camp followers: gaunt women, children in rags, the sick and the lame. The Dutch economy was growing at such a rate that they were easily absorbed into the labour market. The war was good for business in other ways too. As German farmers fled from their land, leaving their crops to rot, Dutch agriculture prospered, as did the Dutch export trade in food and other provisions. Meat, cheese, herring and butter were shipped to Bremen and Hamburg, then up the River Elbe to hungry armies and garrisons, Protestant and Catholic alike. Provisions were also shipped directly into Germany up the Rhine, but only as far as Cologne, because it was dangerous to go any further (William Crowne could testify to that). The extent to which the Dutch dominated trade with the wartorn territories of the German Empire can be gauged from a single statistic: out of 1,121 ships docking at the port of Hamburg in 1633, 944 were Dutch.[23]

The war in the east brought prosperity but it also brought fear. Terrible stories about the conflict went the rounds, told and retold in the inns and taverns and on the passenger barges. Some began as word of mouth, with refugees recounting their lived experiences, while others were published in the popular broadsheets or pamphlets that were the forerunners of the newspaper. The result was an unceasing flow of appalling information. During one of the many famines of the Thirty Years War, a reader of the Dutch news-sheets could learn that in Alsace the people were so crazed by hunger that they tore the bodies of dead criminals from gallows and gibbet; that all across the Rhineland villagers posted sentries in the graveyards lest newly buried corpses be exhumed by marauders in search of food; that in Eichstätt hordes of orphaned children were reduced to killing and eating rats; and that in Würzburg a mother had been discovered feasting on her own son.

The Dutch worried that the contagion of such a conflict might spread to the Republic and expose them, like their neighbours, to the terrors of pillage by roving bands of renegades. That anxiety was manifest in a new type of painting devoted to the subject of modern military men and their behaviour. The guardroom painting, or *kortegarde* as it was in Dutch, was developed in Amsterdam in the late 1620s by a pair of artists called Pieter Codde and Willem Duyster. Within a decade there were numerous painters specializing in such work. Many guardroom paintings portrayed officers and regular soldiers in their barracks, or in temporary accommodation such as stables, engaged in various activities such as smoking tobacco, playing games of chance or simply sleeping: Codde's *Guardroom Scene with Sleeping Soldiers* of around 1630, in the Kunsthalle at Karlsruhe, is a characteristic example. Such pictures were inspired by military life at home rather than abroad, arising in part as a form of wry commentary on the sheer number of troops present all over the Dutch Republic. They make visible the strange world within a world that was the soldiers' garrison. The men in the paintings seem phlegmatic bordering on melancholic. They often look bored, but they are rarely drunk. Loitering in shadowed interiors, they lack all sense of urgency, seemingly afflicted by the tedium of a life spent mostly on call and hardly ever in action.

From the mid-1630s onwards, the *kortegarde* took another and more sinister turn. In the hands of artists including Simon Kick, who was originally from Delft but worked in Amsterdam, and Jacob Duck, who lived and worked in Utrecht, a different type of guardroom picture developed, plainly inspired by the depredations of the travelling armies wreaking havoc in the German Empire. Such paintings were no longer set in guardrooms or barracks, but in the types of building likely to be requisitioned by the officers of an army on the move: a church interior of cold grey stone, the disused refectory of an abandoned monastery, a hay barn or some other farm outbuilding. To these spaces, soldiers have come laden with their loot, which they divide between themselves and their camp followers, who are mostly women. Their treasures include plate of gold, silver and jewellery: a pirate's hoard.

A soldier or group of soldiers actually holding people to ransom would in due course become a subject in its own right, producing a sub-genre of the guardroom scene that has been aptly christened 'the plunder picture'.[24] In such paintings the taking of plunder comes to the fore and the victims are often given more prominence than the soldiers who prey on them. Willem Duyster's *The Marauders* of circa 1635 shows a fair-skinned and well-dressed young woman kneeling before an informal tribunal of cloaked officers. In a whole series of plunder pictures by Jacob Duck, plaintive men and women beg to be allowed to keep their possessions, or at least their lives, only to be met by the cold stare of the officers in charge, confident in their usurped authority. These are the raiding parties described by Grimmelshausen's anti-hero Simplicius, rendered in paint rather than prose.

Such pictures played on the fears of the Dutch. It is no coincidence that the period of their greatest popularity coincided with the grimmest phase of the Thirty Years War, peaking as that conflict reached its end in 1648. Statistics based on contemporary inventories indicate that roughly 10 per cent of all subject pictures painted in the Dutch Republic during the late 1630s and 1640s were *kortegarde* paintings. Of the rest, most were traditional comic (and escapist) depictions of peasant kermesses, musicians and dancers, with a smattering of paintings (perhaps 5 per cent) set in brothels or taverns.[25] So, in the years immediately preceding 1648, the majority of Dutch pictures of people in interiors were depictions of soldiers: soldiers glumly keeping their own company, glorying in their loot, or lording it over their victims.

This striking fact has been largely obscured by the general absence of guardroom paintings from the walls of the world's leading museums of Dutch art. Such pictures were unfashionable in the nineteenth century, when many museum collections were formed, and they have remained so. As a result perceptions of the development of Dutch painting, Dutch taste and Dutch politics during a critical period of history have been skewed. There are many echoes of the guardroom tradition in the work of Vermeer (for example, *Officer with a Laughing Girl*) and his contemporaries, but they are rarely noted.

The terrors of the Thirty Years War had a profound effect on Dutch society as a whole but gave a particular impetus to the Remonstrants and other followers of Jacobus Arminius, including the Collegiants. Their abhorrence of sectarian strife was both amplified and justified by the spectacle of Protestants and Catholics brutally murdering each other in their millions. Dissenting Dutch Christians of many different persuasions called to mind the words spoken by Christ during the Sermon on the Mount: 'Blessed are the peacemakers.' The war was undoubtedly one cause of the rapid growth of the Collegiant movement during these years. The idea of simply reading and reabsorbing Christ's message of peace, in company with a few like-minded souls, must have seemed particularly attractive when the outside world was such a troubled place.

In Rotterdam a resurgent spirit of Christian pacifism led to a revival of interest in the figure of Desiderio Erasmus, who had been born in the city more than 150 years earlier. He had long been revered as one of the founding fathers of the Reformation, having subtly questioned the authority of the Roman Church even while remaining loyal to it. But from the 1620s onwards he was admired above all as a peacemaker, remembered first and foremost as the author of a pioneering pacifist manifesto entitled *The Complaint of Peace*. First published in 1521, it had originally been written in protest against the first wars of religion sparked by the Reformation, but it seemed more topical

CHILDHOOD, EDUCATION, MARRIAGE, 1632–57

than ever in light of the abominations of the Thirty Years War. Adopting the persona of Peace, or Concord, Erasmus had railed against the madness of Christian-on-Christian warfare, in which contesting armies marched against one another under the banner of the cross, professing a faith they violated at every moment.[26]

A stone statue had been erected to Erasmus in Rotterdam in the third quarter of the sixteenth century, one of the earliest European monuments to a man who was neither a king nor a general nor a saint. In 1616 the town council, dominated at that time by Remonstrants, commissioned a larger than life-size bronze sculpture from Hendrik de Keyser to replace it. The Counter-Remonstrants who seized power in Rotterdam after the Synod of Dordt regarded

The controversial bronze statue of Desiderio Erasmus (1466–1536) by Hendrick de Keyser on the Great Market Square in Rotterdam. A liberal Christian humanist whose teachings helped to spark the Reformation, Erasmus was hero-worshipped by the Remonstrants and many other freethinking Dutch Protestants, who admired his spirit of toleration and shared his belief that no war should ever be waged in the name of religion. The statue is still in Rotterdam city centre today.

Erasmus (not without reason) as a Libertine forerunner of Arminius, so the statue was placed in storage during their brief ascendancy. But in 1622, by which time Arminians had crept back into the magistracy, in Rotterdam as in Delft, the statue was given pride of place in the market square at the centre of town. There it has remained, a powerful symbol of the enduring influence of Erasmus on religious and political debate in his native city.

The spirit of Erasmian pacifism was strong among the Rotterdam Remonstrants, and only grew stronger as the decades passed and the sickening excesses of the war in Germany went from bad to worse. The Collegiant groups that emerged from the ranks of the Remonstrants were therefore thoroughly versed in the work of Erasmus. Several of the earliest Colleges in Rotterdam evolved directly from discussion groups originally convened in private houses with the aim of debating his writings.[27] Data for the growth of the Collegiant movement in nearby Delft is far less complete than for Rotterdam, but the pattern was probably the same. In these 'friendship circles' that immediately preceded the founding of Collegiant cells, Erasmus was commonly read together with Coornhert and Camphuysen, a tripartite list that implies a tripartite progression of feeling: horrified pacifism leading to a dislike of confessional religion, leading in turn to disgust, for some at least, with the very institution of the Church.

Opposition to war on moral and religious grounds was made easier in the Dutch Republic by liberal attitudes to military service. Non-resistant pacifism of the kind advocated by Erasmus in *The Complaint of Peace* was tolerated by the Dutch state, which was unique in this respect among the European powers of the day. Notable beneficiaries of the policy were the Mennonites, whose beliefs forbade them from bearing arms under any circumstances, impelling them to refuse service in the civic militia and police, as well as the army. Instead of imprisoning or executing them, which would have been the norm in other countries, the Dutch local authorities allowed Mennonites to supply substitutes for their conscientious objectors. Failing that they could pay a fine of sufficient size to allow the council to hire replacements on its own account.

There was much common ground between the Mennonites and the Remonstrants, as there was between both of those congregations and the Collegiants, the Christians without a church. In Rotterdam and Delft the majority of people attending the newly founded Collegiant meetings of the 1630s were Remonstrants. In Amsterdam, where the first College was founded rather later, in 1646, the majority of its adherents had links with the Mennonite Church.

The Thirty Years War was the most appallingly violent sectarian conflict in history, supported and spurred on by church leaders both Protestant and Catholic. As such it was the main catalyst for Europe's first peace movement, founded by the dissenting Christians of the Dutch Republic. Many such people were naturally attracted to the Collegiant movement, which took the pacifism of Erasmus and Arminius to its logical extreme. They were drawn to the movement precisely because it *was* so radical: a war so dreadful called for drastic remedies. If that meant adopting a whole new way of being a Christian, then so be it.

But there were also plenty of Dutch people who saw the world in a very different light. For much of the 1630s, despite the almost daily reports of atrocities, those in favour of continuing the Dutch war against Spain and perpetuating conflict in the German Empire were in a substantial majority. Chief among them were the leaders of the Reformed Church and Stadtholder Frederik Hendrik, whose Orangist party still enjoyed strong working-class support in the larger towns and cities of the Republic. But gradually, as liberal regents gained the upper hand across Holland, the balance of power shifted in favour of those supporting peace.

A good way to gauge movements in seventeenth-century Dutch public opinion is to consult the surviving trove of popular pamphlets, the 'little blue books', which were published in large print runs for the broadest possible general audience. Between 1606 and 1648, the year when peace was finally declared, some 8,000 of these appeared, offering various perspectives on the most pressing issues of the day.[28] Their authors were for the most part educated men, often state officials, Calvinist preachers or dissenters of various sorts.

As might be expected, war was a subject under constant discussion, but until 1640 the vast majority of pamphleteers opposed any form of peace with Spain. After that date, quite suddenly, the pattern was reversed, and by the mid-1640s, with peace talks at Münster well under way, pamphlets in favour of peace outnumbered those arguing for the continuation of war. Even a rare pro-war pamphlet poem written to mark a Dutch military victory, namely the siege of Sas van Gent, in which Vermeer's uncle had played a part, seemed less than celebratory in tone, prefaced as it was by a dirge-like description of a world devastated by military conflict:

> Mars is different from other carousers,
> His revelling makes laughter die,
> Laughter becomes less than nothing at all,
> One counts only the tears ...
> Men pluck where no feathers remain,
> Men seek from the landsman (who now quivers)
> Goods long since plundered from his empty domain.
> Who can stem this flood of disaster?
> All this sorrow I truly lament,
> But I rejoice in the victory of Sas van Ghent.[29]

THE MAN FROM OUT OF TOWN

Vermeer would have begun serving his apprenticeship when he was around ten or twelve years old, so some time between late 1642 and 1644. His father, Reynier, who was on good terms with many artists, would most likely have had a wide choice when it came to deciding on the painter best qualified to guide and instruct his boy. The name of Vermeer's master is undocumented and by general consensus remains a mystery. A solution to that mystery can be proposed, albeit tentatively, on the basis of two documents from 1653, both found in the Delft City Archives.[30]

The first is dated 29 December 1653 and comes from the Guild of St Luke's '*Register van all de nieuwe meesters*', or register of all newly qualified masters: 'Johannes Vermeer has himself registered as a master painter, being a citizen, and he has paid one guilder 10 stuivers towards his master money; there remain 4 guilders 10 stuivers to pay.' According to guild regulations any painter born in Delft who trained with a painter in the same town was entitled to a 50 per cent reduction on the normal registration fee of 6 guilders. But Vermeer could claim no such

CHILDHOOD, EDUCATION, MARRIAGE, 1632-57

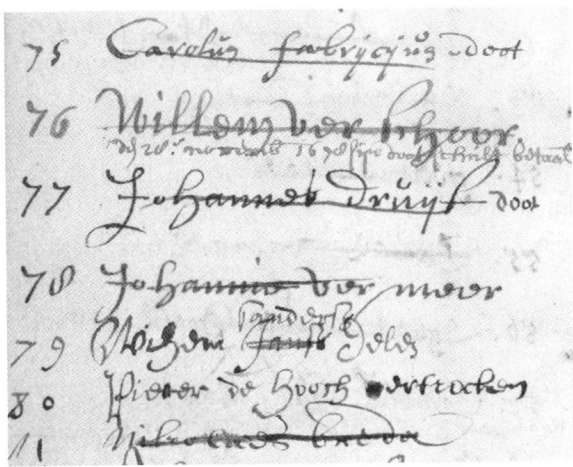

11. A Golden Age for art in Delft: the 'register of newly qualified masters' in the city's Guild of St Luke, covering the years 1652-5, bears the names of no fewer than three famous Dutch masters: Carel Fabritius (75), Johannes Vermeer (78) and Pieter de Hooch (80).

reduction in his 'master money': having paid one and a half guilders, he still owed four and a half. This can be taken as positive proof that he served his apprenticeship with a master outside Delft.[31] Were it not for this document, the distinguished local painter Leonaert Bramer might have seemed a likely master for him. As we shall see, Bramer was close enough to Vermeer to be asked to plead his case with his future mother-in-law. But his workshop was in Delft, so we must rule him out.

The second document is dated a little over eight months earlier than the first, 22 April 1653, and takes the form of an 'act of surety' preserved in the papers of the notary Willem de Langue and recording some business transactions of a captain in the army of the States-General. The content of the document is immaterial but the names of the two men who witnessed it leap off the page. One is Johannes Vermeer, twenty years of age. The other is 'Monsieur Gerrit ter Borch', namely Gerard ter Borch, then thirty-five years old and one of the most accomplished painters of his generation. Ter Borch signed his name directly underneath that of the army captain, in a large and clear hand. Vermeer signed his own name below that of Ter Borch, the handwriting smaller and less certain.

Gerard ter Borch was originally from the town of Zwolle in Overijssel, in the east of the Dutch Republic. According to the early eighteenth-century compiler of artists' lives Arnold Houbraken, he travelled extensively in his youth, visiting England, France, Germany, Italy and Spain. He is then believed to have spent some years working in Amsterdam, among other places. By 1653 he was back living in his native Zwolle. Shortly thereafter he settled in the eastern frontier town of Deventer, where he would spend much of the rest of his life. Other than the one notarial document placing him with Johannes Vermeer in the office of Willem de Langue, there is nothing to suggest that he had any links with Delft. Had that document not been discovered, it would never have been known that he had even visited the town.

There is one other intriguing thing about the act of surety, namely its date: 22 April 1653 was a Tuesday. The Sunday before was the day of Vermeer's marriage. This raises the possibility that Gerard ter Borch may have travelled all the way to Delft from Overijssel to attend the wedding. If so then he was still in town two days later, and still keeping company with Vermeer, when someone – perhaps the notary or the soldier – asked them to co-witness a document. Ter Borch may have stayed on after the ceremony, to exchange news. Is this not how we might expect an older painter to behave towards one of his former pupils, one to whom he had taken a shine?

The trouble with any such extrapolation from bare fact is that it is unprovable. Alternative explanations cannot be ruled out and are not far to seek. Perhaps Gerard ter Borch, like many other artists in the Republic, had known Vermeer's father and stayed at his inn, in which case he might have become a friend of the family, liable to call in from time to time. Reynier had died only six months earlier, so Ter Borch might have been in town to pay his belated respects. But, however we choose to interpret the joint appearance of Vermeer and Ter Borch in that notary's office on that day, it is hard to avoid concluding that they knew each other and shared a bond of some kind.

The known facts of the case boil down to two. First, Vermeer was apprenticed to a painter from outside Delft. Secondly, Ter Borch is the only painter from outside Delft directly linked to Vermeer by documentary evidence. It might not be much to go on, but it is something. Considering that on the day of their one known encounter Vermeer was a twenty-year-old novice and Ter Borch a well-established painter in his thirties, it certainly seems possible that the relationship between them might have been that of apprentice to master.

If we allow ourselves to entertain that hypothesis then the date of their meeting, so soon after Vermeer's marriage day, and not long after the death of his father, becomes fraught with potential poignancy. Might Gerard ter Borch have been invited to Delft by his former apprentice to fill the role of his late father, Reynier, at the wedding? None of this can be presented as truth, only possibility. But bearing that in mind and considering the absence of other plausible candidates for the part of Vermeer's master, there can be little harm in seeing where it leads us.

Vermeer's father would most likely have sought out a master for him in around 1643 or the following year, when Johannes turned twelve. Reynier himself had been apprenticed in Amsterdam, the most populous and competitive city in the Dutch Republic, so it would make sense for him to have placed his own son there too. Ter Borch's movements during the early 1640s are not fully documented, but there is good reason to believe he was living and working in Amsterdam for most of that time.

Reynier was not a rich man and the cost of apprenticeship, which included board and lodging as well as tuition, could be considerable, the more so if a master was experienced and well known. With his picture-dealing business and his extensive clientele of artists Reynier was in a good position to identify an up-and-coming painter, someone to whom he might apprentice his son without bankrupting himself. It would be in keeping with his character for him to have struck a bargain with a younger man like Gerard ter Borch, who was twenty-seven years old in 1644. Reynier may have heard about him directly or indirectly from Ter Borch's father and namesake, Gerard ter Borch the Elder, who had spent seven years in Rome training to be a painter and who knew many of the Birds of a Feather, some of whom gathered regularly at The Mechelen Inn and before that at The Flying Fox. It may have been on that same grapevine that Reynier first heard about the younger Gerard ter Borch as a painter of promise, worth keeping in mind.

Objections have been raised to Ter Borch as a possible master to Vermeer on the grounds that Vermeer's earliest paintings of around

1653–4 bear little resemblance to his. While Vermeer's early works are eclectic, painted in a variety of styles, the same is true of Ter Borch's work of the 1640s, which can be tight and precise on some occasions and loose and expressionistic on others. Ter Borch exhibited no fixed manner that Vermeer might copy, so it would be unwise to read a great deal into any perceived dissimilarity between them. Besides, there may be another explanation for the look of Vermeer's early work, which is not only unlike that of Ter Borch but thoroughly un-Dutch.

It has often been observed that Vermeer's *Diana and Her Companions* of around 1653, which hangs in the Mauritshuis, looks like an Italian painting in a building full of Dutch art. As we shall see, two of his other early pictures are so deeply indebted to works by his Italian contemporaries Andrea Vaccaro and Felice Ficherelli as to suggest that Vermeer must have seen his sources at first hand. Italian pictures so recently painted were not commonly found in the Dutch Republic, so he may indeed have travelled to Italy to see them, just after completing his apprenticeship. If that is the case, we should not be surprised if his early pictures show little trace of Ter Borch's influence, because Vermeer's head would still have been full of Italian art when he painted them.

As time went on, the styles of the two artists strikingly converged. In around 1658 Vermeer painted his *Officer with a Laughing Girl*, a picture manifestly indebted to a new variant of guardroom painting pioneered by Ter Borch, in which soldiers court young women. By 1660 both had become exceptionally skilled painters of light and shade, of fine fabrics, and of the gestures and expressions of figures in interiors. By that date it is hard to tell in which direction the influence ran, although influence there certainly was. It all lends weight to the presumption that a relationship of some kind existed between Vermeer and Ter Borch, one based on mutual respect and an awareness of each other's work.

If Gerard ter Borch was indeed Vermeer's master, there may have been more to the apprenticeship arrangement than business as usual. As we have seen, it seems likely that Vermeer's parents were followers of Arminius and would have wanted their only son to be apprenticed to someone who shared their own tolerant and pacifist beliefs. For this reason, Gerard ter Borch may have taken on the role of accepting Vermeer as his apprentice. No Dutch painter of the time protested more eloquently against the futility and emptiness of war. No Dutch painter of the time was more closely associated with the cause of peace.

Ter Borch's earliest documented composition, painted in around 1634–5 when he was still a teenager, is a startlingly original depiction of a soldier of fortune seen from behind. The man is shown on horseback, hunched in exhaustion, against a lowering sky filled with clouds as dirty as gunsmoke. His black armour glints in the dull light, he wears a feather in his felt hat, his boots are made of impressively supple leather, and his silhouette dominates the horizon; but nonetheless he cuts a pathetic figure. He is in the middle of nowhere, going nowhere: a captive to the ideal of military glory who unwittingly embodies its repudiation. In painting such a knowingly mock-heroic picture, Ter Borch reversed every convention of the Baroque equestrian portrait, the function of which was to aggrandize and elevate the sitter, who was usually royal, like Van Dyck's *Charles I on Horseback*, or at the least aristocratic, like Velázquez's *Count Olivares on Horseback*. In such pictures the man of power astride his spirited horse stares down at the viewer with a haughty expression. Ter Borch's horseman by contrast is seen from the rear and remains anonymous. He is seated on no prancing steed but an exhausted hack. Painted when the Thirty Years War was at its height, the picture perfectly encapsulates that conflict's banality and threat, its lack of direction and pointlessness.

Ten years later, by 1643 or 1644, when Vermeer may have begun his apprenticeship with him, Gerard ter Borch had become a well-travelled artist with an international reputation. According to a eulogy written by his friend and contemporary Joost Roldanus, his pictures had been admired at the royal palace in Madrid, where Philip IV of Spain had sat for him for his portrait. Back in Holland in the early 1640s Ter Borch painted a series of small but intense portraits of distinguished Amsterdammers on copper, restricted to a palette of blacks and browns, which suggest that he had been influenced by the work of Philip IV's court painter Velázquez. Ter Borch was also known at the time for his 'modern' pictures, which included a number of guard-rooms notable for their emphasis on the sheer tedium of garrison life.

Ter Borch was painting weary soldiers in a city weary of war. The Arminian regents of Amsterdam were pushing relentlessly for peace, and eventually led the negotiations for a treaty that would end the Eighty Years War with Spain and establish the United Provinces as a free sovereign state. Ter Borch was regarded with trust by such men, because he was a painter with demonstrably Arminian sympathies. While his subject pictures revealed a profound antipathy to war, his portraits were mostly depictions of liberals and supporters in one way or another of the Remonstrant movement (in later life he would become principal portrait painter to the De Graeff dynasty, one of Amsterdam's leading Remonstrant families). The fact that he had been to Spain and painted a portrait of Philip IV, regarded as the devil incarnate by the pro-war Calvinists, also counted in his favour. He had accepted the Spanish and they had accepted him. He had painted Dutch pictures of Spanish courtiers and Spanish-inspired portraits of Dutch regents. He was cultural diplomacy personified.

In 1646 Gerard ter Borch was invited to join the Dutch delegates to Münster, where he would eventually record the signing of the long awaited peace treaty with Spain. He was the only Dutch painter to whom such an invitation was extended, partly because his previous links to the Spanish court made him diplomatically acceptable. He travelled to Münster with Adrian Pauw, a leading regent who was for many years a leader of the anti-Orangist peace faction. If the young Vermeer were indeed Ter Borch's apprentice, he might have been present, but we have no evidence either way.

Ter Borch's new-found Dutch patron, Adrian Pauw, commissioned him to paint two miniature portraits of his wife and himself as well as a large canvas depicting his arrival in Münster with an impressive entourage. The peace negotiations, which had been painfully slow from the start, took a further two years to conclude, by which time Ter Borch had left the circle of Pauw to join the entourage of the Count of Peñaranda, leader of the Spanish delegation to the peace talks. During his time in Münster, Ter Borch took advantage of his access to delegates on both sides of the negotiating table. He painted numerous portraits of the various Dutch and Spanish ambassadors sent to attend the negotiations, eventually combining their likenesses into a single solemn group portrait commemorating the ceremony that concluded the signing of the peace treaty in 1648: *The Swearing of the Oath of Ratification of the Treaty of Münster*. The picture was not a commission and remained with Ter Borch throughout the rest of his life, so it makes sense to see it as a personal interpretation of the moment when peace was finally made.

In a sombre room lit by an uncertain source, which is perhaps the blessed light of reason, a group of around 100 men are squeezed around a table strewn with documents as they make their solemn pledge:

> Let all persons know that, after a long succession of bloody wars which for many years have oppressed the peoples, subjects, kingdoms and lands which are under the obedience of the Lords King of Spain and States-General of the United Netherlands, the aforesaid Lords, the King and the States, moved by Christian piety, desire to end the general misery and prevent the dreadful consequences, calamity, harm and danger which the further continuation of the aforesaid wars in the Low Countries would bring in their train . . .[32]

Modest in size, Ter Borch's painting is remarkable for its even-handedness, the artist eliding the differences between the Spanish and Dutch delegates to such an extent that both sides seem to become one. The picture is compositionally dull, human concord being naturally uneventful, but alive with optimism. The swearing of the oath of peace is presented as a triumph for the spirit of Christian tolerance.

Many Dutch pacifists believed that the treaty signed at Münster, a prelude to further treaties ending the great war in the German lands, marked nothing less than the beginning of the End of Days, when Christ would come back to rule for a thousand years over an earthly paradise. Apocalyptic excitement reached fever pitch during the years leading up to Münster and would not dissipate for at least two decades afterwards. The sheer ferocity and long duration of the Thirty Years War had convinced many that what they were witnessing was the Final Conflict, legendary harbinger of the Second Coming. Other presumed portents included plague and devastation and signs in the night sky. So when a great comet appeared in the year 1648 many reflected on the melancholy spectacle of Germany in ruins, its people in misery and mourning, and could not help wondering.

1650

The Peace of Münster (ratified May 1648) was followed by the Treaty of Westphalia (October 1648), finally ending the Thirty Years War. Its authors included an 'Amnesia Clause', calling for 'a perpetual Amnesty or Pardon of all that has been committed since the beginning of these troubles ... All that has passed on the one side and the other, as well before as during the war, in Words, Writings and Outrageous Actions, in Violences, Hostilities, Damages and Expenses, without any respect to persons or things, shall be entirely abolished. In such a manner that all be buried in eternal Oblivion.' It was well-intended advice for those who could not bring themselves, as Christ had commanded, to love their enemies. Forget them, forget their crimes. In practice, the memories of war would not be easily erased.

In Holland, the peace was received sceptically by some but warmly greeted by most. All acknowledged that the liberal regents had won a decisive victory over their conservative opponents. Stadtholder Frederik Hendrik had died in March 1647, to be succeeded by his son Prince William II of Orange, a bitter enemy of the peace process. Due to his youth and lack of military experience in the field, William lacked authority and had failed to muster enough support to form a credible opposition to the pro-peace party represented most vocally by the liberal Arminian regents. Unable to block the Münster negotiations, he had not even objected to them, wary of calling attention to his own lack of power.

But by 1650 the situation had changed. By then William had gained the confidence of his troops and formed a strong alliance with the Calvinist hardliners in the Reformed Church, traditional supporters of the House of Orange. As a result the Dutch Republic was riven by the same religious, political and ideological divisions that had caused the crisis of 1618, leading to the overthrow and execution of Johan van Oldenbarnevelt, the defeat of the Remonstrants, and the short-lived military dictatorship of Prince Maurice. The Eighty Years War was barely over but the country was once more on the edge of civil war.

The situation reached crisis point when the Holland regents cut the size of the Dutch standing army, reducing its numbers from a wartime peak of over 70,000 to around 29,000. They presented their policy as part of a fiscally prudent strategy designed to reduce state expenditure while freeing additional labour. For the belligerent William II, who regarded the army as his personal fief, it was the last straw. On 30 July 1650 he attempted a coup d'état, ordering 12,000 troops under the command of his cousin Willem Frederik to march on Amsterdam. The soldiers had almost reached the city when a postal courier bringing letters from Hamburg rode past them and alerted the civic guard to their presence. The gates were closed just in time, the soldiers locked out.

William II may have been temporarily foiled, but he was now in a position to bully his opponents into submission. Within days he had become *de facto* head of state. The arch-leaders of the Arminian faction in Amsterdam were removed from the ruling council of regents, and the military cuts instigated under their regime were reversed. Six other leading regents were thrown into prison and an inquiry was launched into the behaviour of the Dutch diplomats who had led the negotiations at Münster, the insinuation being that they had taken bribes from the Spanish. Adrian Pauw, Gerard ter Borch's former patron and leader of the Dutch embassy, feared for his life.[33] Then as suddenly as it had appeared the threat was lifted. In October 1650 William II contracted smallpox. On 6 November he died. The Calvinist *preciezen*, who had been convinced that God was on their side, were devastated. Pious Dutch pacifists took the prince's death as the clearest sign yet that peace would be permanent, and that those who had supported it enjoyed God's favour.

Nothing is known of the movements of Johannes Vermeer during this turning point in Dutch history. Assuming he had begun a standard six-year apprenticeship in 1644, he would have been obliged to remain with his master for two more years after 1648, the year of peace. Ter Borch himself is thought to have returned to Amsterdam from Münster, so if Vermeer was his apprentice he would have been in the thick of things when the city was threatened and almost taken in the summer of 1650. Assuming that he finished his apprenticeship at around that time, he may then have spent a year or so travelling, as Ter Borch had done when he was around the same age.

Even if Vermeer had never been apprenticed to Ter Borch in the first place, there were plenty of other men in his life who might have inspired him to go forth and see something of the world. Vermeer had grown up around the Birds of a Feather, Dutch painters who had all been to Rome and paraded the experience as a badge of honour. The pattern of his appearances in the archive is certainly consistent with a journey of some kind at this point in his life: no document exists to prove Vermeer's presence anywhere in the Dutch Republic between 1650 and 1652, whereas a flurry from the following year suddenly places him in Delft. Wherever his wanderings may have taken him, he was probably back in his native town by the autumn of 1652. His father died in October of that year, so he may have been called home sometime around then.

After William II's death the Holland liberals took the reins of power and would not relinquish them until 1672. Under the leadership of Johan de Witt, the pre-eminent statesman of the Dutch Republic at its zenith, the role of Stadtholder was abolished and 'The Era of True Liberty' proclaimed. It was during this time and in this watery corner of the northern Netherlands, full of hope, idealism and energy, that Vermeer would paint all of his pictures. But first he got married.

DELFT AND SCHIPLUY, 1653

On the evening of 4 April 1653 three men knocked on the door of a large house in the Oude Langendijk, in the Catholic quarter of Delft, a part of town commonly known as the *papenhoek*, or Papists' Corner. They had come to see a lady named Maria Thins.

Maria was originally from Gouda but had moved to Delft following her acrimonious divorce from an irascible man named Reynier Bolnes, a wealthy brickmaker who had profited from the boom in construction that was a consequence of the surging economy and population of the Dutch Republic during its so-called Golden Age. She was from an old and distinguished family and rich in her own right before her marriage to the brickmaker, which, although unhappy, had made her richer still: her divorce settlement amounted to more than 15,000 guilders. To judge by a later contribution that she was obliged to make to the family levy of Delft – a local tax exacted at the rate of 5 per cent of total assets – her net worth was close to 26,000 guilders.[34] To put it in perspective, Rembrandt at the peak of his fame and fortune overstretched himself by acquiring a splendid house in Amsterdam for 13,000 guilders, most of which he borrowed; the resulting mortgage payments precipitated his subsequent ruin. Maria could have bought that same house without a mortgage, with more than enough capital left over to live on for the rest of her life. She was one of the richest people in Delft.

The men who came to see her that spring evening did not want to discuss money, although it was surely a subtext of the conversation that took place. They were there to talk her into accepting a young painter named Johannes Vermeer, a man with distinctly uncertain financial prospects, as her prospective son-in-law. Maria's daughter Catharina was set on marrying him. Earlier the same day the couple had appeared at Delft Town Hall on the Great Market Square to declare their betrothal. He was twenty, she was a year older. They had evidently acted without Maria's approval. She was a devout Catholic and wanted her daughter to marry a man of the same faith. But Vermeer was either a Protestant by confession or a dissenting Christian who recognized no Church at all, least of all that of the Catholics. It was a stumbling block, hence the evening visit.

Two of the men present were there as young love's advocates. One was a painter, the aforementioned Leonaert Bramer, the other a captain in the Dutch army, Bartolomeus Melling. Both must have been friends of the Vermeer family, associates perhaps of the painter's recently deceased father, whose inn teemed with artists and military officers. The third man was a lawyer, a notary named Johannes Ranck, who witnessed Maria's responses to what may have been a barrage of persuasion. She was accompanied throughout the meeting by her sister Cornelia, who had been one of her main pillars of support during the later years of her troubled marriage.

Cupid's envoys had been personally chosen by Johannes Vermeer and his would-be bride Catharina to speak on their behalf. We know this because when Bramer and Melling both turned up the following day at Johannes Ranck's office, to provide him with a verbatim account of their meeting with Maria, he recorded that their attendance had been specifically requested by 'Jan Reijniersz' (Johannes Vermeer, son of Reynier Vermeer) and 'Trijntgen Reijniers' (Catharina, daughter of Reynier Bolnes). The other man who witnessed their deposition, the notary Willem de Langue, must also have been there at Vermeer's request. He was an old friend of the family, having acted for Vermeer's late father on many occasions.

Notary Ranck's document, written up the morning after the conversation of the night before, is our only source of information for what transpired at Maria's house.[35] Since its sole function was to record Maria's response to the betrothal of her daughter, it reveals nothing of the arguments put forward by Bramer and Melling in Vermeer's favour. Whatever they said had clearly failed to reconcile Maria to her daughter's choice of husband, but she did not dig her heels in. Her attitude was one of pained resignation. Her tersely ambivalent response to the betrothal is recorded in the joint testimony of soldier and painter:

> Captain Melling, about 59 years of age, and Leonaert Bramer, painter, about 58, appeared before the notary Johannes Ranck ... and declared ... that they were present yesterday night on the fourth of this month at the house and in the presence of Joffr. Maria Tints [sic], living in this town, when the question was raised by the aforementioned notary in our presence as to whether the aforesaid Joffr. Tints (assisted by Cornelia Tints, her sister) was prepared to sign the act of consent for the registration of the marriage vows between Joffr. Maria Tints's daughter, named Trijntge Reijniers, and Jan Reyniersz ... in order to make public these vows according to the custom of this town; whom we then heard give for an answer that she did not intend to sign but would suffer the banns to be published and would tolerate it; and she said several times that she would not prevent or hinder them.[36]

The message was clear: the mother of the bride-to-be was not happy about the marriage, but would not stand in its way. Presumably she recognized that Catharina's mind was made up and there was nothing she could do to change it. Maria Thins did not have much to say, but she said it several times, in the manner of someone repeating a well-rehearsed statement. The couple's betrothal, which had taken place at the town hall a few hours earlier, had most likely taken her by surprise. But her response suggests she knew already that it was only a question of when, not if, Catharina tied the knot with Johannes.

Perhaps Catharina had backed her mother into a corner. The clerk who entered the couple's names into the register of betrothals on 4 April was obliged to ask them for their places of residence. This is what he wrote: 'Johannes Reyniersz Vermeer, bachelor, living on the Market Place and Catharina Bolnes, spinster, also there'. Those last two words – *'mede aldaar'* in Dutch – have received little comment in the literature on Vermeer, other than to have been dismissed as a clerical error. But it seems a strange error to have made: clerical mistakes are not usually so precise, nor so open to scandalous interpretation.

At the time of the betrothal, Johannes Vermeer himself was certainly living on the Market Place, namely the Great Market Square, in the inn named Mechelen once owned by his father and inherited by his mother. Maria Thins's house, where it might be expected that Catharina should have been living immediately before her marriage, was in the Oude Langendijk, south of the Nieuwe Kerk: to get there from The Mechelen Inn a pedestrian would have to walk east, to the opposite side of the main square, cross the Langendijk canal and walk on for a block. The two addresses were by no means the same, nor were they close enough, in location or pronunciation, to be easily confused. If Catharina really had been living with her mother on the Oude Langendijk on 4 April 1653, surely the clerk would have noted the fact. Catharina does not seem to have been present in Maria's house that evening, when Captain Melling and Leonaert Bramer came to call. If we take the registration document at face value, we must assume that Johannes and Catharina were together at The Mechelen Inn during the run-up to their marriage.

This is not to suggest that they were living as man and wife. The inn was a hostelry with more than enough rooms for Catharina to be given her own bedchamber. Vermeer's mother, Digna Baltens, would probably have insisted on such an arrangement and the couple themselves must have understood the need for prudence. Delft was a small town where people had a habit of minding other people's business. The Great Market Square was a hub of gossip. Stories about family disagreements would die down but if it got about that a husband and wife had lived in sin before their marriage that would leave a permanent stain on their reputation. If Catharina had moved in with Johannes it would probably just have been to pressure her mother into consenting to her choice of husband. Her aim was to get married, not to live her life under a cloud. Maria Thins was already divorced from her husband and alienated from her only other living child, a son named Willem. Her other daughter Cornelia had died in her teens some years earlier. Perhaps Catharina calculated that her mother, nearly sixty years old, had simply had enough of estrangement and loss. If so she calculated correctly.

Two weeks and two days after their betrothal, Johannes Vermeer and Catharina Bolnes were joined in holy matrimony. We know this because of a brief note scribbled in the margin of the original register of their betrothal: 'Attestation given in Schipluy, April 20th, 1653'. Schipluy, or Schipluiden as it is called today, is a riverside village south-west of Delft, about an hour away by boat. The name of the church where the ceremony took place is not known, but it may have had no official name, being one of the many *schuilkerken*, or hidden churches, allowed to Dutch Christians outside the fold of the Reformed Church. Catholics had long been forbidden by Dutch law to practise their faith openly, so in the early years of the Republic many had resorted to holding their services in out-of-the-way locations, often using agricultural barns. The literal meaning of the term '*schuilkerken*' is 'barn churches' (from the Dutch *schuur*, or barn), indicating their rural origins. A Catholic ceremony was presumably part of Maria Thins's price for allowing the marriage to go ahead.

Some writers on Vermeer have suggested that he took a great risk by marrying a Catholic, as if he were throwing in his lot with a member of a persecuted minority whose very existence was under threat. But neither Vermeer nor anyone else in his immediate family was a member of the Reformed Church, so if Catharina was part of a religious minority then he was too. If he went to church at all, it was most likely to the Remonstrant church on the Oude Delft, which was a hidden church just like those of the Catholics. He may have preferred to attend the meetings of the Collegiants, the Christians without a church. Perhaps he did both.

The situation of Vermeer's bride and mother-in-law as Catholics living in Delft was no more perilous than his own as a Protestant nonconformist. Catholicism was on the rise generally in the northern Netherlands, and had been for more than half a century. The *Missio*

Hollandica, established by Rome in the early 1590s to bolster the old faith in the new Protestant republic of the United Provinces, had prospered to such an extent that by the late 1630s the number of priests ministering to Dutch Catholics had grown from 70 to 482.[37] The number of practising Catholics had risen correspondingly and continued to do so, especially in towns with a strong civic tradition of tolerance, such as Leiden, Haarlem, Rotterdam, Alkmaar and Gouda (where Maria Thins had been born and raised). Precise figures are hard to come by, but by mid-century roughly one in five of Amsterdam's 150,000 inhabitants was a Catholic. In Delft the proportion was even higher, perhaps as high as one-third.[38] There were more Catholics than strict Calvinists living in the town.

Johannes and Catharina came from very different backgrounds. He was from a working-class family, while she was gentry; he had little money, while she was rich; he seems to have been from a family of radical dissenting Protestants, while she was a Catholic. Catharina and her mother, Maria Thins, lived in the heart of Catholic Delft, on Papists' Corner, next to the hidden (but hardly secret) Jesuit church and two doors away from the Jesuit school. Maria's house had originally been purchased in 1641 by one of her cousins, Jan Geensz Thins, a man with strong links to the Jesuits. There is a trail of documents to suggest that he bought it on their behalf and arranged for it to be rented to Maria Thins, the income being used to fund Catholic missionary work in the town. Maria's cousin probably helped to buy other houses in the area: in 1643 the town authorities complained about the Jesuits secretly purchasing property under assumed names. They may have been concerned but they did not put a stop to it. A memorandum of 1686, written by a member of the Jesuit Order, notes that by then no fewer than fifteen houses in Papists' Corner were owned by 'the Jesuit Station in Delft'.[39] The house of Maria Thins was at the centre of a buzzing hive of Catholic activity.

Maria was evidently troubled by her daughter's decision to marry a Protestant. She had taken a Protestant husband herself, and it had ended more than badly. Her only son, Willem, had taken his father's side after the divorce and now both he and her ex-husband were estranged from her: on the rare occasions when she did see Willem he was apt to hurl insults at her, calling her a 'popish swine' and worse. In light of her own unhappy experience of a mixed-faith marriage, it is more than likely that Maria pleaded with her son-in-law to convert to Catholicism before marrying her daughter. Many writers on Vermeer have assumed that he consented to do so and lived thereafter as a Catholic. But, as we will see, he could never in good conscience have proclaimed loyalty to the Church of Rome. It is possible that he feigned conversion, then went through the motions of being an observant Catholic, but he could have gone no further than that. It is more likely that Maria Thins swallowed her reservations and accepted, however grudgingly, that her son-in-law's beliefs were not the same as her own.

As a liberal Protestant living in a town where Catholicism was openly tolerated, Vermeer was breaking few taboos by taking a Catholic bride. He had probably been raised in the Arminian tradition, the core values of which were forbearance and broadmindedness. Catharina may have searched her own conscience before giving him her hand, because according to the teachings of the Catholic Church she would have been marrying a heretic. But, if she had qualms, there is no record of them. Was she just deeply in love with Johannes? Or had she come to share his own tolerant beliefs? An English traveller to the Dutch Republic, Ellis Veryard, remarked that 'it is very ordinary to find the man of the house of one [religious] opinion, his wife of another, his children of a third and their servants of one different from them all; and yet they live without the least jangling of dissension.'[40] Johannes Vermeer and Catharina Bolnes may themselves have aspired to just such a marriage, one in which both husband and wife were free to follow the dictates of their own conscience.

THE BRICKMAKER'S DAUGHTER

Much more is known about the early life of Catharina than about that of Vermeer, because her childhood was so frequently disturbed by discord between her parents that many of its details are preserved in the testimonies made during consequent litigation. She was a young woman with many advantages, but she also had a distinctly troubled past.

On her mother's side Catharina was from one of Gouda's oldest and most distinguished Catholic families. Maria Thins was descended

CHILDHOOD, EDUCATION, MARRIAGE, 1632–57

from the wealthy Van Hensbeeck dynasty, who had a long tradition of public service in the city. Maria's great-grandfather Dirck Cornelisz van Hensbeeck, who held office as burgomaster of Gouda, commissioned one of the many stained-glass windows that still draw visitors to the city's Church of St John. He also gave a generous endowment to the Holy Ghost Hospice, amounting to 3,000 guilders, the annual interest payments on which were distributed to the poor. The Van Hensbeecks were inclined to such charitable acts. Six members of the family gave money to such hospices, or helped to found beguinages, lay convents to which pious Catholic women could retreat and devote themselves to prayer without actually taking vows.[41]

In 1572 Gouda had been one of the first Dutch towns to rise up against Spain in support of William of Orange, and was therefore one of the first to feel the effects of '*De Alterie*', The Alteration, whereby Catholics were forbidden to worship in public and barred from public office. The beguinages founded by the Van Hensbeecks were shut down and no more members of the family were allowed to serve as burgomaster. But still they kept to their faith, as did many others like them in Gouda. The town had a large and active Catholic community and the Jesuit missionaries had a strong presence there. Maria's family was no longer as prominent as it had once been, but remained quietly influential. She grew up in her ancestral home in Gouda, a grand house named *De Trapjes* (The Stairs), which contained a hidden chapel in which Catholic services were held. In 1619, at the height of the Calvinist crackdown, a zealous local policeman reported that he had disturbed a congregation assembled there to celebrate Mass, although no further action was taken.[42]

Vermeer's future mother-in-law, Maria Thins, was born in 1592. She had two brothers, one of whom died in childhood, and two sisters. Her younger sister Elizabeth decided to become a nun as soon as she reached adulthood, taking her vows at the Convent of the Annunciates in Louvain, in the province of Brabant, in the Spanish Netherlands, at the age of just nineteen: further evidence of the family's continued commitment to the old faith. When Elizabeth died in 1640 she was remembered in the convent records as 'a veritable paragon of sisterly love'. None of Maria's siblings would marry, which explains how she came to acquire so many assets during the course of her long life. The inheritance laws of the time meant that any property inherited by her unwed brothers or sisters would eventually devolve on her, so the more of them she outlived, the richer she became. In time she outlived them all.

The limited evidence available suggests that Maria's upbringing was clouded by loss and separation.[43] Her father, Willem Jansz Thins, died in 1601, when she was eight years old. Her mother, Catharina van Hensbeeck, remarried four years later to a man named Gerrit Gerritsz Camerling. He was a prominent Catholic from Delft, where the family lived for some years. But in 1613 he left for the far side of the world, in the service of the Dutch East India Company. How frequently he returned home (if he ever did) is not known. He was away for much of the rest of his life. He was reported drowned off the coast of Ceylon in 1627.

Maria Thins moved back to Gouda not long after her stepfather's departure for the Indies, when she was in her early twenties. She remained there as a spinster until 1622, when she was nearly thirty: too old, as many thought in those days, to marry. But marry she did. At twenty-nine years of age Maria wed Reynier Bolnes, who must have seemed quite a catch to a young lady in imminent danger of becoming an old maid. He was the son of one of the wealthier citizens of Gouda, a brickmaker named Cornelis Bolnes, who contributed the considerable sum of 4,000 guilders to the marital assets of the newly-wed couple. At the time of the marriage Reynier had become his father's partner in the family business, which he would in due course inherit. He was a man with bright prospects, or so it seemed.

Immediately after their wedding, Maria and Reynier set up home in a house near the harbour called *De Engel* (The Angel). Here Maria's prayers for a family were answered. She and Reynier had a son, Willem, and a daughter, Cornelia. Then in 1631, a full nine years after the consummation of the marriage, when Maria was thirty-eight years old, the couple had a second daughter. They called her Catharina, after her maternal grandmother. The future wife of Vermeer was a late arrival to her parents, as he would be to his own.

Over the next few years Reynier Bolnes became implacably hostile to his wife and two young daughters, showing a measure of goodwill only to his son, young Willem. Why he behaved in the way that he did cannot easily be explained. But his conduct was so extreme, so puzzling and so needlessly destructive as to make it seem likely he was suffering from some form of mental illness. Whatever the cause, it scarred Catharina's childhood.

The first reports of his erratic and violent behaviour can be dated to 1635, when his younger daughter was just three years old. On St Jacob's Day of that year, Maria Thins's sister Cornelia visited her at home at The Angel, only to find her in floods of tears, complaining that her husband had hit her so hard with a tin pot that she could hardly walk. When Cornelia complained to Reynier about his behaviour, wishing that he would keep 'a better house with his wife', his answer was 'You black whore, what is it to you?' She had disturbed him at his lunch, and he had a knife in his hand. He got up, still clutching the knife, and grabbed Cornelia by the sleeve, which tore to the elbow as she ran through the door and out of the house to escape. Two days later Cornelia plucked up the courage to pay her sister another visit. She found Maria ill in bed with Reynier standing over her, irate. 'You must get out of bed, you swine!' he yelled at his wife, before grabbing her by the hair and dragging her naked from under the covers, leaving her sobbing on the cold floor.[44]

A little later that same year, 1635, the couple's housemaid heard screaming and shouting upstairs in the house at around midnight. When she went to investigate she found Reynier beating Maria with a stick, 'even though she was pregnant to the last degree'. The housemaid remonstrated with him and asked him why on earth he was beating his wife like that. He explained that it was because she would not lie still and kept complaining about the hens he kept above the bedstead, saying that they kept her awake. When the maid replied that that was no reason to beat a pregnant woman, he flew into a rage and hurled a pair of bellows and an earthenware pot at her. She ducked, the bellows split in half and the pot smashed against the wall. Maria, who was forty-two years old at the time of the reported assault, must have lost the baby she was carrying at the time: there is no subsequent record of the child's birth or baptism. This was probably her last pregnancy. She would have no more children after Catharina.

All of the above witness statements, about Reynier Bolnes's behaviour in 1635, were actually made four years later at Maria Thins's own request, in the offices of her family notary, N. Straffintveldt, in Gouda. Sometime in the second half of 1639 Maria had evidently concluded that her situation was so intolerable that she had better start collecting depositions from anyone she could persuade to testify about the way her husband was treating her. As time passed, his behaviour worsened.

In May 1639 the Bolnes family left The Angel and moved to a house in an area of Gouda mostly inhabited by craftspeople working in branches of the textile trade: tapestry makers, weavers, tailors. It was not uncommon for rich and poor to live next door to one another in the towns of the seventeenth-century Dutch Republic, partly because in this particular corner of Europe, unusually, the rich trusted that the poor would not burgle them. Law and order was so strongly enforced by the civic authorities that urban crime of any kind was rare. The French traveller Jean de Parival noted in 1669 that a person could go more or less anywhere in the towns of the Dutch Republic without fear of being robbed, while a few decades later a Swiss, Albrecht Haller, was surprised to find that the people of Leiden went about their business entirely unarmed, often leaving their houses unlocked while they were out.[45] The civic militia, a strong presence in every Dutch town, was one deterrent to crime. A yet more effective instrument of social control was the comprehensive network of neighbourhood watches organized and run by the townspeople themselves. Little escaped their attention. Anything unusual or irregular would soon be noted and, most likely, reported. This was true day and night: after dark, patrols staffed by members of the local watch would walk the streets, lighting their way with torches and keeping an eye out for trouble.

In such a strictly policed and law-abiding world, anyone regularly causing a disturbance soon made a name for themselves. Reynier Bolnes quickly acquired a reputation for rowdiness (and worse) with his new neighbours. The arrival of the family was followed by a deluge of complaints, witness statements and depositions about his increasingly unsettled behaviour. Almost as soon as they had moved in, a next-door neighbour lamented that Reynier was forever shouting and screaming and banging on the wall. Sometimes this went on all night long, she added, and it happened so often that her family took to greeting each new outburst with the same refrain: 'Hark, Reynier is rumbling again.' Other neighbours reported seeing him hopping about, singing nonsense songs to no one in particular and laughing to himself out loud.

In the autumn of 1639, Maria's brother Jan Willemsz Thins stayed with her and Reynier for several weeks and saw the marriage take another turn for the worse. He overheard a trivial argument between Maria and Reynier – she had a cough, exacerbated by a sputtering candle which he refused to extinguish – as a result of which Reynier moved permanently out of the marital bedroom and went to sleep upstairs with his son, Willem. Henceforth Reynier also refused to eat in Maria's company, insisting that she take her meals in the back room.

To judge by a number of other reports, incidents of domestic violence in the Bolnes household were becoming more frequent and more serious. In October 1639 Maria sought refuge at her sister Cornelia's house, complaining that Reynier had beaten her severely. Following another such beating, in January of the following year, she went to the house of neighbours to recover. After several hours they tried to settle her back at home but Reynier had bolted the door with a piece of wood. The neighbours shouted and knocked until he had to let Maria in, but the next morning she was in distress once more, crying out for help and claiming that 'my husband wants to murder us'. She showed one of her arms to anyone who cared to look: it was black and blue. Some carpenters working on the house next door warned Bolnes that the sherriff (the head of the town's police force) would come to arrest him if he did not mend his ways.

In 1640 Maria applied to the burgomasters of the town for a legal separation, but they refused after Reynier contested her allegations of abuse. So she was compelled to go through the motions of giving the marriage another chance. But by the spring of 1641 it was clear that matters were getting worse, not better. Reynier became ever more violent and controlling. He took to hiding his money in the 'garden house' of the family home, to which he kept the only key. Having stashed away the household cash, he then went to all the shops in Gouda and stopped his wife's credit. When Maria begged Reynier at least to settle the bills for food she had already purchased, he pummelled and kicked her and chased her out of the house with a set of fire tongs. She ran away once again. This time, she did not return.

We have one glimpse of Catharina at this difficult moment in her young life, aged nine, abruptly deprived of her mother and left in the sole care of an impulsive and mercurial father. The day after Maria Thins had left the household for good, at around half-past six in the morning, Reynier took his younger daughter to the door of one of their neighbours, the widow of a tailor. He asked her to look after Catharina, explaining that his wife had suddenly left. He instructed her not to let the child out of her sight until he returned. On his return he took Catharina straight home and confined her to the same outbuilding where he had locked up the household cash. So she spent her first night without her mother, not in the family home, but alone in the cold and dark of a garden shed. She may have passed many more nights in the same way over the months to come. The neighbour whose testimony is the source for this story was struck above all by Catharina's appearance. She was shocked that the daughter of such wealthy parents could look so bedraggled and poor, 'as if she had been a beggar's child'. The implication was that Catharina looked like a street urchin, being dressed in little better than rags – enough to shock anyone, but especially a tailor's widow.

Some six months after leaving her husband, Maria prevailed on the aldermen of Gouda to grant her the legal separation she had previously been denied. In November 1641 she was given custody of Cornelia and Catharina. Willem was to remain living with his father. Within a year Maria had moved with her two daughters to Delft, where she received 24 guilders a week in alimony from Reynier. She still travelled regularly to Gouda during the years following the separation – from Delft it was a journey of four hours by *trekschuit*, with a change of barge at Rotterdam – in order to retrieve her maintenance payments from her sister, who collected them on her behalf. In early 1643 Maria and Catharina made the same trip together, this time to perform the sad duty of burying Cornelia, who had died suddenly of some unknown illness while still only in her late teens. Maria arranged for the coffin to be shipped to Gouda, so that it might be interred in the family grave there. Reynier refused to attend the funeral. Willem followed his father's lead. Riven by death and discord, the Bolnes family was no longer a family.

By 1646 Reynier was having trouble paying Maria's alimony. His brickmaking business was said to be in trouble and he was heavily in

CHILDHOOD, EDUCATION, MARRIAGE, 1632–57

debt to creditors. Nonetheless in 1648 Maria successfully petitioned for her share of the marital assets at the time of the separation, which amounted to the substantial sum of 15,606 guilders. Willem Bolnes, Maria's son, had hardly spoken to her for a decade, but he accosted her in the street after the court hearing that decided the settlement and – in the words of an embarrassed eyewitness – 'with great irreverence he turned his arse towards her (excuse the expression), saying, "That's what you get for it", referring to the sentence of the Court of Holland against Reynier Bolnes'.

She was in fact paid out. But had Maria gone to court much later she would have ended up with nothing. Within a few years Reynier Bolnes fell into insolvency, declaring before the aldermen of Gouda in March 1653 that he could not pay overdue property taxes because he had 'no worldly possessions and now lived at the expense of his brother and sister, as their worships were well aware'. Barely a month after he had reached this low point, his only surviving daughter married a painter from Delft. True to form, Reynier did not attend the ceremony.

Maria Thins, safely divorced from the now penniless brickmaker, must have counted herself lucky to escape him and luckier still to have kept her fortune. Small wonder that she had her doubts about Johannes Vermeer as a suitable husband for Catharina, and not just because he was no Catholic. Vermeer's father had died just six months before the wedding, with so little money that his family had nothing to give to the Charity Chamber.[46] In light of her own experiences of matrimony, Maria Thins would probably have been suspicious of any young man asking for her daughter's hand in marriage, especially a young man with no money to his name.

For her part Catharina Bolnes was plainly set on marrying Johannes Vermeer, solvent or not. She seems to have done everything that she could to ensure that she got her way, tricking her mother with the betrothal and even, it seems, moving out of her family home. She can only have had one motive for behaving in the way that she did: love. Taking into account his apparent unsuitability on the grounds of money, religion and class, Catharina Bolnes must have loved Johannes Vermeer very much. Knowing what we do about her turbulent past, that opens some windows into his character as well as hers.

Catharina's childhood from the age of three onwards was more than merely unhappy. It was a succession of traumas, beginning with the abusive behaviour of her father and culminating in the death of her only sister at an early age. Some people who have lived through a damaging or chaotic upbringing are compulsively drawn to unstable or violent partners in adult life – seeking out the familiarity of problems they have always known – but it is clear that Catharina did not suffer from that syndrome. Although the archives of Delft reveal occasional disturbances in the home she and her husband shared with their exceptionally large brood of children, these were caused by Catharina's disturbed brother, Willem, erupting into the household, and never by Johannes. As far as we can tell, he was never involved in any kind of violent incident. He certainly did not share the misogynist attitudes of the father-in-law whom he probably never met. Vermeer would spend much of his life painting pictures of women that radiate empathy and tenderness.

Catharina must have wanted her own marriage to be everything that her mother's marriage to Reynier Bolnes had not been. She must have wanted a husband who would be everything her father had not been during the years of her childhood: reliable, kind, gentle and loving; someone who made her feel safe. It seems that in Johannes Vermeer she found such a man. Conversely, we can believe that his compassion for the pain that she had suffered, and a desire to help heal it, would have been an important part of the love he felt for her. A small group of pictures that he painted at around the time of his marriage, and in the couple of years following, reveals much about the young artist's temperament and sensibility, and may also shed light on the nature of his own feelings for Catharina as they began their life together.

IN THE COMPANY OF WOMEN

All Vermeer's early paintings tell stories from myth, or the Bible, or the lives of the saints. From the outset he thought of himself as a history painter and therefore an artist to be reckoned with. In the seventeenth-century hierarchy of the genres, history painting stood at the top. This was a legacy of Italian art theory according to which every Old Master from Giotto to Michelangelo had been a painter of history – *istoria* in

Italian, meaning not history in the usual sense but a noble story. The kind of painting that told such stories was the pinnacle of art because it was the work of the mind, not merely the hand and eye.

Vermeer's earliest known picture was inspired by a story told in *Metamorphoses* by the Roman poet Ovid. *Diana and Her Companions* is undated but was probably painted in around 1653, the year of the artist's marriage. It shows the Roman goddess Diana and her nymphs resting in a woodland glade. They are accompanied by a patient dog that sits on a patch of ground close to where a single thistle grows. Many of the picture's effects might have seemed foreign in mid-seventeenth-century Delft. Its composition is frieze-like, with the figures squeezed into shallow space as they might be in a bas-relief on a Roman sarcophagus. Light descends from the top left at a raking angle, sharply illuminating certain details while shrouding others in darkness, in a version of Caravaggio's chiaroscuro. Some figures are sharply defined, like sculptures picked out by spotlight, but overall the modelling is broad and soft.

The palette of the picture is a rich mix of red, blue, orange, russet and gold, more Italian than Dutch. It brings to mind the colour schemes of the Florentine master Andrea del Sarto and his followers. *Diana and Her Companions* may seem far removed from Vermeer's later paintings of people in interiors, but there are affinities between them. The mood of the picture is hushed and its action, if it can be described as such, stilled.

Diana was one of the twelve gods and goddesses of Mount Olympus, a slim and athletic huntress who was venerated by the Greeks and Romans as the personification of chastity. She was also the goddess of the moon, hence the crescent that appears over her brow. Her nymphs were required to be as chaste as Diana herself. But one of them, Callisto, was seduced and impregnated by Jupiter without Diana's knowledge, her pregnant state only being discovered when she refused to disrobe and bathe in a stream alongside the others.

This is the part of Ovid's poem that Vermeer has translated into paint. He shows the moment just after Diana, weary from hunting, calls her companions to rest from their exertions, and just before she discovers Callisto's pregnancy. Seated on a ledge of stone, the goddess is the central figure in the composition, although not necessarily its main focus. At her back perches a nymph in half undress, facing away from the viewer. Another is seated to Diana's left while a third, head bowed and kneeling, is washing the goddess's feet. Slightly behind these figures and standing in deep shadow, we can just make out Callisto. Her eyes are downcast, her hands clasped furtively over her pregnant belly.

Vermeer's treatment of an Ovidian theme is unusually restrained and modest. None of the women are naked or anything close to it: the only hint of disrobing is a fall of orange drapery revealing just a shoulder blade and an expanse of back. There is little sense of drama, no strong suggestion of imminent catastrophe. Lurking in shadow, the unchaste Callisto seems present mainly as a foil to Diana, who seems not even to notice her.

The picture is less narrative than allegory. It was meant perhaps to celebrate an ideal of female purity, embodied by the virginal Diana and her faithful companions and linked by association to two elements so prominently placed – the dog and the thistle – that they must be read as emblems. Dogs personify fidelity, especially dogs that wait as obediently as this dappled terrier. Thistles call to mind the narrow and thorny path of Virtue chosen by Hercules at the crossroads, in preference to the easier path of Vice.

Diana and Her Companions demonstrates that the young Vermeer was a sophisticated and well-read painter who had clearly spent much time looking at art, especially Italian art. It also shows that he was blessed with a natural originality, which most likely stemmed from the integrity of his purposes. Instead of dramatizing the tale of Diana and Callisto, he took it as the pretext for creating a vision of idealized womanhood in which certain attributes were carefully symbolized, then a little clumsily yoked together. Symptomatic of his approach is the fact that Vermeer also distilled Ovid's narrative to the depiction of a ritual nowhere described in it: the washing of feet.

The act is performed with solemnity by the nymph who, kneeling before Diana, gently rubs the goddess's left foot with what appears to be a disc of grey pumice stone. This washing of feet, which is the picture's true focal point, easily draws the mind away from classical antiquity and into a different world of feeling. Christ had washed the feet of his disciples shortly before his death. His devotees, including Mary Magdalene, had washed his feet both when he was alive and after his Crucifixion. Vermeer has included two details that strongly evoke all this: a bright brass basin and a white linen cloth of exactly the kind that appear in countless Flemish altarpieces of the Crucifixion, Lamentation and Descent from the Cross. It might be a trick of the light, but the furled white cloth seems to resemble a dove.

So Diana's kneeling attendant is not only a virgin in the service of the goddess of chastity, but may also be identified with Mary Magdalene, handmaiden of Christ. She has reddish hair like the Magdalene. Her clothes are the colours of earth, rich browns that evoke the Magdalene's robes of penitence. Although the nymph's head is bowed and her role an apparently subsidiary one, the picture seems to be more about her than Diana and Callisto. Everything in it seems quietly to revolve around her, to indicate that in her person are embodied not only the chastity and rigour prized in antiquity, but also the most tender form of Christian humility.

What kind of mythological painting would mould its narrative to the praise of a single woman, and why? The answer to the riddle posed by this mostly Italian-seeming picture may lie within Italian traditions of art. Narrative paintings based on classical legend were an innovation of the early Florentine Renaissance, having their origins in a specific type of marriage gift: a wedding chest, or *cassone*, given to a bride and traditionally decorated with paintings telling carefully chosen stories from myth in which women came out on top, like the tale of Venus conquering Mars. By the late fifteenth century such paintings had been liberated from the sides of linen chests to become large-scale independent works of art, although they were still wedding gifts and turned to the praise of a bride-to-be. The most famous example is Botticelli's *Birth of Venus*, which welcomed a Medici bride into the fold of her new family by personifying her as the goddess of love.

Vermeer's *Diana and Her Companions* seems to be a late and understated addition to this venerable tradition, paying compliment to a bride by emphasizing her qualities of modesty and reserve. Her virtues are not trumpeted, but insisted upon with a kind of forceful reticence. The heroine of Vermeer's story does not stand before us like Botticelli's Venus, but kneels. She is not naked, but soberly dressed in a jacket of muted brown silks, a version of contemporary costume. Her face, shown in profile, is not idealized but has the actuality of a portrait. This suggests that we might be looking at an image of the bride herself, not just a figure symbolizing her.

Who might she have been? Presumably a lady who got married in about 1653, the year of Vermeer's own marriage to Catharina Bolnes. It is tempting to think she might actually be Catharina, in which case the picture would have been Vermeer's first gift to his own bride, and his first portrait of her too. But the possibility is remote. The emphasis on the washing of feet suggests that the woman shown kneeling in the painting felt a devotion to Mary Magdalene. In the case of Catharina Bolnes there is no trace of that in the place where it might have shown up most clearly, the names of her children. Johannes Vermeer and Catharina had no fewer than eleven offspring, the first five of whom were girls, yet none were christened Magdalena. Vermeer's patron Maria de Knuijt was another woman in his immediate circle who married in 1653. She *did* have a daughter named Magdalena, but the kneeling woman cannot be her either because the picture in which she appears was never owned by Maria and her husband. She must have been someone else, or just a pure invention.

Diana and Her Companions is a mythological painting with Christian overtones. Most of Vermeer's other early works are straightforwardly religious pictures. *Christ in the House of Martha and Mary*, which he painted around 1654, is set in what could be the plainly furnished front hall of a small Dutch house somewhere in the country. Mary sits at Christ's feet while Martha stoops to offer him a loaf of bread in a wicker basket. Christ wears a reddish-brown smock and a robe of blue, while Martha and Mary are in modern dress, wearing heavy linen shirts and skirts as if against the cold of a room warmed only by a peat-burning stove.

The figure of Christ, with his shoulder-length hair and straggly beard, was lifted direct from a painting by one of Caravaggio's many Neapolitan followers, *The Death of St Joseph* by Andrea Vaccaro, which is now in the Capodimonte Museum in Naples. The figures are nearly identical in physiognomy and pose, down to the exact position of their hands, the one difference being that Vaccaro's Christ is standing and Vermeer's seated. He addresses the stooping Martha in the manner of a mild and forbearing schoolmaster correcting a pupil who has made an innocent mistake. She has not been paying attention to him, but there is no serious displeasure in his expression. As he explains to her what she has missed by bustling about in the kitchen, he points to her sister Mary, who by contrast has hung on his every word.

Martha is often made out to be a bit of a sulk in other artists' depictions of the subject, notably the version by Diego Velázquez of 1618 in the National Gallery in London, where she scowls at the viewer as she pounds away with mortar and pestle. But Vermeer shows her with lowered eyes and a solemn expression that suggests she has already taken the proffered lesson to heart. She gives the impression of being about to come round to join her sister at Christ's feet. It is not too difficult to imagine the two women in the picture as one and the same person shown in different modes, active and contemplative.

Theological interpretations of the story, which is told in the Gospel of Luke, turned on just such a distinction. According to the venerable St Augustine, Martha's work in preparing a meal for the Lord established her as the archetype of the *vita activa*, or active life, whereas Mary's desire to sit at Christ's feet made her the archetype of the *vita contemplativa*, or spiritual life. According to Augustine, they were not to be contrasted as bad and good but, rather, as better and best. Mary and Martha were also interpreted as complementary embodiments of faith and good works, showing every Christian the twofold way to salvation: belief in God coupled with a life lived practically by Christ's own example.

The relative importance of faith and works was an issue bitterly disputed by Reformed Calvinists and their opponents, who in this instance included not only Arminians but Catholics. Calvinists believed faith alone to be necessary for salvation. Those who stood up to them passionately disagreed, regarding charitable acts as a vital part of every Christian life. *Christ in the House of Martha and Mary* can only have been painted for someone who disagreed emphatically with the Calvinist position. Martha is given similar weight to her sister Mary. She is the meek and humble bearer of a gift, a loaf of bread, which immediately identifies her with the first of the seven Christian Acts of Mercy, feeding the hungry.

Intimate and reflective, *Christ in the House of Martha and Mary* has the feel of a picture painted for people used to reading the Bible and imagining themselves into its stories. It brings us so close to the three figures that we might almost be in the same room as them. It is difficult to escape the impression that the picture is turned more towards a female than a male gaze. After all, its subject is the spiritual education of two sisters. It is large and may once have served as an altarpiece in a private chapel in someone's home. Such spaces existed in Delft, as we shall see.

For whom were Vermeer's early pictures painted? The names of his patrons are not known, but the evidence of the paintings prompts three suppositions. First, they were probably women. Secondly, they may have been Remonstrants, or perhaps liberal Catholics, people at any rate who took a tolerant approach to matters of faith and were relaxed in their attitude to religious images. Thirdly, they were apostolic Christians, people who tried to model their own lives on those of Christ and his apostles, who included in their minds his earliest female followers, Mary Magdalene in particular.[47]

Perhaps the owners of these pictures knew each other. The world in which they lived was certainly small enough for that to have been so. Perhaps they participated in one of the new Collegiant cells that were springing up in private houses in Delft and Rotterdam during the early 1650s, when the numbers of Christians without a church sharply accelerated.

A lost early painting by Vermeer lends weight to such hypotheses purely by virtue of its subject matter. The estate of a prominent art dealer and collector from Amsterdam named Johannes Renialme, who died in 1657, included a picture listed as *The Visit to the Tomb* by 'Van der Meer'.[48] Renialme had first registered as a dealer in Delft's Guild of St Luke in 1644 and was in regular contact with Notary Willem de Langue, who as we know was an old family friend of the Vermeers. So the painting identified in Renialme's death inventory was probably another of the painter's early works. Its subject would have been the visit of the three holy women named Mary to the tomb of Christ, often referred to as *The Holy Women at the Sepulchre*.

Assuming that Vermeer had followed iconographic convention, the lost picture would have shown a pair of angels conversing with the three Marys in the empty sepulchre, as described in the Gospel of Luke. Judged by its theme alone this missing early work appears to have been strikingly congruent with those that have survived.

It suggests that right from the start Vermeer was painting pictures of a deeply pious nature, showing women in search of salvation. Such were the stories he wanted, and was encouraged, to tell.

THUNDERCLAP

On the morning of 12 October 1654 a young clerk named Cornelis Soetens, recently appointed as keeper of the States-General powder magazine in Delft, went to the former Clarissen convent in the Doelenkwartier, beneath which was an arsenal packed with some 90,000 pounds of black gunpowder. His instructions were to remove a two-pound sample as part of a routine inspection. It was a simple task but he had never done it before. Carrying a lantern and accompanied by a fellow clerk from The Hague, he entered the store from the Clares' old convent garden and descended the stairwell leading to the munitions. Neither man would be seen again.

Did sparks fly as a key caught on an ungreased lock? Did Soetens drop his lantern? Whatever the cause, half an hour after the two men had disappeared down the stairs, the magazine exploded with devastating effect. Five successive blasts rocked the north-eastern quarter of Delft, destroying roughly a third of the city. Close to the powder store entire streets were vapourized, while further away the houses were blown to smithereens, the rubble from their walls and the tiles from their roofs scattered far and wide. Heads, arms, legs and other body parts were scattered like bits and pieces of broken dolls. Acrid smoke hung in the air. A foul mist descended, covering the ruins with a layer of slick condensation, the result of water from the town's canals having been blown skywards. The effects of the blast were felt for miles around. Windows shattered in The Hague. It was said that the sound of the explosion was heard on the island of Texel in the North Sea, sixty miles away.

By providence only a hundred people died, although more than a thousand were injured. The death toll would have been far higher had it not been for the autumn pig market in Schiedam and a fair in the nearby village of Voorburg, which meant many people were away from Delft on that particular morning. The Reformed predicant Petrus de Witte was convinced that the devastation was a sign of God's displeasure.

He delivered a penitential sermon subsequently published under the title *Delft Thunderclap, or a short address to the mourning people of Delft, Visited by a Terrible Judgement of God*,[49] in which he blamed his own congregation for the disaster that had befallen them. The Peace of Münster and the end of the Eighty Years War had made them weak and degenerate. They had shown too much tolerance to the Remonstrants, followers of Arminius, as well as to the Mennonites and the Catholics. Such people were heretics. Until they were treated as such the city would continue to suffer the wrath of the Almighty.

Liberal Dutch dissenters agreed that the disaster was a message from God, but to them it was a reminder to keep pushing for peace. Delft had been devastated by the explosion of an arsenal originally created to defend the Republic against Spain. That arsenal was still full of gunpowder because during the 1650s the Dutch had become embroiled in another series of conflicts, this time with their trading rivals across the North Sea, which are now remembered as the Anglo-Dutch Wars. The Thunderclap was God's way of saying that enough was enough. The wars must stop.

The explosion was regarded by many of those who survived it as a terrible aftershock. It was as if all the violence of the Eighty and Thirty Years Wars had suddenly been revisited on a single unsuspecting city. The Mechelen Inn, where Vermeer's mother was still living in October 1654, was buffeted by the explosion, despite being nowhere near the gunpowder store. Digna's name appears on the register of people given compensation by the States of Holland for damage to their houses. Repairs to the tavern cost 150 guilders.[50]

Vermeer's family was affected by the blast and so were many other people he knew, artists among them. One such was the painter Egbert van der Poel, who was related to Vermeer by marriage and whose daughter was killed in the explosion.[51] Van der Poel would subsequently paint numerous views of Delft devastated by the blast, seen from the meadows beyond the town: a city reduced to a pile of smoking ruins. People looking at such images would inevitably think of Magdeburg and the other German towns turned to rubble by the Thirty Years War, before realizing with a shock that what they were actually looking at was a Dutch town here and now. Van der Poel's disaster pictures became well known and a number of them survive. A typically bleak example is in the National Gallery in London. Vermeer doubtless had such pictures somewhere in mind when he painted his own, contrastingly radiant *View of Delft* some eleven or twelve years later.

Egbert van der Poel lost a child to the Thunderclap. Carel Fabritius, another painter with close links to Vermeer, lost his life.[52] When the powder magazine exploded he was painting a portrait of Simon Decker, sexton of Delft's Oude Kerk, or Old Church, while his apprentice Matthias Spoor was grinding colours. Fabritius had his workshop in the Doelen, close to the blast, so none of the three stood a chance.

A former pupil of Rembrandt, Fabritius was one of the most talented painters of his generation. He had moved to Delft in 1652 at the age of twenty-nine. He registered in the Guild of St Luke in October of that same year, fourteen months before Vermeer did the same. His few surviving works include a masterly representation of a goldfinch perched on a bird feeder against a dun-coloured wall, a picture modest in scale but beguiling in its trompe l'oeil effects. The gradations of light and shade between the bird, its perch and the rough plaster wall are rendered with such granular precision as to abolish all sense of the linear definition of forms. There was no true precedent for such a way of painting, although the ideas that lay behind it had been formulated in Italy during the Renaissance.

The supple version of chiaroscuro developed by Fabritius reflects the thought of Leonardo da Vinci, whose optical theories had only just been rediscovered. Leonardo's *Treatise on Painting*, preserved in the Codex Urbinas and first published in Paris in 1651, with illustrations by Nicolas Poussin, contains an exact scientific explanation of the optical effects conjured up in *The Goldfinch*: 'The boundary of one thing with another is of the nature of a mathematical line, because the end of one colour is the beginning of another colour and is not to be called a line ... nothing intervenes between one colour placed in front of another except its end, which is imperceptible even when viewed from near at hand ... the boundary is a thing invisible ...'[53]

There is no such thing as a line: the truth of Leonardo's observation was brought home to Fabritius by the experience of viewing the world projected onto a screen or table in a camera obscura, where the boundaries between one object and another do indeed appear in infinite degrees of gradation. The presence of such devices, originally developed by Dutch military engineers for purposes of reconnaissance, is recorded in Delft in the 1650s.[54] Fabritius, who was interested in optics, was certainly familiar with the images produced by a camera obscura. So was Samuel van Hoogstraten, his friend and fellow apprentice to Rembrandt, who enthused about them in his own treatise on painting.

Vermeer presumably got to know Fabritius between late 1652 and the autumn of 1654. The inventory of Vermeer's own possessions made after his death shows that he owned no fewer than three paintings by his hand: two small *tronie*, which hung in the great hall of the house he shared with his wife, Catharina, and her mother, and another unspecified work in the front hall. He also owned two pictures by Van Hoogstraten, which under the circumstances is unlikely to be a coincidence. There is no proof that Vermeer was formally taught by Fabritius, but he likely knew him. He probably obtained his three pictures direct from the artist himself, along with new ideas.

The formal influence of Fabritius on Vermeer cannot be overstated, so closely does the mature technique of the latter mirror that of the former. It can only have been by studying the paintings of Fabritius that Vermeer eventually arrived at his own approach, which has been eloquently described by Lawrence Gowing:

> ... an almost solitary indifference to the whole linear convention and its historic function of describing ... However firm the contour in these pictures, line as a vessel of understanding has been abandoned and with it the traditional apparatus of draughtsmanship. In its place, apparently effortlessly, automatically, tone bears the whole weight of formal explanation.

That qualifying 'almost' is important, because not only had Fabritius reached identical conclusions about line and tone, he had done so several years before Vermeer. It would not be until around 1657, in pictures such as *Girl Reading a Letter at an Open Window*, that Vermeer would adopt purely tonal painting.

In his *Description of Delft* of 1667, a burgomaster of the town named Dirck van Bleiswijk wrote a short life of Fabritius to which he appended an elegy by Arnold Bon that ends with an explicit comparison between the two artists, one dead, the other still living:

> Thus died this Phoenix, when he was thirty years old,
> In the midst and at the height of his powers,
> But happily arose out of his fire
> Vermeer, who masterfully trod his path.[55]

Vermeer was only twenty-two years old when Fabritius died and had been registered as a professional painter for less than a year. If the older man was indeed his friend and mentor, Vermeer must have felt his loss keenly. The violence and the shock of it were evoked in the opening lines of Arnold Bon's elegy, vivid in the memory more than a decade after the event:

> Thus crushed, bruised and broken,
> Arms and legs unrecognizable,
> Lay Carel Faber, almost suffocated by the ash
> Of the fatal gunpowder; who knows how it was ignited.

BURYING THE DEAD

Vermeer painted another of his early religious pictures in the aftermath of the Thunderclap, and possibly in response to it. The picture in question is a glowing depiction of a grisly subject. It shows *St Praxedis*, pious daughter of a second-century disciple of St Paul, mopping up the blood of early Christian martyrs in Rome.

The painting is a faithful copy of a picture by one of the minor masters of the Florentine seicento, a distant follower of Andrea del Sarto named Felice Ficherelli (1605–1660). It was long considered to be an autograph painting by Ficherelli himself, and only rediscovered as a Vermeer by a stroke of luck. Sent on loan from a private collection to a display of Florentine Baroque painting held at the Metropolitan Museum of Art in New York in 1969, the picture was under examination by the authors of the catalogue to that exhibition when it yielded up its secret: the faint signature of Johannes Vermeer in the bottom left corner of the picture, corresponding to his signature as it appears in other early works, together with the date 1655. Further examination disclosed the presence of another inscription in the opposite corner, 'Meer N/R/o/o', which has been interpreted as indicating a copy by Vermeer after (*nach*) Riposo, the latter being Ficherelli's nickname.

Michael Kitson, who broke the news of the discovery in an article in the *Burlington Magazine*, declared it to be 'one of the oddest surprises ever to be thrown up by a scholarly exhibition'.[56] Those who doubt the attribution to Vermeer argue that the signature and inscription must be later additions to the canvas, but this is not plausible. The paint in which the signature is written appears to be integral to the original surface, and is certainly cracked and old. Besides, the circumstances in which anyone might have added Vermeer's name to a work that looks so unlikely to have been painted by him are hard to conceive. Science is on the side of a positive attribution: when particles of the lead white pigment used in *St Praxedis* were subjected to lead isotope ratio analysis and the results compared with those for the lead white pigment used in *Diana and Her Companions*, the outcome was a match of abundance values so precise as to indicate that the same batch of paint was used for both pictures.[57] *St Praxedis* was painted by Vermeer.

Comparison with the original work by Ficherelli (or an early variant of it), which is in Ferrara, shows that Vermeer's picture is indeed a copy after 'Riposo'. But it is a copy with some telling differences, notably the crucifix held by the saint, which is absent from Ficherelli's painting. Although Vermeer has remained faithful in essence to his source, matching its breadth of handling and vibrant colour contrasts – between for example the raspberry of the saint's draperies and the deep blue sky – he did not create his picture in the manner to be expected of a painter creating a literal copy. The paint has been built up carefully in many layers, as if by an artist creating the prime version of a painting. This technique strongly suggests that Vermeer was recreating Ficherelli's picture from memory (also surely his own notes and drawings) rather than working from it directly. This is most obvious in the case of the ewer, part of which has been painted over a fully elaborated section of the saint's red robes. Vermeer went to the unnecessary trouble of completing her costume before obliterating a part of it: a procedure that would make no sense if he were making a literal copy. The painting also has a freshness and immediacy that sets it apart from the usual journeywork of the copyist, especially in the intensity of the saint's expression, which is humble, urgent and compassionate.

The subject is drawn from the early history of the Church. According to her legend, St Praxedis was a virgin saint living in Rome at the time of Emperor Marcus Aurelius. She and her sister St Pudentiana followed their father, Pudens, a disciple of St Paul, in his devotion to the faith of Jesus Christ. Both risked their lives by caring for the bodies of fellow Christians murdered for their beliefs, St Praxedis collecting the blood of no fewer than twenty-three martyrs. The sponge with which she did so is still purportedly preserved in the Roman basilica dedicated to her.

In Vermeer's *St Praxedis*, as in Ficherelli's original, the main elements of her story are deftly compressed. To the left, just behind her, we see the grisly details of a martyr's severed head and decapitated body, blood still issuing from the neck. To the right, almost lost in the background, a female figure who may be the sister of Praxedis, Pudentiana, is walking beside a circular martyrium, a type of early Christian shrine erected over the burial place of martyrs. Front and centre St Praxedis squeezes out her sponge, from which a broken stream of viscous blood drips into the ewer below. A golden crucifix, carved with the body of Christ, is jammed into the bloody sponge between her hands, the cross silhouetted against the gauzy white material that trims her bodice. This prominent detail, which was Vermeer's own invention, is key to his picture's meaning. The inclusion of the crucifix insists, by way of its blatant symbolism, that the blood of every martyr is mingled with the blood of Christ: all who die for their belief in Christ will be united in Christ and made as one.

St Praxedis has much in common with Vermeer's other early works. Like the *Diana*, it represents an ideal of humble and virtuous womanhood. Like *Christ in the House of Martha and Mary*, it asserts that faith and good works alike are essential to the good Christian life: St Praxedis is performing one of the Seven Acts of Mercy, burying the dead. Implicit in Vermeer's painting, and emphasized by that detail of the crucifix, merging the blood of the martyrs with the blood of Christ, is the ancient belief that all Christians make up a single body, just as the different parts and members of the human body make up a single person. Complementary to that belief was the idea that the body in which all Christians are collectively united was to be understood as the body of Christ himself. St Praxedis was the daughter of a follower of

St Paul, so it is apt that such ideas should have been given their clearest expression in Paul's first Epistle to the Corinthians: 'For as the body is one, and hath many members, and all the members of that one body, being many, are one body: so also is Christ.' (1 Corinthians 12:12)

As we have seen, Corinthians was a text venerated by the Collegiants, as it was by the Remonstrants and all other Dutch followers of Jacobus Arminius. Paul's ideal of unity among Christians, and his hatred of schism, were passionately upheld in the freethinking, liberal circles of the Dutch Republic during the early 1650s; all the more so in Delft in the wake of the Thunderclap.

Painted in 1655, Vermeer's *St Praxedis* may have been commissioned by a woman or group of women who had suffered loss in the disaster of a year before, to help them pray for the souls of the departed. The decapitated Roman martyr behind the saint, whose body still gushes blood and whose head and torso are strewn on the ground, might have recalled to such women the dismembered victims of the powder explosion. But he may also represent the martyrs of the Thirty and Eighty Years Wars, Protestant and Catholic alike, in which case he is all of those dead together, remembered, cherished and buried. Vermeer's picture was there to be prayed to but it was also a prayer in itself. Let there be no more burying like this.

PRODIGAL SON

All three of Vermeer's earliest surviving pictures are marked by the influence of Italy. In the case of *Christ in the House of Martha and Mary* and *St Praxedis* the links to Italian sources are demonstrable and highly specific. The figure of Christ in the former is clearly derived from the Neapolitan painter Andrea Vaccaro's Christ in his *Death of St Joseph*, while the entire composition of the latter is copied from a work by the Florentine master Felice Ficherelli. It has been suggested that Vermeer could have seen those pictures or copies after them in Holland, perhaps in an auction house or with an art dealer in Amsterdam. One such dealer was Johannes Renialme, who held a large number of Italian pictures at his premises in Amsterdam and who as we know probably once owned a painting by Vermeer. They most likely knew each other, so the painter may well have been familiar with the dealer's stock.

Nonetheless it seems unlikely that Vermeer could have seen Ficherelli's *St Praxedis* or Vaccaro's *Death of St Joseph* either on Renialme's premises or anywhere else in the northern Netherlands. The majority of Italian pictures sold in the Dutch art market of the time were Old Masters. This was reflected in Renialme's stock, which listed works by Ribera, Tintoretto and Titian among others. The Italian pictures from which Vermeer borrowed were, by contrast, modern works of art by painters who had strong local reputations but were not internationally celebrated. Ficherelli painted his *St Praxedis* and Vaccaro his *Death of St Joseph* in the mid-to-late 1640s. For Vermeer to have seen them in his homeland, both pictures or variants of them would have had to have been imported to the Dutch Republic within less than a decade of having been painted. There is nothing to show that either work or a version of it has ever left the Italian peninsula. Vermeer's surprising familiarity with these pictures of Florentine and Neapolitan origin not only suggests that he travelled to Italy, it also gives us the probable outline of his itinerary. Going south from Florence to Naples he would surely have stopped in Rome, the city familiar to so many of the artists who frequented his father's inn. It would probably have been his main destination, the place where he absorbed the most.

In 1656 Vermeer painted a picture commonly known as *The Procuress*, which may allude in passing to his years away from home. Its subject, seemingly at odds with those of his other early works, is a seedy sexual transaction taking place in the backroom of some anonymous tavern. A blushing young woman in a yellow bodice and white headscarf grasps a wineglass in one hand while holding out the other to accept a coin proffered by a man in red behind her. She smiles complacently as she does so. The man's tip-tilted hat and woozy expression suggest that he is rather more inebriated than the young lady whose favour he means to purchase. He seems to be having trouble dropping his money into her open palm and stares down at his own unsteady right hand – which seems more inclined to flip the coin than give it over – like a drunk unable to see straight. His left hand fumbles at her breast. As if to mirror his drunken state, the Turkish carpet that serves as a table covering in so many Dutch pictures of this period is extravagantly rumpled.

At the man's shoulder we see the self-satisfied face of the procuress, darting a look at the courtesan. The look is not returned, nor need it be: it is clear that everything is going to plan. Dressed all in black, the procuress is an unholy sister celebrating a black Mass, one where the wine flows too freely, the wafer has been replaced by a coin, and souls are sold rather than saved. Next to her, completing the group of four figures, we see a sharply dressed young man in a beret. Although his face is deeply shadowed, we can see that he is looking directly out at us with a grin that fails to convince and looks more like a grimace of pretended bonhomie. In his right hand he holds the neck of a cittern, a stringed instrument similar to a lute, while with his left he holds up a glass, as if to toast the courtesan and her besotted admirer.

In pose, expression and even clothing, this figure is similar to that of a man seated at the left of a small group in a picture called *The Charlatan* by Frans van Mieris – a picture painted just a few years earlier which may have given Vermeer the idea of including an amused, worldly observer in his own tavern scene. Van Mieris was from Leiden,

Detail from *The Charlatan* by Frans van Mieris of circa 1653, showing the artist's self-portrait. Vermeer probably knew Van Mieris and may have had this picture in mind when including a similar self-portrait in his own painting of 1656, *The Procuress* (Plate 2)

which was just a short hop by public barge from Delft, with services on the hour, every hour. It is possible and even likely that the two painters knew each other. The man catching our eye in Van Mieris's picture is known to be a self-portrait, so maybe Vermeer's sheepishly smiling gentleman is another. The supposition is strengthened by his costume, a dandyish black jacket with slits revealing a white undershirt. The artist wears the same outfit in his one definite self-portrait, *The Art of Painting*, painted more than a decade later.

So perhaps *The Procuress* introduces us to the young Johannes Vermeer: a shifty fellow with a nervous smile, complicit witness to the transitory union of drunken sexual desire and cold money-lust. Why might he have painted the picture, and if he did include himself in it, was he reflecting on the less than perfect life he had sometimes lived while away from home? His costume encourages such speculation, being the garb of travelling Italian musicians. There was encouragement of a kind in Italian art for a painter to cast himself as a character, complicit or inactive, in a scene of wrongdoing: Caravaggio had included himself as a bystander signally failing to do the right thing in his *Martyrdom of St Matthew*, as if to confess to his own sense of unworthiness. Maybe Vermeer intended to make a confession of a similar kind by implicating himself in the sordid goings on at a down-at-heel tavern, and by shrouding his own face in such deep shadow. Perhaps the picture was a *mea culpa*: I have lived in darkness, I have sinned. If so, that would not have been the end of its meanings.

The Procuress might be classed as a 'merry company', to use the term favoured by auctioneers and art dealers of the time. But, knowing the strong appeal that religious themes had for Vermeer, it seems likely that he had in mind the parable of the Prodigal Son recounted in the Gospel of Luke. Crude and bawdy, *The Procuress* is at first sight unlike Vermeer's other, more apparently meditative early pictures. But there is a common thread. *Diana and Her Companions*, *Christ in the House of Martha and Mary* and *St Praxedis* all point the way to salvation, reflecting on the Christian virtues of humility, faith, charity and love. If *The Procuress* is properly understood as a painting of the Prodigal Son, then it does the same thing. It too points along a path to deliverance, albeit a bumpier one: that of the sinner who repents.

Vermeer's reasons for painting the picture are not known, but by casting himself in a leading role he may have given us a sideways glimpse of his own life. Perhaps, like the Prodigal Son, he had travelled, and at his father's expense. Perhaps he felt he had strayed, but returned, made peace with his father (just in time) and repented, taking solace in Christ's affirmation that 'joy shall be in heaven over one sinner that repenteth, more than over ninety and nine just persons, which need no repentance'. On the evidence of his early work Vermeer was a serious young man who spent much time reading and thinking about the Bible, so it would be in character for him to have thought about his own early life in terms of Christian parable.[58]

LOVE REVEALED

One last early picture remains to be looked at. It is one of the most moving and beautiful of Vermeer's paintings, and has been one of the most persistently misunderstood: the *Girl Reading a Letter at an Open Window*, in Dresden. Because it clearly foreshadows the pictures of Vermeer's maturity it should probably be dated after *The Procuress*, perhaps even to as late as 1657. It is more austere than the works that preceded it, or at least it appeared so until restoration brought back an element that had been painted out by an interfering hand. The picture's meaning had been implicit in its incomplete state, but it was confirmed beyond doubt by the missing detail, the return of which made it whole again. It is instructive to consider the work both pre- and post-restoration, because what results from the comparison is an allegory of Vermeer's afterlife as a whole: the story of a long-dead painter asserting his truths despite those who would mask or misrepresent him.

Photographs of the *Girl Reading a Letter* taken before it was restored show a young woman standing by the window of a high-ceilinged room before a blank plastered wall. She wears a jacket of yellow and black satin with piped and pleated sleeves. In her hands she holds a letter. She grips the paper more tightly than necessary. Her cheeks are flushed. A red curtain has been folded over the top edge of the leaded casement window, which opens inwards, her face reflected in its glass. Another curtain, which hangs from a pole at the front of the room, has been three-quarters pulled back as if to reveal a stage set. Pre-restoration there was a little more to the scene, but not much, just a glimpse of a chair and a Delftware dish full of fruit on a table covered with a rumpled Turkish carpet.

Confronted with this spare image, some past writers on Vermeer regarded it as a tease, designed to pique our curiosity about the contents of the letter while deliberately leaving us in the dark. Others grouped it with earlier Dutch pictures of more voluptuous ladies with bowls of fruit, seeing Vermeer's young woman as a modern Eve. To others again she was the personification of vanity, her reflection in the window symbolizing her narcissism. But such interpretations are beside the point because they are based on a fundamental error, which is what logicians call a category mistake. The *Girl Reading a Letter* is not a genre painting at all but a marriage picture, a celebration of the love that leads to wedlock.

There is no ambiguity about it. The letter is a proposal, while all that it portends is indicated in that tumble of fruit, painted in vivid chiaroscuro and placed dead centre of the composition, level with the young woman's womb. Vermeer's still life is a kind of prayer for the union of man and wife to be fruitful. One prominent peach has even been made to resemble the female sex, which is in keeping for pictures of this kind: such visual rhymes had been a commonplace of marriage painting since the time of Botticelli's *Birth of Venus*, in which the long tresses of the goddess's hair and even the loop of the cloak held out to enfold her are shaped like female genitalia, and were a way of acknowledging that sex and procreation were part of conjugal love.

The most obvious predecessor for Vermeer's picture in Netherlandish art is Jan van Eyck's famous and much earlier *Arnolfini Wedding*, of 1434, in which a husband and wife hold hands in an interior furnished with symbols of their true love, including several ripe fruit aligned with her womb. Vermeer has ingeniously adapted the type of that previous marriage portrait, replacing the image of the husband with that of his letter, so that the bride holds his missive rather than his actual hand. The originality of this invention accounts for most of the misreadings that have bedevilled the picture. Love is framed not in the carnal terms of touching or holding but in the more ideal terms of spiritual communication, a message from one heart received by another in the form of a letter. The piece of paper is caught in the light, which gives it an elusive, fugitive quality and makes it seem almost as if the young woman were holding a plume of smoke. What she holds in her hands is essentially intangible, because it is love itself.

In spirit the *Girl Reading a Letter* is another of the young Vermeer's religious paintings. The image of a woman at a window receiving a message of love evokes the Annunciation. Like Mary transfixed by the news brought by Gabriel, Vermeer's young woman is shaken to the core. Her inner turmoil is suggested by the billowing folds of the red curtain at the window. Using drapery to convey the motions of the spirit was a stratagem Vermeer may have learned from Italian painters, especially Caravaggio and followers of his such as Orazio Gentileschi, one of whose best pictures, the *Annunciation* in Turin, might be a prototype for the *Girl Reading a Letter*: reverse it, remove Gabriel and the dove of the Holy Spirit, and it is strikingly similar to Vermeer's composition.

This marriage painting that is also a religious picture declares true love to be sacred, so much so that when a man or woman feels it they are touched by divinity. This aspect of Vermeer's meaning is disclosed by the green curtain that has been pulled back to reveal the scene. It is not to be understood as part of the illusion of a room, because the interior spaces of Dutch houses were not separated in this way, but as a theatrical flourish designed to tell us that what we are looking at is no mere slice of everyday life, but something holy: a revelation.

Similar imaginary curtains can be found in other Dutch paintings of the time. Their associations were quite particular. Almost identical examples appear in two pictures of the early 1650s, both by painters based in Delft, and both showing the city's Oude Kerk as it looked after the changes caused by the Reformation: Gerard Houckgeest's *Interior of the Oude Kerk in Delft with Trompe l'oeil Curtain*, of 1654, and Emmanuel de Witte's *A Sermon in the Oude Kerk, Delft*, of 1651–2. The curtain in each of these staunchly Calvinist pictures is drawn back to show the Oude Kerk as it had been since the Dutch Revolt, purged of Catholic paintings, sculptures and stained glass. What is being revealed and celebrated is the new church, by implication the true Church, created by stripping away the superfluities of the old. While Vermeer's curtain does not disclose the interior of a church but the room of a house, he means us to understand that this is nonetheless a sacred space. No rite is necessary because the ritual solemnity with which the woman reads her letter is enough. Besides, the picture implies, the holiest place of all is part of no building, but lies within: the church of the human heart.

These are the essential meanings of the *Girl Reading a Letter*, as they might have been deduced from the picture in its pre-restoration state. But in 2020 a remarkable discovery was made. It then transpired that Vermeer had underlined his intentions from the start by including a picture within his picture, hanging on the wall directly behind the young woman. Having been painted out in the mid-eighteenth century, this missing element was finally restored to view. It was a painting of Cupid, holding his bow in one hand with the other outstretched, as if to suggest that it is he who has pulled open the curtain to reveal the scene. If there was any doubt about the true subject of the painting before, there could be none now. Having gone missing for the best part of two and a half centuries, Love had stepped back into the room.[59]

So who painted out Vermeer's Cupid in the first place and why? The answer turns out to have been buried in the eighteenth-century provenance of the picture. By 1736 it had entered a distinguished Parisian collection of Dutch paintings. Six years later thirty of them, but not the Vermeer, were offered for sale to King Augustus III of Poland. An agent involved in the deal was a conservator working in Paris named Jean-Baptiste Slodtz, who had his eye on the post of surveyor of the Polish king's paintings in Dresden. To curry favour, he arranged to have one other picture added *gratis* and presented with his compliments to the king. That picture was the *Girl Reading a Letter*, its authorship by Vermeer quite forgotten. Why did Slodtz choose it? Because with a little judicious editing he hoped to pass it off as a picture by the most famous Dutch Old Master of all. He got rid of the Cupid by painting in a blank wall and sent the picture east labelled as a Rembrandt. Despite his efforts he never did get the job.[60]

The restoration of the long-suppressed Cupid is invaluable, not only because it confirms that the *Girl Reading a Letter* is a picture all about love and marriage, but also because it amounts to a gloss by the artist on the meaning of his own work. The inclusion of this particular personification of Love had a precise significance. The emblem books of the seventeenth century offered painters a choice of many Cupids, each with different connotations. A Cupid blowing bubbles signified the pessimistic idea that Love is Transient. A Cupid being chased by Envy, a hag with snakes for hair, stood for Love driven away by Jealousy. A Cupid trampling on the attributes of the arts and sciences, books, telescopes, musical instruments and what-have-you, exemplified the motto *Amor Vincit Omnia*, Love Conquers All. The Cupid in the *Girl Reading a Letter* is none of these. Vermeer's template was an emblem from a book published in Antwerp in 1608, Otto van Veen's *Amorum Emblemata*, which shows Cupid standing in a landscape, with his bow in his right hand, a ring in his left (a detail cropped out by the curtain in Vermeer's painting) and treading down a theatrical mask lying face-up on the ground. According to the caption in the book, this Cupid is '*oprecht*', or upright and sincere: 'Love in all it does cannot be feigned, it wears its heart on its sleeve, never going unseen like Gyges, who could do so through the power of his ring [Gyges was a King of Lydia who could make himself invisible thanks to a magic ring]. Love does not allow us to conceal our thoughts.'

In other words, this is True Love, Faithful Love, Love Despising Dissimulation: the form of human love closest to divine love. Vermeer wants us to understand that this highest form of love has been kindled in the heart of the young woman. The moment will not last, time will flow on, but what she feels right now is so pure that it is incorruptible and therefore part of eternity. The painter completes this idea in the contrast between the woman and her reflection, the secondary image of her that is broken into pieces and darkened by the panes of leaded glass. The woman in the mirror and the woman in the room represent two planes of existence, the ephemeral and the eternal. Her reflection represents her exterior and worldly being, subject to time and change. She herself, shown in regal profile like a queen on a coin, represents her own eternal soul, communing with the soul of another so deeply as to be communing also with God. This most tender element of the painting recalls a passage from St Paul's epistles in which mere reflections are contrasted with higher truths: 'For now we see through a glass, darkly; but then face to face: now I know in part; but then shall I know even as also I am known.' (1 Corinthians, 13:12)

Whose knowing, of God and each other, is commemorated in the *Girl Reading a Letter*? Who were the husband and wife for whom it was painted? In the absence of documentation concerning its early ownership, there is no way of knowing for sure. But it is tempting to speculate that this picture, which seems so charged with personal feeling, might have been dedicated by Vermeer to his own wife, Catharina, in celebration of their courtship and marriage. If that is so the young woman is a portrait of Catharina herself, dressed in her finest – a world away from the 'beggar's child' she had once been, pitied by her neighbours in Gouda – while the heartfelt letter gripped in her hands is a declaration of love from her husband, Johannes Vermeer.

Perhaps the idea of having the composition revolve around the reading of a letter originated in the actual circumstances of their courtship, which may have dictated that the artist woo her by correspondence. If he had been prevented from seeing his future wife, perhaps because he had been *persona non grata* with her mother, or away somewhere, he would have had no alternative but to write. The efficiency of the Dutch postal service, which had no parallel elsewhere in Europe, would have made this possible. One other element in the painting chimes with what we know about Johannes and Catharina. The fruit heaped high in the bowl, so high that it overspills, suggests great hopes for future fertility. It implies a desire for not just one or two but for a whole brood of children, which was certainly what Vermeer and his wife produced: Catharina eventually bore Johannes no fewer than eleven surviving children.

If Johannes did paint the picture for Catharina, it might have been more than just a love gift. It might have been his way of solemnizing their marriage in a space that was sacred but also appropriately free of ties to any particular religious confession. Their physical marriage ceremony had taken place in a hidden Catholic church in Schipluy, but Vermeer's painting, set in a room that is itself another kind of church, with links to no denomination, proposes an alternative idea of what marriage might be: a metaphysical ritual or rite of passage that does not even require the bodily presence of both husband and wife; an annunciation in which love surges up wondrously; a mystical meeting of souls.

One obvious objection to this hypothesis is that no mention of the painting is made in the inventory of movable goods from Vermeer's estate compiled in 1676. But the point of that inventory was to list those goods that Catharina had owned in common with Johannes, and therefore had 'coming to her'; so if he had many years previously given her the painting it would already be hers outright and there would be no reason to list it. Besides, there is reason to suspect that Catharina hid or transferred certain of their joint possessions to keep them out of the taxman's clutches.[61] But in the end none of that really matters. Regardless of who it was painted for, it is what the painting says that counts: what it says, and what it stands for. It is a painting of love like no other.

PART THREE

The Invisible Church, 1657–72

THE ARRANGEMENT

There are few traces of Vermeer in the archives of his time. Admittedly, his name appears in several documents from the year of his marriage. But in the records spanning the seven years between 29 December 1653, when he was enrolled into the Guild of St Luke, and 27 December 1660, when he and Catharina buried an unnamed child in the Oude Kerk, his presence is noted in just four notarial documents.

The first three are routine. On 10 January 1654 he witnessed a statement of debt owed by the widow of an estate auctioneer; on 30 April of the same year he witnessed the debt acknowledgement of a carpenter; and on 14 December 1655 he and his wife guaranteed that they would continue to pay interest on a debt contracted by his father, Reynier.[1] The last of the four documents is yet another debt acknowledgement, but it also records a turning point in Vermeer's life. On 30 November 1657 he and his wife appeared before Notary J. van Ophoven 'to acknowledge that they duly owe Pieter Claesz van Ruijven or his legally empowered representatives the sum of 200 guilders arising from money duly lent and handed over to them this day. They promise to return the sum within a year, by the last day of November 1658, together with the interest on it at 4 guilders 10 stuivers per hundred a year . . .'[2]

From 1657 until about 1670 Vermeer would paint almost exclusively for Pieter Claesz van Ruijven and his wife, Maria de Knuijt. The debt recorded by Notary van Ophoven can be taken to mark the beginning of that arrangement. The apparent loan was really an advance on the acquisition of pictures either in progress or to be painted during the following twelve months. Van Ruijven may have requested that this advance be expressed in the form of a loan to insure himself against the possibility of Vermeer dying, or failing to live up to expectations. As things turned out he and Maria would be repaid many times over in works of art. The fact that no further loans from Van Ruijven to Vermeer are recorded suggests that after a trial period of one year the annuity was paid on trust.

There was a precedent of sorts for such an agreement. In the late 1630s the Swedish envoy to Holland, Pieter Spierincx Silvercroon, paid the painter Gerard Dou an annual sum of 500 guilders for the right of first refusal on a single picture per year. Silvercroon was distantly related to Pieter Claesz van Ruijven, as well as being godfather to Pieter's little sister Pieternella. The two men met on at least one occasion, a baptism in Delft in 1642, so Silvercroon's contract with Dou may have been at the back of Van Ruijven's mind when he made his own deal with Vermeer some fifteen years later.[3] But that was a very different arrangement. Van Ruijven and Maria got more than first refusal on one picture a year from Vermeer. They got all his pictures, or almost all of them. Moreover, those pictures were not merely to appeal to their taste or to please their eyes. They were to express their deepest convictions, their hopes and their dreams. This was so from the outset of the arrangement to its end.

A SOLDIER IN LOVE AND A WOMAN SLEEPING

Vermeer's first two pictures for his patrons would have been painted within a year or so of the artist receiving the advance notarized in November 1657. They can therefore be dated to around 1658. Both were included in the Amsterdam auction of 1696 at which the Van Ruijven collection was eventually dispersed, where they were listed respectively as Lot 11 and Lot 8. Lot 11 is possibly the earlier of the two. Described by the Amsterdam auctioneer as 'a soldier with a laughing girl', the picture is in the Frick Collection in New York. It is commonly known now as *Officer with a Laughing Girl*.

In a corner of a sunlit room a man and woman sit facing one another diagonally across a table. She has a glass of wine in front of her; he probably has one too, but we cannot see it because his body blocks most of the table. They are next to a double casement window with leaded panes, one half of which has been opened to let in the fresh air. A large paper map, torn in places, hangs on the mottled plaster wall behind them. The man, who is shown almost in silhouette, looms large, his out-thrust cocked right arm so close to the picture plane as to seem within touching distance. He wears a broad-brimmed felt hat and red military uniform, the black sash around his shoulder indicating that he is an officer. His white ruffed sleeve adds a touch of swagger. The soldier's expression is inscrutable because lost in shadow, but his gaze is evidently fixed on the face of the young woman opposite him. He is entranced by her. His chair and hers are aligned to face each other, aslant but exactly parallel, so that two imaginary lines drawn from the lion's-head finials on his chairback to those on hers would perfectly enclose the couple. It is a subtle use of perspective, implying that he and she will be together for eternity, and that what he has found in this room – even if he does not yet quite know it, as the bafflement in his body language hints – is true love and a blessed end to all his wandering.

The young woman opens her face and her heart to him at one and the same time. Her smile is radiant and guileless, the smile of a straightforward girl who wants to make her feelings known. She is demurely dressed, in a bodice of glittering yellow and black satin, with a white headdress that evokes the wimple of a nun. She is beautiful but in no stereotypical way. It is the depth of her honesty and the purity of her affection that make her shine so brightly in this stilled instant. She means what her look says and what her left hand gestures as it hovers above the table, caught by the light, beckoning him towards her. The wars are over. The time has come for the soldier to relax his guard and surrender. The time has come for him to be hers.

The picture was probably inspired by some paintings of a strongly pacifist character done by Gerard ter Borch in the wake of the Peace of Münster. During the early 1650s Ter Borch had invented a new type of picture, which it may be helpful to think of as the guardroom painting turned upside down.[4] Such works showed soldiers in interiors, but behaving in far gentler and softer ways than they had ever done in the *kortegarde* paintings of the 1630s and 1640s. The guardrooms of that still recent past, including those by Ter Borch himself, had represented soldiers as vicious idlers or, still worse, plunderers looting the homes of their victims. But in these new pictures they became moonstruck lovers composing letters to the women who had won their hearts.

Characteristic of the type is Ter Borch's *An Officer Dictating a Letter* of 1655, in the National Gallery, in which a melancholy soldier in a broad-brimmed hat, much like that worn by Vermeer's officer, is dictating a love letter to one of his comrades in arms. The latter, wearing a steel helmet and armed with a pen rather than a sword, is committing his friend's words to paper, ready for dispatch by a waiting trumpeter. A similar but slightly later painting by Ter Borch, in the Philadelphia Museum of Art, dispenses with the figure of the amanuensis. Here the soldier himself writes as the trumpeter waits, while a telltale card face up on the floor, the ace of hearts, signifies that the words being set down are words of love. A placid dog completes the scene in both paintings, dozing in the London picture, nuzzling the trumpeter in the Philadelphia version.

In each case Ter Borch has cleverly placed the military man's canopied bed directly behind him, inviting the viewer to note its close resemblance to the bell-tents that Dutch armies set up in the field. The soldier who used to camp out while waging war is now at home in his bedchamber, composing love letters rather than writing dispatches. The dogs of war have been domesticated, tamed into emblems of amorous fidelity.

Vermeer takes the same storyline, of a soldier in love, but makes it yet more vivid and immediate. He brings Ter Borch's letter-writing officer into the same room as the woman who has captured his heart, and he shows the moment when that capturing takes place, through an exchange of gazes: the look of love, sudden as a flash of lightning, which imparts an electrical charge of energy to that small patch of thin air separating the figures. The woman gives, the man receives, and in receiving he is conquered. This is the only type of conquering that needs to happen now that peace has broken out. The map on the wall reinforces this pattern of meaning. It is an exact copy of a real map first published by the Dutch cartographer Berckenrode in 1620, which Vermeer himself must have owned or borrowed. It shows Holland and West Friesland, heartland of the Dutch Republic, once threatened by Spain but now safe and secure in the new European order shaped by the treaties of 1648. Flotillas of warships patrol its paper seas, but they belong to the past just as the map belongs to the background.

The subject of the picture is the victory of Love over War or, to put it in mythological terms, the triumph of Venus over Mars, updated to the present day. It is hard to imagine a more perfectly modern Dutch Venus than Vermeer's wholesome smiling girl, sitting with her rummer of wine in a sunlit room. The allusion to a pagan past is there, but only as an aside. The light that floods the girl's face infuses the picture with Christian significance. The love that has come to pass, now that war is over, is a gift of God.

The other of Vermeer's early paintings for the Van Ruijven household was Lot 8 in the Amsterdam sale of 1696, where it was listed as 'a drunken sleeping maid'. It is now in the Metropolitan Museum of Art in New York, usually described as *A Maid Asleep*. Both the old and the modern title are misleading. The woman is no maid, as her elegant dress indicates, nor is she drunk. She is sleeping, but hers is no ordinary slumber.

With its squashed bird's-eye perspective, with its focus on a single female figure sitting in the corner of a room among scattered objects, and its palette of earth colours, Vermeer's painting is strongly reminiscent of Caravaggio's *Penitent Magdalene* of around 1594. Vermeer may have known that picture through his possible master, Gerard ter Borch. Ter Borch's father had stayed in Rome at the Palazzo Colonna, home to Caravaggio's most steadfast protector, Marchesa Costanza Colonna, shortly after the Italian painter's sudden death in 1610, when he was the talk of the town. Perhaps Vermeer had taken the trouble to see Caravaggio's work for himself on a possible visit to Italy around 1650. However that may be, the image of Caravaggio's Magdalene, eyes closed as she opens her heart to Christ, lies somewhere behind his own image of a sleeping woman.

Something out of the ordinary, something uncanny, is taking place in the silence of this room. A lady dressed in a red satin gown trimmed with white lace has fallen asleep at her dining table in a stiffly upright leather-backed chair. Elbow propped, she rests her head on her right hand while holding onto the table's edge with the fingers of her left. Her dream thoughts are happy ones, to judge by the hint of a smile on her face. She is seated close to a half-open door revealing the glimpse of another room, a detail that encapsulates the world of the painting: a liminal space, a threshold, beyond which lies a mystery.

Not long ago the woman received a visitor, someone who has now disappeared, leaving the signs of his presence behind him like waves in the wake of a swimmer. The chair opposite hers has been pushed back and swivelled the other way. In the act of rising, whoever was sitting in that chair has disturbed the Persian carpet serving as a tablecloth, which is rucked up into peaks and folds like a flat landscape disturbed by an earthquake. A fancy knife and spoon lie discarded by the absent guest, together with a twisted gauzy napkin and a tangled mass of some silky material that might be a scrunched-up veil or shroud. A large rummer, emptied of its contents, lies on its side next to an upright wine pitcher of white porcelain with a hinged tin lid. The someone who is no longer there has been drinking with the lady in red. Her own glass, one-third full, remains on the table in front of her. Beside it is a bowl of fruit containing apples and what appear to be wrinkled plums.

Vermeer's namesake and former family pastor, Johannes Taurinus, had been a strong advocate of private spiritual devotion. 'It is not without reason that our Saviour advises us to go into a room alone when we want to pray devoutly,' he had written in his *Reflections on the Parable of the Samaritan Woman*. 'When we go into a closed room, undisturbed and unperturbed, we can lift our spirits and pour out our need to the Lord.'[5] For Jacobus Arminius, who had inspired the Remonstrant movement, undisturbed meditation and prayer paved the way to Christian enlightenment. The grace of God was not simply granted or withheld by unchangeable decree, as the Calvinists taught. It was up to every man and woman to open themselves up to it or be lost. Only those who bare their souls to Christ, alone and in private, may hope to be visited by his spirit. Arminius justified his position by quoting one of his favourite passages in Scripture: 'Here I am! I stand at the door and knock. If anyone hears my voice and opens the door, I will come in and eat with that person, and they with me.' (Revelation 3:20)[6]

On the wall directly above the sleeping woman in Vermeer's painting, just to the left of the open door, hangs an ill-lit painting, only a fragment of which is visible. In its murk can be deciphered the standing foot of a figure and next to that a theatrical mask: the identifying features of Otto van Veen's now familiar '*oprecht*' Cupid, emblem of a love that is true and honest, hiding nothing. The thin slice of wall to the right of the door is decorated with another map, its bottom edge weighted down by a dark hanging rod attached to a bulbous finial. Only the blank margin of the map is visible, not the map itself.

The world has disappeared, or receded to the point where it is impossible to distinguish between the space of dream and the space of reality. With an open heart the woman has been praying and reflecting, perhaps repenting. We are to understand that she has been visited. Has the spirit of the Lord dwelt with her and held communion with her? The juxtaposition of her wine glass with a bowl of bruised apples and plums may, like Vermeer's overall composition, derive from Caravaggio, in several of whose paintings the same combination occurs, the perishable fruit representing mortal life with all its imperfections, the wine redemption through Christ's sacrifice.

The open door that leads to an empty room may bring to mind the stone rolled away from Christ's empty sepulchre. Whether by accident or design, the legs of the table on the back wall make the sign of the cross. X-rays show that Vermeer had originally included the figure of a man with shoulder-length hair in a broad-brimmed hat, standing in the far room and being sniffed at inquisitively by a dog on the near side of the doorway. Both were subsequently painted out, on this occasion definitely by the artist himself.

Red is a colour associated with Mary Magdalene. Aside from the Virgin Mary, no woman had been closer to Christ than she. She had wept and wailed over his dead body, anointed his feet with oil and conversed with him after his Resurrection, in the garden close by his empty tomb. A Dutch woman who felt a special devotion to her might start her prayers by attempting to imagine herself into the shoes of the Magdalene, then trying to feel what she might have felt during the key moments in her story. This type of intensely private spiritual exercise had a long history in the northern Netherlands but it enjoyed a strong revival during Vermeer's lifetime. It was much practised within the Collegiant movement, many of whose adherents were especially devoted to the inner circle of Christ's first followers. Male Collegiants empathized with the apostles, female Collegiants with figures such as Martha and her sister Mary, whose faith Christ commended, but especially with Mary Magdalene.

Vermeer's picture is such a specific and precise depiction of a moment of visionary experience that it seems possible it was intended to record an actual moment in someone's life, perhaps that of the woman who commissioned the picture, namely Maria de Knuijt. If that is so then the lady in the painting might be a portrait of Maria herself, lost in her devotions. There was a tradition of revering Mary Magdalene in the female line of her family. Her mother's Christian name had been Magdalena. She gave that same Christian name to her daughter, Magdalena van Ruijven, born in 1655.

SISTERHOOD IN ROTTERDAM AND DELFT

Pieter Claesz van Ruijven and Maria de Knuijt had married in 1653, like Johannes Vermeer and Catharina Bolnes. They were definitely living at The Golden Eagle on the Oude Delft by 19 October 1665, because they said so in the preamble to the will that they made on that date.[7] Pieter owned two other properties in Delft, both on the Voorstraat, but one was leased to his sister as a shop and the other was a former brewery, so it is very likely that he and Maria had moved into the house next door to the hidden Remonstrant church immediately after their marriage. It was a grand residence: when put up for sale in around 1670 the price tag was 10,500 guilders, a small fortune at the time.

The majority of Vermeer's paintings would be hung on the walls of that house, its location at the heart of Delft's Remonstrant quarter being apt to their spirit and meaning. The first two, *Officer with a Laughing Girl* and *A Maid Asleep*, set the tone for the rest. They gave new light and life to the liberal beliefs of people raised to revere Jacobus Arminius and schooled in the thought of his followers, Remonstrant and Collegiant alike. They made human and divine love vivid and visible. They also gave expression to an exhilarating optimism. *Officer with a Laughing Girl* proclaims a touching faith in the future of humanity, implying that soon enough every soldier will be a lover, while *A Maid Asleep* concentrates on progress more personal, suggesting the way in which a single human being may cross the threshold leading to enlightenment and inner peace.

Like many of Vermeer's later pictures for the Van Ruijven household, they give the impression of having been painted primarily for women. Women's thoughts and experiences are to the fore. A man is present in one of the pictures, but he is seen from behind. Women's faces are the only faces seen. Might this be because Maria de Knuijt rather than her husband Pieter was the prime mover in commissioning paintings from Vermeer? If so, her motives are likely to have been pious.

Vermeer and the Van Ruijvens came to their arrangement in late 1657. At exactly the same time there was a sharp growth in private prayer groups founded by women, for women, in Rotterdam and nearby Delft.[8] We assume that Maria de Knuijt was godly enough to want to live right next door to Delft's hidden Remonstrant church: it is highly unlikely that she and Pieter lived where they did by chance. We also know that she was sufficiently independent to commission a devotional picture as unique as *A Maid Asleep*. She would commission so many more pictures from Vermeer that it is hard to believe she did not intend them for an audience larger than her own small family.

The inference to be drawn from this is that Maria may already have joined or founded a prayer group of like-minded women when Vermeer started painting for her. His pictures may have been intended to help them in their devotions. Much of what we know about patron and painter points in that direction. The evidence for this will accumulate gradually as the story of their collaboration is told. But first we need to understand the milieu to which it seems they belonged.

What were they like, the women who formed these groups in Delft and Rotterdam from the late 1650s on? They were pious, sociable, well-read, freethinking and fiercely independent. They would meet in each other's houses weekly, and sometimes more often, to read and discuss the Bible. Many of them shared the millenarian beliefs widespread at the time, so the question of what would happen when Christ returned to rule the world was also discussed at their meetings. It was said that in the utopia to come money and property would be redistributed, and women would have the same rights as men. As far as they were concerned, it could not happen too soon.[9]

Some of the women were befriended by English Quakers who had travelled to Holland in the hope of gaining converts to their own recently founded religious movement. The Quakers, whose name was a reference to their trembling spiritual enthusiasm, presented themselves as kindred spirits to the Dutch nonconformists, which in some respects they were. They too believed in the imminent return of Christ and they too had renounced traditional forms of religious observance to gather as groups of 'Friends' without pastors or clergy. They worshipped in pure silence, 'which is to the spirit as sleep to the body' (in the words of one of their leaders, William Penn), hoping thereby to receive truth and illumination directly from God.

The Dutch women were curious about these intensely pious 'inner spirit' Christians from the other side of the pewter sea, and pleasantly surprised to find that they too allowed women's voices to be heard. They would have applauded *Women's Speaking Justified*, a tract composed by one of the more prominent female Quakers, Margaret Fell, who railed against those 'dark Priests who are so mad against Womens Speaking' and pointed to the example of Mary Magdalene, the first person to witness the resurrected Christ: if she had kept quiet, 'then what had become of the Redemption of the whole body of mankind?'[10] Many of the women in the Dutch prayer groups identified with Mary Magdalene.[11] At their meetings they would read and discuss the biblical account of her encounter with Christ in the garden beside the empty sepulchre.

These Dutch women were Collegiants. Ordinarily such people left few traces of their presence for the historian to find. They maintained a low profile to escape the attentions of the Reformed Church, which regarded their gatherings as seedbeds of heresy. But as it happened some of the women who met in Rotterdam were rumbled by the Calvinist authorities. Because those women were themselves members of the Dutch Reformed Church, albeit estranged from it, the Calvinist consistory had the right to call them to account, which it did. Transcripts of the disciplinary hearings that followed still survive in the archives of the Reformed Church in Rotterdam. They paint a vivid

THE INVISIBLE CHURCH, 1657-72

A Quaker woman speaking at a Friends' meeting in London, circa 1678.
Like the Dutch Collegiants, with whom they formed close links, the Quakers met
in each other's homes and allowed women equal rights of speech at their gatherings,
a privilege denied to other Christian women at that time – and indeed during most
periods of history.

picture of the activities and beliefs of a specific group of pious women in that city, and in doing so contribute greatly to our understanding of what might have been going on at the same time in the house of Maria de Knuijt in neighbouring Delft.

For the period between 1657 and 1662, the archives in Rotterdam have yielded the names of twenty-two women known to have participated in Collegiant meetings. Many more remain unidentified, and unidentifiable.[12] The case of one of those women in particular is worth exploring here, because so many of the patterns of her life are mirrored in what we know or can deduce about the life of Vermeer's patron Maria de Knuijt. Her name was Martha Ariens.

Although Martha only began organizing Collegiant meetings at her home in Rotterdam in 1657, she had first become involved with the movement several years earlier. She had started going to the regular Friday meetings at the hidden Remonstrant church in Rotterdam in the late 1640s or early 1650s, when she was around twenty years old. By then the 'Friday School' of the Remonstrants had been so deeply infiltrated by leading Collegiants that it had become a Collegiant meeting in all but name: a leaderless gathering where the Bible was read and free prophecy practised. Martha had been brought up within the Dutch Reformed Church, of which she was a member, but having experienced the freedom of the Collegiant meetings she came to find regular church service stifling and dull. She became permanently alienated from the religion of her childhood.[13]

In 1653 the Calvinist *preciezen* succeeded in making life difficult for Martha and most other Collegiants. By that date the Reformed Church councils had convinced the States of Holland and West Friesland that Collegiant meetings were nothing but a cover for the activities of the Socinians, a sect named after the late sixteenth-century Sienese humanist Faustus Socinus but formed mostly of his Polish refugee followers, notorious for denying the Trinity and questioning the divinity of Christ. Reformed propagandists maintained the strategic pretence that every Collegiant was a Socinian in disguise, and branded their meetings 'Socinian assemblies'. The States swallowed the lie, issuing a placard proscribing all of their gatherings forthwith, on pain of severe penalties.

Its effects were felt immediately. The fledgling College at Amsterdam ceased meeting. In Rotterdam, the Remonstrant Church Council was so spooked by the States' clampdown that it closed down the Friday meetings of the Collegiants with immediate effect. Martha Ariens went underground for the best part of three years, re-emerging in 1657 as the organizer of a tight-knit group of Collegiants who met every week at her home. By that time paranoia about the spread of heresy had receded, the States had relaxed their vigilance and it was safe, or safer, for Martha and like-minded souls to meet once more. The Calvinist ministers were unhappy with this state of affairs but there was little they could do other than harass those of their members whom they believed to have gone astray. It was at this point that the Rotterdam Church Council got wind of Martha's gatherings and called her in to answer for herself.

First they reprimanded her for aiding and abetting the '*t'samensprekinghen*' – literally, 'together-speakings' – of foolish women. Then she was told that she would be well advised to spend less time at home and start coming to church. Secure in the knowledge that the council members had no real power over her, Martha replied defiantly. There was nothing for her at church, she said. If she were going to leave her house, she would visit the houses of the sick and infirm, and help them to pray: 'That's what I do, I call it going to church with people who cannot go to church.' As for the meetings at her house, they were educational and in her view far superior to the catechism classes offered by the Reformed Church. She used to attend catechism lessons but had given up years ago, because it was not God's Word but 'man's mistelling'. She would make sure her children never had to endure them. Sunday service was no better, being just an endless succession of sermons: men with the borrowed authority of the cloth telling women what to do. With that she went back to her world, leaving her interrogators to theirs.

The meetings organized by Martha and her friends were structured around Bible-reading. Together week by week they would read the entire New Testament from beginning to end, in order. So, if at the end of one week they had finished the Acts of the Apostles, the following week they would begin Paul's Epistle to the Romans, then move on to Corinthians I and II, and so on. This was standard practice among all Collegiants, men and women alike: a Calvinist spy sent to infiltrate some of the earliest meetings in Amsterdam in 1647 reported that the Collegiants there gathered in the house of a blind 'Arminian' (i.e. Remonstrant) schoolteacher, and that in successive weeks 'first they read Acts, next they read Romans'.[14] Most Collegiant groups would expect to read the entire New Testament about four times a year.

Conversation at the meetings ranged freely. Sometimes one of the women would have prepared a short sermon of sorts in which she would speak on a theme suggested by a particular text. Together they would sing psalms and, occasionally, more raucous songs proclaiming their freedom from Calvinist patriarchs. Some men, however, they were pleased to see. Martha and her friends attended the 'Great Meetings' that took place every eight weeks or so and were organized by Rotterdam's Collegiant leadership, a group of around half a dozen men with links to the Remonstrant and Mennonite congregations. Those same men or others sent by them appeared regularly by invitation at the meetings in Martha's house. They encouraged the women to bring more people like themselves into the fold of the movement. They also addressed them on subjects such as faith and good works and the imminence of the End of Days.

Martha's group in Rotterdam was small, with a core of just seven women, six of whose names are known: Martha herself, Eva Burgers, Maritge Soemans, Maritge Samuels, Neeltje Jansen, Juffrow Blaeu and Juffrow Blaeu's maid. They were always looking out for opportunities to recruit new participants. Maritge Samuels approached fellow shoppers in the marketplace, while any hawker who came to Martha's door was liable to be invited in for a chat. But sometimes enough could be enough: on one occasion Maritge Soemans turned up with so many newcomers that Martha found the atmosphere too unruly for serious prayer. There was clearly a cap on the ideal number of participants. The women's house meetings were different in character from the 'Great Meetings' in Rotterdam, or indeed the Collegiant assemblies in Amsterdam, which were often attended by a hundred people or more, some of whom explored the farther shores of Christian belief. Martha's far smaller group seems to have contained no one like that. The women were unconventional in their methods of worship, less so in what they believed.

Martha Ariens was evidently well-to-do, living as she did in a house with a front room of sufficient size to accommodate a gathering of twenty to twenty-five people, as it might be on a busy day. So too was at least one of the other women, Juffrow Blaeu, who attended the meetings with her maid. The maid was a participant too and would have been accorded the same respect and rights of speech as all the others. The Collegiants were emphatically egalitarian. In the eyes of Martha and her friends, the rich were no better than the poor. If anything the opposite was true. Knowing that it was easier for a camel to pass through the eye of a needle than for a rich person to get to heaven, Collegiants with money worked doubly hard to make up for their disadvantage and often performed the Acts of Mercy listed in Matthew's Gospel. Not only did they give generously to those in need, they ran charities all over Holland and in at least one case founded a major charitable institution, namely the Oranj-Appel in Amsterdam, an orphanage and foundling hospital paid for and administered by the city's Mennonite Collegiants.

Twice a year, at Pentecost in early summer and again at the end of August, most of the women in Martha's group travelled to the village of Rijnsburg, headquarters of their movement. There they were welcomed to a cavernous, barn-like meeting house where they would partake of the Lord's Supper. Nicknamed the 'Big House', it towered over the other houses in the village. At Pentecost in particular, Collegiants from all over the Dutch Republic would make the same pilgrimage. If the weather was fine, as many as a quarter of all the movement's adherents might attend. Together they would squeeze into the great hall, lit by high windows of plain leaded glass and filled with rows of wooden benches. At the centre was a long refectory table with bread and wine upon it, laid with a white cloth and set with fifteen chairs. A member of the gathering, who might have volunteered or been chosen at random, but who was not to be thought of as priest or pastor, then led the service.

He or she proclaimed that to attend the Lord's Supper at that moment and in that place meant to embrace 'general Christianity'. Toleration was a golden rule. All divisive doctrines were to be set aside. The only thing that those present need bear in mind was the suffering of Christ. A short silence was followed by a brief prayer, after which the speaker invited those present, fifteen at a time, to come to the table, to share the bread and pass the common cup of wine. The room was full, the ceremony long, but patience had been a requirement of Collegiant fellowship ever since the days of the first leaderless gatherings, which often continued through the night.

Dutch Reformed, Lutherans, Mennonites, Catholics, Remonstrants, Socinians, Quakers, Jews and even one or two Muslims were to be found among those who gathered in the Big House. To be part of the movement each man or woman there was required to hold one belief and one alone, namely that the teachings of

Collegiants gathering for the Lord's Supper at the 'Big House' in Rijnsburg. They met there twice a year as 'Christians without a Church', so to them this barn-like building was emphatically *not* a church, but a place where people of all denominations and all shades of belief were welcome. The only qualification for attendance was faith in the saving power of Christ's own commandments such as 'Love thine enemy'. Note the large number of women present: some 70 per cent of Collegiants were female, among them Vermeer's main patron and most of those in her immediate prayer circle.

Christ contained the salvation of mankind. It was not necessary to believe that Christ was the Son of God, or the same as God, or part of a trinity of beings that included God as well as the Holy Spirit (although many of them actually did). It was this latitude that so appalled the strict Calvinists. For their part the Collegiants believed themselves to embody Christianity in its only true, non-sectarian, peaceful form. They also saw themselves as part of a story. They were the faithful followers of Christ who had been scattered and hidden among the different denominations of the post-Reformation world to be recognized only by God. They were the invisible Church.

They would never be numerous. At its peak their movement would claim no more than 4,000 sympathizers. But the Collegiants of the mid-seventeenth century believed their mission was in its infancy, its potential for growth unlimited. Their optimism was reflected in the choice of Pentecost as the day for their largest meeting. Pentecost marked the moment when the spirit of the Lord descended on the apostles, illuminating them with tongues of fire which enabled them to speak every language and take Christ's message to all. The Collegiants saw themselves as latter-day apostles. Every time they gathered at Rijnsburg they were fired up, as if by the flames of the Holy Spirit, for the task that lay ahead. Two of the women in Martha's group, Maritge Soemans and Neeltje Jansen, were said to have returned from the Rijnsburg gathering of 1656 in such a state of elation that they wanted to go straight back.

Many parallels can be found between Martha Ariens in Rotterdam and her near contemporary Maria de Knuijt in nearby Delft. Martha defected from the Dutch Reformed Church to the Remonstrant Church before joining the Collegiants and eventually starting up her own women's group in 1657. Maria de Knuijt seems to have followed a near identical path during the same small window of time. The two women may well have met, if not at each other's houses then at the Big House in Rijnsburg. In the case of Martha and her friends we have copious amounts of precious information: names, dates, even details of what was read and said at meetings. By contrast Maria's Collegiant activities must be inferred from the internal evidence of Vermeer's paintings and a body of strong documentary evidence showing that she and her husband, Pieter, as well as the artist himself, were in close contact with the inner circle of the Collegiant leadership in Rotterdam.

Knowing Martha Ariens's story is helpful when it comes to filling in the many gaps in that of Maria de Knuijt, because the trajectories of their two lives seem to have been so similar. Maria had been born into the orthodox Reformed Church. Her marriage to the prominent Remonstrant Pieter Claesz van Ruijven, together with her decision to live next door to the Remonstrants' hidden church, suggest that she like Martha had recoiled from the Calvinist sermons and catechism classes of her childhood. Maria might have jumped ship and joined the Remonstrants when she was in her late teens, as Martha had done. The dates tally: she was seventeen years old in 1638, when the Remonstrant church in Delft was consecrated and its first services held. They were recruiting; she may have been open to persuasion.

Then in the mid-1640s, not long after turning twenty, Maria may have been introduced to the Collegiants and their egalitarian form of worship. This might have happened at leaderless gatherings held in Delft's Remonstrant church, much like the 'Friday School' in Rotterdam attended by Martha at around the same time. Vermeer's mother, Digna, and his sister, Gertruy, may have been present at those meetings. Considering Digna's documented links to the Remonstrant movement as well as to Johannes Taurinus, Delft's first advocate of free prophecy, it is conceivable that she herself, or her daughter, introduced Maria de Knuijt to the Collegiant way of worship. Digna and Gertruy were Maria's neighbours on Delft's Great Market Square, after all. Such a sequence of events would help to explain why Maria and her husband were quick to hold out a helping hand to Gertruy many years later. Johannes Vermeer may also have joined this Collegiant circle following his return to Delft after completing his apprenticeship. Maria's friendship with the painter seems to have blossomed at just this time. It could not have done so earlier because he was barely resident in Delft between the ages of twelve and eighteen.

Martha Ariens started her women's group in 1657, unable to do so earlier due to the States' placard of 1653 against so-called 'Socinian assemblies'. Because no reports of Collegiant or similar devotional meetings in Delft have come down to us, we can only speculate about Maria de Knuijt's pious activities.[15] But it seems that she began hosting the meetings of just such a religious group at around the same time that Martha did. This is unlikely to have been a coincidence. Maria may have planned to inaugurate the meetings at her home as soon as she moved in with Pieter in 1653 – she may even have bought the house for that purpose – only to be foiled, like Martha in Rotterdam, by the placard of that same year. If so they had both been stuck in the same bottleneck. Just like Martha, who went underground for three years, Maria was forced to wait for the right moment. She ended up waiting so long that she was a mother by the time it came. Her daughter Magdalena was two years old when she and the other women in her group were finally able to convene at 106 Oude Delft, The Golden Eagle.

On that long-awaited occasion it may have been Maria de Knuijt herself who turned to the New Testament and read the first verse of the first chapter of its first book, the Gospel of Matthew. In the interim, she had had much opportunity to think and plan. It may have been during those years that she or her husband, or both of them together, came up with a new idea, one that would distinguish her women's group from that of Martha Ariens or anyone else. At the gatherings held in the house by the hidden Remonstrant church in Delft there would be more than words and music to stir the souls of the faithful. There would be paintings.

LOT 1 AND LOT 2

The meanings of Vermeer's pictures have been forgotten due to a lack of awareness of the religious context for which they were created. For the same reason few questions have been asked about the order in which they might once have been hung, or the relationships between them. The unspoken assumption behind most writing on Vermeer is that his pictures were painted as discrete objects for sale on the open market, when the opposite is true. There are clues in the historical record which lead to the conclusion that a number of Vermeer's paintings for his friends and patrons were planned and painted in pairs. The pictures themselves bear this out.

The catalogue of the Amsterdam auction of 1696, at which all of Vermeer's paintings for Maria and Pieter were finally dispersed, shows that the first two to go under the hammer were *Woman with a Balance* and *The Milkmaid*. They were not given those titles, which are modern inventions, but the auctioneer's descriptions plainly match the paintings in question. Lot 1 was listed as 'A young lady weighing gold, in a box by J. van der Meer of Delft, extraordinarily artful and vigorously painted', Lot 2 as 'A maid pouring out milk, extremely well done, by ditto'.[16]

The Milkmaid hangs in the Rijksmuseum, the *Woman with a Balance* more than two thousand miles away in the National Gallery of

Art, Washington. They have occasionally been brought together for exhibitions devoted to Vermeer, but few serious comparisons have ever been made between them. Both were included in the large retrospective of the painter's work staged at the Rijksmuseum in 2023, but hung in separate rooms, as if to suggest that they had little in common with each other bar Vermeer's authorship.[17] Most scholars place them about five years apart, dating *The Milkmaid* to roughly 1657–8, the *Woman with a Balance* to 1663–4, but this is unlikely to be correct. It seems certain they are a pair, conceived together, painted together, then hung together on the walls of Maria de Knuijt's house. They were paired by the auctioneer, who made them his first two lots. They are the same size as each other, to within a couple of inches, and so intimate are the visual connections between them they might almost be regarded as a single picture painted on two canvases. Assuming that they were done straight after the *Officer with a Laughing Girl* and *A Maid Asleep*, Vermeer would have completed both in the second year of the arrangement with his patrons, namely 1659.

Every element of each composition is repeated or echoed in its pendant. Each picture shows a woman in the act of gauging or measuring. One is carefully pouring milk, the other holding up a small set of scales and waiting for the weighing pans to settle. The women are shown standing, each wearing a headdress of white. Both are half-turned towards the viewer and have downturned eyes, suggesting absorption in their own thoughts as well as in their tasks. Their arms and hands, although engaged in different activities, are in nearly identical positions. Both women exist in the same relationship of scale to the rooms they occupy.

The most striking of the many similarities between the two pictures – the more so because at first sight it seems so odd and arbitrary – is the small single nail that protrudes from the pockmarked plaster wall behind each woman, in each case a little to the left of her and about a foot above head height. Each nail is exactly the same size as the other, has been driven into the wall to exactly the same depth and sticks out of it at exactly the same angle.

Each picture, each woman, is the mirror image of the other. Between them, they complete one another. This pattern is both the beginning of their meaning and its end. The woman weighing is reflecting, assessing, meditating. The woman pouring milk is preparing a meal, working for others, measuring their needs. One woman is thinking, the other is doing. One is contemplative, the other is active. We have met these women before, in different clothes, in a different setting and a different place. We have met them in the Bible and we have met them in another painting by Vermeer. Are they not Martha and Mary, the Active Life and the Spiritual Life, in another guise?

At one and the same time they are Dutch women in the here and now, real people living real lives. The woman weighing is richer than the woman pouring milk, to judge by her jewellery and her blue jacket trimmed with fur, so she has to work harder to get to heaven. The Day of Judgement is on her mind: on the wall behind her is a doom painting thronged with figures of the damned and the saved, beneath Christ the Judge pronouncing his final sentence. But she has no worries on that score. There is a beatific smile on her face, not dissimilar to the smile on the face of the sleeping woman in *A Maid Asleep*, who is perhaps Maria de Knuijt herself. She has looked herself in the eye in the mirror on the wall. She has renounced her jewellery, taken it off and placed it on the table, together with some coins. All will go to charity. Having resisted temptation, her soul remains spotless. According to the description in the auction catalogue, the woman should be weighing gold, but in fact her scales are empty. That is not to say that she is weighing nothing, just that what she is weighing happens to be invisible. She has put her conscience in the scales, and found it so light as to be weightless. She has done no evil, bears no burden of sin.

Such an image might have spoken clearly and directly to pious women gathered in Maria de Knuijt's house, giving a shape and a direction to their prayers, also perhaps acting as a catalyst for their discussions or free prophecies. In the shared traditions of Remonstrant and Collegiant Christianity, much weight was given to the importance of the conscience. Jacobus Arminius's motto had been 'A good conscience is paradise.' Dirck Rafaelsz Camphuysen, evangelist of the Collegiant movement, had declared the conscience to be everyone's personal priest, making the actual priesthoods of the Church redundant. Camphuysen's commentaries describing self-judgement as a prelude to the judgements made by Christ may well have been in Vermeer's mind when he was painting the *Woman with a Balance*.[18]

The pair of women were evidently intended as role models, albeit of an elevated kind. Each represents one-half of a woman's best self. The *Woman with a Balance* embodies faith forever vigilant and also the private, reflective life. By contrast, the so-called *Milkmaid* (it was never Vermeer's own title) embodies the active, evangelical life. She stands for good works, for charity, for feeding others in both the literal and the spiritual sense. In the poor houses of the town a simple preparation of bread crumbled into milk was traditionally served to the indigent, whose teeth were too weak for more solid food. This is the dish she is preparing. While the milk she pours from the jug is real enough, it also calls to mind 'the milk of the word' which all crave 'as newborn babes' (Peter 1:2).

Likewise the bread on the table is knobbly, substantial, dusted with flour, but it also shimmers and sparkles as if blessed by divine light. It is a reminder of the bread on the table at the Last Supper and the loaves miraculously multiplied by the sea of Galilee, 'the true bread from heaven', which is belief and everlasting life (John 6). These are the gifts *The Milkmaid* brings: real food and drink for those who hunger and thirst, but spiritual food and drink too. On the floor at her back is a footwarmer, a symbol of lust according to the Dutch emblem books. A painted Cupid in one of the Delft tiles of the skirting fires off an arrow. These details tell us that she has put romantic love and its temptations behind her.

Performing good works and giving to charity were considered obligatory in Collegiant circles. The people who first gazed at these two pictures by Vermeer hoped to behave like the women depicted in them. In their meetings they prayed and reflected on their own conduct, like the *Woman with a Balance*; in the wider world, they emulated *The Milkmaid* by giving to others, spreading the Christian message of love and tolerance, and working for charitable causes. Maria de Knuijt specifically remembered orphans and the refugees of war in her will, while her husband served for four years as master of the *Kamer van Charitate*, administering lay poor relief in Delft.[19]

Woman with a Balance might almost be floating, so light is her presence in the room where we find her. *The Milkmaid* by contrast is sturdy, steadfast, grounded, the epitome of resilience and dependability. Her domain, like that of Martha in the Bible story, is emphatically the kitchen. She has the brawny forearms of a working woman, tanned by exposure to the weather, whereas the *Woman with a Balance* has slender arms and pale skin and occupies a grander interior, with a painting and a mirror hanging on its walls. The woman who reflects and the woman who acts might be in the same house, in different rooms and on different floors. They are the upstairs and the downstairs of Christian life.

The nail that protrudes from the wall in both pictures is also integral to their meaning. Vermeer may have found the idea for it in a portrait etching of the Mennonite preacher Cornelis Claesz Anslo done by Rembrandt in 1641.[20] The rough wall behind Anslo is unrelieved by

Vermeer probably knew Rembrandt's etching of 1641 portraying the Mennonite preacher Cornelis Claesz Anslo. The prominent nail in the wall was probably meant to symbolize Christ's Crucifixion. Vermeer included an almost identical nail in each of his own later pair of pictures *The Milkmaid* and *Woman with a Balance*, placing it at the exact same spot on the wall in each. (See Plates 28 and 29)

any detail save that of a single nail hammered into the plaster, which is so unusual and so similar to those in *Woman with a Balance* and *The Milkmaid* that it was probably Vermeer's source.

Rembrandt's nail had a double meaning. On the one hand it was a pun: the hidden Mennonite Church in Amsterdam where Anslo preached was nicknamed '*De Grote Spijker*', or The Great Nail, because the building was concealed behind a former ironmonger's warehouse on the waterfront, where nails were kept. On the other hand, it was a reference to the beliefs of a devout Mennonite. Like many Dutch dissenting Protestants, the Mennonites were apostolic Christians who asked of themselves not only that they believe in Christ but also that they try to imagine themselves back to his time and that of the apostles.[21] The nail in the wall is there to remind Anslo of the Crucifixion, when nails were driven into Christ's hands and feet, and to keep its image in his mind's eye.

The nail in the wall in Vermeer's rooms is there for the same reason. It tells us that the two women, as well as embodying the only virtues that matter, are also guardians of the memory of Christ's sacrifice. In any room where these women are found that nail will always be there in the wall, piercing the thin membrane of present time and going all the way back to the mystery of a moment when time itself was conquered and abolished. The wondrous, hushed stillness of the pictures amounts, itself, to a re-enactment of that miracle. Vermeer has poured so much love into creating these illusions of female presence – not just in the painting of the women's forms and faces but in the truly astounding painting of everything that surrounds them, every nuance of light, every object, every visual incident, down to the last chip or stain in the wall – that it is indeed as if the clock has stopped forever. Mortal lives align themselves, in moments like these, with the forces of the divine. The women live in real time but they dwell in eternity.

BOXES

Woman with a Balance and *The Milkmaid* would have hung side by side in the house of Maria de Knuijt. They would probably have been given a prominent position, serving as constant reminders of just what God required from his female followers. Precisely what role they may have played in Collegiant women's devotions cannot be known, although there may be a hint of it in the sales catalogue of the Amsterdam auction of 1696, at which the Van Ruijvens' collection of Vermeer paintings was sold. Of the twenty-one paintings listed, *Woman with a Balance* is the only one described as being 'in a box'. The box in question should not necessarily be thought of as a packing crate allowing for safe transport and storage. It was more likely a case or frame with shutters that could be opened and closed, like the wings of an altarpiece or the folding doors of a portable devotional picture.

It seems that at least two other pictures owned by Maria and Pieter were once displayed in a similar fashion. We know this because the notary's clerk who made an inventory of their collection in 1683 after it had passed to their daughter, Magdalena, observed that three of the eleven Vermeers in her front room were 'in boxes'. Because we know that *Woman with a Balance* was one of those, it seems likely that the same treatment was once given to its pair, *The Milkmaid*.

Before the Reformation the opening or closing of devotional pictures had been an integral part of church ritual throughout Christendom. It was synchronized with particular days in the calendar: Good Friday was a day for covering up images of Christ, hiding them in darkness as Christ had been hidden in the tomb; Easter Sunday was a day for revealing them once more, to celebrate his Resurrection. By the late 1650s such practices were a distant memory for dissenting Protestants in the northern Netherlands. But Maria de Knuijt and the women in her prayer and Bible-reading group may have adapted those old customs to their own different ways of worship, developing specific rituals around Vermeer's paintings, opening and closing them at moments that seemed appropriate to their meaning.

Woman with a Balance would seem an apt image to contemplate during a period of prayer and reflection, perhaps therefore at the start of a meeting. *The Milkmaid*, which is about going out into the world and performing good deeds, would seem suited to the end, when people were about to leave. Their iconography suggests that both pictures might have been hung in the front room of Maria's house, near the entrance. It also suggests a pattern to the opening and closing of the 'boxes' in which they were displayed. Might one picture have bade the women welcome, the other farewell?

We know of one other Dutch painter of the period whose works were displayed in this unusual way, namely Vermeer's contemporary Gerard Dou. In 1665 an avid collector of Dou's work named Johan de Bye put on a one-man exhibition of the artist's work in his home town of Leiden, in rooms hired for the purpose. Twenty-seven pictures by Dou were exhibited, twenty-two of which were displayed in 'boxes'. When visitors arrived all the boxes were closed, the pictures concealed so that they resembled shuttered windows.[22] Anybody wanting to look at one would have to go up to it and physically open the case. Their first experience of the work would be necessarily intimate and close-up. This was apt because Dou was famous as a *fijnschilder*, a painter of exquisitely detailed depictions of the world rendered with a miniaturist's precision.

It is tempting to believe that Dou's patron in Leiden, Johan de Bye, got the idea for his own 'boxes' from Maria de Knuijt and her husband. Born in 1621, he was just a couple of years older than Maria and Pieter. They were no strangers to Leiden and had many friends and associates there, at least one of whom was a prominent Remonstrant with close links to the Collegiant movement.[23] De Bye was the public face and voice of the Remonstrant Church in the city, so he was almost certainly a person they knew and saw. The Van Ruijvens and he had a great deal in common, including at least one mutual acquaintance. The most active collector of Dou's work in Leiden before De Bye had been Pieter Spierincx Silvercroon, who was related to Pieter Claesz van Ruijven, and whose art collection had helped to kindle De Bye's enthusiasm for Dou's work.

In matters of religion, too, they would likely have seen eye to eye. Johan de Bye was a pious man who gave his time and money to charity. Seemingly like Pieter and Maria, he held meetings for prayer and worship at his home. And while they lived in the house next door to the hidden Remonstrant church in Delft, his house was itself the main place of worship for Remonstrants in Leiden. Leiden was a less liberal city than Delft or Rotterdam, its magistrates openly hostile to the still young Remonstrant Church. De Bye's requests to fund and build a *schuilkerk* in the heart of town where he and other followers of Arminius might worship were repeatedly refused by the public authorities, who belatedly granted permission for a hidden Remonstrant church only in 1672, the year of his death. In the interim he made his own house available for Remonstrant religious services, and possibly hosted other kinds of religious meetings there too. The authorities punished De Bye for his defiance by having him removed from the board of the St Elisabethgasthuis, a charity for infirm and homeless women to which, as a good Remonstrant, he had devoted much of his energy. Following public riots outside his home in 1662 and 1664, the magistrates further ordered that the pulpit and other items of church furniture that had been installed there for Remonstrant services be removed.[24]

This was why he hired rooms on the Breestraat, well away from his home, when putting on his public display of Gerard Dou's work the following year. There is no indication that Dou's paintings for Johan de Bye had any strong religious significance for him. De Bye may simply have put them in cases to create a new and interesting experience for visitors to his exhibition, which was in itself a novelty: it has been described as the first one-man show in the history of Western art.[25] The fact that they are the only Dutch paintings known to have been displayed in 'boxes' other than those of Vermeer, which they post-date by several years, suggests that De Bye may have visited Maria and Pieter at home in Delft, seen their altarpiece-style frames and had them copied by his own frame-maker. He and the Van Ruijven family lived fairly close to one another. Using the highly efficient Dutch public-transport system, the *trekschuit*, it was a door-to-door journey from his house to theirs of three and a half hours. It is possible that De Bye also stole the supposedly unprecedented idea of a stand-alone exhibition of work by a single artist from his friends in Delft. After all, the main room of their house, unlike any other, was full of pictures by just one painter.

'GOOD FRIENDS CAN ALWAYS OBTAIN SOMETHING BEAUTIFUL'

The house where Vermeer's pictures hung seems to have been closed to everyone except those sharing the tolerant beliefs and liberal Christian ethics of its owners. So it should come as no surprise that, whenever we discover someone who did know about Vermeer's pictures, that particular someone turns out to have been a Remonstrant, a Collegiant or some other type of dissenting freethinker. The network of those who were familiar with Vermeer's work, or knew about its existence at all, was limited by the milieu for which it was made. There is no better demonstration of this than the story of what befell Lots 1 and 2, *Woman with a Balance* and *The Milkmaid*, when they came under the hammer at the Amsterdam auction of 1696.

Almost forty years after they had been painted both pictures were sold to the same bidder, a person who seems to have known a great deal about them. For a start, he recognized that they were a pair, which makes it likely that he understood how they related to one another, and therefore knew what they really were: part of a unique programme of pictures done for a private house in Delft to assist a group of Collegiant women in their devotions. He clearly believed that they were among Vermeer's best pictures and was prepared to pay high prices to get them. On the day of the sale he secured the first of the pair, *Woman with a Balance*, for 155 guilders. He had to go 20 guilders higher to get *The Milkmaid*. Only one other picture would fetch more at the auction, namely the much larger *View of Delft*, which sold for 200 guilders. But the bidder on Lots 1 and 2 showed no interest in that, or anything else. He had got what he came for.

We know the name of this man. He is in fact the only bidder at the auction of Vermeer's pictures whose identity it has been possible to establish.[26] He was Isaac Rooleeuw ('Red Lion', a Dutch rebel name by origin) and he lived in Amsterdam, where he was known as a connoisseur of paintings as well as a close friend of Jan van Beuningen, one of the most prolific art collectors in late seventeenth- and early eighteenth-century Holland.[27] Rooleeuw's own patient and fastidious approach to buying pictures is conveyed by a letter of his written in 1710, to an acquaintance in Flanders, in which he comments on how hard it is to find good things in the Amsterdam art market – unless, that is, one brandishes the name of a certain famous collector: 'What one finds here in private hands is not exceptional; or what is good is not for sale, unless by chance, in time. However, in the case of Mr Van Beuningen, presently the greatest art lover of the city ... good friends can always obtain something beautiful.'[28]

This is the letter of a man used to waiting for apples to drop from the tree, who knows that good things are not to be had 'unless by chance, in time'. Rooleeuw must have waited a good while to acquire his two pictures by Vermeer. He had probably known about them for years. The steer would likely have come from his own kin and their circle of friends. They were the kind of people, few and far between, who would have known about Vermeer.

More or less every member of Isaac Rooleeuw's immediate family was a Collegiant. Collectively the Rooleeuw clan contributed as much to the movement during the first half-century of its existence as any other family in the Dutch Republic. They were founders and participants in one of the largest Collegiant assemblies, contributed extensively to Collegiant biblical studies, composed music and arranged hymns to be sung at Collegiant meetings and were the principal benefactors behind the construction of the Collegiant headquarters in Amsterdam, namely the orphanage and meeting house known as the *Oranje-Appel*.[29] The family business was the cloth trade, including the manufacture, dying and merchandizing of textiles. Import and export was at the heart of what they did (for money, that is). They travelled widely and had business interests in the major port towns of Holland, including Rotterdam and nearby Delft. Wherever they went they made contact with their fellow Collegiants, attending meetings or holding discussions with them about how to help the movement grow. The Rooleeuws in Amsterdam had links to groups in Rotterdam and its environs.

If anyone was likely to have heard about Vermeer's paintings on their own family grapevine, that person was Isaac Rooleeuw. Someone close to him, perhaps more than one person, had seen those pictures in Delft and been sufficiently impressed by the experience to pass the news on. It could have been a family member, or perhaps a friend: Jan van Beuningen, the art collector, was also from a family with close links to the Collegiant movement. Whoever it was may have been particularly struck by this particular pair of pictures, making it clear that those were ones to buy should they ever come up for sale. Isaac Rooleuw may then have tracked their progress after they passed from Pieter and Maria to their daughter, Magdalena, and then to her husband, Jacob Dissius. However it came about, when Dissius died and the pictures were sent to Amsterdam to be sold, he was waiting for them.

The supposition that most of Vermeer's paintings were devotional pictures, painted to assist Collegiants in their worship, is greatly strengthened by the discovery that someone so strongly linked to the Collegiant movement should have been the first documented person to acquire any of them on the secondary market. Not only was Isaac Rooleeuw the first person in history to buy paintings by Vermeer at auction, he may also have been one of the last people to understand what those paintings were, what they meant, and why they belonged together.

Having had the insight to purchase *Woman with a Balance* and *The Milkmaid* as a pair, Rooleeuw did not enjoy them for long. Within five years he had filed for bankruptcy. On 20 April 1701 his two Vermeers were sold once more at auction, along with the rest of his picture collection. This time they were not bought as a pair, but broken up. *The Milkmaid* was purchased by someone called Jacob van Hoek, *Woman with a Balance* by a certain Paulo van Uchelen, at which point they began their separate journeys through the world and through time. Perhaps one day they may be reunited.

ALL SORTS

The Collegiant movement was nothing if not broad. The plainspeaking Martha Ariens, who wanted freedom to read the Bible with her women friends, was part of it. So too was Baruch Spinoza, the outstanding philosopher of the early Enlightenment. In short, there was no such thing as a typical Collegiant.

So where should we place Vermeer, Maria de Knuijt and Pieter Claesz van Ruijven on the spectrum of Collegiant Christianity? Such evidence as we have suggests that they were conservative in their religious beliefs, however radical their methods of worship may have been. Maria's devotional practices probably included periods of intense private meditation as well as meetings with friends to read the Bible and prophesy on its meanings, to pray and make music. She probably thought of her gatherings as attempts to replicate those of Christ's earliest followers. Many Collegiants were apostolic purists, for whom the highest goal was emulation of the apostles or their female counterparts, such as Mary Magdalene.

Such shades of belief are expressed in the paintings of Vermeer. Many of his pictures for The Golden Eagle also reflect the highly personal and meditative forms of Christianity developed by Dutch spiritualists such as Coornhert in the late sixteenth century. The painter and his patrons are unlikely to have seen themselves as religious rebels or revolutionaries. They may have adopted Collegiant practices primarily to make a space where they might communicate as directly as possible with Christ, as they imagined him to be. It is perfectly possible that they did not even think of themselves as Collegiants by definition, but as dissenting Christians who sympathized with Collegiant ideas among others. Dutch nonconformist religion was so fluid and open-ended that none of these possibilities can be ruled out.

It seems clear from *Officer with a Laughing Girl* and other pictures that the painter and his patrons were strongly opposed to war in all its forms. In that respect they would have had much in common with the Waterlander Mennonites, who were a significant presence at Collegiant meetings in nearby Rotterdam.[30] But we know that Maria, Pieter and Johannes stopped short of the Mennonites' embrace of non-resistant pacifism. Vermeer's possessions included a soldier's pike, breastplate and helmet, while the records of the *Schutters* guild in Delft tell us why he needed them: he was a *wachter* or watchman in the civic militia of the town, a foot soldier in the home guard. Pieter Claesz van Ruijven was also a militiaman, as was Vermeer's brother-in-law Antony van der Wiel. It was one of the few civic roles open to Remonstrants, who were generally barred from public office (the other exception being charity work). Vermeer and his friends and family were prepared to use force, if only to defend themselves and those whom they loved.

Pieter and Maria's attitude to adult baptism is less easy to determine. They christened their daughter, Magdalena, at Delft's Oude Kerk on 12 October 1655, a few days after she was born, but may have done so out of respect for family tradition or to allay any suspicions the Reformed clergy might have entertained about them: many Collegiants attended Reformed Church services for that reason.[31] In light of Maria's apostolic beliefs it seems likely that she would have wished Magdalena to be baptized for a second time, with greater solemnity, when she came of an age to make her confession of faith. This may

A Collegiant baptism in Rijnsburg. Many Collegiants believed that the decision to enter fully into a Christian life could only be made in maturity, so they practised adult baptism by full immersion. Vermeer's *Girl with a Pearl Earring* may have been painted to mark the baptism of his patrons' daughter, Magdalena van Ruijven, at the age of twelve or thirteen.

have happened at the Collegiants' Pentecost meeting at Rijnsburg when she was about twelve years old, so in the summer of 1668. Baptism preceded Communion during the Pentecost celebrations and was an established practice among the Collegiants by that date. It was one of the reasons they met in the summer, when the water in the outdoor pool they used was bearable. There are no lists of the names of those baptized for the simple reason that the Collegiants kept almost no records of their activities.

Maria is likely to have been less aggressively evangelical than her counterpart Martha Ariens in Rotterdam, who openly invited people she met at market or in other public places to attend her own meetings. The Reformed Church in Delft was run by a notably tough council, whose ministers were on the lookout for Collegiant activity and would have come down hard on anyone publicly recruiting for the so-called

'Socinians'. The people attending Maria's gatherings may have been drawn mostly from her friends in the Remonstrant church, their numbers deliberately limited. Such a small and discreet group need not have concerned Delft's Calvinist ministers, even if they had found out about it. Maria and her friends are likely to have worshipped at the hidden Remonstrant church as well as at her home. If the house meetings were timed to coincide with the end of Remonstrant services, it could hardly have been more convenient: turn right out of the alleyway leading from the church to the street, take five steps and you were there.

EDIFICATION

Another early pair of pictures painted by Vermeer for the house on the Oude Delft can be identified from the Amsterdam auctioneer's catalogue of 1696. Once again they were lotted sequentially. They were Lot 32, described in the catalogue as 'A view of a house standing in Delft', and Lot 33, 'A view of some houses'. The first vanished without trace after going under the hammer and is now presumed lost. The second is in the collection of the Rijksmusem and has long been known as *The Little Street*. It was probably painted in about 1660.

Numerous failed attempts have been made to locate the scene depicted in the painting, which has been variously identified as a view from a rear window of The Mechelen Inn, a depiction of step-gabled houses on the Voldersgracht, a topographical record of buildings on the Nieuwe Langendijk, and (in laborious detail) a portrayal of the house on Vlamingstraat once owned by a great aunt of Vermeer's named Ariaentgen Claes van der Minne, a tripe butcher who cleaned and prepared pig's intestines on those same premises.[32]

The chasing of such wild geese is unnecessary. Vermeer was not a topographical artist, a painter of random buildings represented for the sake of picturesque effect or as family mementos. His pictures for Pieter and Maria spoke to their religious convictions. So if he were to create a picture of a particular place to hang on the wall of their house, that place would have to be infused with religious significance for them. In all of Delft there was only one location that Vermeer could have thought, or been asked, to paint for his patrons. *The Little Street* depicts the hidden Remonstrant church on the Oude Delft, together with the houses adjacent to it, including that of Pieter and Maria themselves. Comparison of the picture with the present and past topography of the town bears this out.

A great deal has changed in Delft since Vermeer's lifetime, but the corner occupied by the Remonstrant church is still much as it was when he painted it. The canalside houses that he depicted have been remodelled but they are still in situ and the church itself is still there, albeit deconsecrated. Although it was rebuilt in the nineteenth century it occupies the same footprint as the building where Vermeer and his patrons probably worshipped, and is similar in appearance to it, being a modest two-storey structure large enough for a congregation of about 400 people. It remains hidden, even more so now than in Vermeer's time, because the gap between the houses in front of it has been built over. Having originally been converted from a malting house set behind the main street frontage, possibly with funds provided by the Van Ruijven family's brewing business, it exists in the same relationship to the façades of the houses along the canal as it has for centuries. To get to it you have to pass through a door set into the street front, which leads to an alleyway of about twenty yards in extent. At the end of that alley is a second door, which lets you into the church.

Nearly all of this is visible in Vermeer's painting and what is not can be inferred. On the left of his composition at street level we see a weathered black door set into a rounded arch. Behind it is the alleyway, blocked from sight but architecturally implicit, that still leads to the church today. The church itself is the foremost of the buildings in the left middle distance of the picture, behind the street façade. Its roof slopes at the same angle and has the same square-topped gable as that of the church that has replaced it. In Vermeer's painting, the diagonal formed by the eaves of the church bisects the section of brick wall above the square-topped archway belonging to the house next door. The concealed alley leading to the hidden *schuilkerk* is mirrored by an open passage running alongside the neighbouring house. The entrance to that passage is a square-topped archway with no door, through which we can see a woman with a broom.

The same arrangement of buildings, on the exact spot of the Remonstrant church, is recorded in a map of Delft published by the cartographer Joan Bleau in 1649, about eleven years before Vermeer painted his picture. When mapping the houses on the north-east side of the Oude Delft between Butter Bridge and Pepper Street, a substantial block, Bleau registered a single alleyway piercing the street façade and giving pedestrian access to the buildings behind. As his map shows, that alley's function was to act as a conduit to the hidden church. Despite working on a tiny scale, the cartographer even managed to indicate that the canalside entrance to the passage was guarded by a door set into a round-topped arch: the same black door that Vermeer painted.

Behind the large house to the right of the church, Bleau placed a patch of green. Dead centre of Vermeer's painting a few sprays of foliage creep out from behind the left edge of that same house, at tree height, hinting at the presence of a concealed garden in the place indicated by the map-maker.

In the picture, as most likely it was in reality, the house with the garden is a grand one, with many tall windows of leaded glass and a castellated façade. Dwelling and warehouse combined, it would originally have been the residence of a merchant who needed access to the canal for loading and unloading goods. It must already have been about a hundred years old when Vermeer recorded its appearance, to judge by its architectural style and weathered brickwork. The house survives in a reduced form and altered, without castellations but preserving its original stepped shape. It is described in the Dutch state register of historical monuments as a high-gabled warehouse with many windows, of late sixteenth-century construction.[33] While similar to the building in Vermeer's picture it is not identical, which is hardly surprising given the centuries separating then and now.

This was a type of building once common on the Oude Delft. A three-storey mansion of similar size and design, including the same castellated façade and the same tall, thin central doorway, once stood in the same street less than a hundred yards away on the opposite side of the canal: the topographical painter Jan van der Heyden included it in his view of *The Oude Delft Canal and the Oude Kerk* of 1675, now in the National Museum in Oslo. The house in Van der Heyden's picture may have been erected by the same builder-speculator responsible for the house in Vermeer's painting. But the possibility cannot be ruled out that the painter borrowed elements of the building just down the street, such as its castellations, to make his own depiction of a merchant's mansion seem a little smarter. Pictures of particular places need not be faithful in every detail, as Canaletto's views of Venice demonstrate.

We know that Pieter Claesz van Ruijven and his wife lived in a grand home next door to the hidden church, so it might be assumed that the tall red castle of a house given such prominence in the picture was theirs. But it was not. The Golden Eagle is on the other side of the picture, immediately to the *left* of the black door leading to the church, cropped in such a way by the edge of the composition that less than a quarter of it is visible. While the big red house is open to the world and full of activity, with a woman at her work in the alley, children playing on the front step and another woman sewing in the doorway, this other house seems a more private place, and all the more tantalizing for that. If only we could walk into the picture and peer through the leaded panes of its windows, we would see paintings by Vermeer hanging on the walls inside. Just below those windows there is a rectangular patch of whitewash on which he has emphatically signed his name, in bright red paint.

One thing made particularly clear by the painting, now that its location has been identified, is just how intimately the home of Vermeer's main patrons related to Delft's church of the Remonstrants. Strictly speaking Pieter and Maria's house was (and still is) not next to the church but directly in front of it, like a porter's lodge. Anyone going to service would have had to walk through part of their property to get there. Vermeer has emphasized the commonality between the two buildings by making both seem inconspicuous and reticent. Pieter and Maria's house is shown as little more than an inscrutable fragment bearing the artist's monogram, while the Remonstrant church is so tucked away that only a part of its roof is actually visible.

If it is possible to call attention to the imperceptibility of something, Vermeer has done so in his depiction of the hidden church, which is so hidden that no one would notice it if they did not already know it was there. There was a point to this. Those who had founded the Remonstrant Church as a separate Protestant denomination, in the early 1620s, had made it clear that, since humility was one of their core values, it should also be expressed in their church buildings. As Simon

Episcopius put it in *The Remonstrant Confession*, 'far be it that the character of a true church would be localized in things which the world is accustomed to value ... namely, antiquity, majority, external splendor of congregations'.[34] An old and splendid building to which well-dressed multitudes flock was the Remonstrants' epitome of the Church Magnificent, therefore the Church Corrupt. The corollary of that was the conviction that a true Christian's place of worship should seem as poor as Christ and the apostles themselves. That is how Vermeer chose to present the Remonstrants' own church in his own native town.

Even though to him and his patrons this was an important place, he depicted it emphatically and with a form of contrary pride as nothing much: just a building converted from a brewer's outhouse, lacking in visual distinction. Anyone knowing Delft would also know that less than a minute's walk away stood the great tower of the Oude Kerk, most recognizable of the city's landmarks and one of the two strongholds of the Reformed Church. It is still there today. Stand where Vermeer might have stood to paint the so-called *Little Street*, look left and there it is, looming over you. The contrast between one church and the other could hardly be more extreme.

In some respects it suited the Remonstrants to be a semi-suppressed sect whose churches were required by law to be concealed. In Remonstrant belief a church building ought to be self-effacing, because if it were anything else it would be a fraud: the real Church is not made of stone but of people who truly believe. To the Remonstrants, the measure of a church was its effect on the souls of the people worshipping there and living in its parish. This is the true theme of Vermeer's beautifully optimistic picture. The hidden Remonstrant church and the house that guards it are simply there: quiet, closed, almost unnoticeable. It is the spiritual energy emanating from the church that Vermeer wants us to perceive. That energy animates every corner of his picture, even the sky.

There are clouds above the roof of the hidden church, through which the sun is about to break. Stirrings in the heavens above are confirmed by many signs in the street below that this is a place blessed in the sight of God. The people in the grand house next door to the church are bathed in the light of that benediction. Theirs is a mundane utopia, but a utopia nonetheless. The women are just looking after the children and taking care of the home, sweeping and mending. The children are just together, engrossed in their game. But in a world frequently shattered by war ordinary moments like this are to be treasured. The implication of the picture is that the people in the grand house, quietly caring for one another, have absorbed the spirit of the unobtrusive little church next door. They are doing ordinary things but each one of them has been placed in a posture that a person might adopt while at their devotions. The stooping woman in the alley might be bowing her head in reverence. The woman bent over her sewing might be peering at a Bible. The children playing beneath a bench might be kneeling in prayer.

The hope enshrined in the picture is that this process of transmission will continue, and that the spirit of peace will move from house to house until all of Delft has been transfigured, then all the world. Delft's first Remonstrant pastor, Johannes Taurinus, had compared the building of a church to the construction of a house 'founded on inward truth rather than false ceremonies'. Such a house might be multiplied many times, until the heavenly city be built here on earth.[35]

The brickwork painted by Vermeer with such close attention to detail supports such thoughts. The painter dwells on the area that connects one property to another, the juncture of the square- and round-topped archways, showing evidence of past mends preserved like scars in the irregularities of its construction. The lines of the mortar on the façades of the houses, with the wavy lines of the cobbled street below, form a skein or web thrown across the whole painting, making a pattern that speaks of the collective enterprise involved in the creation of a street, a town, a community. We build each other's houses. We edify one another. Paul's words to the Corinthians were often read out loud at the meetings of the Collegiants: 'What then brethren? When you come together, each one has a hymn, a lesson, a revelation, a tongue or an interpretation. Let all things be done for edification.'

Vermeer may have painted or at least planned his picture from a room on the ground floor of a house on the opposite side of the Oude Delft canal, perhaps one owned by another Remonstrant who made it available to him. If so then even the point of view of the picture, its perspective, communicates fellow feeling. The neighbourliness of Pieter and Maria is gently indicated by the inclusion of their house and the stress placed on its protective relationship to the church behind. We have good reason to believe that their home was also a place of worship, where the message of the New Testament was shared by friends in the Collegiant fellowship and thereby spread to a wider world. This is implied by the vine that climbs vigorously up the façade of the building, proclaiming it to be a house of the Lord, inhabited by the faithful. 'I am the true vine,' Christ had told his followers. Vermeer has placed his signature at the spot where a person would stand to water that vine.

It might seem odd that the artist should have cropped his patrons' house so severely. Why did he not make it more of a focal point? The answer is that he may have done so, but in another picture which has gone missing. The lost pair to *The Little Street* was the preceding lot in the Amsterdam auction of 1696, namely Lot 32, described as 'A view of a house standing in Delft'. Might the single house depicted in that picture have been 106 Oude Delft, The Golden Eagle, the house of Pieter and Maria, with the vine growing on it, shown on its own and in more detail?

The second, missing picture would probably have been hung directly to the left of the picture that does survive, and composed to the same scale as a continuation of its view of the Oude Delft. If so the two paintings would have affirmed the double sympathy felt by Pieter and Maria for the Remonstrant Church and the Collegiant movement. In their world of belief, as in their daily reality, the hidden church and the invisible Church were side by side.

HIDDEN IN PLAIN SIGHT

Most writers on Vermeer have agreed that the artist changed tack early in his career, when he stopped painting religious themes and switched to more modern and secular subjects instead. There has also been general agreement that this turnaround took place around 1657, which happens to be just when he began working for his main patrons, Maria de Knuijt and Pieter Claesz van Ruijven.

Vermeer's work did change at this time, dramatically so, but not quite as suggested. It seems that he never stopped being a religious painter. The distinction that needs to be made is that his early works are religious pictures that look like religious pictures, whereas his later works are religious pictures that do not. They carry religious meanings but do not seem at first sight to be doing so, because they have been given the appearance of other, more secular types of painting. What might the reasons have been for this?

As freethinking dissenting Christians, Vermeer's patrons were part of a liberal tradition that had largely developed within Calvinism. Having rebelled against the stricter interpretations of its confession, people like Pieter and Maria still had much in common with members of the Dutch Reformed Church, including perhaps a distrust of explicitly religious imagery, which they may have considered idolatrous.

To anyone outside their circle Vermeer's pictures appeared to be nothing out of the ordinary. They looked like genre paintings, or topographical views of buildings, or portraits, all the while carrying their deeper meanings within like secrets. This element of disguise helps to explain why Vermeer's pictures have tantalized so many people for so long. They superficially resemble other Dutch paintings of the time, while nagging away at anyone who gives them a second look and wonders at their depths. Ever since Théophile Thoré rediscovered 'the Sphinx of Delft', perceptive admirers of Vermeer (Proust, for example) have felt that there must be something more to his pictures than meets the eye.

COMPANION OF JOY, MEDICINE OF SORROW

Music would have been an important part of any Collegiant gathering at Maria de Knuijt's house. After one of the women or perhaps a visiting man had read the text of the day, and after all had made their comments on it, the meeting would conclude with communal singing. The Psalms were a favourite. By all accounts the singing at Collegiant meetings was beautiful.[36] After the readings and interpretations and spontaneous opinions, the music brought resolution: many voices singing as one.

Another pair of pictures by Vermeer shows us what some of those musical gatherings might have looked like. Each shows figures playing instruments and singing, and each is set in a grand interior with a tall ceiling and decorative leaded glass windows, like those to be found in the houses on the Oude Delft canal. They take us inside the home of Maria and Pieter, or an idealized version of it, and allow us to imagine the harmonies to which the invisible Church once echoed. It is not quite the same as being able to walk into *The Little Street* and look through the windows of the couple's house, but perhaps the next best thing.

These two pictures may have been painted in 1661 or the following year. They were not identified as a pair by the Amsterdam auctioneer who sold them in 1696, although they clearly belong together, being almost exactly the same size and set in what seems to be the same room seen from slightly different angles. The first of the pair was sold as Lot 6, 'A young lady playing a clavecin in a room, with a listening gentleman' and is now in the Royal Collection, where it is known by the title *The Music Lesson*. The second picture was sold as Lot 9, 'A merry company in a room, vigorous and good', and is sadly lost, having been stolen from the Isabella Stewart Gardner Museum in Boston in March 1990, along with eleven other pictures, all so far unrecovered. The title generally given to it is *The Concert*. At least it can still be appreciated in photographic reproduction.

The Concert, which would have been hung to the right in the pairing, shows three people grouped around a harpsichord placed by the far wall of a richly furnished room laid with a floor of black and white marble tiles. Two of the figures are women making music. One is seated at the keyboard of the harpsichord, while the other stands and sings from a songsheet, and gestures as if to express the emotion in the music. Between them a man wearing a sash sits in a chair with his back to us. He too is part of the ensemble, and playing a lute: the instrument's distinctive pegbox, constructed at a right angle to its neck, is silhouetted against the open lid of the harpsichord and the white plastered wall at the back of the room. There is a painting of an Arcadian landscape on the harpsichord's lid, the composition of which is echoed in the landscape painting that hangs on the wall above the lady at the keyboard. The singing of psalms is in this way associated with open vistas that reveal an ideal world, perhaps an earthly paradise.

Above the head of the singing woman hangs a very different painting, the subject of which is difficult to discern because Vermeer has plunged it into deep shadow. It is a picture that still exists and is now in the collection of the Museum of Fine Arts in Boston: a brothel scene by the Dutch follower of Caravaggio, Dirck van Baburen, in which a procuress is pressing the services of a buxom lute-playing prostitute on a leering red-faced man. This same picture was once owned by Vermeer's mother-in-law, Maria Thins, in whose house he and Catharina were living by 1660.[37] The fact that he has transposed a picture hanging on the wall of his home to that of his patrons makes it clear that *The Concert* and its pendant cannot be literal depictions of the interiors of The Golden Eagle. The rooms may have looked much as they do in these two pictures, but not exactly.

Baburen's shadowed *Procuress* borrowed from another place is in the room because the painter needs it to make a point. The three figures lurking in its darkness, one of whom is playing a lute, are in profane contrast to the sacred gathering of music-makers. The singer and the lady playing the harpsichord are both wearing pearls, symbolic here of purity rather than vanity, which gleam softly in the light coming from an unseen window to the left. The white satin dress of the woman at the keyboard, directly illuminated by sunshine, makes shimmering patterns that evoke the shapes in a fire: Vermeer may have sought advice on how to achieve such effects from Gerard ter Borch, the Dutch painter par excellence of satin and its sheen. The scene is completed by a large viola da gamba lying in shadow on the floor, next to a table draped with a Turkish carpet on which rests another stringed instrument, namely a cittern. The musicians in the room are expecting others to join them.

The second picture of the pair, known as *The Music Lesson*, would have hung directly to the left of its pendant, as if continuing and expanding our view of the same one space. To the right of its composition there is a table placed at the same height as the one placed at the left edge of *The Concert*, reinforcing that sense of continuity; it too is draped with a heavy Turkish carpet, of similar colour and pattern to its twin. Once more the musicians are at the back of the room. We see a woman with her back to us, her face obliquely reflected in the mirror hanging above her head, playing a muselar virginal, an instrument with the same action as a harpsichord but with the difference that its strings are plucked at the centre, which produces a pleasingly rich tone but also squeezes the keyboard over to the right side of the instrument. The man who keeps her company is not her teacher but her companion in music-making. He opens his mouth not to instruct but to sing. Just behind him is another painting-within-a-painting, tightly cropped but still recognizable as a depiction of 'Roman Charity': the story of *Cimon and Pero*, the tale of a daughter who saves her imprisoned father's life by giving him milk from her own breast.[38] It was an image associated with good works and charity, being one of the *Seven Acts of Mercy* depicted by Caravaggio in a celebrated Neapolitan altarpiece.

The finely decorated virginal in the picture can be precisely identified. It was made in the workshop of Andreas Ruckers I in Antwerp in about 1640. There is one similar, created by the Ruckers workshop in that same year, in the collections of the Rijksmuseum in Amsterdam, albeit with a different inscription. The words on the virginal in Vermeer's painting are in Latin: 'MUSICA LETITIAE CO[ME]S MEDICINA DOLOR[IS]', 'Music is the companion of joy, the medicine of sorrow.' It would seem likely that Pieter and Maria actually owned the instrument shown in the painting.

Like most of Vermeer's other pictures, *The Concert* and *The Music Lesson* are misrepresented by their modern titles. Viewed as a pair they give us the impression of a Collegiant group of five people, gathered in a single space but distributed across two canvases. It is the end of a meeting, when by singing psalms they express their own togetherness, their fellowship in Christ, in the shape of a musical performance.

Strict Calvinism had all but destroyed Dutch church music by the time Vermeer was born. The *preciezen* believed that a love of music was akin to idolatry, so they banned instrumental music of any kind during their church services, allowing no more than a few short bursts of unaccompanied singing. Even in the congregations of most liberal dissenting Protestants, such as the Mennonites, the music tended to be rudimentary. Collegiants on the other hand took theirs very seriously, and it was only in their circles that Dutch religious music truly thrived.[39] Collegiant composers devised complicated musical settings for the psalm translations of writers such as Joachim Oudaan, which were first performed in Rotterdam and probably Delft too at around the time Vermeer painted these two pictures. Their model was the Baroque *basso continuo*, which required improvising a melodic or chordal accompaniment to a continuous composed bass line. The instruments that could provide that bass line, namely harpsichord, virginal, lute and viola da gamba, were essential to this strictly Collegiant form of music. All are present in Vermeer's paired pictures. His singers are probably singing a psalm in some complex arrangement.

Unlike a service in the hidden Remonstrant church, where a preacher might spell out the importance of mutual understanding in the words of his sermon, a Collegiant gathering was a living physical demonstration of Arminian tolerant values. Because so many different shades of Christian might attend, each of their meetings was a little model of the world at peace rather than war. Putting harmony in the place of discord was the Collegiants' reason for being, which is why the communal singing of psalms was one of the most distinctive expressions of their beliefs. The foundation stone of their movement was Jacobus Arminius's pacifist manifesto, *On Reconciling Religious Dissension among Christians*, at the end of which he had looked forward to a day when all Christians would walk together into the New Jerusalem, joyously singing Psalm 133 in unison.

Vermeer included himself in *The Music Lesson*, or at least a sign of his presence, in the form of the base of his easel, which is shown in reflection in the mirror on the wall. He is part of the circle, not just its resident artist: the same point had been made by his graffito-like signature on The Golden Eagle in *The Little Street*. The empty space in both musical paintings is emphasized by the accelerated perspective of their similar but not precisely matched marble tiles. A viola da gamba lies on the floor in each, waiting for its player to arrive or return. There is a sense of anticipation, of a void waiting to be filled. This is especially true of *The Music Lesson*, where there is also an empty chair beside the discarded viola da gamba, suggesting someone who has gone and needs to come back to bring things into perfect harmony. On the rucked-up carpet draped over the table next to the chair is a white porcelain wine jug with a tin lid. We have seen that jug and that empty chair before.

Men were often present at the women's meetings, but who might the two men be at this particular gathering? The man in *The Music*

Lesson, wearing black with white ruffs and collar, beating rhythm with a stick as he sings, might be none other than the man of the house, Pieter Claesz van Ruijven. It is tempting to think so, and perhaps not altogether fanciful: he has been placed right next to the painting of *Cimon and Pero*, a picture emblematic of charity, which would be apt in light of his documented philanthropy.

There is no way of knowing the identity of the man with the sash and stick who appears in the lost pendant picture *The Concert*. Apart from anything else he has his back to us. But we know the name of the person who may have introduced him to Maria in the first place. Each group like hers was just one small cog in the whirring machine of Collegiant activity. The man who coordinated the movements of that machine was one of the most significant figures in the life of Johannes Vermeer.

ADRIAN PAETS AND FRIENDS

Adrian Paets was the prime mover of the Collegiant movement in Rotterdam and Delft. He is the most influential Dutchman no one has ever heard of, and has claims to be regarded as the greatest all-rounder in the history of patronage. His centre of operations was the port town of Rotterdam, where he was a regent and a magistrate as well as the protector of a circle of friends who called themselves 'Erasmians'.[40] The friends revered Erasmus but their name was essentially a cover. They were Collegiants. From 1656 they met at the bookstore of François van Hoogstraten, who was the publisher of numerous Collegiant texts and the first translator into Dutch of Thomas More's *Utopia*.

Those who gathered at Van Hoogstraten's shop under Paets's patronage included some of the leading figures of the movement. Among them were the pacifist Johan Hartigvelt, whose book *The Truly Defenceless Christian* was an early manifesto for conscientious objection; the Mennonite merchant Jan Dionyssen Verburg, a stalwart defender of women's rights to prophesy; and Jacob Ostens, author of one of the first Collegiant texts published in Rotterdam, *Filial Love*, of 1651.[41] Perhaps the most dynamic member of the group aside from Paets himself was the tile-manufacturer, poet and playwright Joachim Oudaan, who was related by blood to pioneers of the movement: his maternal grandfather was Jan van der Kodde, while his father Frans Oudaan had become a leader of the Rijnsburg Collegiants in the late 1630s.

Any or all of these men may have been among those invited to speak at the womens' meetings arranged by Maria de Knuijt. The mysterious gentleman with his back to us in *The Concert* is possibly one or other of them. Adrian Paets encouraged those in his circle to go out and share their enthusiasm for the ideals of the movement. If he had been aware that a new group had been formed in Delft, he would probably have sought it out.

The Rotterdam friends recognized Paets as the centre of their Collegiant universe, the source of its gravity and energy. When he briefly left Holland for Spain on a diplomatic mission, his friend Oudaan marked the occasion with a poem lamenting that the sun had set on Holland and the light of God would no longer be seen there.[42] Born just a year before Vermeer, Paets was one of the chief orchestrators of the Collegiant movement during the period of its most rapid growth, from the mid-1650s to 1672. In 1664 he was accepted into the party of Johan de Witt, who was Grand Pensionary of Holland throughout the Era of True Liberty. De Witt was in effect prime minister of the Dutch nation, just as Johan van Oldenbarnevelt had been when the Republic was still in its infancy. Paets gained De Witt's confidence, becoming part of his intimate circle: De Witt's last letter would be addressed to him. Paets was also a force to be reckoned with in the world of Dutch enterprise and exploration. In 1668 he was appointed one of the '*Heeren 17*', or 17 Gentlemen, on the board of the Dutch East India Company.

His influence was felt in many fields but he was ruthlessly single-minded. Everything Paets did was directed to one end, the creation of a more tolerant and open society in which old sectarian hatreds and divisions would be dissolved. He had been brought up to revere Jacobus Arminius, having studied at the Remonstrant Seminary in Amsterdam. The Collegiant movement was precious to him because he saw in its meetings a pattern for the ideal society of which he and his friends dreamed. He believed that it was through the spread of such groups, each formed of true Christians from different denominations, that the invisible Church would prevail and the New Jerusalem be built on earth.

THE INVISIBLE CHURCH, 1657–72

Whenever Collegiant meetings were threatened, Adrian Paets acted swiftly. In the aftermath of the States placard of 1653, which had proscribed 'Socinian' assemblies and driven most Collegiants into hiding, he published a string of pamphlets condemning the 'rebelliousness, greediness and rigidity' of 'the new Calvinist Papacy' and proclaiming that all religious opinions no matter how irregular should be tolerated.[43] The ban was lifted, thanks in large part to his efforts.

By the same token, when Collegiant meetings started to flourish, as they did in and around Rotterdam from 1657, Paets was active at street level, offering support to newly formed groups in his own (unofficial) diocese. It is likely that it was Paets who sent Johan Hartigvelt to visit Martha Ariens at her home in that year, where he prayed with her so hard that the two of them 'swam in tears' together.[44] Once Martha had established her Collegiant group for women, Paets continued to send help and boost morale. Hartigvelt and another member of his inner circle, Jacob Ostens, were among the male speakers despatched to speak at the women's meetings. Hartigvelt also accompanied Martha's group on an outing to the Pentecost assembly at Rijnsburg in the summer of 1658. They travelled together on the *trekschuit*, gliding soundlessly along thirty miles or so of canal, locked in conversation. The journey, from Rotterdam to Rijnsburg via Leiden, took around seven hours, and they had to change *trekschuit* twice on the way. The first change was at Delft. Maybe they knew people there who joined them for the rest of the trip.

There is cause to believe that Pieter Claesz van Ruijven, his wife Maria and their friend the painter Johannes Vermeer were part of these same circles. Paets's friends are likely to have been their friends, so they may indeed have celebrated Pentecost together in Rijnsburg. Adrian Paets himself had frequent dealings in Delft at the local Chamber of the VOC (*Vereenigde Oostindische Compagnie*, the Dutch East India Company), a castellated fortress on the Oude Delft, just a couple of hundred yards down from Pieter and Maria's house. As a practising Remonstrant, he may have passed through the weathered black door next to their front door on his way to the hidden church. As a leading Collegiant, he is likely to have been welcomed through their front door as well.

There are documented links between the Van Ruijven family and that of Adrian Paets. When Pieter and Maria made their will in 1665 they did not use the services of their regular notary in Delft but travelled instead to the Leiden office of Nicolaes Paets. He was the son of one of the most prominent Remonstrants in that town, namely Adrian Claesz Paets, who was himself brother to Adrian Paets's father, Vincent Paets. So the Van Ruijvens' notary in Leiden was Adrian Paets's first cousin.[45] Johan van de Bye, patron of Gerard Dou, was part of the same circle of Leiden Remonstrants as Nicolaes Paets. Adrian Paets had friends and family in Leiden, and it seems that Pieter and Maria knew some of them, possibly all.

Few people are definitively known to have visited Pieter and Maria's house on the Oude Delft and to have seen Vermeer's paintings there. One such person is a man called Pieter Teding van Berkhout, who went to the house twice in the summer of 1669, meeting Vermeer each time and recording brief impressions of his pictures in his diary.[46] His relationship with the painter will be examined later, but at this point in the story we are more interested in his potential links to Adrian Paets. In 1668 Van Berkhout had married his third wife, Elizabeth Ruysch, who according to genealogical records was the daughter of Maria Paets, one of Adrian Paets's Leiden cousins. She was also the granddaughter of Willem Paets, a Leiden regent who had married into the family of Johan de Witt and helped advance Adrian Paets's political career. It is plausible to believe that it was Adrian Paets who arranged for his new in-law, Pieter Teding van Berkhout, to visit The Golden Eagle. He could only have done so if he were friends with Vermeer and the Van Ruijvens.

There is evidence too linking Johannes Vermeer to Adrian Paets and his circle, some of it circumstantial, some concrete. From the painter's death inventory of 1676 we know that he owned two *tronien* or character heads by Samuel van Hoogstraten, which aside from three pictures by Carel Fabritius seem to have been the only pictures by any of his contemporaries in his possession.[47] If Vermeer knew Fabritius, which seems probable, he presumably knew Samuel van Hoogstraten as well. He would then probably have known his brother, François van Hoogstraten, the radical Collegiant publisher at whose bookshop in Rotterdam Paets and his inner circle held their meetings.

There is also a possible connection between Vermeer and Paets's friend the ultra-Collegiant Joachim Oudaan. As a baker of tiles and a producer of pottery as well as poetry, Oudaan was entitled to register in Rotterdam's Guild of St Luke. He did so and in 1660 was made a headman, which meant being elevated to the guild's governing board of six, joining two painters, two stained-glass makers and one other maker of faience like himself. A year later Vermeer was made a headman of Delft's Guild of St Luke for the first time. Both men were young to be given such responsibilities, Oudaan thirty-four, Vermeer just thirty. It would be almost inconceivable that they never met.

Besides all this there is a document that dispels all doubt about whether Vermeer and his friends Pieter and Maria were part of the circle of Adrian Paets. The document shows that Paets knew Pieter Claesz van Ruijven and Maria, that he knew Johannes Vermeer, that he was a visitor to The Golden Eagle, the house on the Oude Delft, and that he saw Vermeer's pictures there. Finally it shows that Paets was himself one of Vermeer's patrons.

First published in 1974 by a scholar researching early eighteenth-century Dutch auctions, it is the catalogue of a sale held in Rotterdam on 27 April 1713, in which Lots 10 and 11 were, respectively, 'A painting representing a Mathematical Artist, by van der Meer' and 'A ditto by the same'.[48] The two Vermeers were lots carried over from the previous day's posthumous sale of sixty-one paintings from the collection of Adrian Paets II, son and heir of Adrian Paets I, leader of the Collegiants. The pictures had once belonged to the first Adrian Paets, and had then been passed down to his son.

The auctioneer, as auctioneers usually did, misdescribed Vermeer's paintings. They represent 'Mathematical Artists' only in the most general sense. The two pictures, now known as *The Astronomer* and *The Geographer*, represent male personifications of two sciences that were of great practical importance to the Dutch East India Company, of which Paets was a director. Paets surely commissioned the pair, and would have hung them somewhere prominently in the Delft Chamber of the VOC, perhaps the front entrance hall. They are among Vermeer's most intriguing works and will be looked at in more depth later. It is enough, for now, to know that Adrian Paets commissioned them.

No one asks a painter to paint pictures for them without seeing other examples of that painter's work beforehand, and the only place where anyone could see Vermeer's work in any depth was the house next to the Remonstrant church. Put this together with the circumstantial evidence showing they had friends in common, and it seems all but certain that Paets was on friendly terms with Maria de Knuijt and Pieter Claesz van Ruijven: friendly enough to be invited into their house. He was therefore among the few who knew about Maria's Collegiant meetings and the unusual project of having pictures tailored to the rooms in which prophecy was made. Having seen Vermeer's work on the walls of The Golden Eagle, Paets decided to commission a couple of pictures for himself. *The Astronomer* and *The Geographer* were signed and dated in the late 1660s but doubtless begun earlier. By the time he took delivery of them, Adrian Paets may have known Vermeer and his friends Pieter and Maria for quite a few years.

THE PHILOSOPHER

Aside from Paets's Erasmian friends, who else might Vermeer have met through his new patron? One intriguing candidate is Baruch Spinoza, the outstanding philosopher of the early Dutch Enlightenment. There are grounds to believe that the two men may have known each other, having been introduced by none other than Adrian Paets. Paets was patron to Spinoza, as he was to Vermeer.

Spinoza had appealed to Paets for patronage in late 1660 by sending him a draft manuscript of his *Tractatus Theologico-Politicus*, a work which argued among other things for freedom of thought and expression.[49] Paets had heartily approved of Spinoza's book, singing its praises in a letter to a close friend of his in the Remonstrant Seminary in Amsterdam. Paets may subsequently have helped Spinoza, a lapsed Sephardic Jew at odds with his own community, to move away from bustling Amsterdam to the village of Rijnsburg, heart of the Collegiant movement, so he could think and write in peace. Paets had friends in Rijnsburg and Spinoza moved there in early 1661, soon after soliciting the Rotterdam regent's patronage.

Spinoza's house still exists, on the Katwijklaan, now as then a peaceful street set away from the centre of the village. Its façade bears a quotation from Dirck Camphuysen in which is distilled the Collegiants' collective sense of living in an imperfect world while perhaps standing on the brink of a perfect one:

> Alas, if all humans were wise
> And had more good will
> The world would be a paradise.
> Now it is mostly a hell.

Not long after moving to Rijnsburg, Spinoza took up a new trade to make ends meet and fund his studies. He became known as a grinder of lenses and a maker of telescopes and microscopes. This too may reflect the influence of Adrian Paets, who had contacts in the Dutch East India Company which was, with the Dutch military, one of the main drivers of innovation in optics. Telescopes and other aids to vision, including the camera obscura, were first developed for sailors on voyages of exploration and for soldiers in the field. Two of the VOC's six companies, or chambers, were in Rotterdam and Delft, the centre of Paets's field of influence. Delft in particular had a history of innovation in optics.[50] If Paets had indeed enabled Spinoza's transition to village life, he may also have encouraged him to grind lenses and found him clients in towns nearby. It is an appealing thought: the skippers of Dutch trading missions seeing the New World through lenses ground by a father of the New Philosophy, all thanks to Adrian Paets.

Vermeer the painter of becalmed interiors and Spinoza the radical philosopher might not seem natural bedfellows. But as far as Paets was concerned everyone to whom he showed favour belonged to the same community. All of them were part of the invisible Church. Vermeer and Spinoza, Collegiants both, were no exceptions to the rule. That one happened to be a painter, the other a philosopher, would have been immaterial to Adrian Paets. He may with justice have viewed them as doing different but equally innovative versions of the same thing: Vermeer expressing ancient Christian truths in the codes of a new type of painting, Spinoza reaffirming ancient Christian moral imperatives in the language of avant-garde philosophy. In the imaginary gathering of Adrian Paets's many protégés they form a logical pair.

Doctrinaire atheists caricature Spinoza as a godless man who wanted to free mankind from religious superstition. But Spinoza himself angrily rejected imputations of atheism and wrote about his own 'God, or Nature' with deep reverence. We know that he did not believe Christ to be the son of God because, as he explained to Henry Oldenburg of the Royal Society, the notion that God had taken on human nature made no more sense to him than the proposition that 'a circle had taken upon itself the nature of a square'. But he did believe that Christ's divinely inspired morality contained salvation for the human race. He made this clear in the published edition of his *Tractatus*, the book he had sent in draft to Adrian Paets, in a passage surely written with his Collegiant friends in mind:

> To Christ the ordinances of God leading men to salvation were revealed directly without words or visions, so that God manifested Himself to the Apostles through the mind of Christ ... It may be said that the wisdom of God (i.e. wisdom more than human) took upon itself in Christ human nature, and that Christ was the way of salvation.

Moreover, when Spinoza completed the work by which he wished to be judged, the *Ethics*, he placed at its heart his own formulation of Christ's most difficult moral instruction: 'Hatred is increased by being reciprocated, and can on the other hand be destroyed by love.' Love thine enemy.

It is seventeen miles from Spinoza's house in Rijnsburg to the Remonstrant church in Delft. For Spinoza it would not have been an arduous journey: an hour's walk to Leiden, then three hours more from Leiden to Delft on the passenger barge, no changes along the way. In 1663 Spinoza moved to Voorburg, which brought him even closer to Vermeer's home town: that village was just seven miles from Delft and served by its own *trekschuit* station. He may have made the trip a number of times to meet his patron Adrian Paets at the Dutch East India Company, so that he could deliver whatever optical instruments might have been ordered from him. Paets may have asked Vermeer to join them on one or more of those occasions, the more so on account of the painter's apparent interest in optics and lenses.

For his own part Spinoza dabbled in painting. He was also a gifted amateur draftsman, according to John Colerus, a Lutheran minister who knew him well: 'he apply'd himself to Drawing which he learn'd of himself, and he cou'd draw a Head very well with Ink, or with a Coal.

I have in my Hands a whole Book of such Draughts, amongst which are some Heads of several considerable Persons who were known to him, or who had occasion to visit him.'[51] One drawing in that book or portfolio was a self-portrait of Spinoza as a fisherman. Colerus gave no detail about the rest. All the drawings disappeared hundreds of years ago, so we cannot know if one was a portrait of Vermeer.

If the philosopher and the painter did meet with Adrian Paets at the offices of the VOC on the Oude Delft to talk telescopes, it was the shortest of walks from there to the house where Vermeer's paintings hung. The author of the *Tractatus* could then have admired *Woman with a Balance* in the company of its creator, in Maria de Knuijt's front room. The adage inscribed on the open lid of her muselar virginal by Ruckers of Antwerp, 'music is the medicine of sorrow', is repeated no fewer than three times in Spinoza's collected writings.[52]

LIFE ON PAPISTS' CORNER

Away from his Collegiant friends Vermeer had another life, at home with Catharina and his family. It is not certain where the couple lived during the early years of their marriage, when relations may have been strained between them and Catharina's formidable Catholic mother, Maria Thins. As we know, Maria had barely consented to the wedding and may only have done so to remain on terms with her headstrong daughter. Perhaps Catharina and Johannes stayed at The Mechelen Inn, owned by Vermeer's mother, for some time after exchanging vows.

In light of what we now know about Vermeer's links with the Collegiants, it seems possible that he and Catharina may have fallen in love in the rooms where men and women took it in turn to prophesy. Liberal Catholics were attracted to the Collegiant movement, young female Catholics especially so. If Catharina was among them, she would have been a rebel twice over in her mother's eyes: first in her flirtation with a group of radical Protestant reformers, secondly in her choice of a husband.

Within four years of getting married, Johannes and Catharina had two daughters: the first, named Maria, was born in or around 1654, the second, Elisabeth, in about 1657. That was the year when Vermeer came to his arrangement with Pieter Claesz van Ruijven and Maria de Knuijt. With two more mouths to feed, the annual stipend from his new patrons would have come in useful, all the more so if the young couple were still alienated from Catharina's prosperous mother. Without her financial help, they would have struggled on the salary of a painter. Vermeer's mother could offer little assistance beyond board and lodging.

During those early years money was likely in short supply, which would make sense of why, in this little slice of time, Vermeer painted a few pictures – very few – for people other than his main patrons. We know they were done for other people because they do not appear in the auctioneer's catalogue of the 1696 sale in Amsterdam at which the Van Ruijven collection was sold off. Two such are *The Glass of Wine* and *Young Woman with a Wine Glass*, which were both painted for the same person or family and seem to have been conceived as a pair: a habit with Vermeer.

They are painted on canvases the same size as one another, albeit differently oriented, each representing a scene of modern courtship in which a predatory man is trying to get a vulnerable woman drunk. Each is set in an interior lit from the left by a window glazed in stained glass, which has been left ajar. The decoration in the stained glass is repeated in both, showing among other devices the coat of arms of a man named Moijses Jansz van Nederveen, a *cruytmacker*, or manufacturer of gunpowder, who had made a pile in the bad old days of the Eighty Years War. He died in 1624, but Delft's *Huizenprotocol* allows us to trace immediate descendants of his to a house in Delft called 'The Golden Cloth', where they were still living at around the time when Vermeer painted his two pictures.[53]

Those pictures were almost certainly done for the van Nederveen family. Their house, The Golden Cloth, would have contained the same dynastic stained-glass window duplicated across Vermeer's two canvases. We know where that house was: the south-west corner of the Oude Delft and the Peperstraat, or Pepper Street. That puts it on the same block as the house of the Van Ruijvens, just a few doors away. It would seem a stretch for this to be coincidence. The heirs of the gunpowder tycoon most probably knew their neighbours and had seen Vermeer's pictures hanging in their home. The commission may have been approved by Maria and Pieter as an exception to the exclusive terms of their own deal with the artist. The works were painted in about 1659 or 1660.

There is no suggestion that the owners of The Golden Cloth were part of any Collegiant circle, nor even that they were especially pious. So *The Glass of Wine* and *Young Woman with a Wine Glass* are rare examples of pictures painted by Vermeer that are what they seem to be. They look like genre pictures, or 'urbane elegant modern paintings', to use the terminology of Vermeer's own time,[54] and so they are: no codes or hidden Christian iconography here, or if so only the merest trace. They therefore allow us to measure the gap separating Vermeer the religious artist who painted for Pieter Claesz van Ruijven and Maria de Knuijt at The Golden Eagle from the artist he might have become had he worked for the market.

A note of moral disapproval appears for the first time in his work. It is particularly evident in *Young Woman with a Wine Glass*, where the suitor is characterized as a wincingly unctuous paramour imposing himself on a guileless and hopelessly inebriated girl. The man in *The Glass of Wine* is less of a comic turn, and more sinister, poised to top up the glass of his own victim as soon as she has drained it. Such seduction pictures were a staple of the times. Most are light-hearted but here the comedy seems distinctly sour. It is as if Vermeer could not quite suppress his inner Collegiant and paint genre pictures pure and simple. In each scene of courtship he includes the white porcelain wine jug we know from his paintings for the other house on the Oude Delft, the house more holy, and thereby makes his point. Seduction through wine is like a parody of holy communion. Love like this is a travesty of true love.

By 27 December 1660, at the latest, Johannes and Catharina were living in Maria Thins's large house on the Oude Langendijk, just east of the Great Market Square. They may have moved in considerably earlier, bearing in mind that they had named their firstborn after Maria back in 1654, but there is no way of knowing if her christening had marked a true rapprochement, or just the beginning of family peace talks. We know for sure that they were all in the same house two days after Christmas in the year 1660 for the sad reason that on that date 'a child of Johannes Vermeer' was interred in the Oude Kerk, with the registrar of deaths specifying the Oude Langendijk as the address of the deceased.

The couple had three children by that time. Over the next fourteen years, Catharina would give birth twelve more times. Three of those offspring would die in childbirth or infancy, but eleven would live. By the standards of the time this was an unusually high survival rate. Vermeer's mother-in-law must have played her part in it. Unlike most she could afford to keep her house warm and put plenty of food on the table, summer and winter. Dutch winters in the mid-seventeenth century, which has been dubbed a 'mini Ice Age', were brutally cold.

At the time of their marriage Johannes had one sister, Gertruy, and Catharina had one brother, Willem. They were both from small families, but the similarity ended there. As far as we can see his was in the main happy, and certainly close-knit. Hers was broken beyond repair. Her abusive and mentally disturbed father had lost all his money and was in terminal decline somewhere in Gouda. Her sister Cornelia had been cut down in the flower of youth by plague or another mortal affliction. Her one surviving sibling, Willem, regarded her with such ingrained hostility that the pair had not spoken for years.

The decision to have not just a large but a very large family is more likely to have originated with Catharina than with Johannes. Giving birth in the seventeenth century was hazardous, so it is safe to assume that a person as strong-willed as she was would not have consented to do it so many times had she not deeply desired many children: she was the one at risk, after all. Besides, what better way to obliterate the traumatic legacy of her old dysfunctional family, to erase the pain of its memories, than to create a new one so abundant that it would turn her whole life into a perpetual all-consuming present. To have a huge brood and to be its mother hen, always needed, always busy, was the opposite of what she had grown up with. Two decades later and shortly after Vermeer's death, Catharina would declare in a court hearing that 'she had never concerned herself further or otherwise than with her housekeeping and her children'.[55] She knew next to nothing about her husband's business affairs, she added. *Huyshouding ende kinderen*: that was her world.

Catharina's determination to have such a large family presented

Johannes with a problem. In the absence of inherited wealth no painter in a small town like Delft, no matter how gifted, could hope to feed, clothe and educate numerous children with the proceeds from his work. He probably supplemented his income by running the family art-dealing business, which he seems to have taken on sometime after his father's death in 1652, but it was not nearly profitable enough to cover his needs. The problem was magnified by Vermeer's determination, apparent by 1657, to forgo worldly success and devote himself to painting religious pictures for just one household. Having come to his arrangement with Pieter and Maria in that year, Vermeer subsequently made little visible effort to win further patronage or build a reputation outside the circles of the Remonstrants, the Collegiants and like-minded Dutch dissenting Christians.

The painter was only known within those networks of people and seems to have wanted it that way. Considering his prodigious gifts, this may demonstrate the depth of his attachment to the apostolic ideals embraced by Remonstrants and Collegiants alike. Imitate Christ every day: that was the constant instruction, or self-instruction, to follow. There was even a handbook to help with the task, namely *The Imitation of Christ* by Thomas à Kempis. Not only was it a book that had inspired Jacobus Arminius himself, but it enjoyed a resurgence at mid-century among Christians of all denominations, its popularity increasing in line with the millenarian fervour of those times.[56] On its first page we find the maxims by which Vermeer seemingly lived: 'It is supreme wisdom to come daily nearer to the Kingdom of Heaven by despising the world. It is futile to seek for riches or public approval.'[57] Might *The Imitation of Christ* have been among the thirty books recorded but not specified among the painter's possessions after his death?

The only obvious way to square Vermeer's principled unworldliness with Catharina's desire for a large and thriving family would have been to ask Maria Thins for help. Maria had a house big enough even for the number of children Catharina had in mind. She was also one of the richest women in Delft. Money would be no problem if she was on their side. But how to get her there?

Maria was tough, argumentative and a follower of the Jesuits. She was a supporter of the *Missio Hollandica*, the Jesuit programme of 're-education' that had been established in the southern Netherlands and Westphalia back in the 1570s, in the immediate aftermath of the meetings of the Council of Trent. True to the aggressive spirit of the Counter-Reformation, its goal was not only to promote the re-establishment of Catholicism across Protestant northern Europe, but to bring about the downfall of Calvinism and all other forms of dissenting Christianity. In the future of which the Jesuits dreamed, the Dutch Republic would be reabsorbed by the southern Netherlands, its Protestant population forcibly reconverted and made subject to the Spanish Crown. That dream remained alive in Maria Thins's time, and in her house. Jesuit missionaries and other envoys of the *Missio Hollandica* were welcome there, and called in regularly.

We know that Maria agreed to take Catharina and Johannes and their children back into the family home, and we know roughly when she did so: possibly as early as 1653, possibly as late as 1660, probably somewhere in between. But there had to be a price. It was her house, her rules. It is not hard to guess what the rules might have been. Catharina was to stop going to all Collegiant meetings forthwith (if she had indeed been going to them) and re-dedicate herself to the Catholic Church. Johannes himself was to live and worship as a good Catholic. The children were to be brought up as Catholics and educated insofar as possible by the Jesuits, whether in Delft or elsewhere.

Vermeer cannot have made a genuine long-term commitment to the Church of Rome, for the simple reason that he was part of the circle of Adrian Paets by 1667 at the latest. In the words of an authority on the Collegiants and their networks, 'if a person enjoyed the patronage of Adrian Paets, it is virtually certain that same person was either a Collegiant or a good friend to the Collegiant movement'.[58] As such, Vermeer was bound to espouse toleration and repudiate the authority of any single Church, whether that of Calvin or Rome, from which it follows that he could no more take on the beliefs of a Jesuit than a circle could take upon itself the nature of a square.

Yet somehow he had to come to an arrangement with his mother-in-law that both he and she could live with: it would be his second arrangement with a woman called Maria in a short space of time. His choices were limited. He could feign conversion and become a Nicodemite in his own home, thereby giving Maria Thins the illusion that his beliefs were aligned with her own. Or he could insist on his freedom of conscience and challenge Maria to accept him as he was. The latter is probably what happened, her agreement secured on condition that he give way on the children's education and other things that mattered deeply to her.

However well Vermeer may have played the part of an obedient son-in-law, the chances are that it would have been years before Maria Thins really accepted him. In the meanwhile she probably paid the bills, or gave him the money to do so, and he toed the line. All this inevitably condemned him to a lesser role and lower status than many a husband would aspire to in his own marital home. There is evidence for this in what we know of the home itself.

Thanks to the existence of Vermeer's death inventory we have a fairly complete picture of the house on the Oude Langendijk in which he lived for much of his married life. It was 29 February 1676, Leap Year's Day, when the notary came to visit. It took him several hours to make his lists, because he was thorough and the house was large, with a semi-basement, a ground floor, a first floor and above that an attic. There was an alley next to it, open to the sky, much like the one running alongside the red-brick mansion in *The Little Street*. As in that painting there was a water-cistern or well at the end of it, from which Maria's single female servant could draw water.

Above that alleyway and out of earshot of its bustle, there was a front room on the first floor facing north and looking out over a little canal to the front of the Nieuwe Kerk. Vermeer kept his working materials there, although he painted little during the last years of his life. The room contained two easels, three palettes, ten canvases and a mahlstick for keeping his painting hand steady ('a cane with an ivory knob on it'), among other artist's paraphernalia.

The rest of the house, to judge by its decoration and furnishings, was very much Maria Thins's domain. Coming through the front door, a visitor entered the *voorhuys*, a generous front hall in which were to be found a large linen cupboard, a bench and some chairs, an ebony mirror and, hanging on the walls, some pictures including 'a painting by Fabritius' and 'a large painting of Mars and Apollo in a bad black frame'. The notary was obliged to distinguish between the objects owned by Vermeer and those owned by his mother-in-law and Catharina, placing them in different columns. So we know, for example, that the Fabritius was Vermeer's and the mythological painting belonged to Maria. The *voorhuys* led to the *groote zael*, the great hall, which was the showpiece room of the house, and the one in which the pecking order of its inhabitants was most clearly spelled out.

There were a few things belonging to Vermeer here, including his *schutter*'s pike and 'iron armour with a helmet', as well as his family coat of arms, which was said to have been 'drawn' (by himself?) and 'two portraits of Sr. Vermeer's late father and mother'. Most of the other possessions listed under his name in the great hall were articles of bedlinen or clothing, huge piles of children's clothes especially, stored away in chests and cupboards. Maria Thins on the other hand was so amply represented, by paintings both dynastic and religious, as well as a plethora of other objects including sculpture and furniture, that the room was a veritable shrine to her pre-eminence within the family.

Hung prominently at the centre of the room and striking its keynote was a 'painting representing the Mother of Christ', the Virgin Mary, who was Maria's namesake and patron saint. It was not in her character to identify with the penitent Mary Magdalene, or Mary of Bethany, or any of the other more humble Marys of the New Testament. Nearby was a picture representing Maria's status as Great Mother, namely 'a painting of the Three Kings', or *Adoration of the Magi*, showing the monarchs of the world bringing their gifts to the manger and to the Madonna and her child.

This ensemble was completed by a statuette of Christ on the cross, carved from ebony, and 'nine red-leather Spanish chairs': more than enough to seat the small embassies of Jesuits working for the *Missio Hollandica* who dropped by at the house. Hung on the wall above those chairs, Maria had 'ten portraits of the lineage of the aforenamed Juffr. Tins'. Ten members of her dynasty to two of his: a crushing scoreline.

A similar margin of victory, again in Maria's favour, would have been registered in the birth records of the nearby hidden Catholic church where the babies of Catharina and Johannes were likely to have been christened. The couple's first four surviving children were all girls and all named after ancestors or relations on Maria Thins's side of the family. Little Maria was (of course) named after her grandmother, while her sister Elizabeth was named after one of Maria Thins's sisters, deceased, who had left the Dutch Republic many years before to join the nunnery of the Annunciates in Louvain in Spanish Brabant. Next came Cornelia, named after another of Maria's sisters as well as Catharina's own late lamented sister. Last of the quartet was Aleydis, named in honour of Aleydis van Rosendael, yet another member of the same large clan, an elderly spinster from whom Maria hoped (not in vain, as it turned out) to inherit a further pile to add to her existing one.

An unnamed child was buried in December 1661 so it seems unlikely that Catharina could have given birth again until the end of 1662 at the earliest. Only then, almost ten years into the marriage, was concession made to Vermeer and his forebears. The next three children were all given names that belatedly acknowledged their father's presence in the family. The first to arrive was possibly Beatrix, named after the painter's maternal grandmother Beatrix van Buy, who had died young and about whom little is known. This Beatrix was either followed or preceded by yet another girl, Gertruyd, named after Vermeer's only sister. A year or two after that, Catharina finally gave birth to a boy. His given name was Johannes. This Johannes Vermeer II was born in 1664 or 1665. He cannot have been born any earlier than that, because he was still specified as a minor, i.e. less than twenty-five years old, in a document of 1689.[59]

Some thought must have gone into the choice of his name. It was the convention to name a first-born son after his paternal grandfather, but in this case that was impossible because Vermeer's father had been called Reynier, which by coincidence was also the first name of Maria's abusive ex-husband, therefore off limits. Johannes it had to be. Together with the addition of Beatrix and Gertruyd, this did something to tip the balance of Christian names back towards the painter's ancestry. But the tipping went no further. The last three of the couple's children to survive infancy were named Catharina, Franciscus and Ignatius, the first named after her mother, the last two after St Francis Xavier and St Ignatius Loyola, founders of the Society of Jesus. The final score was a slight improvement on the tally of family portraits, but still marked a resounding victory for Maria, her kin, and her militant Catholicism: seven–three.

Anyone of the time looking through the whole list of names, certainly any friend of the Vermeer family, would have noticed a glaring omission. Yes there was a Gertruyd and a Beatrix, but not one of the seven little girls had been named after Johannes's mother, Digna Baltens. Digna it may have been who attended the Collegiant meetings that first drew Catharina away from her mother and away from the influence of the Jesuits, into Johannes's arms. Digna it was who had offered Catharina a roof over her head following her betrothal to him in the spring of 1653. By the mid-1660s Maria's attitude to her inn-keeping in-law had softened to the extent that she was prepared to purchase a little wine from Digna 'for medicinal reasons',[60] but the fact that she paid for it at all suggests that relations remained frosty.

Nonetheless the naming of Gertruyd and Beatrix and finally Johannes Vermeer II marked a significant shift in Maria's attitudes towards her son-in-law. Things seem to have changed in around 1662 or 1663. By then Vermeer may have played his part well enough, and long enough, for her to believe that he did indeed belong on Papists' Corner. A few years later, in 1667, she granted him power of attorney so that he could collect money on her behalf from notaries in The Hague, and as far afield as Amsterdam. But she always seems to have kept him on a tight leash financially, helping him pay some of his bills but not all of them, and not always in full. She may have drip-fed him his allowance. We know, for instance, that he was constantly in debt with the baker who supplied the household with the large quantities of bread required to feed its many hungry mouths. Even after his mother-in-law began to show Vermeer favour, she would not let him forget that without her, and her money, he and his family would go under.

Maria presumably paid for her grandchildren to be educated on condition that she had the final word on schools. Insofar as we know, they were all schooled in Delft and lived at home, with one exception. Maria decided that her first grandson, Johannes Vermeer II, was a special case. She felt that he had a calling, was destined for the priesthood. So he was to be sent away, given into the hands of those who would truly care for his soul. She sent him to the Oratorian College of the Jesuits in Mechelen, in Spanish Brabant, to be properly instructed in the doctrines of the one true Catholic Church: to be, in the plain literal sense, indoctrinated.[61] His schooling there would have started when he was seven years old.

Either Maria truly believed that her son-in-law was a committed follower of the Jesuits by the time she hatched the plan or it was the sternest test yet of his deferral to her as effective head of the family. Even a Collegiant as devoted to the principle of Christian unity as Adrian Paets found it hard to find a good word for the Jesuit priesthood of the Roman Catholic Church, habitually regarded by Dutch Protestants of the period (who had the scars to show for it) as the advance guard of the papal Antichrist. Paets's friend Joachim Oudaan was ashamed to say that he felt a violent aversion towards the Jesuits, regarding them as the élite but rotten corps of an arrogant, supremacist and thoroughly dangerous ecclesiastical institution.[62] Paets and Oudaan, as we have seen, were likely to have been close to Vermeer. How must Vermeer himself have felt when he learned of Maria's scheme to give his own son into the care of the Jesuit fathers in (of all places) Mechelen, once a rebel town subjected to atrocities by The Spanish Fury, yet now a Spanish stronghold? All we know is that he let his boy go. Perhaps it was his belief in the imminence of the End of Days that allowed him to do so. Soon enough all churches would be united, and all would be for the best.

The notary who wandered round the house on the Oude Langendijk in February 1676 also recorded poignant evidence of just how much care Vermeer took to keep the household running smoothly. Going into the *binnekuken*, or 'inner kitchen', on the ground floor, he listed all kinds of paintings and household goods including a seascape, a couple of character portraits 'in Turkish fashion' and 'two brown footwarmers'. He saw five other things too, and although he did not list them sequentially he should have done so because together they made up an ensemble: 'a large painting representing Christ on the Cross', 'one of Veronica', 'a pair of striped curtains', 'a little sideboard' and 'about seven ells of gold-tooled leather on the wall'. The picture of Christ speaks for itself. That of Veronica would have been a painting of Christ's tearful and bloodied face miraculously imprinted on her veil, an image popularized by the legend of the Turin Shroud. The striped curtains would have been there to conceal or reveal the painting of the Crucifixion. The sideboard was an altar. The gold-tooled leather was for the glory of God, seven ells amounting to about five square metres, which was a lot of glory. What the notary was describing, not so hidden away among the other bric-a-brac in the room, was a small Catholic chapel for private worship in the inner sanctum of the house.[63] Everything in it, moreover, he placed in the column reserved for the possessions of 'the late Sr. Joannes [sic] Vermeer'.

So Vermeer had created a Catholic chapel for the household, where visiting Jesuit priests might celebrate Mass or the whole family might gather to worship. He himself may have sourced and purchased the Crucifixion and the 'Veronica', although he could never have afforded the gold-tooled leather on the walls, so Maria must have paid for that. The effect would have been gaudy, congested and stifling. How inimical such a space would have been to Vermeer's own temperament can be gauged by trying to imagine any of his pictures – *The Milkmaid* or *Woman with a Balance*, say – hanging within it. The whole thing would have been done to Maria's instructions. Yet it was all set down as his personal property. He would disown it some years later, but that is not a story for now.

He made great compromises, but what alternative did he have? To earn enough money to keep his own family Vermeer would have had to paint for the market, rather than for the invisible Church on the Oude Delft, and therefore for God. That was out of the question, so he had no choice. He had to keep Maria onside so she would pay the bills that he could not and thereby keep his wife and children safe.

THE BEQUEST

Pieter Claesz van Ruijven and Maria de Knuijt probably knew Vermeer as well as anyone. His pictures for their house were painted to help her and her friends come closer to God, so she is likely to have had a strong say in the choice of their themes and subjects. They were pictures of a kind that had never been painted before, so there were no templates to follow, no standard iconography: nothing like the Adorations, Flights to Egypt, Crucifixions, Descents from the Cross and Entombments painted by the artists of the Catholic Church. Johannes and Maria de Knuijt were making it up as they went along so they were, perforce, collaborators, and had to be close.

In light of that we can safely assume that Maria de Knuijt knew all about Vermeer's home situation. She certainly knew all about Maria Thins, and probably had her own view of her. This came out in the will she made in the Leiden offices of Notary Nicolaes Paets, first cousin to Adrian, on 19 October 1665.[64] First, Maria de Knuijt specified how she would like the bulk of her estate to be divided in the event of both Pieter and her daughter Magdalena predeceasing her: one-third to the Orphan Chamber of Delft, one-third to the Charity Chamber, and one-third to the relief of the families of preachers displaced by war. As might be expected, the owner of *The Milkmaid* proved herself to be a philanthropist, a woman dedicated to charitable causes. Next, Maria made specific bequests of money to particular individuals, including one of 500 guilders to 'Johannes Vermeer, painter': the only bequest by a Dutch patron to a Dutch artist recorded in the archives of the seventeenth century, and a generous one too. All her other bequests were to blood relations, suggesting she saw Vermeer as family, or all but.

It was the condition she set on this legacy to him that tells us about her likely attitude to Maria Thins in particular and Jesuits in general. In the final draft the notary tacked on the following phrase to the terms of the settlement: 'However, in the case of Johannes Vermeer's predecease, the above aforesaid will be annulled.' In other words the money was only for him, the bequest non-transferable. In composing the document, Notary Nicolaes Paets accidentally left an earlier draft visible at this point, so the words can still be deciphered even though they have been crossed out: 'In the case of his predecease, it will pass neither to his children nor any of his descendants.' At some point Maria or someone else in the room must have decided that this smacked too much of strong feeling for a legal document and had it struck from the record, which makes it all the more informative. It tells us why the bequest was not transferable, and who in particular Maria de Knuijt did not want to get their hands on her money. She did not want Catharina to have it, nor Maria Thins, nor any of her Jesuit-indoctrinated grandchildren, even if they were the children of her friend Johannes.

Maria's words, imperfectly deleted, are all the proof we need that the milieu of Vermeer's friends and that of his family were worlds apart. He was one man when he was at home but quite another when he was with Pieter and Maria at their house on the Oude Delft, or with Adrian Paets and his Collegiant friends. Vermeer painted in twos and lived the same way. But his two lives were not a pair. They were opposites.

A JESUIT IN THE BAKERY

The one person we never meet in Vermeer's story is Vermeer himself. He is like the visitor in the painting of the woman sleeping, who has just pushed back his chair and gone somewhere else. We can see the most important place in his life, the house of his patrons on the Oude Delft, because he included it in a picture. We can see the paintings that he created for it because they still exist: *The Milkmaid, Girl with a Pearl Earring, The Music Lesson* and many others. We can see his family home on the Oude Langendijk, perhaps only in the mind's eye, but in clear detail: there is his armour, on display in the great hall; there is the Catholic chapel he made through gritted teeth; there are his things for painting, so real to us that we might almost pick up the mahlstick he left behind. But however close we come to him, he has always left the room by the time we get there. Gradually we learn to know him by his traces. His every absence has a different shape. It is by following those shapes as they shift that we track him.

There are only two eyewitness accounts of meetings with Vermeer, neither of which tells us anything about him, or at least nothing overt. He does not speak in either account. His appearance is not described. His pictures are barely mentioned and all too briefly assessed. But still there is much to be learned from each encounter. Context is often the only clue to what is going on in a life so hidden, even if it is the context of an apparent void or gap in our knowledge. Vermeer has many different ways of failing to be present. Each reveals a different facet of him.

The second eyewitness account is best kept for later in the story. The first was written by a Frenchman called Balthasar de Monconys. Here it is, his diary entry for 11 August 1663:

> In Delft I saw the painter Vermeer who did not have any of his works: but we did see one at a baker's for which six hundred guilders had been paid, although it contained but a single figure, for which sixty guilders would have been too high a price.[65]

This is a frustratingly truncated report of events. By general consensus, the one significant fact to emerge from it is that the artist was better known than might have been supposed. Monconys fancied himself to be a connoisseur, his journal being peppered with references to the private art collections he had managed to see on his travels. That a French art lover would go out of his way to visit Vermeer has been taken to indicate that the painter's fame had spread wide by the early 1660s.

This is unlikely to be true. Until 11 August 1663 Balthasar de Monconys had probably never heard of Johannes Vermeer. He certainly did not go to Delft on a pilgrimage to meet the artist and see his paintings. He was there on different business, in the company of two associates. The three of them had an appointment not with Vermeer but with his mother-in-law, Maria Thins, among others. Vermeer just happened to be in the house when they got there. When he was introduced as a painter, the Frenchman was intrigued. The rest is as recounted in his diary: after Monconys asked to see some of his pictures Vermeer replied that he had nothing in the house and sent him to see the local baker, Hendrick van Buyten, who had one on his wall.

The meeting was just a chance encounter. Insofar as the episode has a bearing on Vermeer's reputation, it merely confirms something we already knew, which is that almost no one had heard of him outside Remonstrant and Collegiant circles, Monconys included. But that is not to downplay its significance, because it tells us a great many other things about Vermeer, shining a spotlight in particular on some of the difficulties he had to negotiate while living on Papists' Corner. The Frenchman's minimal diary entry is not the small thing it appears to be, but the tip of an iceberg. If we set it in its proper context, if we understand who Balthasar de Monconys really was and what he was really doing in Delft, it fills in quite a few gaps in our understanding of Vermeer. To make a start we need to turn back the pages of the Frenchman's diary by about a week.[66]

At the beginning of August, Monconys was in Rotterdam, where he visited the famous bronze statue of Erasmus as well as various Reformed churches, which struck him as cavernously empty and, shockingly, whitewashed ('*toute blanchie par dedans*'). On the morning of the third, he visited the house of a cloth merchant who was also an amateur painter and an art collector, where he was shown works attributed to Titian, Rubens and Van Dyck, as well as a picture of a woman pouring wine by Gerard Dou, '*excellent Peintre de Leiden*'. Then he climbed more than 300 steps to the top of the great tower of the St Laurenskerk, where he admired the panoramic views of the surrounding countryside ('a vast prairie watered by an infinity of canals') before taking the *trekschuit* to Delft. Monconys was greatly impressed by the passenger-barge system, '*le bateau commun*', as he called it, finding it such a pleasant way to travel that he felt as though he got from A to B in no time. This first trip to Delft, eight days before he met Vermeer, was purely recreational. He took in the main tourist sights, visiting the tombs of Admiral Tromp and William of Orange in the Oude Kerk and the Nieuwe Kerk respectively. If he had known about Johannes Vermeer and his work, he would surely have arranged to meet him that afternoon, which had been earmarked for sightseeing. But he did no such thing. He hopped back on the *bateau commun* and by evening he was in The Hague.

When he went back to Delft for the second time, a week later, Balthasar de Monconys was no longer travelling as a tourist. The identities of the two men with him tell us that much. One of them was Father Léon, a Carmelite priest who enjoyed the special protection of the French ambassador to the Dutch Republic. A friend to the Jesuits, he often accompanied their missions, helping them to carry out their work under the cloak of his own diplomatic immunity. The other travelling companion of Monconys was another Catholic, and a military man to boot, a certain Lieutenant Colonel Gentillo. He was there for protection: a bodyguard for Balthasar.

As a boy Monconys had been educated (or indoctrinated) by the Jesuit fathers at the *Collège de la Trinité* in Lyon. As a man he was a zealot of the Catholic Church Militant: not just a supporter but a participant in the Jesuit missions in infidel territory. Monconys was in Holland as an agent for the *Missio Hollandica*, unobtrusively working for the day when the Dutch Republic would be brought down and the northern Netherlands reconverted to the Catholic faith. Hence his trip to Delft of 11 August, which had precious little to do with Vermeer and everything to do with the appointment of a new Jesuit priest to serve on Papists' Corner. The priest's name was Balthasar

27. *Young Woman with a Water Pitcher*, c. 1662. Vermeer painted this picture for the baker Hendrick van Buyten, who was born in the same year as himself and seems to have been a close friend from childhood: when times were hard Van Buyten provided Vermeer and his family with vast quantities of bread, year after year, all on credit.

28 & 29. *The Milkmaid* (*above*) and *Woman with a Balance* (*right*), *c.* 1659. Like many of Vermeer's pictures, these were clearly conceived and painted as a pair. There is evidence

that the Van Ruijvens originally displayed them in frames with doors that opened and shut, as if they were portable altarpieces.

30. *A Lady Writing*, c. 1665–7.

31. *Woman with a Pearl Necklace, c.* 1665–7. This may be the pendant to *A Lady Writing* (Plate 30), also painted for the Van Ruijvens. The subject has strikingly similar features and is wearing the same clothes, although the mood of the painting is different and more intense. Standing rapt before the mirror, the young lady holding a string of pearls seems hypnotized by a realization that has suddenly come to her.

32. *Girl with a Pearl Earring, c.* 1667–8. This is a portrayal of the Van Ruijvens' daughter and only child, Magdalena, shown in character as her namesake, Mary Magdalene.

33. Despite its modern title, *Study of a Young Woman*, c. 1667–8, is a finished work and may have been painted as a pendant to the *Girl with a Pearl Earring*. The subject is probably one of Vermeer's two elder daughters, Maria or Elizabeth. Looking from one picture to the other we travel from the macrocosm of divine love to its microcosm, a father's love for his daughter.

34. *Girl with a Red Hat*, c. 1668. The identity of the lady who sat for Vermeer in this picture is unknown. Vermeer worked for a very limited group of people, most of whom seem to have known each other. Might the sitter have been one of Maria de Knuijt's friends, who participated in the meetings held each week at her house on the Oude Delft?

35. *The Lacemaker*, c. 1670–71, is another picture painted for the Van Ruijven household. 'Here the painter's theme, as so often, is love, this time the love of a young mother-to-be for her unborn child, expressed in the making of a delicate piece of lace. So abruptly cropped is the composition that we seem to come across the lacemaker quite by chance while she is in the middle of her work.'

36 & 37. *The Guitar Player, c.* 1670 (*above*), and *A Young Woman Standing at a Virginal, c.* 1670 (*right*). Some Collegiants believed that at the End of Days, when peace would descend on earth for 1,000 years, angels would be sent from above to help turn this

world into an earthly paradise. In these two radiant pictures Vermeer is imagining what such creatures might look like. The beatific women playing their musical instruments are messengers from another realm. Both works were painted for the Van Ruijvens.

38. *The Love Letter*, c. 1672–5. A mystery picture, perhaps painted for the open market in the artist's last years. 'A rare instance of pure genre in the work of Vermeer.'

39. *Mistress and Maid*, c. 1668. The true subject of this picture, another for the Van Ruijven household, may be a story from the Bible played out in modern dress: that of Bathsheba receiving King David's letter, urging her to commit adultery with him. 'Vermeer shows us a decent woman shocked by an indecent proposal.'

40. *View of Delft*, c. 1665. ' "And I saw a new heaven and a new earth" ... The unbearably beautiful spectacle of what human life would be if only we would make it so.'

41–44. The Oude Delft, then and now. *The Little Street* (*c.* 1660, *top left*), with the house of the Van Ruijvens to the left, bearing Vermeer's signature in its whitewash, and next to it the single black door leading to the hidden Remonstrant church. A modern photograph of the same spot on the Oude Delft (*top right*), with the gaps between the houses built over and double doors in place of the single black door of old. A detail of *The Little Street* (*lower right*), cropped to show how the rooflines of the scene, past and present, are still essentially aligned; a photograph of the Remonstrant church as it is today (*lower left*), taken by the author from within the alleyway that still runs past the right-hand wall of the Van Ruijvens' former home.

van der Beke and the day of his admission by the magistrates of Delft was 10 August, the day before Monconys came to town.

The document in which this is recorded also tells us where the new priest was lodging at the time of his registration: 'the house of Van der Velde'.[67] This was just around the corner from Maria Thins's house on the Oude Langendijk. Heijndrick van der Velde was, with Maria, one of the most active laypeople in Delft's Jesuit Catholic community. Because he was a layperson the magistracy was more likely to turn a blind eye to his activities, which meant that he could fix things that the Jesuit fathers could not easily fix for themselves.[68] He it was who arranged for the new preacher to be inscribed in Delft's register of 'secular priests'. Everyone knew Balthasar van der Beke was no *'wereltlijck priester'*, but a Jesuit re-educator. That was how it worked: a Catholic priest could always squeeze through the net, as long as the lie was vaguely plausible and the bribe big enough.

Heijndrick van der Velde was also one of the main men behind the Jesuit drive to acquire a substantial property portfolio in and around Papists' Corner. They were buying safe houses, to be turned into Jesuit schools and churches or rented out to provide an income for the mission. The house in which Maria Thins lived with Johannes Vermeer had originally been bought for that purpose by her cousin Jan Geensz Thins, another supporter of the Jesuit mission, before Maria moved in after her divorce.[69] At one point Heijndrick van der Velde had owned the house next door. He was thick with the Thinses. They were all in it together.

Van der Velde and the new priest may have been at the house of Maria Thins on the day when Monconys came calling with Father Léon and the bodyguard Gentillo. The likely purpose of the visit was to brief Van der Beke on the best way to advance the mission in Delft. Including Maria, there would have been at least six people at the meeting, maybe more if other local Jesuits had been invited. So most of the nine red-leather Spanish chairs would have been taken. Perhaps Vermeer pulled one up himself or maybe he just happened to come along at the end, Maria then taking the opportunity to introduce him to her most important visitor, Monconys. We know they met one way or another on the day when Monconys came to Papists' Corner, because he says so in his diary.

The encounter between the two men may have been awkward, for reasons that Vermeer would have known but Monconys could only sense. The Frenchman was working for the *Missio Hollandica*, visiting a house owned by a Catholic family long present in the town who lived just a few doors down from the hidden Catholic church and even had a hidden Catholic chapel in the inner kitchen of their house. He might have expected everyone he met there to be a supporter of the Jesuit mission. But Vermeer was no such thing.

Brief though his diary entry is, it suggests that the Frenchman may have smelled a rat. When he asked to see Vermeer's work he was told that there was nothing to see except a painting at the local baker's. In truth there were plenty of pictures to see, and nearby too, but they were all at Pieter and Maria's place on the Oude Delft, and there was no way on earth that Vermeer was going to invite a militant Jesuit through the door of that house. Was it the evasiveness or the implausibility of his reply that set Monconys on edge? The Frenchman went to the baker's out of curiosity, but he seems to have taken against the painter by the time he did so. He was only too ready to condemn the picture he saw there and leap to the judgement that it was nothing much, and over-priced. Monconys would never normally have been that rude about the friend of Jesuit friends. But that was the end of the affair. Maybe he just bought a loaf of bread and moved on.

We know quite a bit about the baker who owned a painting by Vermeer, but one thing jumps out from the brief account given by Monconys. The baker was probably close to the artist, and someone on his side. Who else would claim to have paid the vast sum of 600 guilders for a single-figure painting? That was three times as much as the price eventually paid at auction for Vermeer's masterpiece the *View of Delft*. The baker was trying to do his friend a good turn by puffing his work and inflating its worth. As he knew better than most, Vermeer was always short of money.

The son of a humble shoemaker, Hendrick van Buyten had chosen to bake bread rather than cobble clogs. Like many others in his line of work, he prospered during the 1650s and 1660s. Grain prices had declined after the end of the Thirty and Eighty Years Wars, but the canny bakers' guilds refused to pass reductions on to their customers, running a cartel to keep the price of bread artificially high, with the result that their profit margins soared.⁷⁰ Van Buyten was already a rich man when late in life he unexpectedly inherited 4,000 guilders from a distant relation. He became even richer by lending his capital out at interest. When he died his estate was worth 24,829 guilders, making him one of the dozen or so richest people in Delft, in the same league as Vermeer's mother-in-law, Maria Thins. He left a widow but no descendants, his estate being administered by the Orphan Chamber of Delft, which made sure that it would be the orphans of the town who ultimately benefited from the baker's business acumen.⁷¹

Van Buyten was the principal supplier of bread to Maria Thins's house on the Oude Langendijk. Bread was the staff of life, an essential part of the Dutch diet, so he was bound to supply more and more with each passing year, as Johannes and Catharina produced more and more children. They were excellent customers in all but one respect. Maria seems to have refused to pay the family's bread bills herself, insisting that Vermeer should do so from a combination of whatever small allowance she gave him plus his own income, which was probably little more than the annuity of around 200 guilders paid by his patrons Pieter and Maria. Payment of the bread bills was an obligation that Vermeer was unequipped to meet, but whenever he struggled the wealthy Van Buyten extended him more credit.

The baker's reserves of generosity and free bread were seemingly inexhaustible, so that by the time of Vermeer's death the amount he owed Van Buyten on tick was a staggering 726 guilders. Bread was sold by the pound in those days, costing approximately 1 guilder for every 11 pounds, which means that by 1675 Vermeer's family had consumed roughly 8,000 pounds, or 4,000 kilos, of Van Buyten's bread without paying for it. Under normal circumstances it was unusual for a tradesman to let an unpaid tab run for as long as twelve months, let alone the two or three years (or more) that it would have taken even a family as large as that of Vermeer to eat all those loaves. John Michael Montias, who discovered the debt, noted that in his extensive searches through the household records of seventeenth-century Delft he had never come across a larger bill for bread.⁷²

Van Buyten cut Vermeer a great deal of slack. Even after Vermeer's death he was unrelentingly kind to the painter's widow Catharina, conspicuously more so than any other creditor with claims on

Vermeer's estate. He was born in 1632, which made him exactly the same age as Vermeer. Seventeenth-century Delft was a small town, little more than a village by modern standards, where no one lived more than a fifteen-minute walk from anyone else. The total population was about 24,000, so during the years when they were growing up there could only have been about 130 boys the same age as the future painter and baker.[73] As children they would have bumped into one another, perhaps literally, in the Great Market Square. As adults they would have marched there together in the parades of the civic militia: both men were *Schutters*, troops in the home guard. Their fathers before them had been *Schutters*, and friends too, to judge by a document of 1631 that has Vermeer's father, Reynier, and Van Buyten's father, Adrian, jointly testifying on behalf of a disgruntled husband whose wife had passed out naked in someone else's house. It seems they had been a party to the low-jinks, not just witnesses: she had been drunk on Reynier's wine when tripping over her own feet in a pair of Adrian's clogs.[74] Altogether there is a great deal to suggest that the men's sons, Hendrick van Buyten and Johannes Vermeer, knew each other from way back and were close.

The baker did the painter many favours, but their friendship was by no means a one-way street. In exchange for bread on tick, Van Buyten got something hardly anyone in history has ever had: a painting by Johannes Vermeer. In the end he got three because Catharina would eventually offer him two more in part settlement of that outstanding bill of 726 guilders, a deal he readily accepted. The picture Monconys saw at the bakery in 1663 had also probably been acquired on account, considering Vermeer's financial circumstances and Van Buyten's willingness to help out. We can work out which painting it probably was, because there are only two known paintings that it could have been. All of Vermeer's single-figure compositions of circa 1657–63 were done for Maria de Knuijt, except for the *Young Woman with a Water Pitcher*, now in the Metropolitan Museum of Art, and the *Woman in Blue Reading a Letter* in the Rijksmuseum. The latter, as we will see, may have had a personal meaning for the painter and his wife, and may have been a gift from him to her. So by process of elimination the former is the best candidate for Van Buyten's Vermeer.[75]

Young Woman with a Water Pitcher is a classic Vermeer, in the sense that it has the look of the pictures created for The Golden Eagle, even though we know that it was not. In other words it looks like a genre picture while hinting strongly at hidden depths of religious feeling. The painter shows us an apparently well-to-do woman in a richly appointed interior holding the handle of a silver-gilt water jug, which is set down in a circular tray on a table draped with a Turkish carpet. Her white headdress and collar give her the look of a holy sister of some description. There is no nail in the wall, only a map hanging from it, but might the woman in this picture be related in some way to the woman whom we know as *The Milkmaid*? She too is shown holding a jug, albeit of water rather than milk. As in the earlier painting, the mood is solemn, which conveys the impression that her actions might have some kind of sacred significance. She has her back to the map on the wall and has left her jewellery box on the table. She has an abstracted expression on her face, as if her mind is full of thoughts but elsewhere. She opens a window, perhaps to look out and down to the street outside.

Like *The Milkmaid* and the *Woman with a Balance*, who are modern-dress reincarnations of the biblical Martha and Mary, *Young Woman with a Water Pitcher* may have been meant to evoke a particular woman described in the New Testament. The most likely contender is the Woman of Samaria, who is strongly associated with water. It may not be a coincidence that her encounter with Christ had inspired Johannes Taurinus, early Collegiant and close friend of the Vermeer family, to write an entire book of religious reflections.

Her story is told in the Gospel of John, much beloved of the Collegiants. On his way to Galilee, Christ meets a Samaritan woman by a well just outside the city of Sychar and asks her to draw some water for him, much to her surprise: 'Jews have no dealings with the Samaritans,' she reminds him. Christ makes it clear that he is no ordinary Jew and explains that the water he will give her in return for her own will be no ordinary water, but will give her everlasting life. Realizing that he is the Messiah, she is filled with the holy spirit and resolves to convert her fellow Samaritans: 'The woman then left her waterpot, and went her way into the city.' (John 4:28)

It is this moment, as she leaves her waterpot to turn back to the city, that Vermeer may have intended to summon up. We are probably not meant to imagine that the woman in the picture actually is the Samaritan woman, any more than we are to imagine that *A Maid Asleep* is Mary Magdalene. It is more likely that we are to understand that she is a pious modern Dutchwoman who has been renewed in her faith through reading the Samaritan woman's story and then acting on it, both in her prayers and in her life.

Young Woman with a Water Pitcher bears all the hallmarks of a picture painted for a Collegiant, or some other kind of intensely apostolic Dutch Christian, to help them reflect inwardly as well as inspiring them to reach out to others. So what was it doing on the wall of the bakery owned by Vermeer's probable friend Hendrick van Buyten? Perhaps either the baker himself or his wife, a lady named Machtelt van Asson, was sympathetic to the ideas that drove the Collegiant movement. We have no firm evidence of Van Buyten's religious beliefs other than that he was brought up within the Dutch Reformed Church,[76] but there were many liberal Reformed Dutchmen in the movement so there is a chance that Van Buyten was one of them. If he was indeed a friend to Vermeer, the latter may have tried to win him round to his own beliefs and introduced him to some of his friends into the bargain. Perhaps Van Buyten went to The Golden Eagle with Vermeer one day, saw *The Milkmaid* with her jug of milk and all her loaves of bread, and asked for a painting along the same lines.

Monsieur Monconys, the Jesuit, was oblivious to the stillness and beauty of Van Buyten's Vermeer: all he could see was something worth 60 guilders that a fool said he had bought for 600. If he had paused for reflection, his grounding in biblical exegesis at the *Collège de la Trinité* might have allowed him to see that the picture was appropriate to its setting. Bread has sacramental and social associations, being linked to the ideas of sacred holy communion and secular community. It is also only ever as pure as the water used in its making. Vermeer's *Young Woman with a Water Pitcher* would have made a fitting patron saint for a bakery.

There may always have been give and take between the baker and the painter. Consider those sparkling loaves on the table in *The Milkmaid*, transformed by the painter's light into the bread of heaven, in what may be the single most beautiful passage of painting in all of his work. They will have started out as real loaves, baked in all likelihood by Hendrick van Buyten. He must have been something of a force in Delft: self-made man, entrepreneur, capitalist and philanthropist. Not only did he bail out Vermeer time and again, feeding his family for next to nothing, he gave generously elsewhere too, much of his fortune going eventually to help children who had lost their parents. Might Van Buyten have known Vermeer's other good friend, Pieter Claesz van Ruijven, master of the *Kamer van Charitate*? Might he have baked loaves for him too, to be ground up with milk and distributed among Delft's poor? – 600 guilders to 60 says he did.

A BLACK SHEEP AND A WOMAN IN BLUE

Sometime around the start of 1663 Maria Thins's only son, Willem Bolnes, reappeared in her life after an absence of several years. He wanted money so she lent it to him, 300 guilders in all, to pay off his debts and leave him with a little cash in hand. The notary who recorded the transaction specified that interest would be charged on the outstanding amount at 4 per cent per annum[77] (Maria would normally have charged 5 per cent, but Willem was family). That was on 17 January. A few weeks later he moved to Delft from Schoonhoven, where it seems he had been living shiftlessly, keeping irregular hours, apparently suffering some form of depression. His address in Delft is not known, but soon after he moved there all hell broke loose in Maria Thins's house on the Oude Langendijk. It broke loose not once but several times.

We know about the ruckuses thanks to a witness statement by three people who had been present at all of them.[78] Willem de Coorde, an innkeeper's son, and Gerrit Cornelisz, apprentice to a local sculptor, were neighbours who had rushed in from outside to help. Tanneke Everpoel was the sole live-in maidservant to Maria Thins, so she had already been in the house when trouble started.

Tanneke and Gerrit began their deposition by jointly declaring that 'on various occasions Willem Bolnes had created a violent commotion in the house, to such an extent that many people gathered before the door as he swore at his mother, calling her an old popish swine, a she-devil, and other such ugly swearwords that, for the sake of decency, must be passed over'. Tanneke added that she had seen Willem pull a knife on his mother and try to wound her with it, 'as well as committing similar violence against the daughter of Maria Thins, the wife of Johannes Vermeer, threatening to beat her on diverse occasions with a stick, notwithstanding the fact that she was pregnant to the last degree'. The innkeeper's son De Coorde confirmed that Willem had repeatedly broken into the house and threatened its inhabitants, especially Catharina. De Coorde had seen him 'several times thrust at his sister with a stick at the end of which there was an iron pin'.

Insult had been followed by aggravated assault, including attempted knifings and a beating with a stick, culminating in an attack on a defenceless pregnant woman with some type of weird improvised lance: all this must have seemed like a nightmare re-run of the family's worst memories. Maria was not having it. She had spent too long putting her past behind her to have her name dragged through the mud again. It may have been the shame of it as much as the actual violence that drove her to have Willem 'set fast' by a Delft magistrate.

Once detained, he was transferred to a place called a *beterhuis* – literally, a house for making people better – run by a local man called Hermanus Taerling. This was a small privately run establishment on Vlamingstraat, not far from the house in which Vermeer's elderly great-aunt Ariaentgen cleaned and sold tripe. There were other butchers and meat merchants nearby: it was not the most fragrant quarter of Delft. But Willem was treated well enough. His confinement was expensive: it cost Maria 310 guilders a year to have her son locked away. That was probably more money than she allowed to her son-in-law each year to pay the household bills.

The *beterhuis* was an institution peculiar to the Dutch Republic, which in matters of healthcare as so much else was in the vanguard of latest developments. *Beterhuizen* were exclusively reserved for the black sheep (*zwarte schapen*) of rich and respectable families.[79] They were small private prisons run on civilized lines, the idea being that confinement there might feel rather like staying at an inn or tavern, albeit one that it was impossible to leave. Prisoners could read, smoke a pipe and receive visitors. The better behaved and more stable inmates were allowed one bottle of wine per day, or the equivalent in beer: Willem's 'medicinal' wine was supplied from The Mechelen Inn on the Great Market Square by Vermeer's mother, until her death in 1670; after that date Vermeer himself probably took care of it. Thanks to the survival of a copy of the weekly menu at 'De Drie Taarlingen', a slightly later incarnation of the establishment founded by Hermanus Taerling, we know more or less precisely what Willem was given to eat: from Sunday to Thursday lunch consisted of fresh meat, smoked meat or ham, with fish being served on Fridays; the evening meal was smaller, often just a salad with some eggs.

Willem's post was censored both in and out. Access to pen, ink and paper was a privilege that could be forfeited if abused. Breakouts were not unknown and often arranged by letters to and from accomplices on the outside, although not in Willem's case. When he briefly escaped, in 1665, it turned out to have been an inside job. Hermanus Taerling's maid seduced Willem and then persuaded him to run away with her so that they could get married. Somehow he managed to get hold of his father's mourning mantle, which she pawned for 16 guilders to fund their getaway. The two of them got as far as Gouda before he concluded that she was only after his money and returned to the house on Vlamingstraat, where he stayed.

When Willem Bolnes was first committed, in 1664, the *beterhuis* was a new invention. Social historians have traced its origins to Delft in around 1660, so Hermanus Taerling's little house of correction was one of the first of its kind and perhaps even the first. Maria Thins was therefore a pioneer herself: one of the first Dutch mothers to send a mentally disturbed son into private care rather than letting the state have its way with him. Before the advent of *beterhuizen* people like Willem would have been locked away in a government-run institution, most likely housed in a repurposed monastery or convent: there was the *dolhuis* for mad people, the *gasthuis* for sick people, and the *tuchthuis* for criminals requiring corrective rehabilitation.

The conditions were much worse in such places, but their greatest drawback from Maria's point of view would have been their lack of privacy. People went to stare at the inmates of the *dolhuis*; people gossiped if somebody's son was a convicted criminal in the *tuchthuis*. Rather than suffer such embarrassment and humiliation, she preferred to place her own black sheep in the care of Hermanus Taerling. Leave him there long enough and the world might forget he had ever existed. So it proved. After his brief elopement with Mary Gerrits, Willem Bolnes spent the remaining ten years of his life in the tavern with no way out. When he died in 1676, not long after his brother-in-law Johannes Vermeer, his mother had him interred in the family grave in the Oude Kerk.

A year or so after his brother-in-law's attack on the heavily pregnant Catharina, 'with a stick at the end of which was an iron pin', Vermeer painted the picture known as *Woman in Blue Reading a Letter*, now in the Rijksmuseum. Like *Young Woman with a Water Pitcher* it is a rare example of a picture by Vermeer that looks every inch as though painted for Maria de Knuijt, although it was not, as we know by its absence from the Dissius sale. The picture's early provenance is unknown, but we can make a guess at it. At the time when Vermeer painted the picture his wife would have been pregnant with their first son, Johannes Vermeer II. He may have painted it for her.

The artist does not often repeat himself, but here he has done so. The painting is a reprise, on a smaller scale, of the *Girl Reading a Letter at an Open Window* in Dresden. There are certain differences, the most obvious being the replacement of Cupid on the back wall by a map of Holland and West Friesland, but they are outweighed by the many strong similarities. Like its predecessor in Dresden, the picture in the Rijksmuseum shows a woman intently reading a letter in a room illuminated by light entering from the left. The air of hushed expectancy is the same, so too the woman's expression of absorption. To judge by her profile and high forehead the woman herself is the same person as in the earlier picture, although some years older and evidently pregnant. On the table beside her there are some pearls and the floppy slab of a book.

It is probable but not provable that Vermeer had painted *Girl Reading a Letter at an Open Window* as a declaration of love and therefore a marriage gift to Catharina, his bride. This is made more likely by the existence of the *Woman in Blue Reading a Letter*, which makes a convincing sequel to the earlier picture. Once again Vermeer has implicitly included himself in the painting, in the form of the letter Catharina holds in her hands. Thanks to the painter's trick of the light that small rectangle of paper is emphatically prominent, its sharply folded upper edge picked out like a white ace of diamonds against the wrinkled ochre of the map.

Like Calvinists, Collegiants observed just two of the traditional sacraments, baptism and communion. For Vermeer, it seems, painting was a third: a ritual infused with love and faith, never more so than here. The letter in her hands tells Catharina that Johannes is thinking of her. It tells her he will not forget she is with child, just as she must not forget that he is its father. It tells her how much he regrets not having been there when her brother descended upon her like a demon. The painting has something of an ex-voto about it, recalling the images put up in Catholic churches on behalf of people who had survived accidents, thanks to God. It may have been Vermeer's way of blessing his wife and their unborn child.

AWAY

The tenderness of Vermeer's picture of Catharina heavy with child, if it is indeed her, allows us to believe that he and his wife were still close, ten years into their marriage. So why was he never there to protect her when she was visited by her brother in the depths of his psychosis? Not only was he away when the attacks took place, his absence was barely remarked. In the deposition made by those who had been present at the scene, Catharina was described as 'the daughter of Maria Thins'. The reference to her other status as 'wife to Johannes Vermeer' was tacked on like an afterthought. All three witnesses made it sound as if he were someone they associated with the household but did not see very often. None of them expressed surprise that he was not there. In the moment of each attack, when Willem Bolnes went berserk, no one thought to get him. Once again, the one person not in the room is Vermeer himself.

Even when he was busy painting a picture the artist probably spent little time in the house on the Oude Langendijk. The idea that he worked from home is based on the knowledge that he had a room full of painting equipment there at the end of his life, in late 1675. But between 1657 and around 1670, when he worked all but exclusively for Maria de Knuijt and her husband, it is hard to believe that

Vermeer would have kept his main workshop anywhere near Papists' Corner, let alone in the house he shared with Maria Thins. He was living in a nest of Jesuits while painting for the opposition: those two things had to be kept apart. The last thing he wanted was Maria Thins interfering in his studio and asking questions about his work. That aside, it would have been difficult for Vermeer to paint in the way that he did in the house he shared with his family on the Oude Langendijk. Painting for him was a form of religious contemplation. Pictures as still and solemn as his could not have been easily meditated, let alone executed, in a house teeming with children.

Where Vermeer's actual studio was remains a matter for conjecture. It is possible that he himself revealed its location by inference in his picture of the hidden Remonstrant church on the Oude Delft, known as *The Little Street*. The implied point of view from which the church is seen in that painting places the artist in a room on the first floor of a house on the west side of the Oude Delft, on the other side of its little canal. As we have seen, he may have been allowed to set up his easel there by one of the many Remonstrants who lived in the vicinity of their church, and perhaps the arrangement was a long-standing one.

Interior of the hidden Remonstrant church in Delft. If Johannes Vermeer regularly attended any church it was probably this one, just behind the house of his patrons on the Oude Delft.

He had plenty of friends and patrons in the neighbourhood, including not just Maria de Knuijt and her husband, Pieter, in the house opposite but also the supportive Dirck van Bleiswijk,[80] who lived just down the street, as well as Adrian Paets, often to be found a few hundred yards away in the local Chamber of the VOC. It would make sense for Vermeer to have taken a studio in that part of town. A home on Papists' Corner and a studio on Remonstrant Row: even the geography of his life was fractured.

None of this fully explains why Vermeer was away from home whenever Willem Bolnes came looking for trouble. According to the witnesses the attacks occurred on multiple occasions, the implication being that they took place by day and by night. Yet the painter never made an appearance. If he were working in his studio on the other side of town he would presumably have come home in the evening most of the time. But during the months of Willem's outbursts he apparently did not do so. He must have been away on business, and often, to miss Willem every time he came. So where was he? What could he have been doing?

It is a question worth asking, not just in connection with the violent events of 1663. Elementary maths tells us that Vermeer must have been doing something with his life other than paint pictures, not just in that year but most others. During the entire period of his arrangement with Pieter Claesz van Ruijven and Maria De Knuijt, which lasted some thirteen years, he painted around twenty-one pictures for them plus a handful for other people, including himself and his wife. That is a little over two paintings per year. Even if allowances are made for his painstaking technique he can only have been painting for six months of the year, if that. His obligations as a twice-elected headman of the St Luke's Guild, which involved a two-year stint each time, can hardly have been demanding. Delft was a relative backwater, with a dwindling economy and a shrinking population of artists. The duties of a *schutter*, which Vermeer also performed, were mostly ceremonial. He must have been doing something else, and doing it a lot.

His depictions of becalmed interiors have contributed to a general preconception that he himself must have been an unadventurous, stay-at-home type. The opposite is more likely true. We know from the internal evidence of Vermeer's pictures that he travelled throughout the country a great deal. He borrowed motifs and compositional ideas from the work of many painters who lived and worked outside Delft, including Gerard Dou and Frans van Mieris in Leiden, Nicolaes Maes and Gabriel Metsu in Amsterdam, Caspar Netscher in The Hague and Jacob Ochtervelt in Haarlem. An analysis of his influences purely by geography has led to the conclusion that he spent as much time on the Dutch passenger barges as any of his contemporaries.[81]

It seems unlikely that Vermeer would have crossed the length and breadth of the country by *trekschuit* purely to visit the studios of other painters from whom he might borrow an idea or two. If he visited artists in other Dutch towns he most likely did so in passing while on other business, perhaps while acquiring pictures for the family art-dealing concern. Other than that, however, there is little to be said about his journeys, save that there seem to have been a great many of them. We know that he was out of Delft a lot but have no idea of exactly where he went, or why, or when.

A THOUSAND YEARS

We cannot accompany the painter on his travels, but we can explore the range of his thought by examining the beliefs of his fellow Collegiants, in particular their preoccupation with the Apocalypse. This seems to hold the key to several of Vermeer's later paintings.

During the 1660s many devout Christians took a keen interest in the prophecies handed down in the Book of Revelation. One passage in particular held their attention:

> And I saw an angel come down from heaven, having the key of the bottomless pit and a great chain in his hand.
> And he laid hold on the dragon, that old serpent, which is the Devil, and Satan, and bound him a thousand years. (Revelation 20:1–2)

There was a long tradition of finding in these verses a prediction of the End of Days. At that moment, evil would disappear from the face of the earth for a single perfect millennium. For a thousand years Christ and the resurrected saints would rule over an earthly paradise, human beings would sin no more, and all would live together in harmony. Thanks to another gnomic phrase in Revelation, 'the number of the beast is six hundred threescore and six' (13:18), many believed that all this would come to pass in the year 1666.

During the middle years of the seventeenth century belief in the prophecies of Revelation was by no means restricted to fringe groups or exotic freethinking sects.[82] A great many Christians, especially the pious Protestants of northern Europe, truly believed that the promised thousand years of blessed peace would arrive soon. The question was not whether this would happen, but how it could be hastened. It was an important part of millenarian legend that the Last Days could not arrive until all the Jews were converted. This mass conversion would be triggered by the rediscovery of the so-called 'Lost Tribes' of Israel, ten tribes descended from Jacob who had disappeared from history. Once found, they would turn to Christianity and travel to Jerusalem. Inspired by their example, all the other Jews in the world would follow suit, and soon after that the Messiah would come.

The discovery of unfamiliar peoples and tribes in the New World fanned the flames of such millenarian enthusiasm. Native Peruvians, with their dark hair and supposedly aquiline noses, were acclaimed as one of the Lost Tribes of Israel, as were the supposed 'Indians' of North America. In 1650 a Norfolk preacher named Thomas Thorowgood published a tract entitled *The Jewes in America or Probabilities that the Americans are of that Race*. The idea that the Lost Tribes had been rediscovered in New England was enthusiastically taken up by the Scottish ecumenical churchman John Dury, who wrote an appendix to Thorowgood's text in which he imagined hordes of 'Red Indians' marching on Jerusalem to seal the end of history. Dury was a friend to the Dutch Collegiants. Rumours about the Lost Tribes soon spread through the Netherlands. They were discussed in the Erasmian circles of Adrian Paets and formed part of Vermeer's mental landscape. He would touch on the theme of the Lost Tribes of Israel in a pair of late pictures, as we shall see.

As 1666 approached there was great excitement in England and the Dutch Republic alike about the prospect of converting the Jews. Because there were no Jews in England to convert, the Quakers sent a mission to Amsterdam to accomplish that purpose. In the late

1650s the lapsed Jewish philosopher Spinoza, who may have been in Vermeer's circle, had been recruited by the Quaker leadership in Amsterdam. They had employed him to translate some pamphlets written by Margaret Fell, in the hope that the people of his community might be moved to convert. Urging the Jews of Amsterdam to turn to Christ, the renowned 'mother of the Quakers' had decorated her arguments with metaphors so bizarrely graphic they cannot have been easily rendered into Hebrew: 'if ye come into the *light*, by which the Lord God *teacheth his People* ... you will come to have your heart *Circumcised*, and the fore-skin of your heart taken away.'[83]

Spinoza translated such texts probably to earn a little money, knowing full well that they would fall on deaf ears. He himself felt little affinity with the Quakers, because they denied that reason had any role to play in religion. Collegiants likewise clashed with Quakers over their dogmatic belief in 'inner spirit' illumination, resulting in a deep rift between the two movements. By the early 1660s, when he petitioned Adrian Paets for support, Spinoza had already taken the side of the Collegiants. A philosophical pantheist who believed that God is coterminous with the universe, therefore neither good nor evil, he was hardly a conventional Christian. But he could claim without dishonesty to be a Collegiant Christian, in that he genuinely regarded the morality of Christ as a precursor of his own rational ethics.

By force of personality and lucidity of thought Spinoza would have a powerful impact on the movement. So, whether he knew Vermeer personally or not, he was probably an influence on him. Spinoza himself was no millenarian, but he became close friends with a number of Collegiants nonetheless and sought to shape their thinking. He encouraged them away from a belief in mystical personal illumination (which most of them in any case distrusted) and towards what he as a philosopher regarded as the true light of reason. The clearest example of how he managed this is a text written not by Spinoza himself but by one of his close friends, Pieter Balling. A merchant from Amsterdam, Balling devoted the later part of his life to the Collegiant movement. He has been remembered for *The Light upon the Candlestick*, of 1662, a set of meditations clearly written under the influence of Spinoza's belief in divinely inspired reason as the lodestar of human life. In its time it was widely read and admired in dissenting circles, in England as well as the Dutch Republic. A contemplative and poetic piece of writing, suffused by the imagery of light and the idea of illumination, it has affinities with the paintings of Vermeer.

Many Collegiants came to embrace a form of rational Christianity, that had also been advocated by Camphuysen and Coornhert, influential figures within the liberal Arminian tradition.[84] This gave a particular colour and tempo to their apocalyptic hopes. Most other millenarians awaited the second coming of a decidedly vengeful Messiah, who would be their Saviour and no one else's. But the Collegiants' idea of the Apocalypse was more inclusive and less dramatic. They believed the earthly paradise might materialize gradually, rather than all at once, that it might even sneak up on the world without the world noticing. People would be changed subtly, from within. They would learn to see the light of moral truth more clearly, and grasp for themselves the lessons taught by Christ. It just needed a little twist, a tweak in the fabric of human consciousness, for all this to happen. Christ himself need not even come back to earth in person.

The earliest and most vivid description of the Apocalypse as imagined by a Collegiant was Daniel de Breen's *Of the Triumphant Spiritual Kingdom of Our Lord Jesus Christ*, of 1653. De Breen was a founder of the Amsterdam College who had been close to Joachim Oudaan, a key member of Adrian Paets's circle. In 1664, the year of De Breen's death, his prophecy of the End of Days was republished in Rotterdam by François van Hoogstraten, in whose bookshop Paets's Erasmian friends gathered. The timing of this was deliberate. Less than eighteen months before the beginning of 1666, members of the invisible Church were being reminded of what might lie ahead.

De Breen was not one of those who believed that Christ would physically return to earth when the new millennium dawned. He predicted that Christ would come back in a purely spiritual sense to rule within the souls of true believers. The first sign would be that all the Jews of the world would be converted. Then those sowing war and division, including churches, kings and nations, would surrender their power. The meek would inherit the earth. Christ's work would be accomplished by angels, his earthly power exercised from heaven above. All this would not necessarily happen at once, or in a single year such as 1666. The process might be slow and the way long but eventually the New Jerusalem would appear. All the blessed would gather there, to live in peace.

We cannot prove that Vermeer was familiar with Pieter Balling's ideas about the light within mankind, with Spinoza's belief in the power of reason to improve the world, or with De Breen's gentle prophecies of a blessed future. But it seems that he was, to judge by one of his largest and most ambitious pictures.

VIEW OF DELFT

Near the end of *The Adventures of Simplicius Simplicissimus*, the hero of Grimmelshausen's tale briefly escapes the combat zone of the Thirty Years War and travels to Switzerland. A place that has seen no fighting, suffered no atrocities, and experienced no pillaging or arbitrary acts of violence strikes him as extraordinary. Having lived for so long in a world turned upside down, Simplicius does not know what to make of one where everything is the right way up:

> The country looked odd to me after the German states . . . People were going about their business in peace. Cattle sheds stood full of livestock, farmyards teemed with hens, geese and ducks, inns with people having a good time; the roads were safe to travel on, no man went in fear of the enemy or of being attacked and robbed or of losing his property or well-being or even his life; everyone lived in safety under his vine and under his fig-tree . . . To me, it was like heaven on earth.[85]

After dwelling for so long in death and destruction, the traumatized veteran of war is enthralled by the sights and sounds of ordinary life, by the eerie calm of a normality he has barely known until now: a world in which farmers can plough their fields in peace, in which people can go to the shops without having to step over dead bodies, in which there is actual bread for sale at the bakery. It is so strange to him that he feels as if transported to the other side of the world: 'We might have been in Brazil or China.'

The same stunned or rapturous appreciation of everyday life lies behind a great many Dutch paintings created after the peace treaties of 1648 and during the Era of True Liberty, when optimism about the future was at its height. It is the feeling that animates the soldiers' courtship pictures of Gerard ter Borch and Vermeer's own *Officer with a Laughing Girl*, likewise the panoramic landscapes of Phillips de Koninck and the peaceful interiors of Pieter de Hooch. The first people to contemplate such pictures, the inhabitants of the Dutch Republic, circa 1648–72, would have been struck first and foremost by what the artists who painted them did *not* include: predatory men, armies, ruins, gunsmoke, housebreakers, evidence of pillage. Having absorbed the blessed absence of such things those same people could then, but perhaps only then, take in what actually *was* before their eyes: people in love, a man walking with his dog under a vast sky filled with scudding clouds, a mother delousing her child's hair in a room lit up by morning sunshine.

The most radiant of all such quietly Dutch annunciations of peace is Vermeer's *View of Delft*. He painted the picture most likely around 1664 or 1665 for his patrons Maria de Knuijt and Pieter Claesz van Ruijven. One of his largest works, it must have hung in a prominent position in their house on the Oude Delft. It is of the same scale and shape as a small altarpiece. It was probably kept in a 'box', that is to say displayed behind folding doors that could be closed or opened. It may have been one of just three paintings treated in that way, the other two being *The Milkmaid* and *Woman with a Balance*.

When first sold at auction, some thirty years after Vermeer painted it, the picture was given the title 'The Town of Delft in perspective, to be seen from the South'. Ever since then it has been persistently miscategorized as a topographical painting and classed with other 'city views' by Vermeer's contemporaries, including Jacob van Ruisdael, Jan van der Heyden and Jan van Goyen. But it does not take much looking to realize that Vermeer's picture is far more than the painstaking portrayal of a town viewed from a point just outside its walls. Marcel Proust, who was nothing if not sensitive, declared it to be the most beautiful picture in the world, which would seem an extremely eccentric thing to say if it really were just a representation of some buildings seen across a stretch of dullish water, however well done. People have always instinctively known that there was more to the *View of Delft* than its overt subject matter, although none (certainly not Proust, despite the depth of his admiration for it) has ever claimed to put their finger on what that might be.

The key to the picture is the story that it tells: a story of the weather. The giveaway clue is a small detail in the making of it: the very specific feel and texture of the paint that has been used by Vermeer to describe the red-tiled roofs of the buildings in the scene. The pigment has been prepared to a recipe unusual in Vermeer's time, but commonplace in the cathedral workshops of the Middle Ages. The medieval painter whose job it was to add colour and life to the statues on the west front of a Gothic cathedral ground his pigments to varying degrees of coarseness. The figures lower down, close to worshippers as they entered the building, were often those of the apostles and evangelists, so to make them seem welcoming and lifelike the colouring of their hands and faces had to seem as smooth as skin itself. Higher up the figures became naturally more remote, reflecting the hierarchies of the heavenly host. Here the painter of statues would use progressively coarser pigment, deliberately leaving angular shards of unground mineral embedded in the final preparation to make the figures sparkle in the rays of the sun, as if haloed by otherworldly radiance.

Vermeer used a version of the same technique for his red-tiled roofs, leaving a residue of grit in the paste of his paint so that it looks almost tacky to the touch. It is possible that he ground actual red terracotta tiles in with his pigments and oil to get the required result.[86] Adrian Paets's close friend the Rotterdam poet Joachim Oudaan was a tilemaker by profession, so he could have helped with that. Vermeer was after the same effect achieved by the medieval painter of statuary, whose grains and granules of coarse-ground pigment caught the light. He achieved it. When we look carefully at his red roofs, especially the roof directly to the left of the Schiedam Gate with its clocktower, we see that there is a gritty, glittery speckle to them. They seem to gleam and sparkle.

The point of all this effort was to make us understand one thing: the roofs of the town are *wet*. More than half of the composition is sky, a blue sky through which clouds are moving quickly, blown by the same wind that has whipped up the waters of the Kolk Harbour. The cloud nearest to us, passing directly overhead, is dark grey in colour. It has just shed its load of rain on the town, hence the glitter on those red tiles. They are still slick from the downfall and are now glistening in the sun, which has just come out. What Vermeer has painted with such utter precision is the aftermath of a storm. He even has us sensing that which we cannot see but must be there: a rainbow at our backs.

The sunlight flooding the scene is at its brightest, by implication, in the concealed centre of town, somewhere behind the clocktower of the Schiedam Gate. That way lies the Remonstrant church, next door to the home shared by Pieter Claesz van Ruijven, Maria de Knuijt and their daughter Magdalena: the house with the vine climbing up it, inside which Vermeer's *View of Delft* once hung. We know exactly where we are in relation to those unseen buildings because the long red roof to the far left of the composition is that of East India House, headquarters of the VOC, marking the southern end of the Oude Delft, the street in which they stand. We deduce that the hidden church and the invisible Church alike are lit by blessed sunshine, and we see with our own eyes that the same is true of the Nieuwe Kerk, the spire of which is flooded with light as it rises into the cloud-filled sky. In the world the picture dreams of there will be no distinction between one church and another, no more sects, no more division. The sun will shine on all alike.

This is the heart of it. The picture is not a representation of reality, not a picture of a real town after a real storm. It is the translation, into paint on canvas, of a dream. It is a prophetic vision. The gunmetal cloud that looms above us, as we stare at the unbearably beautiful spectacle of what human life would be if only we would make it so, is not the kind of cloud that a meteorologist could describe. It is the dark stormcloud of the seventeenth century, a century of death and destruction, within it swirling the shades of a dirty, atrocious history. But one day, Vermeer tells us, one day that cloud will pass, and this will be what we see.

There will be no thunderbolts from heaven, no fluttering of angels' wings, and it may well be that everything will seem exactly the same as it did before. The wind will blow, making shapes that fan out like whispers on the water. People will go down to the harbour, the usual family groups, including perhaps a mother carrying her child on her back, to wait for the *trekschuit* boatmen to let them on. Women will do their shopping and stop to chat. It will look like nothing special but that is exactly what will make it so special. An ordinary day in an ordinary town, a place blessed but in a simple and achievable way, by love and happiness, where war is just a memory: that is what heaven on earth looks like through the eyes of Johannes Vermeer.

The miracle envisaged by the picture is re-enacted in the brilliance of its making. It is perfectly preserved because it was made with such care in the first place. The artist's green trees have been turned blue by a fickle pigment, but otherwise time has barely touched it. Nothing that Vermeer included in this picture – sky, clouds, buildings, water, boats, bare ground, people simply being – has ever been painted with a deeper sense of truth or desire. It is a picture so lovingly dwelt upon it seems made of love itself: a dream of the new millennium, made to last a thousand years.

The Delft of Vermeer's prophecy, or a place like it, is described at length in the Bible's last book, Revelation. A city with high walls and many gates, shining with an unforgettable brilliance, appears to St John the Evangelist:

> And I saw a new heaven and a new earth: for the first heaven and the first earth were passed away ... And I John saw the holy city, the New Jerusalem, coming down from God out of heaven, prepared as a bride adorned for her husband ...
> (Revelation 21:1–2)

Transfigured in painting, Vermeer's home town, for all its deceptive ordinariness, is that same holy city. He has imparted to it the airborne, spectral quality of a vision, so that it seems to hover between the sky above it and the waters below, rising up from its own slate-grey reflections in the harbour like a person waking from a dream.

A BOOK MARKED WITH THE LETTER 'A'

It was in the autumn of 1665 that Maria de Knuijt and her husband travelled to Leiden to make their last will and testament before Notary Nicholas Paets, to whom they had probably been introduced by his cousin and their friend, Adrian Paets. Pieter had other business in the town at the time, involving the purchase of shares in the Dutch East India Company, which further connects him and his wife to the

Rotterdam regent, who had his own close links to the VOC.[87] It will be remembered that this was the occasion on which Maria made her generous bequest to Vermeer, treating him as if he were a member of her own family.

The date on which the couple testified seems significant. By late 1665 they had probably taken delivery of the *View of Delft*, completed to mark the hoped-for dawn of the new millennium. Adding that picture to all the others in The Golden Eagle, they could have had little doubt about what the painter had done for them, the magnitude of what they had all done together. It makes sense that they should have chosen this moment to reward Vermeer and to show how grateful they felt towards him. But Maria's testament, which did exactly that, was not the only document they signed that day. They also signed a joint will, together with a statement in which they appointed guardians to any underage child surviving them, and in which they gave instructions for how their pictures were to be treated in the event of their deaths.[88] This statement, fascinating and tantalizing in equal measure, reveals by inference just how precious Vermeer's paintings were to them.

Its opening clauses are mundane, dealing with the nuts and bolts of guardianship: against the possibility that Pieter and Maria should die before their only surviving child, Magdalena, had reached majority, they appointed the Masters of Delft's Orphan Chamber to care for her, stipulating that any gold, silver and fine linen was to be held in safekeeping and passed on to her when she reached legal age. There was nothing surprising or unusual in any of this, but there was in the declarations that followed, in which the couple insisted that special care was to be taken of certain paintings or examples of 'the art of painting' ('*schilderkonst*') that would be found in their house after their deaths. So precious were those pictures that an entirely separate set of instructions relating to them had been written down, and put in a safe place for when needed. Magdalena's guardians were to act:

> according to the dispositions specified in a certain book marked with the letter 'A', on which would be written 'Disposition of my "*Schilderkonst*"' and other matters.

This book, which would be found in their house, was to be considered 'an integral part' of their testament.

The book has vanished without trace, maybe destroyed or lost by Magdalena van Ruijven herself, once she had read its contents. She survived both her parents, lived into adulthood, and received her inheritance without the involvement of guardians. The book marked with the letter 'A' would have been part and parcel of the picture collection they bequeathed to her. The gist of it is not hard to guess. The pictures were more precious than money. They were painted to be together, so it was important to keep them together for as long as possible. If those were indeed the instructions, they were obeyed to the letter. Magdalena kept every painting ever done by Vermeer for her mother and father. After her death, her widower and heir, Jacob Dissius, did the same.

The inscription on the cover of Book 'A' is said to have referred to the disposition of 'my "*Schilderkonst*"': *my* art collection, not *our* art collection. This suggests that, although both parties clearly took a great interest in it, they also acknowledged that it belonged more to one of them than the other. We know enough now to say that the primary owner was surely Maria de Knuijt. Maria had known Vermeer since he was a little boy, back in the days when they lived as next-door neighbours. Most of Vermeer's pictures for the house on the Oude Delft are depictions of women, probably part of a scheme of devotional art conceived for the rooms where Maria and her female friends met. Admittedly some of them, including the *View of Delft* and the music paintings, are no more aimed at women than men. But most are. All in all it seems overwhelmingly likely that this unique collaboration between patron and painter was the brainchild not of Pieter Claesz van Ruijven but of his wife. One last piece of evidence strongly suggests that this was indeed the case. It was she alone, in her sole will, who left the generous legacy of 500 guilders to 'Johannes Vermeer *Schilder*'.

A YELLOW JACKET TRIMMED WITH FUR

Between about 1665 and 1670, at around which time Vermeer stopped painting for Maria de Knuijt and her husband, he created nine more pictures to hang on the walls of The Golden Eagle. In eight of those a single female figure is depicted. In the other one we see a lady and her maidservant. More than ever, it seems, he was painting for women.

Three of these pictures date from around 1665–7 and may be thought of as a group, because in each we find a woman wearing a distinctive garment: a lemon-yellow morning jacket trimmed with spotted white fur. The painter presumably borrowed it from his wife each time he wanted to paint it, because just such a piece of clothing is listed as hers in the inventory of their possessions made after his death. It is possible that Catharina herself, or one or other of the painter's older daughters, modelled for these pictures. The repetition of a single striking detail (and colour note) across three compositions seems calculated to plant the idea that some connection exists between them. This would have been particularly noticeable when they were hung in The Golden Eagle, among the many other pictures there by Vermeer.

The young woman who looks up from her desk to catch our eye in *A Lady Writing* sits in a leather-backed chair with lion's-head finials. The chair is familiar from Vermeer's earlier paintings: one just like it had appeared in *A Maid Asleep* and *The Music Lesson*, without anyone sitting in it. As well as her yellow morning jacket, the woman wears fancy ribbons in her hair and sits at a table on which we see a jewellery box and a single string of pearls. She might easily be mistaken for an 'urbane elegant modern' sort of person, someone who loves dressing up and composing flirtatious letters to her admirers. If this were a straightforward genre picture that would perhaps be so, in which case its creator might be inviting us to indulge in a small sneer at her. But Vermeer is not that type of artist, and it is not that type of picture. The lady's gaze is frank and forthright and she holds her pen with serious intent. She is someone to reckon with.

The picture on the wall behind her, less visible now than it once was, is a still life with musical instruments, including a viola da gamba. If music has the same import here as elsewhere in Vermeer, this indicates the young lady is attuned to celestial harmonies. The image of a man or woman writing had long been associated with divine inspiration, especially in Italian painting, whether it be Carpaccio's St Jerome working at his Vulgate Bible, Caravaggio's St Matthew writing by dictation from an angel, or Michelangelo's mighty prophets and seers, such as the Delphic Sibyl, who clutches a mystic scroll while nervously awaiting illumination. Vermeer's lady with her quill pen is a domesticated version of the same exemplary figure: a sibyl for the Collegiant movement.

The juxtaposition of the piece of paper on which she writes and the string of pearls she has put aside recalls the biblical adage that wisdom is more precious than rubies, coral or pearls (Job 28:17–19). Pearls harvested from the sea are dead to her, because she is harvesting pearls of wisdom. Those pearls may be her thoughts on whichever passage from the New Testament is to be discussed at the next meeting. If that is so then she is writing notes in preparation for prophecy, and the edification of others.

A Lady Writing was Lot 35 in the Dissius sale of 1696: 'A writing young lady, very good'. Lot 36 was described as '*een paleerende*', which literally means 'a bepearling one', but is more accurately rendered as 'A young lady adorning herself with pearls'. The picture, in Berlin's Gemäldegalerie, is now usually known as *Woman with a Pearl Necklace*. It is not hard to see why the Amsterdam auctioneer paired these two pictures: not only is the lady in the second wearing the same yellow morning coat as the lady in the first, they look more or less the same age, have the same fair complexion, and are even wearing similar ribbons in their hair. They might be sisters, or even the same person in different situations.

Woman with a Pearl Necklace is a more solemn picture than *A Lady Writing*. The lady in the latter is having serious thoughts, but we can tell by her expression that she is calm and self-possessed. By contrast, the lady in the former is experiencing a life-changing revelation. She stands rapt, as if hypnotized by the import of a realization that has come to her. Holding the strings that fasten the pearl necklace gleaming at her throat, she gazes at her own reflection in the mirror on the wall. Light floods in from the window next to that mirror. Like the merchant in Christ's parable of the pearl of great price, she has realized that the only true pearl is the kingdom of heaven. She was putting the last touches to her toilette but, having looked herself in the eye, has decided to undo it all instead, starting with the string of pearls.

Originally Vermeer had thought to emphasize the spiritual nature of the young woman's meditations by including a map on the far wall behind her, emblem of the world to which she has suddenly become oblivious. It can still be seen in X-ray. Without it, the picture acquired another dimension of meaning. The unrelieved blankness of the wall where the map would have been gives the room the feel of a chapel, within which the young woman takes on the character of a priest at the altar. Her gesture even resembles that of a priest praying over the consecrated host. The picture implicitly proclaims the superiority of the invisible Church to the visible churches of the world. The woman looking in the mirror is by implication a Christian without a Church, in that her revelation has taken place at home, by inference when she was least expecting it. She is not elevating the host but taking off her pearls, not going through the motions of a church ritual but making an active change to her life.

There is a defiant edge to a number of Vermeer's later pictures for the house on the Oude Delft. This may reflect the embattled mood of Maria de Knuijt and other Collegiant women during the middle years of the 1660s. They had fought hard for the freedom that men had forever enjoyed, to speak out in religious assemblies, and were proud of their victory. Their freedom was restricted, however, to their own private house meetings. If and when Maria and her friends attended regular service at the Remonstrant church next door to her house, their voices would not be heard there, liberal though the Remonstrants were.

Even in Collegiant gatherings a woman's right to debate and discuss the Bible was threatened during the mid-1660s. The Calvinist consistories had kept up their attempts to close down 'Socinian assemblies' wherever they became aware of their existence. Interference from that side was only to be expected, but as the millennial year of 1666 approached conservative male Collegiants were emboldened to speak out against the practice of 'women's speaking'. They argued that if Christ had meant to sanction female edifiers or evangelists he would have included women among his apostles. Determined to preserve their independence and convinced that they had right on their side, the Collegiant women typically countered with two examples. What about the woman of Samaria, they asked, to whom Christ had given the water of salvation before bidding her to spread the word of his coming among her fellow Samaritans? What was she if not an evangelist, appointed by the Saviour himself? And what about Mary Magdalene, to whom the risen Christ entrusted the task of enlightening the apostles with the news of his Resurrection?

Despite such stout defence, the rumblings of patriarchal discontent continued to be heard. In Amsterdam the leader of the Mennonite Collegiants, Galenus Abrahamsz, had to resist attempts to stop women speaking during worship. In Rotterdam, Adrian Paets's close friend Jan Dionysus Verburg was forced to take a similar stand against male chauvinist elements within the ranks of Collegiants there.[89] During the same period there was unrest within the Quaker movement, in Holland and England alike, over the same issue: hence the publication of Margaret Fell's incandescently indignant pamphlet, *Women's Speaking Justified*, which came out in the year 1666.

By modelling the posture of his *Woman with a Pearl Necklace* on that of a Catholic priest at Mass, Vermeer was probably having a subtle dig at the Church of Rome and its ceremonies, but he was also by implication making the bold assertion that a woman who has seen the light is just as entitled as any man to become a minister of Christ. Who is the truer *predikant*, the picture rhetorically asks, a woman alone meditating change in her life, or a man in church performing a ritual that may mean little more to him than a job? Beneath the still surface of the picture a blow was being struck in an important struggle, albeit one still in its infancy. Vermeer's work is many things, including a vindication of the rights of women.

The third of his paintings to include a lady wearing a yellow fur-trimmed jacket is also the largest of the trio by some distance, being painted nearly life-size. Once more the woman in yellow is the primary focus of attention, but this time she is not alone. She looks up from the writing table at which she is seated, pen in hand, as a maidservant enters with a letter. In the catalogue to the Dissius auction the picture was listed as Lot 7, 'A young lady who is being brought a letter by a maid'. Now in the Frick Collection in New York, its modern title is a short form of the same description, *Mistress and Maid*.

This is probably a misnomer, because its actual subject may be a story from the Bible played out in modern dress, namely that of Bathsheba receiving King David's letter. Rembrandt had told this tale of a virtuous woman corrupted by a king in his ominous picture of 1653, *Bathsheba at her Bath*, showing the heroine naked as she reads David's troubling letter and struggles to absorb its implications. It remained a popular theme among Vermeer's contemporaries: Caspar Netscher depicted Bathsheba, no longer naked but still revealing a single bare breast, taking David's letter from her maidservant in a painting of around 1667. Vermeer's version is more decorous, which is unsurprising in view of its intended audience. He shows us a decent woman shocked by an indecent proposal.

Like Mary Magdalene, for whom Maria de Knuijt seems to have felt a special devotion, Bathsheba was a powerful woman with a strong presence in the Bible. Her story was complicated, to say the least. King David lusted after her and sent for her to come to his bedchamber, even though she was married to another man. She was persuaded to do so against her better judgement and bore David a son, but the child was taken by God as punishment for their sins. Having repented, David made Bathsheba his queen and she bore him another child, Solomon, from whose line Christ himself would be descended. The tale is long and not easily moralized. Christians have commonly interpreted it as a parable of sin and repentance leading to redemption. But it is also a classic instance of the Old Testament God moving in mysterious ways. He decrees a destiny for Bathsheba that leads her at the last into the light, but only after she has spent much time in darkness.

As if responding to the chiaroscuro in Bathsheba's story, Vermeer has plunged the heroine and her maidservant into something close to pitch darkness, having their forms emerge into light from a dark background. As in the work of Caravaggio the impenetrability of the shadows, coupled with the sharpness of the illumination, has the effect of simplifying the composition to the essential expressive elements of faces and hands. The maid holds out the letter with uncertainty. Bathsheba, if this is she, clearly knows who sent it: she looks stunned and serious and uncertain all at once. She is on the threshold of a fate that she cannot resist but is yet to understand. It is unclear whether we are meant to think of the lady in the painting as the actual biblical figure of Bathsheba, or a modern woman who finds herself in a similar, troubling predicament.

Bathsheba's face is the best thing in it but the picture as a whole is not entirely successful. It is a brave attempt by Vermeer to work against the grain of his own gift. The result is perhaps more melodramatic than dramatic, the poses and expressions of both figures seeming a little contrived. It will have added something nonetheless to the collection of pictures in the house on the Oude Delft.

Vermeer did a number of different things in his cycle of pictures for Maria de Knuijt. He provided her and those in her circle with role models: exemplary images of female piety such as *The Milkmaid*, embodying charitable works, or *Woman with a Balance*, representing the more inward spiritual life. He alluded to stories in the Bible that touched on their lives in various ways. He painted their places of worship, as in *The Little Street*, showing the hidden church of the Remonstrants. He painted their home town of Delft as a vision of the world as it might be some day.

The programme of paintings for the invisible Church on the Oude Delft was clearly different from any cycle of pictures painted for the visible Christian churches of the past. Taken as a whole, Vermeer's work for The Golden Eagle is of the same order of achievement as Giotto's Arena Chapel frescoes in Padua, or Michelangelo's paintings for the Sistine Chapel ceiling in the Vatican; but unlike them it follows no chronology and tells no single clear story. A great deal of medieval and Renaissance religious art was painted to bring the tales of the Bible to people who could not read, but the pious dissenting Protestants for whom Vermeer was painting read the New Testament at least four times a year and knew their Bible inside out. They did not want an art that reframed narratives they already knew, but one that helped them to think and pray. Like Collegiant free prophecy, Vermeer's work was open and discursive. There was no fixed pattern of prescribed belief into which his paintings were supposed to fit. They were mostly designed as pairs, but the pairs could seemingly be looked at in any order.

Anyone attempting to understand the milieu for which Vermeer's pictures were made, more than three centuries after the fact, would be wise to keep an open mind. We can be confident that they were painted to assist the devotions of Maria de Knuijt and her female friends, who were most likely Remonstrants with strong Collegiant leanings. But to suggest that they were painted solely for those people seems unduly limiting. To borrow a Dutch distinction, it is better in such matters to stand with the *rekkelijken* than the *preciezen*: better to be flexible than over-precise. Such evidence that we have, including the generous spirit of the paintings themselves, suggests that they were also meant for the wider appreciation of many other dissenting Protestants, friends to Maria de Knuijt and her husband, who would have come to the house to see them, not necessarily in the context of religious devotion.

This broader audience for Vermeer's pictures cannot be limited to any particular group or groups. They would have been part of that large and diverse mass of Dutch freethinkers who did so much to shape the Republic in its Era of True Liberty: people with a liberal outlook who longed for peace and an end to the terrible wars of the time, who were deeply pious but mistrustful of dogma, so reluctant to commit to any one Church or confession. As we will see presently, there is good reason to believe that such unaffiliated Christians were made welcome at The Golden Eagle, to admire and reflect on the paintings that hung there. We know that Vermeer himself was in direct contact with a number of people fitting that description.

Despite their evident variety, there was a common thread to all of the artist's pictures for the house on the Oude Delft. They were without exception set in a world that any Dutch person of the period would have recognized as their own. Buildings, people, clothes and objects: everything in them was grounded in lived reality. As we have seen, this may have reflected a residual Protestant wariness of explicitly religious imagery. But Vermeer probably had deeper reasons too for updating ancient Christian themes and stories, and making them seem part of modern experience.

While each of the 'morning coat' paintings has something different to say, the underlying message of hope remains the same across all three. It is possible for a Dutchwoman of today, writing at her desk, to be visited by divine inspiration. It is possible for a modern woman with a complicated life and perhaps some skeletons in the closet to be chosen by God, as Bathsheba was once chosen by David. It is possible for a young lady at her dressing table to be enlightened by a flash of wisdom, as the merchant in Christ's parable once was. For Vermeer and those closest to him it was axiomatic that the truths of the Christian faith were as nothing if not kept alive, every day, in the thoughts and actions of Christ's followers. That message was brought vividly to life in what has become his most famous painting of all.

GIRL WITH A PEARL EARRING

When Vermeer's pictures for Maria de Knuijt and her husband were dispersed at auction in 1696, three *tronien* were the last lots sold. Lot 38, the first of this trio of animated portraits to go under the hammer, was advertised as the best of them. Described in the auction catalogue as 'a *tronie* in antique dress, uncommonly artful', this picture can be confidently identified as the *Girl with a Pearl Earring* now in the collection of the Mauritshuis. The girl portrayed is certainly wearing 'antique dress', in the form of an oriental turban fashioned from scarves of yellow and ultramarine blue, of the kind in which Dutch artists of the period were apt to clothe biblical characters. The picture is so beautifully painted that its every last detail proclaims Vermeer's uncommon artfulness. The expression on the girl's face is hauntingly immediate, the artist's treatment of light and shade beguilingly delicate. The painting of the highlights in her limpid light-brown eyes is brilliant, so too the recreation of the reflections trapped in the pearl of otherworldly size that she wears as an earring.

Not only does the girl seem on the point of utterance, she has the air of someone about to say the most urgent thing they have ever said. It is a picture of a moment preserved in stillness, but which is also full of motion. The girl's feelings are shifting and turning, in transition. She is moving in the literal sense too, turning around to look someone in the eye. She has only just realized who that someone is.

To understand the painting we need to know three things: the identity of the real live girl who sat for it; the identity of the character in the Bible whose part she plays; and the identity of the person to whom she turns, as if to speak. The first two are fairly easy to establish. Once they are known, the third follows logically and all becomes clear. *Girl with a Pearl Earring* has a reputation for being insolubly enigmatic but in truth it is one of Vermeer's most straightforward pictures. Its messages are piercingly direct and demanding.

The painter shows us a girl of about twelve, maybe thirteen. Vermeer's eldest daughter, Maria, was born in 1654, but why would he paint a biblically inspired portrait of his own child for the house of his patrons? Considering that the picture was made for Maria de Knuijt and her husband it is a fair assumption that the sitter was someone they knew and cared about. There is only one plausible candidate, namely their daughter, Magdalena van Ruijven.

Magdalena was born in October 1655, so would have reached the age of twelve in the autumn of 1667. Assuming that she participated in the Collegiant movement she would probably have solemnized her commitment to Christ at that age, possibly undergoing baptism by full immersion at the summer gathering at Rijnsburg the following year. Vermeer's portrait of her in character may have been painted to mark that rite of passage. It could have been done either before or after the baptism itself, so it was probably completed sometime in 1667 or 1668.

If the girl who sat for the painting is Magdalena van Ruijven, which figure in the Bible might she reincarnate? Again, there can only be one answer. Magdalena had been named for Mary Magdalene, like her grandmother before her. There seems to have been a family tradition of venerating Mary Magdalene, to judge by the fact that one of the first pictures commissioned from Vermeer by Magdalena's mother, the *Sleeping Maid*, was directly inspired by her legend. So *Girl with a Pearl Earring* brings us face to face with Magdalena van Ruijven in the persona of Mary Magdalene, follower of Christ.

Towards whom does the girl in the picture turn with such depth of feeling? The answer to the last of our three questions is to be found in that passage in John's Gospel where Mary goes to Christ's tomb in search of his body. A text close to the hearts of many Collegiant women, it is worth quoting in full. *Girl with a Pearl Earring* is an imaginary representation of the Magdalene as she appears in the words of its final verse, emphasized here in italics:

> But Mary stood without at the sepulchre weeping: and as she wept, she stooped down, and looked into the sepulchre, and seeth two angels in white sitting, the one at the head, and the other at the feet, where the body of Jesus had lain. And they say unto her, Woman, why weepest thou? She saith unto them, Because they have taken away my Lord, and I know not where they have laid him.
>
> And when she had thus said, she turned herself back, and saw Jesus standing, and knew not that it was Jesus. Jesus saith unto her, Woman,

why weepest thou? whom seekest thou? She, supposing him to be the gardener, saith unto him, Sir, if thou have borne him hence, tell me where thou hast laid him, and I will take him away. *Jesus saith unto her, Mary. She turned herself, and saith unto him, Rabboni; which is to say, Master.*

Vermeer conjures up Mary Magdalene in this instant, as she turns back towards the gardener whom she has just understood to be Jesus Christ. The look on her face expresses dawning recognition and wonder, mingled with awe, humility and love. There is the suggestion of tears recently shed in her bright, liquid eyes. The pearl at her ear is impossibly large because it is no simple jewel but a reflection of the state of her soul, bursting with joy and irradiated with divine light. She is the first person in all of history to see the risen Christ, to speak with him, to grasp the enormity of all that his presence embodies. Once she has got over the sublime shock of it, she will tell the rest of the world what she, and only she, has been given to know.

To have been christened Magdalena was to have been charged with preserving that meeting in the memory. Vermeer's picture was there to summon and sustain that moment daily, directing Magdalena's prayers and placing her always in the presence of Christ, near his empty tomb. The picture would also have spoken powerfully to those who visited or prayed in the house where she lived with her parents. Deeply affecting, yet conceived in a spirit of ruthless conceptual purity, it accomplishes something that several of the other pictures painted for those rooms could represent only in terms of desire or longing: the return to earth of the resurrected Christ.

Magdalena as Mary Magdalene uttering the word 'Master' brings Christ by implication into the same room as her and therefore us. He remains invisible, like the unseen rainbow summoned by the *View of Delft*, but is nonetheless present as the focus of her gaze. This turns the picture into a kind of challenge. If we are looking at her and she is looking at Jesus, then we must be standing in his shoes.

THE INVISIBLE CHURCH, 1657–72

THE END OF THE ARRANGEMENT

We know from the Amsterdam auction of 1696 that Lot 38, the 'uncommonly artful' *Girl with a Pearl Earring*, had been one of three *tronien* in The Golden Eagle, but we have little information about the other two. They are simply described in the auction catalogue as Lot 39, 'another ditto Vermeer' and Lot 40, 'a pendant of the same'.

One possible candidate for Lot 39 is the *Girl with a Red Hat* in the National Gallery of Art in Washington. But since that appears to be a secular portrait, innocent of religious meaning, it is unlikely to have been part of the invisible Church. Vermeer accepted outside commissions on a few rare occasions, so perhaps *Girl with a Red Hat* is an instance of that practice. It would make sense for the sitter to have been a participant in Maria de Knuijt's Collegiant group. We should hardly be surprised if a woman who went to the meetings at The Golden Eagle on the Oude Delft every week should want a Vermeer for herself.

The presumption therefore is that Lot 39, sadly, is lost. Lot 40, 'a pendant of the same', can tentatively be identified with a picture still extant, the so-called *Study of a Young Woman* in the Metropolitan Museum of Art in New York. Despite its modern title this is actually a finished work, which may indeed have been painted as a pendant to the *Girl with a Pearl Earring*. The canvas is the same size, the lighting is similar and so is the scale and position of the sitter, who turns to face the viewer with a smile. But here there is no drama, just a sense of peace and well-being: what this second picture lacks, compared with the first, is any sense of the momentous. Looking from one to the other we travel from the macrocosm of divine love, irradiating the entire world, to its microcosm. The subject is a fresh-faced happy girl, perhaps a little older than Magdalena in the other picture. She has the same slightly prognathous jaw as the young man in *The Procuress*, who is possibly Vermeer's self-portrait.[90] Might this actually be one of the painter's own daughters, Maria perhaps, or Elisabeth? They were close in age to Magdalena. If so, the picture would present another more down-to-earth version of the love that nurtures and protects: not the love of Christ for Mary Magdalene and all mankind, but a father's unqualified love for his daughter. She basks in its radiance like a cat in the sun.

Vermeer would paint only three more pictures for the house of his patrons. They were probably all completed by the end of 1671, by which time Pieter Claesz van Ruijven had put 106 Oude Delft on the market, thus marking the end of the women's meetings there.[91] The paintings were likely to have been done earlier than that. Two of the three are now in London: A *Young Woman Standing at a Virginal*, in the National Gallery, and *The Guitar Player*, in Kenwood House. The third is in Paris, in the Louvre: it is the picture known as *The Lacemaker*. All three appeared in the 1696 auction, where they were described respectively as Lot 37, 'A lady playing the clavecin', Lot 4, 'A young lady playing the guitar, very good', and Lot 12, 'A young lady doing needlework'.

The two pictures of women playing musical instruments are hauntingly beautiful. There are differences between them but their function seems to be the same. The guitar player wears the lemon-yellow morning coat that belonged to Vermeer's wife. As she plucks the strings of her instrument she smiles and looks off to her right. Her coiffure is a playful arrangement of tumbling ringlets that hang in the air against the back wall of the room like some new form of musical notation. There are books on the table in the corner. At her back hangs a picture in a brilliant gilt frame, a tranquil landscape seen under blue skies, dominated by a single elegant tree shaped like a sprig of parsley. This painting-within-a-painting may have been based on an actual picture of a woodland scene by Pieter van Asch, who was registered as a landscape painter in Delft's Guild of St Luke. If so Vermeer improved the original to represent an ideal world, an earthly paradise, to which the lady with the guitar holds the key. One day she might take us there.

When he came to paint the girl's face and form Vermeer invented an early version of what would later be known as Impressionism. Her clothes are webs of gossamer, the pearls at her throat droplets of light, her face a blur. She is more vision than person. She resembles the angels who make music at the feet of the Virgin and Child in the *Sacra Conversazioni* of Bellini. There is a point to the resemblance, which is not coincidental. She is herself an angel. Such messengers were expected by Collegiants. Their arrival had been foreseen by Daniel de Breen in his prophetic text *Of the Triumphant Spiritual Kingdom of Our Lord Jesus Christ*, according to which angels would be sent from above to bring about the great change and turn this world into an earthly paradise. Vermeer is imagining what they might look like, perhaps doing a little more than that. To paint something is also to summon it into being.

A Young Woman Standing at a Virginal occupies a room more minutely observed than that in which we find the guitar player, but equally idealized. Once more there is an arcadian landscape on the wall, framed in gold. Its image is doubled in the painting on the open lid of the virginal that the lady is playing. A large painting of Cupid with his bow and arrows, brandishing the ace of hearts, hangs directly behind her. He is the symbol of faithful love, the lover who cleaves to just one beloved. In the foreground, angled towards the player of the clavecin, is an empty chair.

This room is like a temple filled with votive signs and symbols. The woman at the clavecin is like a caryatid set free to walk in temple precincts. She stands perfectly upright, the folds in her white silk gown giving her the appearance of a fluted marble column. She too has ringlets that dance and play at the margins of her face. Her expression is welcoming but also remote. It is as if we see her through mist or fallen cloud. Like the lady playing the guitar, she has a string of pearls around her neck. She is another angel with ancestors in Italy: she looks like Piero della Francesca's angels in the *Senigallia Madonna* and is lit by transverse light just as they are. The empty chair pulled up to face her tells us the identity of her beloved: empty chairs in Vermeer mark the place of Christ. Like the guitar player she is one of those sent to help us get to that perfect place, that paradise, framed like a vision in gold. It will not be long now, she seems to say.

The last painting for the house of his patrons, *The Lacemaker*, is the smallest of them all. It is also one of the most brilliant and surprising. Here the painter's theme, as so often, is love, this time the love of a young mother-to-be for her unborn child, expressed in the making of a delicate piece of lace. So abruptly cropped is the composition that we seem to come across the lacemaker quite by chance while she is in the middle of her work. She is utterly absorbed by the activity in hand, as she weaves a simple pattern with the threads held taut by two bobbins squeezed between her fingers. Like the *Guitar Player* she wears yellow, and like her she wears her hair in lively coiling ringlets, but the resemblance stops there. She is not an otherworldly being but someone of this world. She is pregnant and probably nearing the end of her term. Hence her complete concentration on the piece of lace. It is for the baby and she needs to get it done on time.

We know the lacemaker is pregnant because Vermeer has set the image of a woman's womb, veins and arteries pulsing with blood, in the foreground. Lightly disguised as a *naaikussen* or sewing cushion, where seamstresses kept their thread, this fruitful object of the painter's imagination spills a little stream of white strands or fibres, and a startling torrent of fine red filaments, pooling crimson on the carpet-draped surface of a table. They look more like trails of spilt blood than threads: Vermeer laid his canvas flat and dripped red paint on it from above, using a loaded brush, so that it splashed and splattered. The sewing cushion's function as metaphor is sealed by the fact that such an object has no part to play in a lacemaker's work, which involves the meticulous separation of threads, not their entanglement in a matted pile. There are many other lacemakers in Dutch art, none of whom has a *naaikussen* at her side.

So, while the girl is working away at her little piece of lace, with her full attention and her busy hands, another piece of far finer lace is taking shape within her body. What she makes herself, she makes with her love for her child. But the child being made within her is being formed by the love of God, whose miraculous powers of creation are responsible for the complex systems of the human body. Those systems are figured in the sewing cushion and the red threads that pour into it, like the arterial flow of a mother's blood nourishing the placenta. We can sense Vermeer's wonder at the complex beauty of it all. Might this be how a mother's love is made in the first place? Does it all happen in the blood?

After *The Lacemaker*, Vermeer would paint no more pictures for the house on the Oude Delft. Shortly after completing the picture, it would seem, his special arrangement with Pieter Claesz van Ruijven and Maria de Knuijt came to an end. Why this happened we do not know. Vermeer remained on good terms with the couple, to judge by a document that places him in Pieter's company, in The Hague, in the summer of 1672. Pieter and Maria had probably moved out of their house on the Oude Delft by then. They were certainly living in The Hague by June 1674 at the latest.[92] Pieter may have been in poor health during these years. He did not have long to live.

Maybe it was that, combined with the move to another city, that finally put an end to the project. Maria's meetings probably stopped when she went to live in a new town. Her friends had been Vermeer's audience, so in their absence adding more pictures to the collection might have felt pointless. The project may already have lost some of its momentum by the time Vermeer was painting *Girl with a Pearl Earring*. By then the year 1666 had come and gone, with none of the signs that millenarians had hoped to see: no mass conversion of the Jews, no sudden spread of fellow feeling among the warring sects of Christianity. Despite the repeated failure of the new millennium to materialize, optimistic Collegiants continued to believe that the Last Days were at hand. But they were no longer holding their breath.

Having lost some of its messianic urgency, the Collegiant movement changed character. Beginning in the late 1660s complaints were heard that the meetings for free prophecy had lost their intensity, and had become too cerebral and remote. This was especially true of the Rotterdam College, according to one of its number, Barend Joosten Stol, who in 1676 felt moved to write *Den Philosopherenden Boer*, or *The Philosophical Farmer*, a dialogue in which a devout farmer rebuked a Cartesian philosopher for turning Collegiant worship into an intellectual exercise. Half the words spoken at the meetings were in Latin, the farmer complained, calling for a return to the heartfelt Bible readings of the old days: 'the apostles taught trust and belief, not philosophy'.[93]

Vermeer's creative life had been strikingly in step with the life cycle of the Collegiant movement all the way through. His unique sequence of paintings for the house on the Oude Delft had been conceived when the movement was at its zenith, the number of enthusiasts for it increasing and new groups multiplying across the Dutch Republic. That period of peak energy lasted for the best part of ten years, during which time he created most of the pictures for which he is now famous. Once that moment had passed, and the movement had entered a more introverted phase, Vermeer ceased painting for his most important patrons. All this may be highly significant, or just a coincidence. No creative collaboration lasts forever. Altogether Vermeer had worked for Maria de Knuijt and her husband, Pieter, for the best part of thirteen years. Few artists have been blessed with greater continuity of patronage.

The painter underwent no great personality change after the termination of the arrangement, so far as we can tell. Such evidence as we have indicates that his links and affinities with freethinkers and religious liberals remained as strong as ever, and that he continued in his millenarian beliefs. But he no longer painted as he had done before.

He may have realized that the project was nearing its end by around 1667 or 1668. After that he would find a few ways to carry on working, but not many. He did some painting for himself, and at least one new patron turned up. But gradually he spent less and less time in the studio. Perhaps in his heart he knew he was done, the best of his life's work complete.

Realistically the only way he could have expected to carry on would have been to find another patron or patrons as uniquely congenial to him as Maria and Pieter. But this did not happen. Leaving aside his late pictures for the Van Ruijvens, from about 1668 until his death in 1675 Vermeer created just four significant works of art. There were a few other odds and ends, but those four works were his last meaningful things. He painted them, as was his way, in pairs.

THE GEOGRAPHER AND *THE ASTRONOMER*

Vermeer's interest in the science of optics is well documented, and richly demonstrated in his pictures. The tonal subtlety of his painting is such that all linear description is abolished in favour of exquisitely nuanced gradations of light and shade. That no drawings survive by his hand is a measure of his dedication to the principle that there are no lines in the human field of vision. As we know, he was probably helped to arrive at this truth by looking through lenses and viewing the moving images projected within a camera obscura.

Vermeer was a creator of scientifically informed optical illusions. But he was also a profoundly religious artist who seems to have regarded painting as a form of devotion. There was no contradiction in this. The scientific revolutions of seventeenth-century Europe are often taken to have brought the ascendancy of a desanctified and mechanical world view, although that is far from the truth. Vermeer's contemporary Isaac Newton was the exemplary scientific figure of the early Enlightenment, known for formulating the laws of motion and universal gravitation, and for establishing classical mechanics. He also spent many years speculating on the meanings of the Book of Revelation and calculating the date 'when the end of time might be', as he expressed the problem in his *Observations on the Prophecies of Daniel and the Apocalypse of St John*.[94]

For Vermeer, as for Newton, the revelations of science complemented the prophecies of religion. If Vermeer's illusions seem as lifelike as reality itself, it is not because he was bent on recording empirical fact, but because he was trying to make that which can only be dreamed of look so real you might touch it. He painted for the same reason that people pray: to make things come true.

Optics was not the only branch of science to attract Vermeer's notice during the later years of his life. The meaning of one of his most deeply affecting pictures, *The Lacemaker*, rests on an allusion to placental blood supply that might not easily have occurred to the artist had he not been aware of William Harvey's discovery of the circulation of the blood. Harvey's descriptions of pulmonary and systemic circulation had first been published in Latin as *De Motu Cordis* in Frankfurt in 1628. The text included a discussion of the many veins that 'strike into the placenta like roots of a tree into the ground'.[95] Harvey's findings were by no means common knowledge by the late 1660s, but Vermeer was well placed to be aware of them. He was part of the circle of Adrian Paets, whose interests extended to scientific discovery, through whom he may have come to know Spinoza. The philosopher undoubtedly knew Harvey's work. He corresponded about it with Henry Oldenburg of the Royal Society and alluded to it several times elsewhere, notably in Book IV of the *Ethics*.[96]

Two other scientific disciplines caught Vermeer's attention during the late 1660s, namely astronomy and geography. We know this because he was called to personify them in the pair of paintings commissioned by his patron Adrian Paets, director of the Dutch East India Company and much else besides. *The Astronomer* and *The Geographer* were dated by the artist, the former to 1668, the latter to 1669. They were clearly commissioned as a pair and painted as such, although time has since separated them. *The Astronomer* is in the Louvre, *The Geographer* in the Städel Museum in Frankurt.

During the seventeenth century astronomy and geography were considered complementary fields of study, for good reason. The vast profits of the Dutch East India Company depended on both. Knowledge of the stars was essential to maritime navigation, because it helped to determine latitude. Knowledge of the world's different continents made possible the exploration and exploitation of faraway places. In short, astronomy led a ship's captain to his destination while geography showed him where to go when he got there. The idea for *The Geographer* and *The Astronomer*, which are so different from the rest of Vermeer's work, presumably originated with Adrian Paets. He is assumed to have commissioned them to hang in East India House, the Delft offices of the VOC.

The Astronomer is shown in his study, half-rising from his chair in order to rotate his celestial globe in its stand. The crumpled folds of a Persian carpet have been pushed impatiently to the edge of his desk, making room for the book that lies open before him. Affixed to the cabinet on the back wall is a celestial planisphere, a chart with rotating paper discs for identifying stars and constellations and for plotting their future alignments. There is a painting on the wall behind him, cropped by the right edge of the composition. His study is a contemporary Dutch room with high ceilings, lit from the left by watery sunshine entering through a leaded glass window. But the astronomer himself looks like someone from another time. His voluminous robe and long, lank hair give him the air of an ancient prophet or holy man. He might almost be one of the Three Wise Men, who had themselves studied the heavens to plot a course for Christ's birthplace. The modern scientist is also a magus.

The Geographer is likewise shown in his study, which is much like the room in the picture next door. The light enters from the left. There is a desk with a rolled-up carpet again hastily shoved to its edge, forming thick folds that catch the light from a window set into the wall on the left. There is a cupboard pushed against the back wall, with a terrestrial globe perched on top. That globe is turned to reveal the Indian Ocean, where many of the VOC's ships sailed. The map hanging on the same wall, only a third of which is visible, is a sea chart of Europe originally published by Willem Jansz Bleau in 1600. Unlike the astronomer, the geographer has no chair and stands over his desk, on which two books and a map can be seen. Dividers in hand, he pauses for thought and stares into space as he contemplates whatever is in his mind's eye.

Vermeer's scientists are descended from an illustrious line of deep thinkers as portrayed in painting. The tradition to which they belong is partly Flemish but mostly Italian. The pictorial celebration of intellect *per se* was born in the studies of Renaissance men like the scholar-soldier Federigo da Montefeltro, whose intimate *studiolo* in the Ducal Palace in Urbino was furnished by Justus of Ghent in the 1470s with portraits of famous Greek and Roman exponents of Astronomy, Philosophy, Geometry and other disciplines. The concept of a painted pantheon of intellectual heroes was then appropriated and transformed by Raphael, himself born in Urbino, when he created his *School of Athens* for the far grander papal library of Julius II some forty years later. Raphael's innovation was to dramatize the advancement of human knowledge by placing all the sages of time past on a single stage, at a single moment, then having them interact with one another in a spectacular tableau vivant inspired by the transmission of ideas. Side by side at the centre of the *School of Athens* he placed two famous philosophers: Plato, who points upwards to heaven and the realm of Ideal Forms, and Aristotle, who gestures to the ground as if to say that this world is all he intends to study.

Vermeer's geographer and astronomer do not communicate with one another across the divide that separates them. But, insofar as they are animated embodiments of their respective intellectual disciplines, they are not so distant relations to Raphael's jostling throng of thinkers. They even bear a trace memory of the contrasting gestures of Plato and Aristotle in their own body language: in the act of examining the constellations on his celestial globe the astronomer reaches upwards, as if to the stars; whereas the geographer leans forward heavily and pushes downwards onto his desk.

The atmosphere of both paintings is portentous, suggesting that there may be more afoot in these scholars' rooms than meets the eye. Vermeer had always dealt in codes and clues, never more so than here. The first clue to his meaning is so well concealed that few can have noticed it without prompting, even in Vermeer's time. It lies within the open book in front of the astronomer. When the picture is viewed closely, the book's pages can be seen in sufficient detail to allow for its identification. It is the second edition of Adriaen Metius's textbook on astronomy and geography, *Institutiones Astronomicae & Geographicae*, which was published in Amsterdam in 1621.[97] Because it is open at an illustration showing a cartwheel astrolabe, we know that Vermeer's astronomer must be reading the first words of Book III, 'On the Investigation or Observation of the Stars'.

Those words themselves cannot be read from the impressionistically blurred squiggles that are the painter's shorthand for text, so the only way to hunt the clue down is to obtain a copy of Metius's actual text: a high barrier, even by Vermeer's standards. The passage at the beginning of Book III begins:

> The first observers and investigators of the situation and course of the stars have been, as history points out, our ancestors the patriarchs who through inspiration from God the Lord and the knowledge of geometry and assistance of mathematical instruments have measured and described for us the firmament and the course of the stars.

Metius went on to explain that it was 'the children of Seth', revered in Jewish tradition as the righteous ancestors of Noah, who had 'founded the science of the stars and the knowledge of the heavens'.

The one person who would definitely have been alive to the inclusion of this hidden text was the man who commissioned the picture. Metius's words would have spoken to one of Paets's particular concerns, as a leading Collegiant and millenarian, namely the finding of the Lost Tribes of Israel, a necessary precondition for the mass conversion of the Jews that was to inaugurate a thousand years of peace. According to a millenarian legend preserved in the Apocrypha, it was thanks to their prowess in astronomy that the exiled tribes of Israel had managed 'to leave the multitude of the nations and go to a more distant region where mankind had never lived' (II Esdras 13:41–2). If that were the case, the only way to find them would be to read the stars as well as they had done many centuries ago.

A further gloss on this idea is to be found in another detail of *The Astronomer*. The painting on the back wall of the room is a depiction of *The Finding of Moses*. It tells the tale of how Pharaoh's daughter took in Moses after his mother had set him adrift in a basket, to escape Pharaoh's order that all newborn Hebrew boys be drowned in the Nile. This story of an Egyptian caring for a Jew was a favourite of Remonstrants and Collegiants, who saw in it a prefiguration of their tolerant attitude towards those of other faiths. But that is perhaps not its primary meaning on this occasion. The picture hangs on the astronomer's wall to remind him and us of the mission at hand: Moses must be found all over again, this time in the New World.

Perhaps the most emphatic reference to the millenarian beliefs cryptically embedded in the two paintings has been obscured by the fact that they no longer hang together as a pair. But it is easy enough to reconstruct, with reproductions of the pictures to hand. Picture them side by side as they once were, with *The Astronomer* on the left and *The Geographer* on the right. It then becomes apparent that together they form a pictogram of the most famous verse in the Book of Revelation, also evoked in the *View of Delft*: 'And I saw a new heaven and a new earth . . .'

The year 1666 had been and gone but for Adrian Paets the discovery of the Lost Tribes may still have been a matter of pressing concern: one of the main priorities, perhaps *the* main priority, for millenarians like himself attempting to hasten the increasingly overdue End of Days. The secret message embedded in Vermeer's two paintings *The Astronomer* and *The Geographer* is that it is their priority, too. We who are in on the secret are to understand that these two men, so intent on their work, are not merely thinking great thoughts in the abstract. They are working together, albeit in separate rooms, on a single project. They are trying to calculate where the Lost Tribes of Israel might be, so that a squadron of VOC ships can be dispatched to bring them back: because it surely follows that if the raison d'être of the two scientists is to locate the missing Jews of legend, that of the

Dutch East India Company must be to retrieve them. It may be wondered how such an enterprise was to be explained to the shareholders.

The pictures remain something of a puzzle, even after their meanings have been excavated. Why might Adrian Paets have wanted Vermeer to include such cryptic symbolism in paintings probably intended for prominent display in the offices of the Dutch East India Company? Was Paets pretending to himself, and anyone else he made privy to the pictures' meanings, that Dutch colonialist trade and all the violence that went with it was somehow justified by its role in God's great plan for the Lost Tribes? Or, as a director of the VOC, did he genuinely dream of repurposing that hard-nosed enterprise as a vessel of world peace?

The information needed to answer such questions is lacking. But it is clear, mainly from the letters and journals of Christian missionaries active in the New World, that strong belief in the legend of the Lost Tribes persisted for decades after the millennial year of 1666 had come and gone. William Penn, the leading Quaker who left England to found Pennsylvania in 1682, persuaded himself that he had seen so many signs of Judaism among the native Indians there that he might almost be living among the Ashkenazim in one of London's newly created Jewish quarters: 'I find [the Indians] of like countenance, and their children of so lively a resemblance, that a man would think himself in Duke's Place or Bury Street . . .'[98] Apocalyptic fantasies clearly died hard. Vermeer's two pictures for Adrian Paets are the relics of outlandish hope, and remind us that sometimes the past really is another country.

THE WELCOME GUEST

Just as Vermeer was finishing the second of his pictures for Adrian Paets he received a visit from a gentleman by the name of Pieter Teding van Berkhout. Van Berkhout arrived in Delft from The Hague on 14 May 1669 with the express purpose of seeing the permanent exhibition of Vermeers on display in the house on the Oude Delft canal. He had made an appointment with the artist, who received him cordially and showed him around the rooms where his pictures hung. Van Berkhout must have been impressed and intrigued, because six weeks later, on 21 June, he was back to meet Vermeer again and to take another look at his work. He noted both encounters in his journal. Those two diary entries are the only first-hand accounts of meetings with Vermeer other than the one written by the Frenchman Balthasar de Monconys six years earlier. Here is what Van Berkhout wrote:

> 14 May, 1669. I rose rather early in the morning ... then took a ride to Delft on a yacht ... Upon my arrival I saw an excellent painter named Vermeer, who showed me a few curiosities made with his own hand.
>
> 21 June, 1669. I ... went out and visited a celebrated painter named Vermeer who showed me some examples of his art, the most extraordinary and most curious aspect of which consists in the perspective.[99]

Van Berkhout's descriptions are if anything even more frustratingly abbreviated than that of Monconys. But they are revealing nonetheless, not least because they show the world of difference between the way in which Vermeer received two very different people.

Monconys the militant Jesuit was persona non grata, full stop. When he surprised Vermeer by turning up without notice, the painter gave him short shrift and sent him off to see Hendrick van Buyten the baker. He never got a sniff of the only collection of Vermeer's work that mattered, the one at the house of Pieter Claesz van Ruijven and Maria de Knuijt. Pieter Teding van Berkhout, by contrast, got special treatment. Vermeer met him at the house where his pictures hung, and stayed with him while he took them all in. This happened not once but twice. Vermeer and Van Berkhout may also have popped down the street to see *The Geographer* and *The Astronomer* at the offices of the VOC. They never went near Papists' Corner, because they had no reason to do so.

Why was Van Berkhout shown such favour? Because he was on the same side as Vermeer and his friends, part of their network. He had recently married one of Adrian Paets's cousins and probably came calling with an introduction from Paets himself. But he was also an exemplary liberal in politics and religion alike, therefore Vermeer's sort of person in every way. We know quite a lot about him and the company he kept.

Not long after Van Berkhout's two visits to see Vermeer, he and his new wife settled in Delft. They would set up home there in the autumn of 1669, in a grand house that was itself on the Oude Delft, just a stone's throw away from The Golden Eagle and the hidden Remonstrant church. Word soon got around that Van Berkhout was immensely rich (which he was, by inheritance) and also that he was intensely pious. He was soon befriended by a well-connected Reformed predicant named Johan van Bleiswijk, who played an important part in the fluid religious life of Delft during the 1670s. This Van Bleiswijk was no advocate of toleration, but, as a passionate exponent of the so-called 'Further Reformation' of the Calvinists, he shared many of the values of the Remonstrants and even the Collegiants, outcasts though they were from his Church.[100] An admirer of Thomas à Kempis, he encouraged his Reformed congregation to read the Bible at home and gave Van Berkhout a self-help manual he had written for people wanting to read Scripture for themselves. Among other things this contained a plan that required reading the Old Testament once and the New Testament four times every year.

We know what kind of people read the New Testament four times a year. Keeping track of his progress in his journal, Van Berkhout adhered to the prescribed programme more or less exactly. He also encouraged his large family to meet regularly in his home on the Oude Delft to read the Bible and pray together. Like the meetings of the Collegiants, such homespun gatherings were occasions for prayer and free prophecy away from clerical supervision.

Our main source of knowledge about the detail of Van Berkhout's beliefs is his journal, which gives us a preciously comprehensive account of his reading, and therefore a snapshot of the interests of a well-educated dissenting Dutch Protestant. It is all the more valuable because it paints such a clear picture of someone to whom we know Vermeer was happy to show his work: a welcome guest.

Van Berkhout read a great deal about contemporary events, buying newspapers and also periodicals such as the *Mercure Galant*, which were filled with court news, anecdotes, poetry extracts and so on. He acquired popular pamphlets, or blue books, by the dozen. He also bought books about history and geography. But around a quarter of his books were about religion or religious history, his greatest preoccupations.

His library was particularly well-stocked with literature lamenting the divisions caused by the Reformation and calling for an end to sectarian division. He diligently ploughed through the first two volumes of Gerard Brandt's *History of the Reformation*, which celebrated the triumph over adversity of the Remonstrants. He also read and admired *The History of the Edict of Nantes*, which was written by one of his close friends, Elie Benoist, the exiled French Huguenot historian. Benoist believed that the evils besetting French Protestants had their origins in the French state's refusal to embrace religious toleration. If only the French had been as flexible as the Dutch there would have been far less bloodshed and the displacement of the Huguenots into a refugee sect would have been avoided. Van Berkhout's comments on Benoist's book suggest that he heartily concurred with such views. Within a few years the historian's forebodings would be fulfilled, with the revocation of the Edict of Nantes leading to an exodus of the French Huguenots: yet another mass migration caused by religious persecution.

Van Berkhout was reading Brandt and Benoist in the mid-1670s and 1680s, but his journal also gives us a taste of what was on his mind at around the time of his meetings with Vermeer. In about 1670 Van Berkhout acquired a copy of *La Réunion du Christianisme* (*The Reunification of Christianity*) by Isaac d'Huisseau, one of the leaders of the beleaguered Reformed Church of France, soon to be extinguished altogether. In that text, d'Huisseau urged a reunification of all Christian churches on the basis of a simplified creed, decrying the deaths of so many millions of Christians over minor points of doctrine. Much of d'Huisseau's book was plagiarized from Jacobus Arminius's famous oration *On Reconciling Religious Dissension among Christians*, foundation stone of the Remonstrant Church and the Collegiant movement.[101] Van Berkhout may or may not have been aware of the source of d'Huisseau's ideas, but he loved the ideas themselves: it was 'a very fine book', he commented.

Van Berkhout's journal is not written in a confessional style, mostly just listing the things he has done, the people he has seen, or the books he has read. His cursory remarks on Vermeer's work reflect this matter-of-fact approach. He probably had far more detailed and interesting thoughts about the artist's paintings that he simply never wrote down. The fact that he arranged to meet Vermeer for a second time suggests that the pictures had gained his full attention. The dates of his two visits, which took place in 1669, mean that he must have been one of the few people in history to have seen all of the paintings done for the invisible Church in situ.

Van Berkhout's description of the painter as 'celebrated' is intriguing and has been misconstrued as evidence of Vermeer's fame. But it should not be taken to imply that he was truly well-known, a name to be conjured with. To be celebrated is not the same as being famous. It is possible to be celebrated by a small group of people, and this was the case with Vermeer. Van Berkhout was a man of few words but he chose them carefully.

His two visits to The Golden Eagle confirm that there were people with a keen interest in Vermeer's paintings who were *not* part of the group formed by Maria de Knuijt and her female friends. The fact that he was received twice, and by the artist himself each time, suggests that Van Berkhout typified this broader audience for Vermeer's pictures. So how might we describe him? He was a pious freethinking Christian who felt a strong affinity for the Remonstrants and seems to have adopted some of the practices of the Collegiants when worshipping at home. But as far as we know he was part of no established Collegiant group, nor does he appear to have worshipped at the hidden Remonstrant church in Delft. He was, furthermore, prepared to accept spiritual guidance from a strict Calvinist minister such as Johan van Bleiswijk, albeit without ever becoming a member of the Reformed Church.

All in all, Pieter Teding van Berkhout was someone to whom it would be unwise to affix any label. What can be said for certain is that he was independent of mind and ecclesiastically unaffiliated. There were many others like him in the Dutch Republic: people who floated between one allegiance and another but settled on none.

'THE VAST SEA OF THESE SIGNS'

Vermeer's final pictures were not painted for Maria de Knuijt and Pieter Claesz van Ruijven but for other people. This allows us to see or infer other sides of him through what can be discovered about them. We already know much about Adrian Paets, and we can piece together a reasonably complete picture of Pieter Teding van Berkhout. Paets was exceptional, a man of great energy and intellect who played a major role as patron and protagonist in the development of early Enlightenment thought. Van Berkhout was a lesser light of seventeenth-century Dutch civilization, but nonetheless well read across a number of subjects. It was probably Paets who introduced Van Berkhout to Vermeer. Both men belonged to the uppermost echelon of Dutch society. Both were sincere in their religious beliefs and passionate in their political convictions. They were plainly comfortable in the painter's company, as he most likely was in theirs.

It is clear that Vermeer was a highly educated and sensitive man. His pictures for The Golden Eagle tell us that he knew the New Testament inside out, that he was deeply read in Dutch dissenting literature, and that he was able to translate radical Protestant theology into movingly humane pictorial terms. A number of his later pictures are also rich in allusions to the new science of his time, suggesting that he understood William Harvey's contributions to anatomy and was familiar with texts as abstruse as Adrian Metius's Latin commentaries on the origins of astronomy. Taken all in all, the sheer range of Vermeer's interests and knowledge suggests that by the time he entered the last decade of his life he had made numerous friends among the circle of Collegiants and Remonstrants orbiting the influential figure of Adrian Paets. He may also have owed some of his Remonstrant friendships to the influence of his mother, who appears to have been friendly with the Rombouts family. It was probably through her that he knew Jacob Rombouts, the grandson of Jacobus Arminius.

Direct documentary evidence of Vermeer's friendships and alliances is hard to come by, so thoroughly did he hide his traces. But we can identify one more admirer of his work thanks to an announcement made in the pages of a local newspaper, the *Amsterdamsche Courant*, on 24 February 1699. Here it was stated that:

> The beneficiaries of Hermann van Swoll, postmaster during his life, will, on Wednesday 22 April 1699 in Amsterdam, sell by auction to the highest bidder, at the home of the deceased, on the Herengracht, opposite the Leidsegracht ... artful and excellent paintings, collected with lots of effort and money over the years ... many top pieces ... and an artful work by Vermeer van Delft.

Hermann Dircks van Swoll, who had commissioned the said 'artful work' from Vermeer some thirty or so years earlier, was at the time of his death one of the richer men in one of the world's richest cities. He seems to have been intellectually curious and driven by ambition. He liked pictures and was widely read. The son of a baker named Stoffel Dircks, he had risen to become controller of Amsterdam's Wisselbank, one of the leading financial institutions of seventeenth-century Europe and the first bank to introduce an international reserve currency, the bank guilder. He had also served as principal postmaster of the Hamburger Comptoir, a position fondly associated by native Amsterdammers with the saving of their city: it had been a courier riding for the Hamburg postal service who had warned the city watch of William II's approaching army in the eventful summer of 1650. As a lucrative sideline Van Swoll had also speculated in property, making a fortune on the Amsterdam housing market.

Many of Vermeer's friends and patrons turn out to have been close to his own age. Van Swoll was born in 1632, the same year as the painter. He married Hendrijke Verhoef in 1656, and by 1666 he had prospered sufficiently to buy the plot of land on which his home, number 413 on the sought-after Herengracht canal, would eventually be built. The land alone cost 3,600 guilders. The house, which was a grand one, took several years to construct. The couple had probably just moved in when Van Swoll persuaded Vermeer to paint a picture for him, in about 1670.

The banker, postmaster and property investor had taken a discerning interest in art from an early age. The best man at his wedding had been Gerard Reynst, the pre-eminent art collector in the Dutch Republic at that time.[102] Reynst had acquired numerous masterpieces from the dispersed collections of King Charles I of England, sold to him direct on the orders of Oliver Cromwell. After the collector's death in 1660, the Dutch state purchased twenty-four of his best Italian paintings and a dozen of his finest classical sculptures, presenting them as a diplomatic gift, 'the Dutch Gift', to the restored Stuart King Charles II. Reynst was more than thirty years older than Van Swoll at the time of the latter's wedding, so may have been his mentor in matters of art.

Van Swoll was buried in Amsterdam's Noorderkerk on 23 December 1698.[103] The Noorderkerk was a Reformed church, but as we have seen that need be no indication of Swoll's faith: public churches were also public graveyards, where anyone had the right to be interred. A more useful guide to his religious orientation may be the document that places him in the home of a recently deceased merchant named Isaac Swartepaert, together with the well-known Amsterdam art dealer Gerrit Uylenburgh, on 17 January 1671.[104] Van Swoll and Uylenburgh were present to give an evaluation of the paintings in the dead man's estate. Uylenburgh was an art professional who regularly assisted in the compilation of such inventories, while Van Swoll was one of the most prominent bankers in Europe with no apparent business being there. The presumption is that the latter was present as a friend of the family to ensure fair play.

Not much is known about the Swartepaerts, other than that they were merchants and most probably Mennonites, like Uylenburgh. But one member of the family did achieve notoriety as a radical Collegiant. In 1678 Adrian Swartepaert published his *Revelation of the True Universal Belief*, in which he used rationalist arguments borrowed from the Socinians to question the doctrine of the Trinity: 'whatever contradicts reason contradicts God himself'.[105] If Hermann van Swoll was linked to the Swartepaert clan, which it seems he was, he may also have had links to the Collegiant movement.

Van Swoll's Vermeer was duly sold in Amsterdam, as his heirs had promised, on 22 April 1699. It was described in the auction catalogue as 'a seated woman with several meanings, representing the New Testament by Vermeer of Delft, vigorously glowing and painted'. Bidding was competitive and had reached 400 guilders by the time the hammer went down, twice as much as the sum paid for the *View of Delft* at the Dissius auction three years earlier. The picture still survives today and can be seen at The Metropolitan Museum of Art in New York. Its modern title is *Allegory of the Catholic Faith*, which might give the impression that it was painted as pro-Catholic propaganda. Vermeer's actual theme is the Catholic faith in crisis, blinded to the truth of Christ's message by a surfeit of unnecessary doctrines. Van Swoll must have asked him to paint a picture that clearly exposed the deficiencies of the Roman Church.

The setting is a space very like the secret chapel that Vermeer had created for the inner kitchen in Maria Thins's house on the Oude Langendijk. The artist pulls back a floor-to-ceiling curtain, which has one of the Three Magis' camels lurking in its folds, to reveal with a flourish his *mise-en-scène*. The room is more or less exactly as described in the inventory of Leap Year's Day 1676. On the back wall we see the notary's 'large painting representing Christ on the Cross', to its right 'about seven ells of gold-tooled leather' (cut down to roughly two by cropping); while a 'little sideboard' is being used as an altar on which, for good measure, has been placed the 'ebony wood crucifix' that Maria kept in her great hall, near Vermeer's armour. At the centre of the scene, hand on heart and with eyes uplifted, we find a female figure seated awkwardly on a chair set on a carpeted dais beside an open copy of a book of saints' lives placed on a lectern. She is derived from images of the personification of 'Catholic Faith' in Cesare Ripa's emblem book the *Iconologia*. She wears robes of white and blue, symbolizing the purity to which she aspires and the heaven to which she would ascend. She is destined to be disappointed, the artist insinuates.

The German Renaissance master Albrecht Dürer had embodied Melancholy as a woman sitting slumped in a barren landscape, surrounded by symbols, codes and devices: how empty the world turns when we try to impose our interpretations and meanings onto every last inch of it. Vermeer's *Catholic Faith* is a close cousin to Dürer's *Melencolia II*, as that image is known: she too is a woman tyrannized by a profusion of emblems. The black-and-white tiled floor of her room is littered by imagery thrown down in an almost desultory way by Vermeer. A slab of stone (the Church of Christ) crushes a serpent (Satan). An apple with a bite taken out of it (Original Sin) has been dropped and is rolling away, like a child's ball discarded.

Each of these articles of Catholic faith was questioned by Dutch dissenting Protestants. At their meetings Collegiants doubted the value of churches, debated the existence of the devil, and refuted the doctrine of Original Sin, many preferring to believe that human beings could achieve perfection by following Christ's commandments. To Vermeer, as presumably to the freethinking banker and entrepreneur Hermann van Swoll, the doctrines embodied by the emblems on the floor were obstructions, things that got in the way of true faith. That is why they are where they are, scattered like trip hazards.

The biggest trip hazard of all is the globe on which the doll-like figure of Catholic Faith balances her unsteady right foot. This object, we know from Cesare Ripa's extended explanations, symbolizes 'the world under her feet', thereby expressing the Church of Rome's autocratic conviction that the world should bow down before its authority. Vermeer puts all this in his own sceptical perspective by having the globe disable rather than empower his anti-heroine. The archetype of Catholicism is hobbled by the sphere of her own arrogance.

The open book on the lectern has been painted in such close detail that it can be identified, along with the page at which it is open. The book is the 1640 edition of *Legende der Heylighen*, an anthology of legends of the saints by Pedro Ribadineira and Heribert Rosweyde. It is open at page 546, which includes an account of the life of St Hugh of Lincoln. Like the similarly exact representation of a particular page in a particular book in Vermeer's *Astronomer* for Adrian Paets, it is a detail that may have been included at the suggestion of the patron, in this case Hermann van Swoll.[106] St Hugh was a twelfth-century English saint known for his deep devotion to Mary Magdalene, who might well have been of interest to a pious, tolerant, freethinking Dutchman (and indeed his wife). It was also an important part of the saint's legend that he had on many occasions protected the Jews of medieval Lincoln from violent persecution. But Vermeer's embodiment of Catholicism pays no attention to the book and is therefore oblivious to the life story of the saint, whose faith and forbearance she would do well to emulate.

Her gaze is directed instead towards the second sphere in the painting, a transparent glass globe that dangles from the ceiling. Where the painter got this from is debated, but it does not come from Cesare Ripa's book of emblems and is probably intended to represent the idea of true faith as 'the invisible world' that only a few can see. (The phrase comes from Samuel van Hoogstraten, who some years later included a similar transparent sphere in the self-portrait frontispiece to his treatise on painting.) Vermeer's embodiment of Catholicism is shown failing to penetrate its mysteries, the implication being that all she can see is the reflection of her own sorry self, adrift in her cabinet of clutter.

Some years later, Adrian Paets composed a memorable repudiation of Catholic claims to universal authority, in which he so perfectly caught the spirit of Vermeer's picture that it may be wondered whether he had it in his mind's eye as he was writing:

the marks by which Protestants are expected to recognize the authority of the Roman Church are not only more obscure than the thing they are intended to indicate, but also so awkward that one would rather learn all the arts and sciences than come to grips with the vast sea of these signs.[107]

In Vermeer's sea of signs one last detail catches our eye. There is a chair pulled up to face Catholic Faith, by the bottom of the curtain that has been pulled aside to reveal the scene. In any of the artist's paintings for The Golden Eagle it would have been empty, as such chairs always are in those pictures. But here a fat blue cushion has been placed on the seat, yet another obstruction.

Defenders of the impossible idea that Vermeer was a follower of the Jesuits, and the improbable notion that this picture is a hymn to Catholicism, are obliged to suppose that Hermann van Swoll bought it on the secondary market from some original devoutly Catholic owner. But the idea for the painting almost certainly originated with Van Swoll himself. He had a confirmed taste for pictures with 'several meanings' and a track record of commissioning allegories. As well as Vermeer's *Allegory of the Catholic Faith*, he commissioned Nicholas Berchem's *Allegory of the Four Seasons* and *Allegory of the Four Elements*, completed in the early 1670s, and Gerard de Lairesse's *Allegory of Amsterdam Flourishing*, of around 1680.

Van Swoll seems to have been a patron of new literature as well as painting, to judge by an intriguing notice that appeared in the *Amsterdamsche Courant* of 3 April 1700, a year after the posthumous sale of his paintings. Reporting the recent untimely death of 'the author Hendrik Doedijns, bachelor', the announcement recorded that the deceased had been living on the Herengracht, 'in the house of the late postmaster Van Swoll'. The postmaster's family still owned the house at that time so may have been honouring an arrangement made by Van Swoll himself. Doedijns was a self-published writer who could not possibly have afforded to rent rooms in the most expensive quarter of Amsterdam. The presumption is that Van Swoll was giving him help in the form of board and lodging. Doedijns's writings, characterized by the author himself as allegories of modern life, with a twist of caricature, were likely to have been much to Van Swoll's taste.

Doedijns's death at the age of forty-three cut short the promising career of one of Holland's most daringly outspoken journalists. Founder and sole author of the satirical periodical known as the *Haegsche Mercurius*, or *Hague Mercury*, he has been remembered as one of the first Dutch essayists in the mould of Joseph Addison and Richard Steele, authors of *The Tatler* and *Spectator*. He wrote from an extreme liberal standpoint, defending the political philosophy of Spinoza as well as embracing the cause of religious toleration, standing up for the rights of women and campaigning for freedom of speech.[108] He wrote with a comic touch that infuriated the Calvinist leaders of the public Church, who succeeded in imposing a lengthy ban on publication of his periodical, the demoralizing effect of which may have played a part in his early death.

It would be through *agents provocateurs* like Doedijns that the beliefs and principles of the Collegiant movement, unmoored from their original Christian context, would enter the mainstream of European Enlightenment thought. If Hermann van Swoll was part of that process, he not only commissioned a rare painting from Vermeer but passed on his liberal values to the next generation, like a relay runner passing a baton.

THE ART OF PAINTING

Vermeer bids his farewell to painting with a picture in which he himself appears, brush in hand, in his own studio. Finally he is in the room with us. But so engrossed is he in his work that he only has eyes for his canvas. Evasive to the last, he shows us his back. He is painting a young woman in blue, wreathed with laurel and holding a book. On the wall behind her is a large map. Light comes in from the left, bathing the room in its glow. The air is the colour of honey.

The picture, which hangs in the Kunsthistorisches Museum in Vienna, is called *The Art of Painting*. For once we can say with confidence that this is the artist's own title for his work: a notarial document of 1676 exists in which Catharina referred to 'a painting by her late husband wherein is depicted "The Art of Painting" '.[109] Vermeer painted it for himself, and bequeathed it to her. He spent many months working on it. It is the largest painting done in his mature style, and it evidently meant a great deal to him. It may or may not be his actual last painting, but it is his final account of himself.

Its composition is strikingly reminiscent of the *Allegory of the Catholic Faith*, a comparison sealed by the presence of the dramatic device of the pulled-back tapestry curtain in both works. They are a pair, like so many of Vermeer's pictures, but a pair with a difference, in that the artist knew they could only ever be coupled in his own mind and would never hang together. He thought of things in twos by instinct, a habit that helped him to sharpen his ideas. The picture for Hermann van Swoll was false religion personified. The picture done for himself was to be its opposite. It was to be an image of 'The Art of Painting' as Vermeer had always conceived it: an act of faith.

His starting point can be traced to a passage in Leonardo da Vinci's *Treatise on Painting* which was part of the *paragone*, a comparison between sculpture and painting in which painting came off much the better. Taking aim at his rival Michelangelo, Leonardo had disparaged the work of the sculptor as rudely mechanical, all sweat and strain, 'making him look like a baker, smeared all over with marble powder'. By contrast he had described the painter, by implication himself, in the following terms:

> He sits in front of his work at perfect ease. He is well dressed and handles a light brush dipped in delightful colour. He is arrayed in the garments he fancies, and his home is clean and filled with delightful pictures, and he often enjoys the accompaniment of music or the company of men of letters who read to him from various beautiful works to which he can listen with great pleasure without the interference of hammering and other noises.[110]

The Art of Painting is so faithful to this description that it may have been directly inspired by it, or at least by one of the several versions of it circulating in Vermeer's time. The painter in the picture is dressed in the garments of his fancy (the same slashed black jacket and beret he had worn in his other presumed self-portrait, in *The Procuress*). He handles a light brush which has evidently just been dipped in a delightful laurel-green colour. His home could hardly be cleaner. Although the wall is filled with a map, rather than pictures, it is a splendid map. Music is hinted at in the instrument, a trumpet or trombone, held by the lady in blue who is posing for him, while the reading of beautiful works is implied by the presence of the large gold-coloured book she holds.

Reinforcing the theme of painting's superiority to sculpture, Vermeer has placed a careful arrangement of different objects and stuffs on and around the low table in the left middle ground of the picture. The plaster cast of a man's face is an allusion to sculpture, perhaps monumental statuary of the type associated with Michelangelo, but it is merely a dead fragment compared with the face of the painter's model, which thanks to the painter's art is like life itself. Next to the mask the painter has with consummate skill depicted three types of fabric that a sculptor could never conjure up, namely a tapestry, a bolt of silk-satin cloth, and a flowing silk scarf done in two colours that pours off the edge of the table. Perhaps the most masterful example of the art of painting is the great map of the seventeen provinces of the Low Countries. Raked by light from the unseen window at left, its brittle varnished surface seems palpable, every crack and tear rendered with minute care. Held up by strings hung from two small nails near the top of the wall, it seems too heavy for its supports, the paper forming pull-ripples that descend at a diagonal from the map's moorings above.

Vermeer was not the sort of artist who would spend months painting a picture simply to show off his technical skills. Like the *Allegory of the Catholic Faith*, *The Art of Painting* is a picture with something to say, a story to tell. The map is central to that story. Produced by Nicolaes Visscher sometime in the 1650s, from old plates, it shows the seventeen provinces of the northern and southern Netherlands as a single political entity, as if the Dutch Revolt had never happened and the region had never been divided into the Spanish Low Countries and the Dutch Republic. The artist has contrived a crease running down the centre of the map, which coincides more or less exactly with the line of division separating Protestant north and Catholic south. It is like a scar on the skin of an old person. Perfectly centred on the figure of the painter, the map represents the history Vermeer and his contemporaries have had to live through. It is an apt emblem of all that, this battered piece of paper, stretched and cracked by time, its central feature a fold made by murderous schism.

The map, however, is not what the painter is painting. He has turned away from it. He is painting the young woman in blue robes. She is Clio, Muse of History, whose conventional attributes are exactly as he shows them, namely a book, a laurel crown and a trumpet. But why would he turn from the map, eloquent image of history and all its traumas, to a figure who stands in allegorical form for the same thing? Why turn from history to History?

The answer is that Vermeer's Muse of History is not like those painted by other artists of the seventeenth century. When Artemisia Gentileschi, Johannes Moreelse or other painters of Vermeer's time depicted Clio, they showed her with an open book, to symbolize that time never stops and the next page of history always needs to be written. But Vermeer's Clio holds a closed book, to which she gives a downwards glance, as if to say that her work is done. By this Vermeer means us to understand that she is no longer the Muse of History. What she represents is History's end, the End of Days. She used to hold a trumpet to proclaim the deeds of famous men, but now she holds it as if she were the seventh angel in the Book of Revelation, about to herald the time of wonders. There is an empty chair in the foreground of the room, handily placed for someone to watch Vermeer at work, should that someone choose to come.

The moment has not arrived yet, but the painter hopes it is imminent. That is why he has placed a beautiful candelabrum above the tattered map that is like a skin to be sloughed off. There are no candles in its holders for now but when the change comes and the world is made fresh there will be a light upon every candlestick. Meanwhile the artist paints Clio with her shut book, steadying his hand with his mahlstick, the one with the ivory knob on it. When he finishes there will be nothing more to do but wait. His gifts are undiminished, his powers undimmed, but the time for making pictures is over.

PART FOUR

Disaster, Death, Legacy, 1672–5

RAMPJAAR

History did not come to an end. Clio was unable to lay down her pen and close her book. Powerful forces were ranged against the Dutch Republic. A storm was brewing, one that would finally break in 1672. It would be remembered as the *Rampjaar*, or Year of Disaster.

The trouble started in the summer of 1670, when Louis XIV of France entered into a secret alliance with Charles II of England with the aim of bringing down the Dutch and ending their dominance of world trade. Three years earlier Louis's plans to invade the Spanish Netherlands had been foiled by a military coalition formed by the Dutch statesman, Johan de Witt. The King of France had born a grudge ever since. He fumed at the temerity of this upstart state, David to his Goliath, which had dared to thwart his plans. He detested the Dutch Republic on principle because its mere existence was a challenge to the principles of absolute monarchy. He grudgingly recognized the Dutch genius for trade, by virtue of which one of the world's smallest nations had become its richest, but he was also suspicious of it. The Dutch were merchants, not empire builders, but Louis convinced himself they had designs on world domination. It was a misunderstanding that would have large consequences.

Money lay at the root of it. To an absolute monarch such as Louis, excess capital meant only one thing: stored-up military power. Large amounts of money meant large armies, therefore conquests of territory. By contrast Dutch merchants thought of their territory as a refuge, a safe haven, and had little interest in expanding it through military aggression. To them, money did not mean power to dominate others but prosperity for themselves and their families, by extension serving the interests of society at large as it trickled down to pay for orphan chambers, poor houses, old people's refuges and all the other newfangled social institutions of the Dutch Republic. This was simply incomprehensible to the French. So when a political theorist such as Pieter de la Court tried to explain the perspective of the Dutch wise merchant in books such as *The Interest of Holland*, his words were met with scepticism at the court of Versailles. As the French Minister of State, Jean-Baptiste Colbert, put it in a private memo to his sovereign:

> Upon trade they base the principal doctrine of their government, knowing full well that if they but have the mastery of trade, their powers will continually wax on land and sea, and will make them so mighty that they will be able to set up as arbiters of peace and war in Europe, and at their pleasure set bounds to the justice and all the plans of the princes.[1]

The Dutch failed to grasp how offensive their mere existence was to the established monarchies of Europe. Even as Louis strengthened his secret alliance by recruiting both the Elector of Cologne and the Prince-Bishop of Münster, Christoph Bernhard von Galen, a follower of the Jesuits who dreamed of restoring Catholicism to the fractious Republic, seasoned Dutch observers discounted the threat of invasion. Despite the fact that there had been wars between England and the Netherlands as recently as the late 1660s, when English ships had been burned on the Medway in a daring Dutch raid, those same observers persisted in believing that the friendship symbolized by the Dutch Gift would survive any French attempts to undermine it. On New Year's Eve 1671 Pieter de la Court wrote to his English friend and fellow republican James Harrington to inform him that Charles II would have to be mad to join with France in an attack on the Republic, being more likely in his view to form an alliance with the Dutch:

> According to the interest of the king of England and his subjects it is totally unadvisable to form an alliance with the king of France to subdue the Free Netherlands. On the contrary, it very well suits the

interests of the king of England and his subjects to form with other close neighbours and especially with the State of the Free Netherlands an alliance for mutual protection against that all-powerful and otherwise all-swallowing France.[2]

With such arguments did the Dutch comfort themselves as they sleepwalked towards disaster.

In the autumn of 1671, as these stormclouds gathered, Vermeer had been elected a headman of the St Luke's Guild in Delft for the second and last time.[3] He was required to remain in post for two years but would have little time for the administrative work demanded by the role, such as registering new members or ensuring that frail or impoverished artists received support from guild funds. For much of his tenure the town would be in a state of emergency, or nervously readying itself for war.

By March 1672, it was apparent to all that Louis had formed a military coalition which completely encircled the Dutch Republic and was about to attack on several fronts. Even without the additional troops pledged by Münster and Cologne, the French army numbered 118,000 infantry and 12,500 cavalry. The Dutch could only muster a quarter as many men, softened by years of peace and dispersed around the nation's defensive ring of fortresses and garrison towns. In addition to the French land offensive the Dutch were to be harried and blockaded at sea, their trade disrupted and their fisheries brought to a standstill. This task fell to the English navy, which announced its intentions on 23 March by attacking a flotilla of Dutch ships bringing goods from the Levant as it passed by the Isle of Wight. Two weeks later, on 6 April, Louis XIV declared war on the Dutch Republic. On 18 May Münster did the same, followed soon after by Cologne. Enemy forces were poised to strike.

On 21 May 1672, as the nation held its breath, Johannes Vermeer was summoned from Delft to The Hague to assist in the resolution of what must have seemed under the circumstances a decidedly trivial conflict: a dispute over the authenticity of a group of Italian paintings.[4] The twelve pictures at the centre of the row had once formed part of the collection belonging to the famous connoisseur Gerard Reynst. In May 1670 the bulk of the Reynst collection had been sold at an auction in Amsterdam organized by the art dealer Gerrit Uylenburgh (whom we met in Part Three). Uylenburgh had retained a number of lots for himself, some of which he subsequently sold to a delegation of art buyers working for Friedrich Wilhelm, the Elector of Brandenburg. When those pictures arrived in Berlin, the Elector's court painter Hendrick Fromantiou pronounced them to be copies, if not outright fakes. Fromantiou was promptly ordered to take the paintings back to Amsterdam, make his case with Uylenburgh, and extract from the dealer the sum he had been paid on account.

The negotiations did not go smoothly. Uylenburgh accused Fromantiou of character assassination and issued a counter-claim for the unpaid balance owing to him for works of art sold in good faith. He categorically refused to take the pictures back. It was then agreed that they should be placed on display in a tavern on Amsterdam's Kalverstraat so that the opposing parties might gather expert testimonies for and against their authenticity. When the exhibition duly opened on 13 May numerous painters were called in by both sides, but, since their contrasting opinions neatly coincided with the interests of whoever had invited each of them to testify, the exercise proved indecisive. A week later the twelve pictures were sent to The Hague, where they were displayed in the 'confreres' room' of the painter's guild. Hendrick Fromantiou induced Vermeer and Johannes Jordaens, an older member of the St Luke's Guild in Delft, to make the short journey to The Hague and express their views, which they did on Saturday 21 May.

It is possible that Vermeer was invited to give evidence purely because he happened to be in post as headman of his guild, but more likely because he knew about Italian art and could speak about it with authority. The affair of the Italian pictures strengthens the hypothesis that Vermeer himself had travelled to Italy as a young man. Johannes Jordaens, his fellow deponent, had spent many years there, as had several other artists called to testify in the case.

Like most witnesses called by Fromantiou, Jordaens and Vermeer took his side. Their scathing judgement of the Italian pictures, recorded two days later, would have been music to his ears:

> The aforementioned paintings being sealed with the signet of His Serene Highness the Elector of Brandenburg, which paintings are not only not outstanding Italian paintings but, on the contrary, great pieces

of rubbish and bad paintings, not worth by far the tenth part of the aforementioned proposed prices, which they, the deponents, cannot estimate, since the items have no value.[5]

The statement was recorded by Notary P. van Swieten and is still preserved in The Hague Municipal Archives. Overlooked until recently was a signature at the bottom of the page, that of the man who witnessed Vermeer's (and Jordaens's) scathing judgement of the paintings. He turns out to have been none other than Pieter Claesz van Ruijven.[6] Van Ruijven may have travelled with Vermeer from Delft to The Hague on the regular *trekschuit* service, or he may have already been living in The Hague by May 1672, in which case he would have met the artist there. Whatever the case, the document strongly suggests that Vermeer remained close to his friends and main patrons, even after their arrangement had come to an end.

The dispute over the allegedly dubious pictures would rumble on, but eventually Friedrich Wilhelm successfully returned most of them, keeping just a few things including a *Beheading of John the Baptist* by José de Ribera to reflect the modest sum already paid to Uylenburgh on account. He let the dealer keep the deposit, allowing him to salvage a little pride. We do not know whether Vermeer knew Uylenburgh, but he probably knew of him. Vermeer's one known patron during these lean years, Hermann van Swoll, was someone who did know Uylenburgh personally: we know this thanks to the document putting them together in the house of Isaac Swartepaert in January 1671. Van Swoll had also known the previous owner of the disputed paintings, Gerard Reynst, who had been best man at his wedding and may have kindled his enthusiasm for art. Such connections confirm the impression we have of the Dutch Republic as a small world formed of many networks, in which almost everyone is linked, somehow or other, to almost everyone else.

On the artists' grapevine it was rumoured that Uylenburgh was a chancer. Arnold Houbraken later alleged that Fromantiou had himself painted fakes for Uylenburgh to pass off on his clients. That was why he distrusted him, Houbraken added: 'he knew how the fox did business.' Vermeer's motives for foiling the fox remain unknown. Bizarrely it was the second time a member of his family had done a favour for an Elector of Brandenburg. In 1619 Vermeer's grandfather Balthasar Gerrits had been arrested for forging counterfeit coins probably intended to help Elector George William pay for the acquisition of the Duchy of Cleves. Half a century later Vermeer was helping George William's son, Friedrich Wilhelm, get out of paying for some counterfeit pictures. If the country had not been on the verge of war, he might have smiled at the coincidence.

On 22 May 1672, a day after Vermeer had visited the exhibition of dodgy art with his old friend Pieter Claesz van Ruijven, Louis XIV led his great army through the Spanish Netherlands and across the Maas towards Maastricht. The Dutch fleet under Admiral Michiel de Ruyter won a small victory against the English at Solebay, but otherwise the situation went from grim to worse. The weather was clement in early June, ideal for marching. Louis's soldiers continued their advance, travelling north-east in a right-flanking movement that would bring them to the vulnerable easternmost edge of the Dutch Republic. Their way was barred by the chain of Dutch garrisons in Cleves, their names made famous by the events of the Eighty Years War. Rheinberg, Orsay, Emmerich and Wesel had held out against the might of Spain for many long years, but now they fell to Louis in a matter of days. Further east the Münsterites took the fortress of Grol and advanced on Zutphen, just as the Duke of Alva's infamous army had done more than a hundred years before.

It was in this dark hour that Adrian Paets, apostle of Dutch toleration, was despatched to Madrid in the hope that he might broker a military alliance with Spain. It was one of the key diplomatic missions of that turbulent time. The fact that Paets was chosen for it shows how much confidence De Witt and his inner circle had in him. If anyone could make a friend of the Republic's oldest enemy, Paets could. He had spent his life preaching reconciliation, after all. It was on this occasion that his friend Joachim Oudaan gloomily compared his departure to the setting of the sun.

On 12 June 1672 the French crossed the Rhine at Lobith. They had outflanked the IJssel line, the main outer defence of the Dutch Republic, and had victory in their grasp. The Dutch pulled back to their last line of defence, the *'waterlinie'*, or waterline, running north to south from the fortress of Muiden, on the edge of the Zuiderzee, to Gorinchem on the River Waal. If the French got that far, the Dutch would open the dykes and flood the land so that at least the two seaward provinces of Holland and Zeeland might be saved. The invasion was scarcely two weeks old but Louis and his allies had already conquered more than half of the Republic's territories and were still on the march. Having taken Arnhem without a struggle, on 19 June they entered Amersfoort. Barely fifteen miles westwards lay Utrecht, gateway to Holland. The town authorities there ordered the people to prepare for a lengthy siege, but they rebelled and resolved to let the French enter unopposed. Prince William III of Orange, who had been appointed captain-general of the Dutch forces against the will of Johan de Witt, ordered a further retreat, staking all on the defence of Holland and Zeeland.

The succession of Dutch military reverses led to political turmoil bordering on insurrection. Calvinists and Orangists rediscovered their kinship of old, encouraging the people at large to blame Johan de Witt and the liberal regents who supported him for sleeping at the wheel of the ship of state. On the evening of 21 June, as De Witt was walking home from the Binnenhof in The Hague after a meeting of the States of Holland, four young men armed with knives made a botched attempt on his life. He escaped with a minor stab wound, but was incapacitated for several days. Calls for stronger leadership were heard on all sides. The days of the Era of True Liberty were numbered.

On 23 June the French army entered Utrecht in triumph. On the same day, Münsterite forces entered Zwolle and Kampen, opening a passage westward towards Amsterdam. William III ordered the flooding of the waterline, but his troops were in such disarray that the garrisons of men needed to complete the task were not yet in place. The Castle of Muiden, which occupied a key strategic position at the northern end of the flood plains, was still unoccupied as enemy forces approached along the eastern corridor of their advance. A detachment of Dutch troops was sent to secure it, arriving just two hours before the vanguard of the invading army. They closed the castle and released the floodwaters. Had they not done so, Holland would have been lost.

Opening the dykes was a measure of last resort, reflecting the collapse of the land-defence system. It was particularly unpopular with peasant farmers subsisting along the length of the waterline itself, whose land

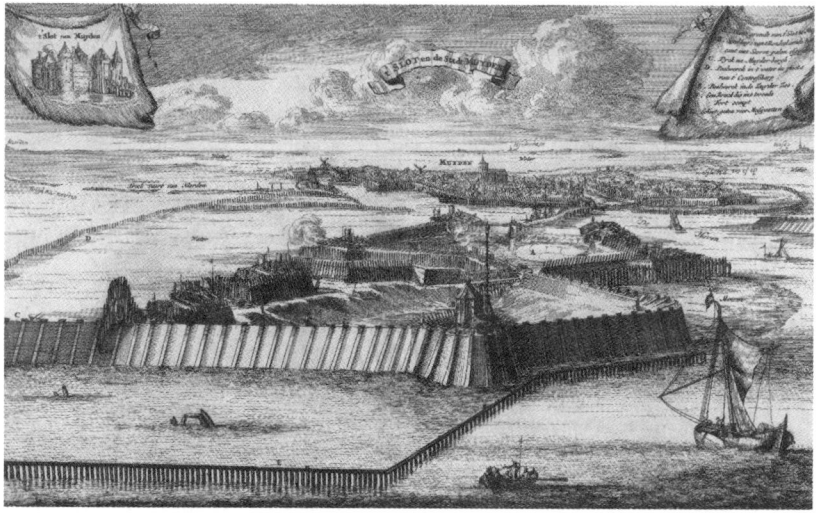

The fortress of Muiden, which was (and is) on the edge of the Zuiderzee, marking the northernmost end of the waterline, the Dutch Republic's defence of last resort. After the opening of the dykes controlled by the fortress, the fields became lakes, as shown here, protecting the seaward provinces of Holland and Zeeland from any further advance by the armies of Louis XIV and his allies.

would be ruined for years as a result. A group of armed peasants in and around the fortress town of Gorinchem formed themselves into a ragtag army and tried to prevent the Dutch military from opening the sluices there. A detachment of 300 civic militiamen was despatched from Delft to help quell the uprising, leaving the town itself with few reinforcements. Johannes Vermeer's name is listed in a register of Delft's *schutters* compiled in 1674, so he may have been among those sent on the long march to ensure the land was properly inundated.[7] If so, he probably had one or two friends for company: the names of Pieter Teding van Berkhout and Pieter Claesz van Ruijven also appear in the lists, as does that of Vermeer's brother-in-law, the frame-maker Antony van der Wiel. Whether any or all of them were personally involved in putting down the short-lived peasants' revolt at Gorinchem, the sluices there were eventually opened. The negative side effects of saving the nation in this way would be felt shortly afterwards in the household of Maria Thins on the Oude Langendijk. She depended for part of her income on some farmland she owned near Schoonhoven, a few miles west of the waterline. As the land was turned to bog, her rents dried up. Over time she would lose more than 1,500 guilders.

The Dutch were lucky that the French did not understand the workings of their defence system. The summer of 1672 was hot and dry, as a result of which the waters released by the dykes rose at an agonizingly slow pace. If Louis XIV had marched on Amsterdam at once, he would have crossed the waterline without difficulty and conquered the Dutch Republic. Instead he tarried in Utrecht for a fortnight, by which time it was too late. By the start of July the inundations had turned the land to a treacherous sludge of salty mud, impassable by any army. Meanwhile the towns of Holland and Zeeland were seized by a mixture of fear and rage: fear of what Louis might do next, rage against De Witt and his fellow regents for their failure to keep the French wolf from the door.

In Delft there were riots in the last week of June, an ugly crowd calling for what had once been unthinkable, the instatement of William III, Prince of Orange, as Stadtholder. The rioters were a motley crew of the disaffected, including out-of-work tanners, carpenters and builders, laid-off fishermen from the port of Delfshaven, and peasants from out of town who could no longer till their flooded land. They were joined by thousands of women: farmers' wives, fishwives, housewives and many low-paid textile workers. On 30 June the expeditionary force of Delft militiamen that possibly included Vermeer and friends was urgently called back from the waterlogged plains around Gorinchem to deal with this larger insurrection. Whether they got back in time or not, they can have made no difference. The angry crowd had its way, surrounding the town hall on the Great Market Square and pressuring the regents into setting aside the so-called Perpetual Edict of 1667. This had been the jewel in the crown of True Liberty legislation, abolishing the role of Stadtholder forever and thereby – as De Witt and his liberal supporters had hoped – forever removing the threat of a return to monarchy from the Dutch political landscape.

Perpetuity had lasted just five years, one of the shortest forevers recorded by Clio, Muse of History. The city fathers were given no choice but to vote for the restoration of the Stadtholderate, then for William III's election to the role. The same pattern was repeated across what was left of the Republic, and by the first week of July the Prince of Orange was duly proclaimed Stadtholder of Holland and Zeeland, those being the only two provinces of the former United Provinces not by then under French control.

Record numbers of popular pamphlets appeared in the summer of 1672, more than 600 all told, the great majority railing against De Witt and anyone perceived to be on his side. This flood of publications was propelled by a tidal wave of conservative, Calvinist, Orangist complaint. Most writers agreed that the root cause of the Republic's problems was the Arminian cancer that had been allowed to spread through the body politic. By encouraging freedom of speech and allowing publishers to print books without fear of censorship, De Witt had nurtured a devil's library of impious literature, endangering the souls of his people. He had turned the country into a safe haven for atheists and 'new upcoming philosophers' whose poisonous ideas had infected the bloodstream of the nation.[8]

One particularly virulent clutch of pamphlets accused De Witt of cultivating an entirely new system of religious belief, using the Dutch Republic as his laboratory for a dangerous experiment with the Christian faith. Instead of ensuring that the Reformed Church of the Calvinists was the only Church to flourish, he had pursued a policy of unlimited toleration, allowing 'Jews, Turks, heathens, atheists, Socinians, papists, Arminians, Lutherans, Mennonites, Quakers' and those of every faith under the sun to flourish.[9] Such Calvinist propaganda made the Republic itself sound like one huge Collegiant meeting. The anonymous author of this last tirade was indeed insinuating that De Witt's entire regime, the regime of True Liberty, was a front for the Collegiant movement. His pamphlet was published in Rotterdam, Adrian Paets's fiefdom.

On 4 August Johan de Witt resigned as Grand Pensionary of Holland. Eight days later he wrote to his old friend Adrian Paets, who had just arrived in Madrid, to tell him the news.[10] De Witt lamented that despite the recent attempt on his life by 'four armed persons', and despite his many efforts to save the Republic from its enemies, no one had any sympathy for him. The people at large held him accountable for all the misfortunes of the nation. Their attitude 'has confirmed to me more and more the truth of what used to be said in the Republic of Rome: "in prosperity all claim credit for themselves, whereas in adversity they blame someone else".' Under the circumstances he felt compelled to resign: 'I thought it my duty to inform you of this, so that henceforth you will no longer send any letters concerning the notification of the state to me, but will for the time being send them with the caption: "to the Lord Pensionary of the land of Holland and West Friesland or whoever may hold this said office nowadays".' He remained, as always, 'Your humble servant, Johan de Witt.'

It was the statesman's last letter. On 20 August he went to visit his brother Cornelius in prison. Cornelius de Witt had that same day been acquitted of plotting to assassinate William III, a trumped-up charge invented by Orangist enemies of the regime. Johan was planning to bring his brother home. But, as he arrived, a hostile mob gathered at the gate of the prison. When the two men tried to leave, the cry of

Johan de Witt, Grand Pensionary of Holland, was the pre-eminent statesman of the Dutch Republic at its zenith. He and his brother Cornelius were murdered by an Orangist mob in The Hague in August 1672.

'Traitors' went up from the crowd, so they were forced back inside to take refuge in Cornelius's prison cell. Their supposed guardians were Hague militiamen with Orangist sympathies who allowed the seething crowd into the prison and then assisted in the acts that followed. Johan and his brother were pushed down the stairs and bundled outside, where they were attacked with knives, guns and clubs. The intention had been to hang them but they were already dead by the time they reached the scaffold. Their killers hung their bodies upside down, like carcasses in a butcher's shop.

The story of what happened next would be told and retold, even reaching the ears of an English visitor to The Hague, Ellis Veryard, ten years after the event.[11] According to his informants:

> their bodies stripped naked ... were dragged out of town and hung up by the legs at the common gallows, where their bowels were pulled out and their limbs minced into a thousand pieces, everyone present endeavouring to get his share; some got a finger some a toe and others a piece of their flesh, which they preserved in oil and spirits of wine as trophies of their matchless vengeance.

Eyewitnesses reported that once the bodies had been dismembered some of those present at the scene of the murders cooked and ate various of the De Witts' sensory organs, including their eyes, ears and lips. This was probably not an act of frenzied rage but a deliberate ritual of retribution: a symbolic punishment enacted on the remains of the dead for all that they had seen, heard and said while still alive. A market soon developed for their remaining body parts, not all of which were preserved as 'trophies of vengeance'. The Hague Historical Museum still holds one of their tongues and the bone of one of their fingers, displayed as they have been for centuries in a miniature coffin made of glass: preserved as secular saint's relics. In Remonstrant and Collegiant circles especially, Johan de Witt and his brother were remembered as martyrs to the cause of True Liberty and toleration. In 1705 an English student at Utrecht University was shown one of Johan de Witt's fingers, which was the property of a pious Remonstrant minister named Altenus.

The deaths of the De Witts appalled everyone in the circle around Adrian Paets. Spinoza was so enraged on the day of the massacres that he wrote out a placard in Latin saying *'ultimi barbarorum'*, meaning in effect that 'the greatest of barbarians did this', which he intended to place next to what was left of the victims' bodies. His landlord locked the house to prevent Spinoza from going out, reasoning that the philosopher would be beaten up or even killed if he were allowed to make his protest.[12] Joachim Oudaan wrote a tragedy inspired by the events of 20 August 1672, *Fratricide at The Hague, or Mad Joy*, in which he exposed the murders as an Orangist plot (which in truth they were) and remembered Johan de Witt as a heroic freedom-fighter martyred for his liberal beliefs.[13] Under the censorship rules of the new regime, as he well knew, Oudaan's play could neither be performed nor published. He seems to have written it primarily to be read by his friends, and to exorcize his feelings.

In the summer of 1672 life suddenly became much more difficult for liberal writers and philosophers such as Oudaan and Spinoza. The former found himself regarded with suspicion and unable to publish, while the latter found himself the victim of a smear campaign which asserted that his *Tractatus Theologico-Politicus* was not a work of political theory, but devil's bile. The demoralizing effect of such attacks, added to Spinoza's sense that the Republic was in moral decline, may have exacerbated the chronic tuberculosis to which he would succumb less than five years later. In early 1673 Spinoza considered emigrating to Switzerland. He was offered a post at Heidelberg University, but he eventually declined it.

Six months earlier, just after the death of the De Witts, when the backlash against True Liberty was at its most violent, the liberal political theorist Pieter de la Court actually did emigrate, leaving his home in Leiden for a safe haven in Antwerp. A few days earlier a gang of Orangists spoiling for a fight had knocked on his door while he was out. Failing to find him at home, they caught and killed a stray dog, slicing its belly open, putting a candle in the cavity, and nailing its body to the tree in front of his house, with a note: 'De la Court, if you won't shut your mouth, we'll treat you as we did this dog.'[14]

The second half of 1672 offered the Dutch hope at least of retaining their independence. Having failed to take Holland when he had the chance, Louis XIV gradually realized the scale of the task facing him and his troops. What should have been a short sharp victory had turned into a war of attrition: the kind of war that suited the Dutch.

By autumn they had formed an alliance that brought powerful support from Brandenburg-Prussia and, thanks in no small part to Adrian Paets, King Charles II of Spain. The tide had turned in their favour, although there was a shock at the end of the year when severe frosts resulted in the freezing over of the waterline. On 27 December one of Louis's generals, the Duc de Luxembourg, made it halfway over the ice with 8,000 soldiers before a sudden thaw forced them to turn back. They had hoped to sack The Hague and enrich themselves, like the Spanish soldiers who had once sacked Antwerp. On their retreat to Utrecht they gratuitously massacred the civilian populations of Bodegraven and Zwammerdam. Romeyn de Hooghe made engravings of the atrocities which were put up in taverns across Holland: images of decapitated babies, women violated and bonfires of human bodies, broadcasting the news of another Massacre of the Innocents taking place on Dutch soil. Thus 1672 was like 1572 all over again.

Atrocities committed by soldiers under the command of the Duc de Luxembourg, one of Louis XIV's generals, in the winter of 1672. From a series of engravings by Romeyn de Hooghe.

We can only imagine what effect all this may have had on Johannes Vermeer. To a millenarian optimist inspired by a belief in the spiritual progress of mankind, the times must have seemed brutal indeed. Encouraged by more than two decades of peace to imagine that his world was becoming more enlightened, he was now condemned to watch it slipping into darkness and barbarism. War had seemed a thing of the past, but not so. It was as if, in writing these latest pages of it, Clio had taken the Dutch all the way back to the bloody beginnings of their story.

LAST YEARS

Vermeer turned forty in late October 1672. He was the last surviving member of the small, nuclear family of four into which he had been born. His father had died twenty years earlier. His mother and sister had passed away within a few months of each other at the start of 1670. Meanwhile the large family he and his wife had made grew just a little larger. Catharina continued to bear children during these years but not always with a happy outcome. A son, Ignatius, was born to the couple in 1672. He would survive into adulthood. Another unnamed child was delivered the following year but died in infancy, while the last of their offspring, born in 1674, was probably a sickly child, since he or she lived only four years.

Also in 1674 Johannes and Catharina's eldest daughter, Maria, got married. Her husband was Johannes Cramer, the son of a wealthy silk merchant, who had presumably been vetted by Maria Thins for adequate levels of commitment to the Church of Rome. The marriage took place in Schipluy at the hidden Catholic church there, a Jesuit priest presiding over the ceremony. A couple of months later, in August, Pieter Claesz van Ruijven died, either in The Hague or in Delft, it is unclear which.[15] He was forty-nine years old. Vermeer is likely to have felt the loss of his friend and patron keenly, but we have little evidence about his state of mind during his last few years. Most of what can be gleaned about this period of his life takes the form of bare archival fact.

During the final three years of his life Vermeer left more traces of his presence in notarial and other records than he had done in the previous forty. This sudden increase in activity is largely to be explained by the economic consequences of the Year of Disaster. Most of Vermeer's notarial appearances were made on behalf of his mother-in-law, Maria Thins, whose affairs had been thrown into disarray by the flooding of farmland on which she was normally paid rent. One or two of them were made on his own account.

In July 1673 Vermeer raised 800 guilders by selling two bonds.[16] One of these bonds had been issued in the name of Magdalena van Ruijven, daughter to Pieter and Maria. No further details are known, but we may speculate that Maria herself gave this bond to Vermeer in lieu of the bequest she had already made to him in her will. In other words, knowing that he needed money sooner rather than later she resolved to give it to him straightaway. This would suggest that she continued to have an eye out for Vermeer's interests after he had stopped painting for her. Whether that is the case or not, the selling of interest-bearing bonds to raise capital is clearly the act of a man in need of cash.

Vermeer remained dependent on his mother-in-law for the money needed to support himself, Catharina and their children. To judge by the size of the bread bill he ran up with the ever-obliging Hendrick van Buyten between 1672 and the end of 1675, she may have put the squeeze on his allowance during these years of slump and recession. There are signs that even Maria was feeling the pinch, or feeling nervous. Accordingly she kept her son-in-law busy on her behalf, sending him from place to place to maximize her income from rents, inheritances, debts and other sources.

On 4 April 1674 Maria Thins's first husband, the brickmaker Reynier Bolnes, finally gave up the ghost. She promptly sent Vermeer to Gouda, where he leased out Reynier's house for 140 guilders a year. The money fell due to Maria and Reynier's son Willem Bolnes, who had inherited and on whose behalf Vermeer was in theory acting. But since Willem was still confined subject to a restraining order, and Maria was his guardian, she was the actual beneficiary of the arrangement. The rent on the house in Gouda will have helped with the considerable cost of Willem's continuing detainment in the *beterhuis* run by Hermanus Taerling.

Money was being gathered in. At the end of May of the same year,

Vermeer appeared with his mother-in-law before a notary in Delft to settle another inheritance, due jointly to Willem and Catharina from the estate of a distant relation.[17] Eleven months after that, on 5 March 1675, Maria Thins gave Vermeer power of attorney to act on her behalf in the division of Reynier's estate, and to collect any assets owed to Willem.[18] Once more, these were assets that she as his guardian would control.

On 26 March Vermeer took the *trekschuit* to Gouda once more, to renew the leases and collect the rent due on some farmland that Maria had herself inherited from her late husband.[19] This trip was less remunerative than the others. The tenant farmer explained to Vermeer that since much of the land had been underwater from 1672 until 1674 he had been unable to pay rent on it for those years. Vermeer duly agreed that the outstanding balance for that period would be forfeited 'due to the war times'. The land was still unproductive, and the adjusted rent for the year ahead reflected that, being only 72 guilders for three *morgen* of meadow, with a further deduction for the cost of a mud dyke to prevent further flooding: slim pickings.

In July 1675 Maria instructed Vermeer to return to Gouda on her behalf. This time he was to go to the Orphan Chamber armed with a note of obligation, collect 2,900 guilders that had been placed on trust there by her late aunt Dieuwertje van Hensbeeck[20] and bring it back to the house on the Oude Langendijk. But 'the honourable Johannes Vermeer', as he had been described in the power of attorney of 5 March, did no such thing. Instead he travelled to Amsterdam, where he met Jacob Rombouts. They made a deal whereby the merchant Rombouts agreed to accept the interest-bearing obligation in exchange for a loan of 1,000 guilders. Maria Thins would eventually be forced to repay the loan to recover the obligation, so that she could duly return it to the Orphan Chamber, as the law required. She would then have to reapply for the moneys in the Van Hensbeeck trust to be transferred to her possession, all over again. She did not do so until after Vermeer's death, which suggests that he may not have told her what he had done, or at least not straight away.

Vermeer's accomplice in this apparent betrayal of Maria's trust, Jacob Rombouts, was as we know the grandson of Jacobus Arminius. The painter's mother, Digna, had been offered shelter and employment by the staunchly Remonstrant Rombouts family in Amsterdam, when she had first arrived in the Dutch Republic as a refugee more than fifty years earlier. Vermeer most likely knew Jacob Rombouts through such family connections, but we cannot rule out the possibility that he had met him through mutual friends in Collegiant circles or the Remonstrant Church. One thing does seem clear from the incident. There was still a fault line running through Vermeer's life. He was one man on Papists' Corner, another with his friends in the dissenting movements.

Vermeer must have been hard pressed for funds to take such drastic action. Perhaps he had applied to Maria for more money but she had denied him. Perhaps he felt helpless and angry, for other reasons: he and Catharina probably had a sick infant on their hands at this time, having just buried another. We simply do not know what lay behind the pawning of the debt obligation. What we do know is that, if he really needed money at this time, he had few ways of getting it. At the beginning of 1673 he had leased out The Mechelen Inn, which he had inherited from his mother, for 180 guilders a year, but he still had mortgage payments to meet out of that income.[21] He was also attempting to trade as a dealer in pictures, but the business was failing. When he died in mid-December 1675 he had a stock of twenty-six paintings which, according to his widow, he had been unable to sell due to the financial crash. The Year of Disaster had crushed the Dutch art market. Even the most established dealers struggled: Gerrit Uylenburgh was forced into bankruptcy and left Holland for London, where he landed the job of Surveyor to the King's Pictures. The Dutch and the English had made their peace by then, with the signing of the Treaty of Westminster in February 1674.

Smaller fry like Vermeer had no choice but to stomach their losses. He could have tried to find buyers for his own work, and he may have made one or two desultory efforts in that direction. But, aside from these few last gasps, he stayed true to his decision of some years earlier to give up painting. The room on the upper floor of the house on the Oude Langendijk was not often disturbed by his presence, and he cannot have earned much by his brush.

The Love Letter, which is something of a mystery picture, was perhaps one of those painted during his last years. It shows a smirking maid who has just passed a letter to an evidently surprised young

45–48. Patrons, friends and kindred spirits: Pieter Teding van Berkhout (*top left*), who met Vermeer twice in person at the house of the Van Ruijvens for a guided tour of the rooms in which most of the artist's pictures hung. A year before, Van Berkhout had married Elisabeth Ruysch (*top right*), his third wife, who was a cousin of Adrian Paets (*lower left*), the prime mover of the Collegiant movement, to which many of Vermeer's friends and family probably belonged. Paets, who commissioned two paintings from Vermeer, was also a patron to Pierre Bayle, John Locke and Baruch Spinoza (*lower right*), one of the leading philosophers of the early Enlightenment and himself a member of the Collegiant movement. Paets may have introduced Vermeer and Spinoza to one another. Sadly, no pictures exist of Vermeer's principal patrons, Maria de Knuijt and her husband, Pieter Claesz van Ruijven.

49 & 50. *The Astronomer*, 1668 (*above*), and *The Geographer*, 1669 (*right*). These two pictures embodying the spirit of scientific inquiry were conceived as a pair. They were commissioned by Adrian Paets, leading light of the Collegiant movement and a director of the Dutch East India Company, or VOC. They were probably hung in East India House,

the VOC's headquarters on the Oude Delft. 'The vast profits of the Dutch East India Company depended on the complementary sciences of astronomy and geography: knowledge of the stars was essential to maritime navigation, because it helped to determine latitude, while knowledge of the world's different continents made possible the exploration and exploitation of faraway places.'

51. *Allegory of the Catholic Faith*, c. 1670–72. The picture's modern title gives the misleading impression that it was painted as pro-Catholic propaganda, when Vermeer's true theme was the Catholic faith in crisis, blinded to the truth of Christ's message by a surfeit of unnecessary doctrines. The most stiflingly claustrophobic of Vermeer's pictures, it was commissioned by the Amsterdam banker and postmaster Hermann Dircks van Swoll, a freethinker with links to the Collegiants.

52. *The Art of Painting*, c. 1670–72. Vermeer painted this picture for himself and bequeathed it to his widow Catharina, who was forced to sell it by the executor of his estate, to her great distress. We see the painter at work in an airy, elegant room, painting Clio, the Muse of History. Usually, Clio's book is open and she is writing in it, but here it is shut, her work by implication done. History is over, the time of wonders about to begin. Like the *View of Delft*, the picture is a dream of the End of Days.

53 & 54. *Lady Writing a Letter with Her Maid*, c. 1672–5 (*above*), and *Woman with a Lute*, c. 1662–5 (*right*). Both of these pictures were acquired from Vermeer's widow, after the painter's death, by the baker Hendrick van Buyten. Neither show the artist at

the peak of his powers, although the earlier of these two studio remnants, the *Woman with a Lute*, is touchingly intimate, despite the awkwardness of its composition. It seems to be another picture of the girl portrayed in *Study of a Young Woman* (Plate 33).

55. *Young Woman Seated at a Virginal*, *c.* 1665. One of the artist's last pictures, acquired by a certain Diego Duarte sometime before 1682. We do not know how he came by it. It resembles the earlier 'messenger' pictures for the Van Ruijvens but lacks their spirit and conviction. 'It looks like a Vermeer, but with the lights switched off.'

woman, who holds a guitar and wears the fur-trimmed lemon-yellow jacket familiar from Vermeer's earlier work. The painting on the wall behind mistress and maid depicts a ship on stormy seas, traditional emblem of love's turbulent adventures. This is a rare instance of pure genre in the work of Vermeer. Its one singularity is the strange, tunnel-like perspective that has us viewing the scene through an open door and seemingly from within some kind of cupboard or storeroom, the stacked shelves of which dominate the foreground and take up a third of the picture, creating a claustrophobic effect. We have no idea who the first owner of this painting may have been. Nowadays it is in the collection of the Rijksmuseum.

One other picture possibly from these final years, 'A little piece with a lady playing the clavecin with accessories by Vermeer', was listed among the possessions of a jeweller and banker from Antwerp named Diego Duarte in July 1682.[22] The painting is probably the *Young Woman Seated at a Virginal* now in the National Gallery, London. It belongs to the same group of pictures as the National Gallery's one other work by the artist, *A Young Woman Standing at a Virginal*, and *The Guitar Player* in Kenwood, but unlike those it was not painted for the house of Pieter Claesz van Ruijven and Maria de Knuijt. *Young Woman Seated at a Virginal* does not appear in the catalogue of the 1696 Amsterdam auction, and how Diego Duarte came by it we do not know. It may have been painted for him on commission, or he may have acquired it on the secondary market. Either way it is a sad thing. The girl who plays the piano is a wan ghost. The handling is coarse, the picture as a whole lacking in spirit or conviction. It looks like a Vermeer, but with the lights switched off.

On 13 or 14 December 1675 Johannes Vermeer died, of causes unknown. He was forty-three years old. It happened suddenly, according to his widow and his mother-in-law. The two of them included an account of his death in a petition filed with the High Court of the States of Holland and West Friesland a year and a half later.[23] This is what they said:

> The petitioners reverently inform the States that Johannes Vermeer, during the ruinous and protracted war, not only was unable to sell any of his art but also, to his great detriment, was left sitting with the

paintings of other masters that he was dealing in, as a result of which and owing to the very great burden of his children, having nothing of his own, he had lapsed into such decay and decadence, which he had so taken to heart that, as if he had fallen into a frenzy, in a day and a half he had gone from being healthy to being dead.

Those were the bare bones of it: having been driven to distraction by money worries, Vermeer had a seizure of some kind, a stroke or a heart attack.

It is a plausible story, but almost certainly a fabrication. Maria and Catharina's account needs to be taken with a pinch of salt, because of its context. They filed their petition before the court in the summer of 1677 because Maria had by then paid back the 1,000 guilders borrowed against her will by her late son-in-law, redeemed the pawned obligation for 2,900 guilders, and returned it to the Orphan Chamber in Gouda as required. Now she wanted to get her hands (at last) on the large sum of money her son-in-law Johannes and his Arminian friend Jacob Rombouts had kept from her. She and Catharina were in court trying to secure an immediate order for the Orphan Chamber to release those funds.

Their petition was a tearjerking lament with a mercenary subtext. Having begun with the account of Vermeer going crazy with stress because he could not sell any pictures, it went on at length about the many children needing to be looked after in the household on the Oude Langendijk, the shame and humiliation of having to beg family members to help, and the dire situation facing Maria and Catharina and all their little ones. Then came the inevitable punchline. All this would be instantly remedied if the Orphan Chamber would part with 'the sum of 2,900 guilders, deposited there in the form of interest-bearing obligations'.

The story about Vermeer being desperately anxious for money was just part of a bigger story in which his whole family was portrayed as being desperately anxious for money, told with one purpose in mind: to make sure that a much-coveted sum was finally paid over, after many a slip between cup and lip, to Maria Thins. There is no reason to believe the part about Vermeer, because we know that the whole story was essentially untrue. No one in the household of Maria

Thins was panicked about where the next meal was coming from, about how to pay the bills or heat the house or feed all those children. In 1674, two years after the Year of Disaster and in the middle of a deep recession, Maria Thins's wealth was assessed by Delft's officers of the family levy and calculated at 26,000 guilders.[24] That was a huge amount of money and probably did not include all of her assets. Maria Thins might have lost some rent here and there, but the slump had barely dented her. The truth was that she wanted to stay rich and get a fair bit richer. But of course that was not what the High Court needed to be told if she were to be paid out.

It is hard to believe that Vermeer was overwhelmed by money worries in December 1675. He knew that in the last resort Maria Thins would always look out for her grandchildren and Catharina, and that she had the means to do so. She might have caused him stress by withholding the money he needed day to day, for baker's bills and such, but if so he had already vented that frustration by taking the 1,000 guilders that was not his to take. That betrayal in itself could have caused problems. Might she have discovered his double-dealing sometime just before Christmas and given him such a hard time that he had a seizure? Maria Thins had a sharp tongue: it cannot be ruled out. Another more prosaic possibility is that he contracted an illness of some kind. A serious outbreak of flu, or some like virus, felled a great many people in the winter of 1675. In October the English diarist John Evelyn reported catching 'an extreme cold, such as was afterwards epidemical, not only in this island, but was rife all over Europe'.[25]

All is speculation at this point in Vermeer's story, but he may have fallen victim to a different sort of malaise. Knowing what we do about the patterns of his life it would make sense for him to have suffered a crisis at this low point, to have succumbed to some form of 'decadence', as two of the women in his life delicately put it. Demoralized by the return of war, saddened by personal loss, and dispirited by the realization that a thousand years of promised peace was not going to begin any time soon, he may have been so deeply disappointed there was no coming back from it.

AFTERMATH

Ever mindful of public appearances, Maria Thins paid for her son-in-law to be given a rich man's funeral. He was carried to the Oude Kerk from Maria's house on the Oude Langendijk with great pomp and ceremony, his coffin borne by no fewer than fourteen pallbearers.[26] It was the most costly send-off ever given to a painter from Delft. Leading the procession were Catharina and the eleven children, three of whom were now adults. As Vermeer was laid in the family grave the small remains of one of his children, the infant who had died in 1673, were placed on top of his coffin. Then the bell in the great church steeple was rung a single time. Everyone in Delft heard it, heard the echo fade. He was gone.

In the aftermath there was a lot of scrambling, mostly by Maria Thins. Having spent lavishly on the funeral she was set on getting value elsewhere. In due course there would be the Van Hensbeeck trust money to pursue and the sob story to write, but first she made it known that any debts accruing to Vermeer were Catharina's sole responsibility. That way no creditors could come running to her, even though she was the one who had always paid them in the past and the only one with any money.

First in line to get his dues from the painter's widow was the baker, Hendrick van Buyten, who as we know was owed a small fortune for bread supplied to the family. He accepted two paintings by Vermeer in lieu of his large bill of 617 guilders and 6 stuivers. The pictures were itemized as 'Two personages one of whom is writing a letter' and 'One person playing on a cittern'.[27] The first of these studio remains can be identified as the large canvas now known as *Lady Writing a Letter with Her Maid*, in the National Gallery of Ireland, a stale picture in which various elements familiar from Vermeer's earlier work have been recombined as if by rote, without urgency or purpose. The light that enters the room from the window at the left is hard as stone, as are the two women illuminated by it: the standing maid is stiff as a statue, her face frozen in a half smile, while the woman writing resembles a portrait bust set on a tabletop rather than an actual human being. The second work acquired by Van Buyten is likely to have been the awkwardly composed but nonetheless touching *Woman with a Lute*, in the Metropolitan Museum of Art, which seems to be another picture of the girl portrayed in the same museum's *Study of a Young Woman*, who was perhaps one of Vermeer's older daughters. Neither painting shows the artist at the peak of his powers, so Van Buyten was being more than generous when he agreed to value them at over 300 guilders apiece. At auction they would have fetched a quarter of that sum, on a good day.

Van Buyten was equally accommodating in allowing Catharina an option to repay her debt and reclaim the paintings. He allowed her to do so over a period of twelve years at 50 guilders a year without interest. In the event, the debt was never repaid and he kept the pictures. But if further evidence were needed of the friendship between the painter and his baker, this is surely it. Van Buyten's treatment of the recently bereaved Catharina suggests he knew how much Vermeer had loved her.

Catharina also owed a lot of money to a supplier of clothing, which she raised by selling Vermeer's unsold stock of twenty-six paintings by other artists to a picture dealer in Amsterdam named Jan Coelenbier, who took delivery of the consignment at a shop called The Three Lemons.[28] He gave her a sour deal, 500 guilders for the lot. That was on 10 February 1676. On 22 February Catharina took the *trekschuit* to The Hague and appeared before a notary to transact some transparently crooked business. She made a gift 'in full and free property' to her mother, Maria Thins, of 'a painting by her late husband wherein is depicted "The Art of Painting"', as well as a certain amount of land and some life annuities.[29] This transaction, it now appears, was part of a systematic attempt to defraud the remaining creditors of Vermeer's estate, a scheme most likely cooked up by Maria Thins in order to reduce her own liabilities and preserve as many assets as possible within the family. Maria had the cooperation of her daughter, whose main priority seems to have been to make sure her husband's self-portrait and last statement *The Art of Painting* remained in the house on the Oude Langendijk. The plan was simple: once Catharina's principal assets had been transferred to her mother she could apply for bankruptcy and request a moratorium on all debts still owing to the creditors of her late husband.

This would be exactly what happened, but first, on Leap Year's Day 1676, less than a week after Catharina's return from The Hague, a notary came to the house on Papists' Corner to compile the inventories required by the laws governing inheritance. These are the same inventories that have already permitted us to peek inside the house in which Vermeer lived. But they are not complete. The notary was obliged to list everything previously owned by Vermeer now 'due' to Catharina, and everything that Catharina and her mother owned in common, but he was not obliged to list anything that belonged solely to Maria Thins, because there could be no call on her sole possessions by creditors of Vermeer's estate. This is why there is no mention of *The Art of Painting* in the inventory, even though that painting was certainly in the house when the notary came to call: it had been formally transferred from Catharina to Maria Thins in the deed drawn up days earlier.

It is likely that other items went missing by the same subterfuge.[30] If so they would have been attributed to Maria verbally on the day the notary came, he taking it on trust that he was being told the truth by two respectable ladies, mother and daughter. There is no mention, for example, of the fine clothing decorated with lace that a woman of Catharina's standing would probably have possessed. This suggests that many of her better things had either been put away, or were made out to belong to her mother on the day the notary came to visit. The two pictures possibly painted by Vermeer as portraits of Catharina, and given to her as love gifts, the *Girl Reading a Letter at an Open Window* and the *Woman in Blue Reading a Letter*, may also have escaped the inventory in this way. It would not have been hard to do. Hang a picture in a dark corner, say it belongs to Maria, hope no questions are asked.

On 24 April 1676, according to plan, Catharina requested and received 'Letters of Cession', which meant that she was legally insolvent and therefore entitled to plead with the High Court for a moratorium on all her debts.[31] The resulting petition presented an advance version of the same tale of woe that would be put before the magistrates of Gouda fifteen months later, omitting only the details of the painter's death:

> the supplicant, charged with the care of <u>eleven living children</u> [underlined in the original], because her aforementioned husband during the recent war with the King of France, a few years ago now, had been able

to earn very little or hardly anything at all, but also because the works of art that he had bought and with which he was trading had to be sold at great loss in order to feed his aforementioned children, owing to which he had then run so far into debts that she, supplicant, is not able to pay all her creditors . . .

The stratagem might have worked if the executor of the estate, appointed in consequence of the letters of cession, had not smelled a rat. He was Anthony van Leeuwenhoek, a man who has been well remembered for reasons other than his involvement in the tangled post-mortem affairs of Johannes Vermeer. A correspondent, like Spinoza, of Henry Oldenburg of the Royal Society, he was a self-taught natural scientist who contributed to the empirical observation of natural phenomena by grinding short-focus lenses through which he viewed bacteria, blood and his own spermatozoa, among other things. Numerous writers on Vermeer have wondered if the painter and Van Leeuwenhoek might have been friends, exchanging ideas about optics and other common interests. But Van Leeuwenhoek's appointment as curator of Vermeer's estate argues against that hypothesis. As steward to the Chamber of Aldermen, with a duty of impartiality in affairs of inheritance, he was obliged to recuse himself had he been familiar with the painter. Besides, having taken the job he showed no favour to Vermeer's widow: quite the opposite.

Van Leeuwenhoek was appointed on 30 September 1676.[32] Within a month he had come to the conclusion that Maria Thins was up to no good. On 9 November he sent an attorney named Christiaen van Vliet to question her about allegedly undeclared assets belonging to Catharina.[33] Speaking for Van Leeuwenhoek, attorney Van Vliet put it to Maria that she had conspired to conceal some of Catharina's assets by pretending they were her own. A month later Maria made a deposition denying that she done any such thing: 'She had kept no assets of her daughter or her daughter's deceased husband Johannes Vermeer in her possession *in fraudem creditorum* [to defraud creditors], neither is she in bad faith.'[34]

Maria was not believed, but the scam was hard enough to prove that in the end she and Catharina got away without paying most of the creditors, and came to favourable terms with the rest. The grit in the oyster, which may not have hurt Maria but certainly wounded Catharina, was that the sceptical Van Leeuwenhoek refused to accept the deed of gift by which *The Art of Painting* had been transferred out of Vermeer's estate. He seized the picture, then advertised that it would be publicly sold at the Guild of St Luke in Delft on 15 March 1677. Maria warned him by notarial deposition that he was under no circumstances to go ahead with the disposal, citing her daughter's transfer of its ownership to her, but he seems to have ignored her bluster and gone ahead anyway. Maria could have bought the picture ten times over and not noticed a material difference, but chose not to do so. It must have been a great loss to Catharina. At least she may have managed to keep the two paintings by her husband of herself reading letters.

Maria Thins outlived her son-in-law by five years. She made the last of her many wills in January 1680, a document from which it can be inferred that she was no longer on speaking terms with Johannes Cramer, the husband of her oldest granddaughter, Maria. Argumentative to the last, Maria passed away in December of that same year, her near neighbour the Jesuit priest Philippus de Pauw giving her the last rites.[35] Fourteen pallbearers carried her to the family grave, the same number as had borne the coffin of Vermeer. For Maria the great bell tolled not once, but twice.

Vermeer's widow, Catharina, died seven years later, on 30 December 1687, aged fifty-six. Father Philippus anointed her too with holy oil. She too was carried to the grave by many pallbearers. Her son-in-law Johannes Cramer, in whose house she was cared for in her last days by her daughter Maria, footed the bill. Maybe Maria Thins had been wrong about him. It would not have been the first time she misjudged a man's character.

Johannes and Catharina's many children gradually disappeared into history. The son who had been intended for the priesthood, Johannes, never did take holy orders. Injured in a gunpowder explosion on a boat taking him from Jesuit school in Mechelen back to Delft, he seems to have given up his religious studies. He later changed his name to plain Jan. He was last heard of practising as a notary in Bruges, in the southern Netherlands, in 1708.

LEGACIES

Vermeer's true legacy was his body of work, above all the pictures which he painted in little more than a decade for the household of Pieter Claesz van Ruijven and Maria de Knuijt: the house with the vine growing up its façade that we can still visit, in imagination, every time we stand before his picture of *The Little Street* in the Rijksmuseum.

John Ruskin may have had that same picture somewhere in the back of his mind when he delivered his damning judgement on Dutch art: 'the patient devotion of besotted lives to the delineation of bricks and fogs, cattle and ditchwater'. The idea that Dutch painting is first and foremost an art of literal representation, an art of describing, has stood unchallenged for too long. It is a preconception based on the assumption that Dutch art reflected the materialistic attitudes of the mercantile society in which it was produced. Sometimes it did, often it did not. One of the main aims of this book has been to show that Vermeer was a painter not of things but of ideas. Its other closely related aim has been to give him back his rightful place in history, to locate him as part of a religious and intellectual movement driven by the desire to reform society and make the world a fairer and a better place.

These key aspects of his legacy have long remained hidden due to a lack of knowledge of the various religious milieus to which Vermeer belonged. Much evidence has been produced here to indicate his probable links to the Remonstrants, who rebelled against the doctrines of the Reformed Calvinist Church, and his likely sympathy with the Collegiant movement, itself an extension of Remonstrant Christianity. So many Remonstrants and Collegiants turn up in so many different corners of Vermeer's life story (and that of his parents too) that their presence cannot be put down to happenstance. Moreover, the pictures that he painted for people we know to have been Remonstrants and Collegiants reflect their hopes and beliefs with uncanny exactness.

Understanding Vermeer's legacy has been made all the more difficult because the legacy of the Dutch freethinkers with whom he associated has itself been obscured by a form of amnesia. This is neatly illustrated by the history of an idea central to their thinking: toleration.

Since the late eighteenth century, when religious toleration was made a cornerstone of European Enlightenment thought, the English philosopher John Locke and the French encyclopedist Pierre Bayle have been widely credited as its principal early advocates. But, as both men themselves acknowledged, it was an idea of Dutch origin, the importance of which had been brought home to them by none other than Vermeer's patron, the leading Collegiant Adrian Paets. Locke spent the best part of five years as an exile in the Dutch Republic between 1683 and 1689, while Bayle spent most of his adult life there. Paets was Bayle's principal protector and patron, paying him a generous annuity for many years. Through Bayle he came to know Locke, whom he not only befriended but also persuaded to attend at least one Collegiant meeting. Locke's journal entry for 30 July 1684 is one of the few surviving eyewitness descriptions of Collegiants at worship:

> The Collegiants pray both in the beginning and end and conclude with the Lord's Prayer; the rest of their prayer is extempore. Anyone that finds himself moved, has the liberty to speak. One sang a psalm alone; he that sang or spoke or prayed stood up and was bare [headed] ... They admit to their communion all Christians and hold it our duty to join in love and charity with those who differ in their opinion.[36]

Locke and Bayle were both familiar with Paets's main publication on toleration, his *Letter of Mr van Paets on the latest disturbances in England, in which the tolerance of those who do not follow the prevailing religion is discussed*, of 1685. It was Bayle who first translated and published it. Each drew on it when composing their own thoughts on the same subject, subsequently published as Bayle's *Philosophical Commentary* (1686) and Locke's *A Letter Concerning Toleration* (1689).[37] Bayle openly acknowledged Paets's text as his own inspiration, even singling it out as the essential short read on the subject: 'without undertaking to read a long-winded work, one need only read a small piece written at London in 1685 by an illustrious magistrate of a town in Holland'.[38] Bayle came to regard toleration as an absolute prerequisite of any civilized and morally grounded society: 'Toleration is the very Bond of Peace, and Non-Toleration is the Source of Confusion and Squabble.'

Toleration was made an international *cause célèbre* by Voltaire, whose caustically witty (and best-selling) *Treatise on Tolerance* of 1763 was inspired by the judicial torture and murder of a French Protestant merchant at the hands of reactionary Catholic magistrates in Toulouse. Voltaire reached many more readers than his predecessors, while drawing heavily on their arguments, especially those of Locke, who had himself been inspired by the Dutch tolerationists who had preceded him. So it was that toleration, implicit in the thought of Erasmus, fully developed in the late sixteenth-century disputes of Coornhert and Arminius, and nurtured within Dutch Remonstrant and Collegiant circles, became part of Enlightenment thought by a process of clear and direct transmission. Having begun as a primarily religious idea it became a political and humanitarian one too, an important strand in the weave of thought that eventually produced the concept of human rights and contributed to the abolition of slavery.

Whether Pierre Bayle was aware of it or not, the 'Bond of Peace' he celebrated in those lines of his *Philosophical Commentary* was essentially a gift from Jacobus Arminius to the modern world. Adrian Paets had been brought up on Arminius's lecture of 1606, *On Reconciling Religious Dissension among Christians*, which was the founding text of the Dutch toleration movement, and had passed it on in turn. It had a millenarian subtext for Paets, as for Arminius before him: to both men toleration was God-given love, the spirit of Christ reigning in man, its diffusion a necessary prelude to the End of Days.

Such histories of thought may be distasteful to some modern observers of the past, especially those who view it from a purely secular perspective. The proposition that certain basic tenets of the Enlightenment might first have been hatched by a group of intensely pious Christians, millenarians to boot, is anathema to those who consider religious belief to be inherently inimical to human progress. But the many buzzing mosquitoes of Dutch dissenting Christianity did indeed play a major part in developing the core values of the Enlightenment, and therefore the core values of more or less every free modern society. They included not just Collegiants and Remonstrants but many other freethinking Dutchmen and women besides. Collectively such people dreamed of a world in which men and women would be treated as equals, in which all would be free to worship as they wished, and in which all would enjoy freedom of thought and speech. The Collegiants created that dreamed-of world, in microcosm, each and every time they met.

Spinoza's posthumous celebrity ensured that the Collegiants' belief in freedom of thought and expression, and their corresponding distrust of churches as institutions of power, became enshrined in Enlightenment thought. The rights of women to speak their minds and be treated as equals to men were promulgated by Dutch journalists and freethinkers such as Hendrick Doedijns, and taken up in England, France and Germany by the middle of the eighteenth century. The Dutch cult of freedom, and corresponding hatred of tyranny, was brought into the mainstream by Pierre Bayle and others of his ilk. Dutch freethinkers may have felt crushed by Louis XIV and his invading armies in the Year of Disaster, but their legacy would long outlast that moment.

Likewise, Vermeer's life may have ended in a sad way but there is nothing sad about it in its totality. His paintings have made sure of that. His art is the most tangible and beautiful legacy of the liberal Dutch tradition exemplified by the Collegiants. With great depth and poignancy Vermeer made manifest many of the things in which such people believed. In a world of political and spiritual upheaval, his pictures implicitly regret the horrors of war, especially religious conflicts, which had claimed millions of lives and brought devastation to Europe during the years of the painter's youth. His paintings dream of a world where people of all faiths (or none) might be reconciled, so that no one need die for what they believe. They speak for the equality and the dignity of women. Above all they radiate a belief in the power of love, that redeeming emotion placed at the heart of his *Ethics* by Vermeer's fellow Collegiant Spinoza, to heal the wounds we do to ourselves and others.

At times the pictures also hint at a powerful strain of radicalism implicit in Dutch liberal thought. This is especially true of Vermeer's two surviving paintings of architecture, *The Little Street* and the *View of Delft*, which are by implication pictures of society as his more millenarian contemporaries envisaged it, albeit done with a light touch. Each shows us a world built, brick by brick, by people working together, in which all are equal and everyone looks after everyone else, free from government or indeed any form of institutional oversight. They stand in perfect opposition to the architecture of autocracy, epitomized in Vermeer's own time by Louis XIV's palace at Versailles.

It may be wondered whether it was this aspect of Vermeer's thought-world that touched a nerve in Théophile Thoré and sowed the seeds for the obsession that drove him to rediscover the painter's work in the middle of the nineteenth century. Thoré was no friend to the *ancien régime*, being himself a radical intellectual and revolutionary activist who had taken part in an attempted coup in Paris just after the revolution of 1848. Travelling to the Low Countries as an exile, banished by Louis Napoleon, he adopted the pseudonym of William Bürger to write many of his essays about Dutch art, *burger* being Dutch for 'The Citizen'. Might Théophile Thoré-Bürger, as he thus became known, have had some intuition about Vermeer's affiliations, despite knowing nothing, or next to nothing, of the painter's life? Might he have looked at Vermeer's pictures and felt, without ever quite knowing why, that he had come home? Many other people have had that same feeling, entranced before their magic. That is one thing that can never be explained.

THE MIRACLE

Most of the people who had known and supported Vermeer during his lifetime were dead within ten years of his passing. Adrian Paets died in 1686, having returned to the Dutch Republic after negotiating the military alliance with Spain that helped to preserve his nation's independence. By the time of his death he had been patron to, among others, Baruch Spinoza, Johannes Vermeer, John Locke and Pierre Bayle. Yet there are no monuments to him. His biography has never been written. Even in the Netherlands, he has barely been remembered.

Maria de Knuijt, whose Collegiant meetings were likely to have been encouraged by Paets and possibly attended by him on occasion, died in 1681, seven years after her husband, Pieter Claesz van Ruijven. Might she have added one more picture to their collection of Vermeers, sometime between her husband's death and her own? Lot 3 in the sale of 1696 at which the pictures were dispersed was 'The portrait of Vermeer in a room with various accessories uncommonly beautifully painted by him'. This might be a description of *The Art of Painting*, the picture sequestered from Vermeer's widow by Anthony van Leeuwenhoek and sent to be sold at the Guild of St Luke on 15 March 1677. It would make sense for Maria to have bought it. She and Vermeer had been close for many years and she would have been one of the few people likely to have understood the symbolism of the painting. If that was not a description of *The Art of Painting*, then somewhere, overlooked under old varnish in some bad black frame, there may still be a missing self-portrait by the artist.

We know what happened to all Maria de Knuijt's paintings by Vermeer after she died. They went to her daughter Magdalena, whom we believe to have been the real *Girl with a Pearl Earring*, who took them with her to the home and printing establishment owned by her husband, Jacob Dissius, on the Great Market Square: the Golden ABC. Magdalena herself possessed them for less than a year, dying in the summer of 1682, still in her twenties, of causes unknown. Like many young women in those days, she perhaps died in childbirth.

Magdalena must have believed it was important to keep the Vermeers together, because that is exactly what she had done. We know this from the notarial inventory of the house made just after her death, which as we have seen includes a description of one of the most unusual displays in the history of art: in her 'front room' eleven paintings by Vermeer were hung in a sequence disturbed only by the presence of two pictures by other artists: an anonymous landscape and a seascape 'by Porcellis'. Three of those Vermeers were said to be in 'boxes', likely meaning that they were displayed in frames with doors like those of an altarpiece. Elsewhere in the house the pictures by Vermeer appear to have been more evenly distributed among those by other artists. But the arrangement of the eleven in the front room may lead us to suspect that those paintings in particular had continued to serve a devotional purpose, for Magdalena and whoever may have joined her on occasion in that space in her house. Her parents had left her instructions about what to do with their paintings in that 'book marked with the letter "A"'. One of those instructions must have been to keep the pictures by Vermeer as a group. Might another have been to continue worshipping in their presence?

Following Magdalena's death, her widower, Jacob Dissius, kept the pictures together himself. The collection of Vermeers remained intact for another fourteen years, which is in itself remarkable and cannot be put down to inertia, because Dissius actively disposed of a number of paintings by other artists bequeathed to him by his wife. We know this because several of them, including the Porcellis, failed to appear in the auction of 1696 at which his pictures were finally sold. By contrast, he made sure that all of the twenty-one Vermeers that had been passed down to him remained in his possession until his dying day. Once again we may wonder whether Dissius not only kept Vermeer's paintings together but continued to respect their devotional character.

More or less everything about Vermeer's afterstory is remarkable. But most remarkable of all is the fact that such an astonishingly high percentage of those pictures should have survived at all. On the day that they were sold in Amsterdam, following the death of Jacob Dissius, Vermeer was a painter of distinctly minor repute. Within a few decades he had been forgotten: his name is absent from the biographies of Dutch Golden Age artists written by Arnold Houbraken in the early eighteenth century. Yet somehow only a handful of the twenty-one pictures that were abruptly dispersed into the world on 16 May 1696 have *not* survived. If we dare to hope that *The Concert* stolen from Boston may one day be recovered, the most notable casualties include a picture in which 'a gentleman is washing his hands in a see-through room with sculptures'; a portrait of an unidentified young woman; and 'a view of a house standing in Delft'.

The rest can still be seen today. What that means is that almost all of those twenty-one pictures – sent into the world without a meaningful name attached to them, without demonstrable financial value, without anything to protect them from the disregard that leads to loss and destruction, other than the brilliance of their being – have made it through centuries of time, with all its dangers, not only unscathed but as radiant as they were when the painter finished putting his brush to them. By rights they should have disappeared, should have sunk into the humus of history, as a buried body is dispersed into the soil. But the body of Vermeer's work kept its integrity, each part surviving so that they might once again be seen as a whole.

This is the miracle of Vermeer, made possible because the painter transcended himself in the act of creation. He produced something so beautiful that it insisted on being preserved, persuading all who saw it to recognize, instinctively, that it was too precious to be lost. Vermeer lived and died in the watery world of the Dutch Republic, a place of red-brick houses standing by reflective canals, a world of huge skies and flat horizons. But he escaped it too. Like the women he painted so long ago, the women in the room with a nail in the wall, he leapt the bounds of here and now to dwell in eternity.

Appendix 1

The act of ownership document for 106 Oude Delft bears the signature of Pieter Claesz van Ruijven: it is near the top of the page, eight lines down and in the middle.

The pledge diagram for the block (*overleaf*) between the Boterbrug and the Peperstraat on the Oude Delft shows the hidden Remonstrant Church standing directly behind the house of Vermeer's patrons.

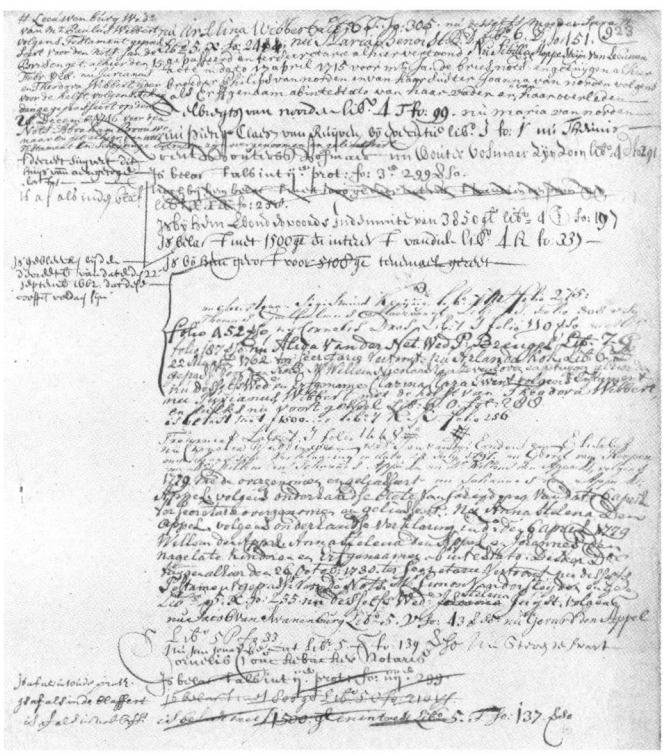

APPENDIX I

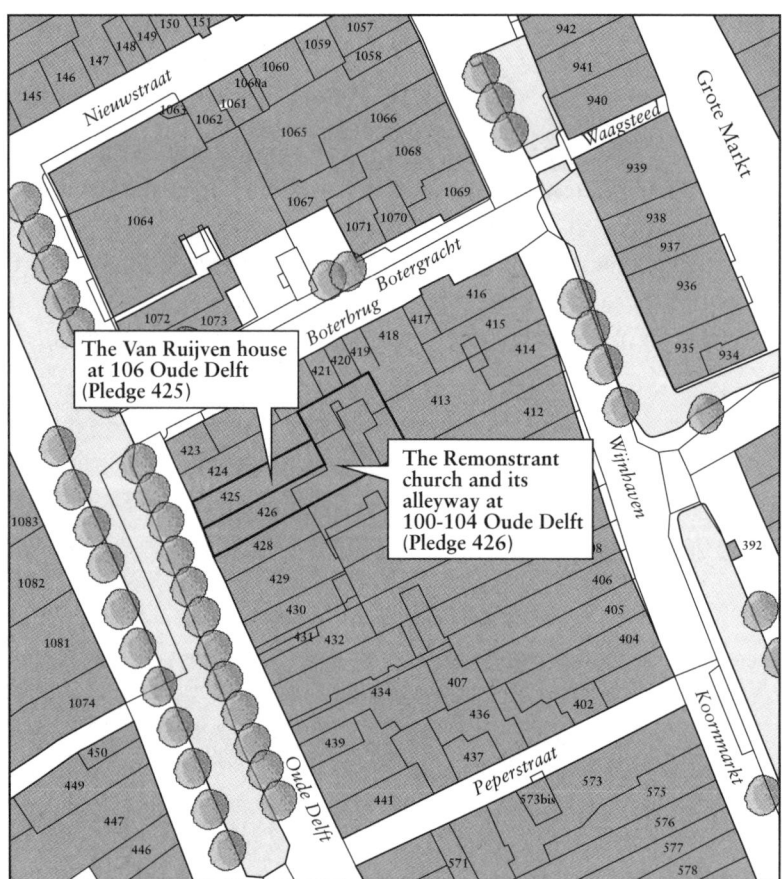

Note: *the street numbers have changed since the seventeenth century and no longer correspond*

Source: Gemeentearchief Delft; the relevant pledges are 034D426 and 034D425

Appendix 2

The *trekschuit* network was the first truly reliable mass-transportation system in Europe: a countrywide grid of canals traversed by horse-drawn barges, enabling the Dutch to travel safely to almost anywhere they wanted within their own country. In the words of Maximilien Misson, an exiled French Huguenot who travelled widely by *trekschuit*: 'Nothing could be more convenient. The Boats are drawn by Horses, and go off at set hours [*see timetable overleaf*]. You are seated as quietly in them as if you were at home, and sheltered both from Rain and Wind: So that you may go from one territory to another almost without perceiving that you are out of the House.'

Schedule of trekschuit service from Rotterdam and in the second half of the seventeenth century.

From/To															
Rotterdam	-	-	-	-	5:00	6:00	7:00	8:00	9:00	10:00	11:00	12:00	13:00	14:00	
Delft	-	-	-	-	6:45	7:45	8:45	9:45	10:45	11:45	12:45	13:45	14:45	15:45	
Maassluis	-	-	-	-	-	6:00	-	-	8:00	-	-	-	-	11:30	-	-	-	-
Delft	-	-	-	-	-	8:00	-	-	10:00	-	-	-	-	13:30	-	-	-	-
Delft	5:30	6:30							and every half hour to						
The Hague	6:45	7:45													
Delft (also The Hague)	-	-	6:30	7:30	-	-	9:00	10:30	-	-	-	-	13:30	-	-	15:00	-	-
Leiden	-	-	9:30	10:30	-	-	12:00	13:30	-	-	-	-	16:30	-	-	18:00	-	-
Leiden	-	-	-	-	-	-	-	13:00	-	-	-	-	-	-	-	-	-	-
Utrecht	-	-	-	-	-	-	-	21:00	-	-	-	-	-	-	-	-	-	-
Leiden	-	-	10:00	11:00	-	-	13:00	14:00	-	-	-	-	17:00	-	-	-	-	20:00
Haarlem	-	-	14:00	15:00	-	-	17:00	18:00	-	-	-	-	21:00	-	-	-	-	|
															via
Haarlem	-	-	-	-	-	-	-	-	-	-	-	-	-	-	-	-	-	Alphen
Alkmaar	-	-	-	-	-	-	-	-	-	-	-	-	-	-	-	-	-	|
															|
Haarlem	-	-	15:00	16:00	17:00	18:00	19:00	20:00	-	-	-	-	-	-	-	-	|
Amsterdam	-	-	17:15	18:15	19:15	20:15	21:15	22:15	-	-	-	-	-	-	-	6:00
Amsterdam	-	-			Every hour a ferry				-	-	-	-	-	-	-	-
Buiksloot	-	-							-	-	-	-	-	-	-	-
Buiksloot	-	-	19:00	-	-	-	23:00	-	-	-	-	-	-	5:00	6:00	7:00
Monnikendam	-	-	21:00	-	-	-	|	-	-	-	-	-	-	7:00	˘	9:00
Purmerend	-	-	-	-	-	-	|	-	-	-	-	-	-	˘	8:30	˘
Edam	-	-	-	-	-	-	˘	-	-	-	-	-	-	8:00	˘	10:00
Hoorn	-	-	-	-	-	-	5:00	-	-	-	-	-	-	10:00	11:00	12:00
Hoorn	-	-	-	-	5:00	-	-	8:00	-	-	-	-	-	-	-	13:00
Alkmaar	-	-	-	-	9:00	-	-	12:00	-	-	-	-	-	-	-	17:00
Hoorn	-	-	-	-	-	6:00	-	-	10:00	-	-	-	-	-	-	-
Enkhuizen (coach route)	-	-	-	-	-	8:00	-	-	12:00	-	-	-	-	-	-	-

Maassluis to Alkmaar and Enkhuizen

```
15:00  16:00  17:00  18:00  19:00   -    20:30   -     -     -     -     -     -    -    -    Rotterdam
16:45  17:45  18:45  19:45  20:45   -     -    22:15   -     -     -     -     -    -    -    Delft

14:00  16:00   -     18:00   -     -     -     -     -     -     -     -     -    -    -    Maassluis
16:00  18:00   -     20:00   -     -     -     -     -     -     -     -     -    -    -    Delft

              19:00   -     -     -     -     -     -     -     -     -     -    -    -    Delft
              20:15   -     -     -     -     -     -     -     -     -     -    -    -    The Hague

17:00  18:30   -     -     -     -     -     -    22:00   -     -     -     -    -    -    5:00   Delft (also The Hague)

20:00  21:30   -     -     -     -     -     -     1:00   -     -     -     -    -    -    8:00   Leiden

21:00   -     -     -     -     -     -     -     -     -     -     -     -    -    -    9:00   Leiden
 5:00   -     -     -     -     -     -     -     -     -     -     -     -    -    -   17:00   Utrecht

  -    -    23:00   -     -     -     -     -    4:00   -    6:30   -     -    -    -    9:00   Leiden
  -    -     3:00   -     -     -     -     -    8:00   -   10:30   -     -    -    -   13:00   Haarlem

  -    -     -     -     -     -     -     -    9:00    -     -     -     -    -    -           Haarlem
  -    -     -     -     -     -     -     -   14:00    -     -     -     -    -    -           Alkmaar

  -    -    5:00    -     -    6:00   7:00  8:00  9:00 10:00 11:00 12:00 13:00 14:00       Haarlem
  -    -    7:15    -     -    8:15   9:15  10:15 11:15 12:15 13:15 14:15 15:15 16:15      Amsterdam

                      Every hour a ferry                                                     Amsterdam
                                                                                             Buiksloot

 8:00   9:00   -    -    -   11:00   -     -   13:00  14:00  15:00  16:00  17:00  18:00    Buiksloot
   ˘   11:00   -    -    -     ˘    -     -   15:00    ˘    17:00    ˘    19:00    ˘       Monnikendam
10:30    ˘    -    -    -   13:30   -     -     ˘    16:30    ˘    18:30    ˘    20:30     Purmerend
   ˘   12:00   -    -    -     ˘    -     -   16:00    ˘    18:00    ˘    20:00    -    -  Edam
13:00  14:00   -    -    -   16:00   -   18:00 19:00  20:00  21:00    -     -     -        Hoorn

  -     -    -    -   16:00    -    -     -     -     -     -     -     -     -            Hoorn
  -     -    -    -   20:00    -    -     -     -     -     -     -     -     -            Alkmaar

14:00   -    -    -   16:00    -    -     -     -     -     -     -     -     -            Hoorn
16:00   -    -    -   18:00    -    -     -     -     -     -     -     -     -            Enkhuizen (coach route)
```

Notes

PROLOGUE

1. See John Nash, *Vermeer* (London, 2002), pp. 102–4, with citations.
2. Gemeentearchief Delft, records of Notary D. van der Hoeve, no. 2359, 20 June 1682. Cited in John Michael Montias, *Vermeer and His Milieu: A Web of Social History* (Princeton, 1989), p. 252.
3. Magdalena had a younger brother and sister but neither survived infancy: see the family tree of the Van Ruijvens in the front matter.
4. John Michael Montias, *Verneer and His Milieu*, pp. 251–5.
5. Ibid., Document 417.
6. Ibid., p. 254.
7. S. A. C. Dudok Van Heel, *Jaerboek Amstelodanum 37* (Amsterdam, 1975), p. 159.

PART ONE: THE INHERITANCE, 1560–1632

1. Owen Feltham, *A Brief Character of the Low Countries* (London, 1648), pp. 3, 5, 91.
2. Ibid., p. 85.
3. Jonathan Israel, *The Dutch Republic: Its Rise, Greatness and Fall* (Oxford, 1995), p. 74.
4. Peter Limm, *The Dutch Revolt, 1559–1648* (London, 1989), p. 33.
5. William I of Orange was also known as William the Silent. He is not to be confused with William III of Orange who became Stadtholder of the United Provinces in 1672 and later King of England.
6. Peter Arnade, *Beggars, Iconoclasts and Civic Patriots* (Ithaca and London, 2008), p. 228.
7. Ibid., p. 233.

8. Peter Limm, *The Dutch Revolt, 1559–1648*, p. 42.
9. See Christopher Duffy, *Siege Warfare: The Fortress in the Early Modern World* (London, 1979), p. 61.
10. Ibid., p. 60.
11. For this quotation and an interesting discussion of Herod's place in Dutch rebel propaganda, see David Kunzle, *From Criminal to Courtier: The Soldier in Netherlandish Art, 1550–1672*, in particular Chapter 6, 'Spanish Herod, Dutch Innocents: Anti-Spanish Satires 1569–1578'.
12. Cited in ibid.
13. See Christopher Duffy, *Siege Warfare*, pp. 70–82.
14. Ibid., p. 64.
15. Ibid., p. 45.
16. The seven provinces forming the United Provinces were: Holland, Zeeland, Utrecht, Gelderland, Friesland, Overijssel and Groningen.
17. See Michael Pye, *Antwerp* (London, 2021), for an illuminating account of the city's rise and fall, including much on the sack of Antwerp and its subsequent mixed fortunes.
18. *Dudley Carleton to John Chamberlain, 1603–1624, Jacobean Letters*, ed. Maurice Lee, Jr. (New Jersey, 1972), pp. 212, 218.
19. P. C. Hooft, *Nederlandsche historien sedert de ooverdraght der heerschappye van Kaiser Karel den Vufden op Kooning Philips zynen zoon* (Amsterdam, 1642), pp. 463–5.
20. See 'The Duke of Alba: The Ideal Enemy' by Daniel R. Horst, in *Arte Nuevo: Revista de estudios áureos* 1 (2014), pp. 130–54.
21. See George Renier, *The Dutch Nation* (London, 1944), p. 23.
22. W. P. C. Knuttel, *Catalogus van de pamfletten-verzameling berustende in de Koninklijke Bibliothek*, 9 vols. (The Hague, 1899–1920; reprinted Utrecht, 1978). Pamphlet 2310 A2vo (1614).
23. On Nicodemism, see Diarmaid MacCulloch, *A History of Christianity: The First Three Thousand Years* (London, 2009), pp. 189–99; and idem., *Lower Than the Angels: A History of Sex and Christianity* (London, 2024), pp. 187–91.
24. For an excellent account of the Vogelsangh affair, see Carl Bangs, *Arminius: A Study in the Reformation* (Nashville, 1971), pp. 155–67.
25. City Archives, Leiden, Municipal Archives 1575–81, inv. no. 73; see Carl Bangs, *Arminius*, p. 46.
26. Jacobus Arminius, 'Oration V: On Reconciling Religious Dissensions among Christians', in *The Works of James Arminius, D.D., Translated from the Latin by James Nichols*, 3 vols. (London, 1825), I, pp. 372ff.

Given on 8 February 1606, in the Hall of Leiden University, on the occasion of Arminius resigning the office of *Rector Magnificus*.

27. They had indeed sent their own Counter-Remonstrance to the States of Holland.
28. For Digna's place of employment, see John Michael Montias, 'A Postscript on Vermeer and His Milieu', in *The Hoogsteder Mercury* (Etten-Leur, 1985–91), p. 415; for the mills of Amsterdam, see Violet Barbour, *Capitalism in Amsterdam in the Seventeenth Century* (Ann Arbor, 1983), pp. 68–9.
29. Gemeentearchief Amsterdam, Register van Huwelijken; cited in Albert Blankert, *Vermeer of Delft* (London, 1978), p. 145.
30. In 'New Documents on Vermeer and his Family', *Oud Holland*, vol. 91, no. 4 (1977), pp. 267–87, John Michael Montias asserted that the presiding minister was the ultra-orthodox Jacobus Triglandius, without giving a source for the information. This has proved impossible to verify.
31. The author is greatly indebted to the article on this subject by Paul Abels, 'Church and Religion in the Life of Vermeer', in *Dutch Society in the Age of Vermeer*, ed. Donald Haks and Marie Christine van der Sman (The Hague, 1996), pp. 68–78.
32. For the links between the Vermeer family and the Rombouts family, see John Michael Montias, 'A Postscript on Vermeer and His Milieu', pp. 415–19, note 12; see also the detailed notes on Jacob Rombouts and family in the online resource 'The Montias Database', Inv # 292.0021.
33. See John Michael Montias, 'New Documents on Vermeer and his Family', pp. 267–87.
34. In the autumn of 1617 he had opposed the appointment of the orthodox Calvinist preacher Henricus Swalmius to the Delft Church Council, and when Swalmius was nonetheless confirmed Taurinus refused to recognize him as his fellow minister. He subsequently organized a petition against Swalmius's appointment, which he persuaded many of Delft's disaffected Remonstrants to sign. He was suspected of allowing Remonstrants into the Delft ministry without the usual examinations and was accused by one member of his own congregation of 'viciously traducing' the Reformed religion. See F. Wouters and P. H. A. M. Abels, *Nieuw En Ongezien: Kerk en samenleving in de classis Delft en Delfland 1572–1621*, A. Ph., 2 vols. (Delft, 1994), I, pp. 491–4.
35. There it was charged that he, together with his fellow Remonstrant minister Petrus Cupus, had persistently upheld the freedom of each individual to interpret the Bible in his or her own way, rather than be guided by the authority of the Church: 'P. CUPUS affirmavit Ioanni Taurino,

esse inter REMONSTRANTES, qui dubitent de *autopistia* S. Scripturae.' From F. Hommius, *Specimen controversiarum Belgicarum, seu Confessio ecclesiarum reformatarum in Belgio* (Leiden, 1618), p. 12. Cited in H. van der Belt, *Autopistia: The Self-Convincing Authority of Scripture in Reformed Theology* (Leiden, 2006), p. 167.

36. Gerard Brandt, *History of the Reformation*, trans. John Chamberlayne (London, 1721), II, p. 557.
37. Ibid., pp. 566–9.
38. The trail of documents concerning Taurinus's relations with the Reformed Church after 1619 is recorded by F. Wouters and Paul Abels in their survey of the Delft classis cited above, *Nieuw En Ongezien*, I, pp. 491–4.
39. See John Michael Montias, *Vermeer and His Milieu*, p. 65.
40. Gerard Brandt, *History of the Reformation*, IV, p. 327.
41. See John Michael Montias, *Vermeer and His Milieu*, pp. 246ff.
42. Ibid., Document 94 (8 December 1623).
43. See Jonathan Israel, *The Dutch Republic*, pp. 469–88.
44. For the counterfeiting affair, see John Michael Montias, *Vermeer and His Milieu*, Chapter 2, *passim*.
45. Ibid., Document 134 (17 April 1632).
46. Simon Episcopius, *The Remonstrant Confession, 1621*, trans. Mark Ellis (Oregon, 2005), p. 28.
47. Ibid., p. 76.
48. Ibid., p. 12.
49. Ibid., p. 122.
50. Paschier de Fijne, *Kort, Waerachtigh, en Getrouw Verhael van het eerste Begin en Opkomen van de nieuwe Seckte der Propheten ofte Rynsburgers in het Dorp van Warmont, Anno 1619, en 1620*, or *A Brief, Truthful, and Faithful History of the Beginning and Origin of the New Sect of the Prophets of Rijnsburg in the Village of Warmont in the Years 1619–20* (Waer-Stadt, 1671).
51. Ibid., pp. 14, 21.
52. Gerard Brandt, *History of the Reformation*, IV, pp. 53ff.
53. Ibid., pp. 49–59.
54. For the text of it, see Dirck Rafaelsz Camphuysen, *Stichtelijke Rijmen*, ed. Dr J. van Vloten (Schiedam, 1861), pp. 78–9.
55. Dirck Rafaelsz Camphuysen, *Vant onbedriegelik oordeel tusschen goede ende quade* (Infallible Judgement), in *Theologische Werken, bestaande in drie Deelin* (Amsterdam, 1699), Chapter XI, p. 57.
56. Women played an important part and exerted considerable authority in the early Christian communities to whom St Paul wrote his epistles.

Paul offers his greetings to several such women in those letters. The prominence of those women is probably linked to the fact that the early Christian communities gathered in private houses, the household being a space identified more strongly as female than male in those times. The fact that the Collegiants also met in private houses and also allowed women much authority is unlikely to be a coincidence: they modelled their gatherings on those encouraged by Paul. Women also took leading roles in the Anglo-Saxon Church from the late sixth to the early eighth century. Otherwise, from the third century to the seventeenth (and beyond) officially sanctioned Christian worship was conducted in most times and at most places more or less exclusively according to 'a more normal pattern of male dominance'. The phrase is that of Diarmaid MacCullough, whose *Lower Than the Angels* contains a great deal of fascinating information on the role of women (and its curtailment) in Christianity: see especially pp. 87–9, 226–7 and 308–9.

57. Dirck Rafaelsz Camphuysen, *Predicatien VI*, in *Theologische Werken, bestaande in drie Deelin* (Amsterdam, 1699), p. 206. For a brilliant account of Camphuysen's theology, and for the best general introduction to the rich and varied traditions of Dutch nonconformist religious thought, see the scintillating study by Pierre Kolakowski, *Chrétiens sans Eglise* (Paris, 1967). The author is deeply indebted to Kolakowski's pioneering work.
58. Johannes Taurinus, *Bedenckingen Op d'Historie van't Samaritaensche Vroutjen*, or *Reflections on the Parable of Samaritan Woman* (Delft, 1625, 1630), vol. I, p. ii.
59. Ibid., p. 20: 'we adhere to the Evangelical teachings only, we reject the traditions of the followers, the councils and the synods that aim to turn Christians against the Gospel and the Holy Script. We reject the abhorrent choice of going by the laws and testimonies of the synods and councils, instead of acknowledging the truth of what is written.'
60. Ibid., pp. 238–42: 'It is quite clear that an internal divine service pleases God, and that an external service – mindless, heartless – is vanity to God . . . However, a Christian must also be holy on the outside – his face, his words, his ways together must show that God lives in his heart. And it must be quite clear that it all comes straight from the heart in order to please God.'
61. See Jonathan Israel, *The Dutch Republic*, p. 493.
62. Paul Zumthor, *Daily Life in Rembrandt's Holland* (London, 1959), p. 95.
63. John Michael Montias, *Vermeer and His Milieu*, p. 63 and Document 136.

64. A regent in Delft named Cornelis Adriaensz Boomgaert, who was a great admirer of Coornhert's spiritualist Christianity, used the Reformed Church in precisely the same way. See Paul Abels, 'Coornherts trouwste discipel. Cornelis Adriaensz Boomgaert als zijn literair executeur testamentair', in *Tijdschrift voor Nederlandse Kerkgeschiedenis* 25 (2022), pp. 110–22.

PART TWO: CHILDHOOD, EDUCATION, MARRIAGE, 1632–57

1. Notaries often wrote their contracts in inns or taverns, so the innkeeper was frequently called upon to witness them.
2. The quotation is from 'The New Guild Letter' of 1611, cited in John Michael Montias, *Artists and Artisans in Delft: A Socio-Economic Study of the Seventeenth Century* (Princeton, 1982), p. 75.
3. John Michael Montias, *Vermeer and His Milieu*, p. 64.
4. Ibid., Document 156.
5. Ibid., Document 186; see also John Michael Montias, 'A Postscript on Vermeer and His Milieu', pp. 415ff.
6. John Michael Montias, *Vermeer and His Milieu*, p. 69 and Document 149.
7. Ibid., Document 364.
8. This hypothesis was put to the author in conversation with John Michael Montias; see also his *Vermeer and His Milieu*, p. 73.
9. See Gregor Weber, *Johannes Vermeer: Faith, Light and Reflection* (Amsterdam, 2023), p. 49.
10. See H. G. Slager, 'Johannes Vermeer and his Neighbours' (Ommen, 2017), *passim*.
11. The details of the bequest will be discussed in detail below.
12. John Michael Montias, *Vermeer and His Milieu*, pp. 204–5 and Document 329.
13. The evidence for this will be presented below, in Part Three.
14. See John Michael Montias, 'Recent Archival Research on Vermeer', *Studies in the History of Art*, vol. 55, Symposium Papers XXXIII: Vermeer Studies (98), p. 98.
15. The author is extremely grateful to all those at the Remonstrant church in Rotterdam for helping to find this information, especially Titus van Hille, who generously spent a great deal of his time in the Gemeentearchief Delft specifically searching for the house's exact location, for the purposes of this book.

16. See Andrew Cooper Fix, *Prophecy and Reason: The Dutch Collegiants in the Early Enlightenment* (Princeton, 1991), Chapter 2, *passim*.
17. See Jori Zijlmans, *Vriendenkringen in de zeventiende eeuw: Verenigingsvormen van het informele culturele leven te Rotterdam, or Friendship Circles in Amsterdam* (The Hague, 1999), pp. 99–125.
18. Many historians have understandably baulked at the label, notably the Dutch philosopher of history Johan Huizinga, who protested that 'if our heyday must needs have a name, let it be about timber and steel, pitch and tar, paint and ink, daring and piety, spirit and imagination'. See Johan Huizinga, *Nederlands Beschaving in de Zeventiende Eeuw* (Haarlem, 1941), pp. 175–6 (trans. here Beverley Jackson). For a classic account of this period of history, focused on Dutch prosperity and its reflections in art and society, see Simon Schama, *The Embarrassment of Riches: An Interpretation of Dutch Culture in the Golden Age* (London, 1987).
19. For Reynier Bolnes's career as a military engineer, see John Michael Montias, *Vermeer and His Milieu*, Chapter 5.
20. For an invaluable account of this subject, see Maria Francisca Davina Eekhout, *Material Memories of the Dutch Revolt: The Urban Memory Landscape in the Low Countries, 1566–1700*, PhD dissertation, Leiden University (2014).
21. For a useful summary of the facts and figures, see Kevin Cramer's introduction to Hans Jacob Christoffel von Grimmelshausen, *The Adventures of Simplicius Simplicissimus*, trans. J. A. Underwood, ed. Kevin Cramer (London, 2018), pp. vii–xxviii.
22. C. V. Wedgwood, *The Thirty Years' War* (1st edn. 1938) (New York, 2005), p. 506.
23. See Jonathan Israel, *The Dutch Republic*, p. 335.
24. See David Kunzle, *From Criminal to Courtier: The Soldier in Netherlandish Art 1550–1672* (Brill, Leiden, Boston, 2002).
25. See John Michael Montias, *Artists and Artisans in Delft*, p. 245.
26. This is the passage in question: 'What a shocking sight! Lo! Crosses dashing against crosses, and Christ on this side firing bullets at Christ on the other; cross against cross and Christ against Christ . . . Let us now imagine we hear a soldier, among these fighting Christians, saying the Lord's prayer. *Our Father*, says he; O hardened wretch! Can you call him father, when you are just about to cut your brother's throat? *Hallowed be thy name*: how can the name of God be more impiously unhallowed, than by mutual bloody murder among his sons? *Thy kingdom come*: do you pray for the coming of his kingdom, while you are endeavouring to establish an earthly despotism, by spilling the blood of God's sons and subjects? *Thy*

will be done on earth as it is in heaven: his will in heaven is for peace, but you are now meditating war. Dare you say to your Father in heaven, *Give us this day our daily bread*, when you are going, the next minute perhaps, to burn up your brother's cornfields. With what face can you say, *Forgive us our trespasses as we forgive them that trespass against us*, when, so far from forgiving your own brother, you are going, with all the haste you can, to murder him in cold blood . . .' *The Complaint of Peace, translated from the Querela Pacis (A.D. 1521) of Erasmus* (London, 1917), p. 29.

27. See J. Zijlmans, *Vriendenkringen in de zeventiende eeuw*, p. 149.
28. The complete surviving corpus of 'little blue books' is reprinted in W. P. C. Knuttel, *Catalogus van de pamfletten-verzameling berustende in de Koninklijke Bibliothek*, 9 vols. (The Hague, 1899–1920; reprinted Utrecht, 1978). For statistics concerning the pamphlets and an illuminating analysis of their treatment of war, see Craig Harline, 'Mars Bruised', *BMGN (Low Countries Historical Review)* 104 (1989) afl.2, pp. 184–208. The author is greatly indebted to this article.
29. Jan van der Veens, *Zege-Sang over het Sas van Ghent* (1644). Kn. 5128, in W. P. C. Knuttel, *Catalogus van de pamfletten-verzameling berustende in de Koninklijke Bibliothek*.
30. John Michael Montias, *Vermeer and His Milieu*, Document 256.
31. For an explanation of the guild regulations and the implications of Vermeer's fee, see Jaap van der Veen, '*De Delftse kunstmarkt in de tijd van Vermeer*', in Donald Haks and Marie Christine van der Sman (eds.), exh. cat., The Hague Historical Museum, *De Hollandse samenleving in de tijd van Vermeer* (The Hague, 1996), pp. 124–35.
32. Quoted in Geoffrey Parker, 'The Economic Costs of the Dutch Revolt', in *War and Economic Development: Essays in Memory of David Joslin* (Oxford, 1975), p. 66.
33. See Jonathan Israel, *The Dutch Republic*, pp. 606–9.
34. For Maria's divorce settlement, see John Michael Montias, *Vermeer and His Milieu*, p. 126; for her family levy payment, see *Dutch Society in the Age of Vermeer*, ed. Donald Haks and Marie Christine van der Sman (The Hague, 1996), p. 61. Maria made her family levy payment (of 130 guilders) in 1674, in other words after the French invasion and during a period of extreme economic recession; so her net worth in the more buoyant 1650s and 1660s must have been considerably more than the 26,000 guilders implied by the sum she paid. It is also likely that she under-declared the size of her taxable assets.
35. John Michael Montias, *Vermeer and His Milieu*, pp. 99–102, and Document 249 (5 April 1653).

36. Ibid.
37. See Jonathan Israel, *The Dutch Republic*, p. 328.
38. See Willem Frijhoff and Maria Spies (eds.), *Dutch Culture in a European Perspective*, vol. 1, *1650: Hard-Won Unity* (Assen, 2004), p. 352, where it is estimated that 35 per cent of Delft's population was Catholic in 1650; Jonathan Israel, *The Dutch Republic*, pp. 328 and 380, contains an estimate for the year 1656, which puts the figure a little lower, at 25 per cent, counting some 5,500 Catholics out of a total population of about 21,000.
39. John Michael Montias, *Vermeer and His Milieu*, pp. 175–7.
40. Ellis Veryard, *An Account of Divers Choice Remarks Taken in a Journey through the Low Countries, France, Italy and Part of Spain* (London, 1701), p. 23. Cited in C. D. van Strien, *British Travellers in Holland during the Stuart Period* (Amsterdam, 1989), pp. 148–9.
41. See John Michael Montias, *Artists and Artisans in Delft*, pp. 108–10.
42. Ibid., p. 111.
43. For Maria Thins's early life and marriage, see John Michael Montias, *Vermeer and His Milieu*, Chapter 7, 'Family Life in Gouda', *passim*.
44. The turbulent events leading to the breakdown of Maria Thins's marriage are reported extensively in John Michael Montias, *Vermeer and His Milieu*, Chapter 7, 'Family Life in Gouda', pp. 116–28.
45. See Jonathan Israel, *The Dutch Republic*, p. 678.
46. John Michael Montias, *Vermeer and His Milieu*, p. 96 and Document
47. Beyond alluding to Mary Magdalene's humility in *Diana and Her Companions*, Vermeer understood *Christ in the House of Martha and Mary* to depict Mary Magdalene as well, because he and his contemporaries identified her with Martha's sister Mary of Bethany.
48. John Michael Montias, *Vermeer and His Milieu*, p. 140.
49. *Delfschen Donder-slagh Ofte Korte aensprake aen de bedroefde gemeente van Delf. By een schricklijck oordeel Godts besocht [...]* (Delft, Ian Pietersz, Waelpot, 1654).
50. The document, dated 9 July 1655, is in the Gemeentearchief Delft. It is reproduced in the exhibition catalogue *Vermeer's Delft*, ed. David de Haan et al. (Delft, 2003), p. 107.
51. Egbert's father, Lieven van der Poel, had taken Vermeer's maternal aunt as his second wife, which meant that Digna's sister, Tanneken Baltens, was his stepmother. See John Michael Montias, 'A Postscript on Vermeer and His Milieu', p. 416.
52. For an engaging account of the Thunderclap, intertwined with an appreciation of the art of Fabritius (and much else besides), see Laura

Cumming, *Thunderclap: A Memoir of Art and Life and Sudden Death* (London, 2023).
53. See Leonardo da Vinci, *Paragone*, ed. Irma A. Richter (Oxford, 1949), p. 85.
54. See Huib J. Zuidervaart and Marlise Rijks, '"Most rare workmen": Optical Practitioners in Early Seventeenth-Century Delft', *The British Journal for the History of Science*, vol. 48, no. 1 (March 2015), pp. 53–85.
55. Dirck van Bleyswijk, *Beschryvinge der Stadt Delft*, 2 vols. (Delft, 1667), II, p. 852. See Christopher Brown, *Carel Fabritius* (Oxford 1981), Appendix B.
56. See Michael Kitson, 'Florentine Baroque Art in New York', *Burlington Magazine*, vol. 111, no. 795 (June 1969), pp. 409–10.
57. See Christie's sale catalogue, 'The Barbara Piasecka Johnson Collection', Lot 39, pp. 142–3. More recent tests carried out by the conservation department at the Rijksmuseum have produced the same results. Arie Wallaert, a conservator there, kindly shared the results of his own isotope research into *St Praxedis* and *Diana and Her Companions*, undertaken in 2019, with the author: these produced the same results as those printed in the Christies' sales catalogue.
58. It is also worth noting that the parable of the Prodigal Son, with which he chose to identify, was a particular favourite both of Jacobus Arminius and of at least one leading figure in the Collegiant movement during Vermeer's lifetime. The Mennonite preacher and Collegiant Galenus Abrahamsz held it up as the perfect biblical riposte to Calvin's doctrine of predestination, because, if repentance is effective, as the tale insists, then every human being is free to choose salvation at any moment. For Galenus it justified the Collegiant belief in a Christianity without churches, the Prodigal exemplifying a radical's idea of the Reformation, namely reform of the individual from within, as opposed to reform of any external institution.
59. The existence of the Cupid beneath the surface of the painting had been known since the mid-twentieth century, when X-rays had revealed it. But the assumption among art historians had always been that Vermeer himself had had second thoughts and painted it out. The restoration of 2020 proved that this could not be the case by revealing some seventy years' worth of dust trapped between the original paint layer and the overpaint, thereby demonstrating that the alteration had been made many years after Vermeer's death.
60. See Stephan Kocha, 'The Inner Cohesion of the World: Vermeer's Paintings as Spaces of Reflection', in *Johannes Vermeer: On Reflection*, exh. cat., Staatliche Kunstsammlungen Dresden (2021), pp. 14–27.
61. This will be explained in further detail in the section entitled 'Aftermath' in Part Four.

PART THREE: THE INVISIBLE CHURCH, 1657–72

1. John Michael Montias, *Vermeer and His Milieu*, Documents 258, 259, 262.
2. Ibid., Document 271.
3. See John Michael Montias, 'Vermeer's Clients and Patrons', *The Art Bulletin*, vol. 69, no. 1 (March 1987), p. 68.
4. For an excellent account of Ter Borch's innovations see Alison McNeil Kettering, 'Gerard ter Borch's Military Men: Masculinity Transformed', in *The Public and Private in Dutch Culture of the Golden Age*, ed. Arthur K. Wheelock, Jr., and Adele Seeff (Newark and London, 2000).
5. Johannes Taurinus, *Bedenckingen Op d'Historie van't Samaritaensche Vroutjen*, or *Reflections on the Samaritan Woman* (Delft, 1625, 1630), II, pp. 186–90. The quotation continues: 'There is a proverb that says "A blind man is a poor man" but in truth the blind may meditate internally and contemplate more deeply than those who see. If a person has a special need or concern, withdrawing to pray in solitude, with eyes closed, will protect their thoughts from distractions and confusion.'
6. There are numerous references to Revelation 3:20 in Arminius's collected works: see for example *The Writings of James Arminius*, ed. and trans. William and James Nicholls, 3 vols. (Grand Rapids, 1853), II, pp. 18, 59–60, 631, 664, 743–5. For an illuminating account of what the passage meant to him in different contexts, see Keith D. Stanglin and Thomas H. McCall, *Jacob Arminius: Theologian of Grace* (Oxford, 2012), pp. 151–64.
7. John Michael Montias, *Vermeer and His Milieu*, Document 301.
8. For a fascinating account of these women's groups see Jori Zijlmans, *Vriendenkringen in de zeventiende eeuw*, pp. 99–125. The account of their activities presented here owes a great deal to Zijlmans' pioneering research in the Rotterdam church archives. Unless otherwise noted, most of the detail here is drawn from her transcripts from those archives as given, especially in Parts Three and Four of her book.
9. See Jori Zijlmans, ibid, Chapter 5 in particular, which describes women's meetings at their homes.
10. Margaret Fell, *Women's Speaking Justified* (London, 1666), p. 7.
11. This was part of a tradition shared by Dutch Calvinists and Dutch dissenters from strict Calvinism. Calvin's biblical commentaries reveal that he himself viewed Mary Magdalene in an extremely positive light,

although he would never have condoned the practice of free prophecy or allowing women to speak out in religious gatherings.

12. The archives in Delft that might have yielded more names, perhaps even that of Maria de Knuijt, are sadly incomplete for the years in question, but the iceberg of Collegiant women's groups was certainly not confined to the tip of Martha Ariens' Rotterdam circle.

13. For Martha Ariens and her group, the main source is Jori Zijlmans, *Vriendenkringen in de zeventiende eeuw*, esp. pp. 101–8, 113–22, 124–6.

14. See Francesco Quatrini, *Adam Boreel: A Collegiant's Attempt to Reform Christianity* (Leiden, 2021), p. 100.

15. There are no documented sightings of Collegiant meetings taking place in Delft, either at The Golden Eagle or anywhere else. The Reformed Church Council of the town was notably wary of such assemblies and would have been on the lookout for them. That their reports contain no mention of such activity does not mean that it was not present in the town: Collegiants were discreet, and the great majority of their meetings across the Dutch Republic went unnoticed by the Calvinist Church. It is also possible that Maria and her circle were helped to escape the attentions of the Delft Church Council by the fact that their meetings took place right next to the Remonstrant hidden church, which was known to the Calvinist authorities and considered by them a low-level or even non-existent threat to public piety by the 1650s.

16. John Michael Montias, *Vermeer and His Milieu*, Document 439.

17. *Woman with a Balance* was also loaned to the Rijksmuseum in 2009 and displayed alongside other works in its collection, including *The Milkmaid*. But the close connection between the two works was not noted.

18. As previously quoted, p. 63 above: 'The conscience is like the vicar of God within our hearts; And if, when we scrupulously consult it, and put ourselves to the test according to the Law of Christ, and find then that our conscience does not condemn us, we have the right to believe without hesitation that God has passed a favourable judgement on us.' Dirck Rafaelsz Camphuysen, *Predicatien VI*, in *Theologische Werken, bestaande in drie Deelin* (Amsterdam, 1699), p. 206. Camphuysen's collected works were avidly read in Collegiant circles and especially so in the late 1650s and early 1660s. The Amsterdam publisher Jan Rieuwertsz, a deeply committed Collegiant himself who became in effect the in-house publisher of the movement, embarked on a new edition of Camphuysen's works at this time, publishing the first volume

19. For Maria's will, see John Michael Montias, *Vermeer and His Milieu*, Document 301. For Pieter Claesz van Ruijven's charity work in Delft, see Paul Abels, 'Church and Religion in the Life of Vermeer', in *Dutch Society in the Age of Vermeer*, ed. Donald Haks and Marie Christine van der Sman (The Hague, 1996), p. 71.

(including the sermons of Camphuysen, which contain the passage about conscience quoted here) in 1661.

20. Trompe l'oeil nails appear in painted walls in other Dutch pictures of the period, but without the Christian implications given to the motif by Rembrandt. There is a somewhat similar but less emphatically placed nail in Carel Fabritius's *Portrait of Abraham Potter* in the Rijksmuseum, but Vermeer is less likely to have known that unique painting than he is to have known the Rembrandt etching.

21. The Mennonite form of Christianity was very close to that of the Remonstrants and Collegiants. Many Mennonites were to be found in Collegiant meetings.

22. See Arthur K. Wheelock, Jr., 'The Framing of a Vermeer', in *Collected Opinions: Essays on Netherlandish Art in Honour of Alfred Bader* (London, 2004), pp. 233–8; Wilhelm Martin, *Gerrit Dou* (London, 1902), pp. 145–7, contains a transcript of the contract made between De Bye and a private citizen in Leiden for the rental of rooms in the town, which specifies that the first twenty-two paintings to be displayed there are to be shown 'in cases'. Other Dutch artists of the time including Samuel van Hoogstraten are known to have displayed their pictures in special constructions designed to create particular effects of perspective: Hoogstraten's peep-hole construction with a painting inside can still be seen at the National Gallery in London. The 'boxes' enclosing the paintings of Vermeer and Dou were not of this kind, however, and seem to have been unique.

23. Their notary in Leiden, Nicolaes Paets, came from a line of Remonstrants and was closely in touch with at least one of the most influential Collegiants in Rotterdam, namely his first cousin Adrian, about whom more will be revealed imminently.

24. For Johan de Bye's links to the Remonstrant community in Leiden, see S. P. Perdijk, 'De opkomst der Remonstrantsch-Gereformeerde Gemeente te Leiden, 23 August 1618 tot 7 Augustus 1679', *Leidsch Jaarboekje* 12 (1915).

25. 'Perhaps the first monographic exhibition ever organized', suggests Arthur K. Wheelock, Jr., in 'The Framing of a Vermeer', p. 233. If the idea for it came from the pre-existing display of Vermeers at The

Golden Eagle then it was, strictly speaking, not the first such exhibition but the second.

26. Just one other bidder can be tentatively identified on the basis of old inventories. Jacob Oortman (1661–1738), a manufacturer of guns from Amsterdam, may have purchased the Frick Collection's *Mistress and Maid* at the Dissius auction in 1696. But it is also possible that he acquired the picture some years later. It was sold at his estate auction in 1738.

27. Isaac Rooleeuw is identified as the purchaser of the paintings on the basis that both appeared at the auction of his paintings held in Amsterdam on 20 April 1701, as Lots 6 and 7, less than five years after the Dissius sale.

28. See Koenraad Jonckheere, *The Auction of King William's Paintings 1713: Elite International Art Trade at the End of the Dutch Golden Age* (New Haven, 2008), p. 44.

29. See the entry under 'Rooleeuw family' in the online Global Anabaptist Mennonite Encyclopedia: https://gameo.org/index.php?title=Roleeuw_family. To give a single example, Reinier Rooleeuw, one of Isaak Rouleeuw's several devout uncles, composed hymns and songbooks for Collegiant groups in Amsterdam and Rotterdam, wrote new melodies for Dirck Camphuysen's much-loved book of poetry, the *Stichtelike Rymen*, translated the New Testament into Greek, and wrote a dense tract called *The Treasure of the Soul*, in which some of his contemporaries detected a lack of belief in the Trinity.

30. I am indebted to Francesco Quatrini, author of a forthcoming history of the Collegiant movement, for this information.

31. See Jonathan Israel, *The Dutch Republic*, p. 460.

32. For a useful summary of such hypotheses see Walter Liedtke, *Vermeer: The Complete Paintings* (London, 2008), p. 90; see also Frans Grijzenhout, *Vermeer's Little Street: A View of the Penspoort in Delft* (Amsterdam, 2016), *passim*.

33. The building's identification number in the state archives is Rijksmonument ID 12086.

34. Simon Episcopius, *The Remonstrant Confession, 1621*, trans. Mark Ellis (Oregon, 2005), Chapter 22, paragraph 9, p. 46.

35. Johannes Taurinus, *Bedenckingen Op d'Historie van't Samaritaensche Vroutjen*, II, pp. 186–90.

36. See Andrew Cooper Fix, *Prophecy and Reason*, pp. 151–3. Also E. Van Nijmegen, *Historie der Rijnsburgsche Vergadering*, (Rotterdam, 1775),

p. 266, where the author states: '*De gezangen, welke men meestal gewoon is te Rijnsburg te gebruiken, zijn de psalmen, door Kamphuizen berijmd, en de liederen van Oudaen en Rooleeuw, voormaels Leden van dit Gezelschap.*' ('The hymns usually used in Rijnsburg are the psalms rhymed by Camphuysen and the songs of Oudaen and Rooleeuw, foremost Members of this Society.') This latter quotation was noted by Rosa Ricci in her doctoral thesis (see note 40, below, for citation).

37. An inventory of the possessions owned in common by Maria Thins and her husband Reynier Bolnes was made at the time of their divorce, with the painting by Baburen specified as 'A painting wherein the procuress points to the hand'; Maria is presumed to have taken the picture with her when she moved to Delft. See John Michael Montias, *Vermeer and His Milieu*, pp. 122ff.

38. See ibid., p. 139. Montias notes that Maria Thins owned such a picture at the time of her separation from Reynier Bolnes, in Gouda. He speculates that this picture, by Gerrit Honthorst or Dirck van Baburen, may have remained in her possession and served as Vermeer's model for the picture-within-the-picture in *The Music Lesson*.

39. 'Only among the Collegiants did the ancient songs of David resound to harmonious Baroque music, complete with basso continuo and musical rhetoric': Louis Peter Grijp, of the Meertens-Institut in Amsterdam, writing in his sleeve notes to 'Grace and Peace: 16th and 17th Century Mennonite Music from the Netherlands', performed by Camerata Trajectina. The CD in question contains performances of settings of Oudaan's extensions of Psalms 50, 67, 28, 69, 7, 17, 61 and 9.

40. See Rosa Ricci, *Religious Nonconformity and Cultural Dynamics: The Case of the Dutch Collegiants*, a doctoral thesis submitted to Der Fakultät für Geschichte, Kunst- und Orientwissenschaften der Universität Leipzig (2014), p. 116.

41. Jacob Ostens, *Liefde-son, omstralende de hoedanigheyt der tegenwoordige genaamde christenheyt* (Rotterdam, 1651).

42. *Gedichten van Joachim Oudaan* (Delft, 1734), p. 2.

43. In Dutch: '... *heersucht, oproerigheyt, precijsheyt, geltgierigheyt &c ... dese hervormde Papen*'. See the following three pamphlets, all by Adrian Paets, all published anonymously, the first and last without specifying the location of publication, presumably to avoid risk of prosecution: *Antwoord, van een Gereformeerdt Hollander, op een klaagbrief van N.N. Over zommige onrustige Rotterdamsche*

Predicanten, en voornamentlijk Iacobus Borstius (n.l. 1654); *Sedig antwoord van N.N. Gereformeerd Hollander ... Waar in bewesen werd dat de dwalende als soodanige niet strafbaar zijn door uyterlijk geweld* (Leiden, 1655); *Fabula vetus actores novi. Dat is, de oude paep onder een nieuwe kap* (n.l. 1656).

44. For the relationship between the Rotterdam women's groups and the circle of Paets, see Jori Zijlmans, *Vriendenkringen in de zeventiende eeuw,* chapters 5 and 7, *passim.*
45. See John Michael Montias, *Vermeer and His Milieu,* Document 301; see also Walter Liedtke, *Vermeer: The Complete Paintings* (New York, 2008), p. 152.
46. See John Michael Montias, 'Recent Archival Research on Vermeer', p. 99.
47. See ibid., *Vermeer and His Milieu,* Document 364.
48. See J. G. van Gelder, 'Het kabinet van de heer Jacques Meyer', *Rotterdams Jaerboekje* 2 (1974), pp. 167–83.
49. See H. W. Blom and J. M. Kerkhoven, 'A letter ...', in *Studia Spinozana* (Hanover and Louisville, KY, 1985), I, pp. 371–8.
50. In 2014 what may be the world's first telescope was discovered at the bottom of one of the town's canals. Reported in the *NL Times* (14 May 2014).
51. John Colerus, *The Life of Benedict Spinoza* (London, 1706), pp. 33–4.
52. Following the commonly used system for citing Spinoza's work, the references occur at 4Pref, 4P45Sch, and TTP 1.25. See also Christopher Davidson, 'Music, Melancholia, and the Artistic Production of Disobedience: A Spinozist Aesthetics', paper presented at the 2017 Interstices Under Construction symposium, The Arts of Spinoza + Pacific Spinoza, organized by the School of Art and Design at Auckland University of Technology, and the School of Architecture and Planning at the University of Auckland.
53. See Huib J. Zuidervaart, 'Een nieuwe theorie over twee schilderijen van Johannes Vermeer (1632–1675)', *Jaarboek Delfia Batavorum* 28 (2018), pp. 9–34.
54. The first published use of this term occurs in the third book of Gerard de Lairesse's *Groot Schilderboek* (Amsterdam, 1707), but it was probably in use some decades earlier; the term 'genre painting' is a later invention.
55. See John Michael Montias, *Vermeer and His Milieu,* Document 383.
56. See 'Religion and Belief' in *Dutch Culture in a European Perspective,* vol. 1, ed. Willem Frijhoff and Marijke Spies, pp. 362ff.

57. Thomas à Kempis, *The Imitation of Christ*, ed. and trans. Robert Jeffrey (London, 2013), p. 5.
58. Francesco Quatrini, in conversation with the author, September 2023.
59. See John Michael Montias, *Vermeer and His Milieu*, Document 430.
60. Ibid., Document 301.
61. Ibid., Document 393.
62. See J. Melles, *Joachim Oudaan, Heraut der Verdraagzaamheid* ('Joachim Oudaan, Herald of Tolerance') (Utrecht, 1958), p. 102.
63. The existence of the chapel within the inventory has also been noticed by Gregor Weber, who first published it in his book *Johannes Vermeer: Faith, Light and Reflection* (Amsterdam 2023), pp. 31ff. Contrary to the view presented here, Weber argues that it is proof of Vermeer's conversion to Catholicism.
64. Gemeentearchief Leyden, records of Notary N. Paets, no. 676, act no. 99. See also John Michael Montias, *Vermeer and His Milieu*, Document 301, and idem., 'Vermeer's Clients and Patrons', p. 70.
65. Balthasar de Monconys, *Journal de Voyage de Monsieur de Monconys*, 2 vols. (Lyon, 1666), II, p. 149.
66. Ibid., pp. 136ff.
67. See H. E. van Berckel, 'Priesters te Delft en Delfshaven 1646–1696', *Bijdragen voor de geschiedenis van het Bisdom van Haarlem* 25 (1900), pp. 230–63.
68. It was common for rich and influential lay people to carry out property transactions for Jesuits, and indeed other priests, who were proscribed from doing so by law.
69. See John Michael Montias, *Vermeer and His Milieu*, p. 120 and Document 160.
70. See Jonathan Israel, *The Dutch Republic*, p. 632.
71. See John Michael Montias, 'Vermeer's Clients and Patrons', p. 74.
72. See idem., *Vermeer and His Milieu*, p. 217.
73. The population is an estimate based on the various population charts cited in Jonathan Israel, *The Dutch Republic*, p. 631.
74. See John Michael Montias, *Vermeer and His Milieu*, Document 132.
75. The documented facts of the case point strongly to this conclusion, although the reasoning that leads there is, by necessity, somewhat drawn out. We know that when Van Buyten died he owned three paintings by Vermeer, because they were listed in an inventory made by order of the administrators of his estate, the Orphan Chamber of Delft, in 1701. The first of these was identified only as 'a large painting by Vermeer' in

the front room of the late Van Buyten's house. The others were listed only as 'two little pieces by Vermeer' (*'stuckjes van Vermeer'*) in a side room adjoining the main hall. (For more detail on this document see Montias, 'Vermeer's Clients and Patrons'.) Van Buyten acquired two of these three pictures long after 1663, when Monconys visited him, as we know from a document of 1676 (reprinted in Albert Blankert, *Vermeer of Delft: Complete Edition of the Paintings* [London, 1978], pp. 149–50), which records the arrangement by which Vermeer's widow gave those two pictures to Van Buyten in part payment of debts owed by the painter's estate. There it is stated that these paintings were 'one [picture] representing two persons one of whom is writing a letter, and another [picture] with a person playing the lute'. These can be identified as (almost certainly) *Lady Writing a Letter with Her Maid* now in Ireland and (possibly verging on probably) *Woman with a Lute* in the Metropolitan Museum of Art, New York. Going back to the three Vermeers hanging in Van Buyten's house when he died, the 'large' picture in his front room would therefore have been *Lady Writing a Letter with Her Maid*, which is indeed a big picture by Vermeer's standards. The much smaller *Woman with a Lute* would most likely have been one of the two 'little' Vermeers in the adjoining room. The other 'little' one must have been the only other Vermeer we know Van Buyten to have owned, namely the one he had shown to Monconys in 1663. Monconys tells us that 'it contained but a single figure', while the inventory of 1701 confirms the impression this gives that it was 'little'. As stated in the main text, we only know of two pictures of a modest scale and containing but a single figure by Vermeer that are *not* listed in the Dissius sale and therefore were *not* part of the Van Ruijven collection: *Woman in Blue* owned by the Rijksmuseum, and *Young Woman with a Water Pitcher* in the Metropolitan Museum of Art. As argued later in this book, the former may be a portrait of Vermeer's wife, Catharina. For this reason and also by inference from its iconography, which seems apposite for a baker, it seems most probable that the picture Van Buyten showed to Monconys was indeed *Young Woman with a Water Pitcher*. No other extant work fits. The other possibility, on balance a remote one, is that the picture Monconys saw at the baker's was a different small single-figure composition by Vermeer that has now been lost. If that is so, *Young Woman with a Water Pitcher* was painted for someone else altogether, in circumstances of which we know nothing. There are few absolute certainties in the case of Vermeer.

76. His death inventory lists a copy of Calvin's *Institutes of the Christian Religion*, which is no proof that he was a strict Calvinist – Maria de Knuijt and probably Vermeer too would have read Calvin and respected many of his views – but probably reflects his confessional inheritance. See Montias, 'Vermeer's Clients and Patrons', p. 74; for details of Van Buyten's estate, see Gemeentearchief Delft, Orphan Chamber, Estate papers (*boedel*) no. 265.
77. See John Michael Montias, *Vermeer and His Milieu*, Document 292.
78. See ibid., Chapter 9, *passim*.
79. See Pieter Spierenburg, *Zwarte Schapen: Losbollen, dronkaards en levensgnieters in achttiende-eeuwse beterhuizen*, or *Black Sheep, Loose Women, Drunkards and the Unmotivated in Eighteenth-Century Beterhuizen* (Hilversum, 1995). Spierenburg's focus is on the eighteenth-century *beterhuizen*, but his book contains an illuminating account of the origins of the institution in seventeenth-century Delft (and much other fascinating information besides).
80. Like more or less everyone who showed familiarity with Vermeer's work during his own lifetime, Dirck van Bleyswijk was allied with the 'Arminians' and Remonstrants and firmly opposed to the strict Calvinists. As a magistrate of Delft, he was unwavering in his insistence that the state-privileged Church remain subordinate to the secular civic authorities. Dutch liberals regarded the separation of Church and State as a necessary precondition of toleration and therefore freedom of speech (with the usual necessary constraints for keeping public order, and so on). The apparent inkling of wider recognition implied by Bon's praise of Vermeer in Van Blejswijk's *Description of Delft* confirms once again how very small was the constituency of those who ever saw, let alone admired, his work. As we have seen, Dirck van Blejswijk was a liberal magistrate, Arminian in his politics and probably Remonstrant in religion; he also happened to live just three doors away from Vermeer's patrons Pieter and Maria on the Oude Delft, at number 93. Arnold Bon was a liberal poet, printer and publisher with a shop nearby; the stricter Calvinist preachers of the day would fulminate against his verse.
81. See the exhibition catalogue 'Vermeer and the Masters of Genre Painting' (Dublin, Washington, Paris, 2017–18), in particular the essay of that same title by Adriaan E. Waiboer, p. 7, in which the author stresses that many painters of 'elegant modern' genre pictures were a great deal more mobile than many art historians have tended to assume, viz: 'their extant paintings – certainly Vermeer's – suggest that

they regularly travelled to other Dutch towns to study works by other masters.'

82. As a striking instance of this, a statistical survey of 112 publications by English clergymen between 1640 and 1653 has shown that 70 per cent of them were fully convinced millenarians, who all believed in the imminence of a kingdom of glory, ruled by Christ here on earth. See B. S. Capp, *The Fifth Monarchy Men: A Study in Seventeenth-Century English Millenarianism* (London, 1972), p. 38. Equivalent analyses of opinion among Dutch Protestant ministers, or indeed among the rabbis of Amsterdam, would likely yield similar results.

83. Cited in Steven Nadler, *Spinoza: A Life* (Cambridge, 1999), pp. 159–61; see also Richard Popkin, 'Spinoza, the Quakers and the Millenarians, 1656–8', *Manuscrito* 6 (1982), pp. 113–33; and *Spinoza's Earliest Publication? The Hebrew Translation of Margaret Fell's 'A Loving Salutation, to the seed of Abraham among the Jews, where ever they are scattered up and down upon the face of the Earth'* (Van Gorcum, 1987).

84. For an illuminating account of Balling and his precursors, especially Coornhert, see Ruben Buys, 'Pieter Balling, the Radical Enlightenment and the Legacy of Dirck Volckertsz Coornhert', *Journal of Church History and Religious Culture* 93 (2013), pp. 363–83.

85. Hans Jacob Christoffel von Grimmelshausen, *The Adventures of Simplicius Simplicissimus*, trans. J. A. Underwood, ed. Kevin Cramer (London, 2018), p. 377.

86. The conservator Jørgen Wadum, who headed the restoration of the *View of Delft* and *Girl with a Pearl Earring* that took place over a number of years at the Mauritshuis, kindly shared many of his insights in a meeting with the author that took place in the summer of 1999. It was his idea that tile-dust might have formed part of the composition of the pigment used to paint the red roofs in the picture. He was also the first to help the author understand the importance of the weather in the picture.

87. See John Michael Montias, 'Vermeer's Clients and Patrons', footnote 12.

88. Ibid., pp. 68–70.

89. See Rosa Ricci, *Religious Nonconformity and Cultural Dynamics*, p. 124.

90. This idea originated with John Michael Montias, who pointed out the resemblance in conversation with the author.

91. Gemeentearchief Delft NA 2177, fol. 161r and 161v. For comment on this 'insinuation' for sale, see John Michael Montias, 'Recent Archival Research on Vermeer', p. 98, note 29.

92. Ibid., p. 98.
93. Barend Joosten Stol, *Den Philosopherenden Boer* (Rotterdam, 1676), p. 28.
94. See Isaac Newton, *Observations on the Prophecies of Daniel and the Apocalypse of St John* (London, 1733), pp. 113–14. Cited in Stephen D. Snobelen, '"A Time and Times and the Dividing of Time": Isaac Newton, the Apocalypse, and 2060 A.D.', *Canadian Journal of History* XXXVIII (December 2003), pp. 537–51.
95. See Billy F. Andrews, MD, 'William Harvey in Perinatal Perspective', Chapter 26 of *Historical Review and Recent Advances in Neonatal and Perinatal Medicine*, ed. George F. Smith, MD, and Dharmapuri Vidyasagar, MD (online publication, 1980), n.p.
96. See Spinoza, *Ethics* 4, Propositions 38–52, and Ep. 32 (a letter of 1665 to Oldenburg).
97. See James Welu, 'Vermeer's Astronomer: Observations on an Open Book', *The Art Bulletin*, vol. 68, no. 2 (June 1986), pp. 263–7.
98. See William Penn, *His Own Account of the Lenni Lenape by Albert Cook Myers* (Philadelphia, 1737), n.p. Cited by Tudor Parfitt, *The Lost Tribes of Israel: The History of a Myth* (London, 2002), p. 78.
99. For a first-rate account of his reading habits, as reflected in his journal, see Jeroen Blaak, *Literacy in Everyday Life: Reading and Writing in Early Modern Dutch Diaries* (Leiden, 2009), Chapter 3 *passim*.
100. On Johan van Bleiswijk as a Pietist, see J. M. Müller, *Exile, Memories and the Dutch Revolt: The Narrated Diaspora, 1550–1750* (Leiden, 2014), pp. 188–93; on his Erastian opposition to Calvinist political ambitions for state control, see Frank Daudeij, '"Let no citizen be treated as lesser, because of his confession": Religious Tolerance and Civility in De Hooghe's *Spiegel van Staat* (1706–7)', in *Enlightened Religion: From Confessional Churches to Polite Piety in the Dutch Republic*, ed. Joke Spaans and Jetze Touber (Leiden, 2019). For much the most detailed account of him see T. Brienen, 'Johan Cornelisz Van Bleiswijk (1618–96), in *Figuren en thema's van de Nadere Reformatie* (Kampen, 1987), vol. 1, pp. 71–82.
101. See Alfred Soman, 'Arminianism in France: The D'Huisseau Incident', *Journal of the History of Ideas*, vol. 28, no. 4 (October–December 1967), pp. 597–600.
102. Gemeentearchief Amsterdam (35–90 DTB 475, fol. 285).
103. Ibid. (13513 DTB 1075, fol. 28).
104. Ibid. (1997, filmnr. 2163, fols. 264–80).
105. Adrian Swartepaert, *Openbaringe van het ware algemeen geloof* (no location of publication given, probably Amsterdam, 1678), p. 54.

NOTES TO PP. 287–97

106. The identification of the book and page number was made by Evelyne Verheggen of the University of Antwerp, who also observed that Hugh of Lincoln's feast day was 17 November, according to her the same day on which the French were forced to withdraw from Utrecht in 1673 following their invasion of the Republic. Verheggen hypothesized on that basis that the picture might have been painted to celebrate the deliverance of the Republic. But Catholics celebrated the saint's feast day on 16 November, not the day after, and Vermeer's picture is in any case unlikely to have been painted as late as 1673. He was painting little at that time and was much occupied by the business affairs of his mother-in-law, as will be shown in Part Four below. For Verheggen's findings, see the online report at https://projecthighart.net/findings-from-the-vermeer-symposium-in-amsterdam/?utm.
107. *Lettre de Monsieur van Paets sur les derniers troubles d'Angleterre, où il est parlé de la tolérance de ceux qui ne suivent point la Religion dominante*, or *Letter of Mr van Paets on the latest disturbances in England, in which the tolerance of those who do not follow the prevailing religion is discussed* (Rotterdam, 1686), p. 32.
108. For Doedijns on his admiration for Arminius and the tolerance of those who follow him, see the *Haegsche Mercurius* of 14 January 1699. On the wisdom of women, see the editions of 12 April 1698 and 1 November 1698. On women wearing the trousers in most Dutch homes (rightly so according to Doedijns), 15 April 1698. Judging by his lengthy attack on the Calvinist doctrine of predestination, and his equally lengthy defence of the Arminian position, in which he asserts that human beings must have free will in order to exercise moral judgement, Doedijns sympathized with the Remonstrants and may well have attended one of their hidden churches. For this, see the *Haegsche Mercurius* of 27 May 1699.
109. See John Michael Montias, *Vermeer and His Milieu*, Document 363.
110. See Leonardo da Vinci, *Paragone*, ed. Irma A. Richter (Oxford, 1949), p. 95. The passage was not published in this form until the nineteenth century but was known in its essentials in the time of Vermeer.

PART FOUR: DISASTER, DEATH, LEGACY, 1672–5

1. Quoted in G. J. Renier, *The Dutch Nation* (London, 1944), p. 133.
2. Quoted in Arthur Weststeijn, *Commercial Republicanism in the Dutch Golden Age: The Political Thought of Johan & Pieter de la Court* (Leiden, 2012), p. 2.
3. John Michael Montias, *Vermeer and His Milieu*, Document 334.

4. For details of the dispute, see Anne-Marie Logan, *The 'Cabinet' of the Brothers Gerard and Jan Reynst* (Amsterdam, 1975), and Friso Lammertse and Jaap van der Veen, *Uylenburgh & Son: Art and Commerce from Rembrandt to De Lairesse, 1625–1675* (Zwolle, 2006).
5. John Michael Montias, *Vermeer and His Milieu*, Document 341. Montias had not seen the original of this document when he wrote his book about Vermeer. The fact that the statement was witnessed by Pieter Claesz van Ruijven would doubtless have interested him greatly.
6. Van Ruijven's presence was discovered by Jaap van der Veen and published in 2006. See Friso Lammertse and Jaap Van der Veen, *Uylenburgh & Son*, footnote 168, p. 87.
7. See John Michael Montias, 'Recent Archival Research on Vermeer', pp. 100–104.
8. *Staat-Kundige Droom* (1672), Kn. 10,493, in W. P. C. Knuttel, *Catalogus van de pamfletten-verzameling berustende in de Koninklijke Bibliothek*, 9 vols. (The Hague, 1899–1920; reprinted Utrecht, 1978). Cited in Jonathan Israel, *Spinoza: Life and Legacy* (Oxford, 2023), p. 871.
9. *Hydra of Monster-Dier* (Rotterdam, 1672) Kn. 10,602, in W. P. C. Knuttel, *Catalogus van de pamfletten-verzameling berustende in de Koninklijke Bibliothek*. Cited in Jonathan Israel, *Spinoza*, p. 871.
10. N. Japikse en R. Fruin (ed.), *Brieven van Johan de Witt, vol. 4: 1670–1672* (Amsterdam, 1913), p. 421. The letter was copied to Admiral Michiel de Ruyter, Constantijn Rumpf and Coenrad van Beuningen, burgomaster of Amsterdam and a passionately committed Collegiant. The author is grateful to Jane Choy-Thurlow for pointing out the existence of this letter to him.
11. See Ellis Veryard, *An Account of Divers Choice Remarks*, pp. 80ff.
12. Spinoza told the story of how his landlord saved him to the philosopher and polymath Leibniz, in 1676. See J. Freudenthal, *Die Lebensgeschichte Spinoza's in Quellenschriften, Urkunden und Nichtamlichen Nachrichten* (Leipzig, 1899), p. 201.
13. See Nigel Smith, 'The Politics of Tragedy in the Dutch Republic: Joachim Oudaen's Martyr Drama in Context', Chapter 8 of *Dramatic Experience: The Poetics of Drama and the Early Modern Public Sphere(s)*, ed. Katja Gvozdeva, Tatiana Korneeva and Kirill Ospovat (Leiden, 2021), pp. 220ff.
14. See Arthur Weststeijn, *Commercial Republicanism in the Dutch Golden Age: The Political Thought of Johan & Pieter de la Court* (Leiden, 2012), p. 2.

15. In June 1674 he went to a notary in Delft and passed a codicil to the will he had made in the office of Notary Adrian Paets in Leiden nine years before. The notary who drafted the codicil of 1674 noted that Van Ruijven was residing in The Hague but added somewhat ambiguously that he was also 'lodged' on the Voorstraet in Delft (where he is known to have owned a house). See John Michael Montias, 'Vermeer's Clients and Patrons', p. 71.
16. John Michael Montias, *Vermeer and His Milieu*, Document 344.
17. Ibid., Document 351.
18. Ibid., Document 354.
19. Ibid., Document 355.
20. For details of the Van Hensbeeck trust, see ibid., p. 109; the family tree of Catharina Bolnes in the front matter is also helpful.
21. Ibid., Document 340.
22. See Albert Blankert, *Vermeer of Delft* (London, 1978), Document 60.
23. John Michael Montias, *Vermeer and His Milieu*, Document 383.
24. Algemeen Rijksarchief, Rekenkamer ter Auditie, no. 15, *Kohier van het Groot Familiegeld van 1674 voor de Stad Delft*.
25. See H. S. Carter, 'Medical Gleanings from the Diary of John Evelyn', *Glasgow Medical Journal*, vol. 34, no. 10 (October 1653), pp. 463–75.
26. For facsimile versions of the two surviving burial documents for Vermeer, see *Vermeer's Delft* (Delft, 2023), p. 109. Both documents are in the Gemeentearchief Delft, the latter being a fresh discovery which has put paid to the myth that Vermeer died a pauper. Bas van der Wulp, who found the document detailing the number of pallbearers, also did extensive research into the funerals of other Delft painters and found none as grand as Vermeer's.
27. See John Michael Montias, 'Recent Archival Research on Vermeer', p. 103.
28. John Michael Montias, *Vermeer and His Milieu*, pp. 218–20.
29. Ibid., Document 363.
30. Foul play was certainly suspected by John Michael Montias. See *Vermeer and His Milieu*, p. 222.
31. Ibid., Document 367.
32. Ibid., Document 370.
33. Ibid., Document 371.
34. Ibid., Document 375.
35. See A. J. J. M. van Peer, 'Was Jan Vermeer Katholiek?', *Katholiek cultureel tidjschrift* 2 (1946), pp. 469–70. The information that Father Philippus anointed Maria Thins and her daughter Catharina is cited

from a Catholic register of deaths. It has not been possible to locate the document in question so the information must be taken on trust. Van Peer is considered a reliable source.
36. See Cornelis Daniel van Strien, ed., *British Travellers in Holland during the Stuart Period* (Amsterdam, 1989), p. 216.
37. Locke's *Letter Concerning Toleration* bore the stamp of Dutch collaboration at the moment of its release into the world: the first edition was printed in Gouda, thanks to the intervention of the leading Remonstrant minister Philippus Limborch.
38. See John Marshall, *John Locke, Toleration and Early Enlightenment Culture* (Cambridge, 2006), pp. 545–80, for an excellent account of Paets's influence on Bayle and Locke.

Index

Abrahamsz, Galenus, 260, 344n58
adult baptism, 195–6
Aemilius, Theodore, 40
Aesop's fables, 81–2
Alva, Duke of, 21–5
Amsterdam: plague outbreaks, 43, 63
  rise as commercial centre, 30–31, 35–6, 51–2
Anglo-Dutch Wars, 145–6, 312
Anslo, Cornelis Claesz, *187*
Antwerp, 21, 28–30, 30–31, 33
Ariens, Martha, 175–83, 194, 211
Arminianism, 46–7 *see also* Remonstrant movement
Arminius, Gertruyd, 54
Arminius, Jacobus, 40–46, 170, 185
  On Reconciling Religious Dissension among Christians, 44–6, 208, 281, 323
Arundel, Thomas Howard, Earl of, 101
Asch, Pieter van, *Wooded Landscape*, 268
Asson, Machtelt van, 238
Augustine, St, 143
Augustus III, King of Poland, 159

Baburen, Dirck van, *The Procuress*, 206, 349n37
Balling, Pieter, *The Light upon the Candlestick*, 248–9, 250
Baltens, Digna, 32–3, 51–2, 57–8, 59–60, 77–8, 98, 127, 182, 226, 311–12
Baltens, Reynier, 60–62, 86, 96–8
Baner, Johan, 104
Bayle, Pierre, 322–4, 325
Bellini, Giovanni, *Sacra Conversazioni*, 268
Benoist, Elie, *History of the Edict of Nantes*, 281
Bentivoglio, Cardinal, 24–5, 29
Bentvueghels (artists' association), 87–8
Berchem, Nicholas
Berckhout, Pieter Teding van, 212, 278–83, 302
beterhuizen, 240–42
Beuningen, Jan van, 192–3
Beza, Theodore, 42–3
Blaeu, Juffrow, 178
Bleau, Joan, 199
Bleau, Willem Jansz, 275
Bleiswijk, Dirck van, 148, 245, 353n80
Bleiswijk, Johan van, 280, 282

INDEX

Bloemart, Abraham, 83
Bolnes, Catharina
   background and family, 130–38
   marriage to Vermeer, 124–30, 217
   children of, 220–21
   in Vermeer's paintings, 257
   attacked by her brother Willem, 240–42
   and *The Art of Painting*, 289
   account of Vermeer's death, 313–15
   settlement of Vermeer's debts, 316–20
   death, 320
Bolnes, Cornelia, 128, 132
Bolnes, Reynier, 124, 132–7, 310
Bolnes, Willem, 132, 137, 239–42, 310–11
Bon, Arnold, 148–9
Borch, Gerard ter, 115–21, 123, 167–8, 206, 251
   Man on Horseback (c.1634), 119
   The Swearing of the Oath of Ratification of the Treaty of Münster, 121
Botticelli, *Birth of Venus*, 141, 157
boxes, as frames for paintings, 188–91, 347n22
Bramer, Leonaert, 88, 115, 125–6
Brandenburg, Friedrich Wilhelm, Elector of, 298, 299
Brandenburg, George William, Elector of, 61, 300
Brandenburg, Johann Sigismund, Elector of, 61
Brandt, Gerard, *History of the Reformation*, 56, 58, 69, 71, 281
Breda, 95, 98
Breen, Daniel de, *Of the Triumphant Spiritual Kingdom*, 249–50, 269
Burgers, Eva, 178
Buyten, Hendrick van, 231, 234–9, 310, 316–17, 352–3n75, 353n76
Bye, Johan de, 190–91, 212
Bylandt, Willem van, 63

Callot, Jacque, *The Hanging*, 103
Calvin, John, 38, 42
Calvinists, 38, 94, 207, 346n11
camera obscura, 4, 147–8, 215, 272
Camerling, Gerrit Gerritsz, 132
Camphuysen, Dirck Rafaelsz, 71–5, 83, 112, 185, 215, 249, 339n57, 346n18
Caravaggio
   chiaroscuro, 139, 261
   influence on Dutch artists, 87
   influence on Vermeer, 158, 171
   Martyrdom of St Matthew, 155
   Penitent Magdalene, 169
   Seven Acts of Mercy, 207
   St Matthew and the Angel, 257
Carleton, Sir Dudley, 31, 77
Carpaccio, Vittore, 257
Catholicism, in the Dutch Republic, 128–30, 131
Charles II of England, 295
Charles II of Spain, 308
chiaroscuro, 139, 147, 157, 261
Cleves, Duchy of, 61
Codde, Pieter, *Guardroom Scene with Sleeping Soldiers* (c.1630), 108
Coelenbier, Jan, 317
Colbert, Jean-Baptiste, 296
Colerus, John, 216–17

Collegiant movement
    Adrian Paets' role in, 209–11
    in Delft, 194–7
    growth of, 93–5
    hidden meetings, 346n15
    influence of Erasmus, 112–13
    and millenarianism, 248–9
    and music, 204–5, 207–8, 349n39
    origins of, 67–71
    reaction to Thirty Years War, 110
    at Rijnsburg, 179–80
    and Vermeer's work, 271–2
    women's role in, 74, 174–8
Coorde, Willem de, 239–40
Coornhert, Dirck Volckertszoon, 43, 67, 83, 112, 195, 249, 323, 340n64
Cornelisz, Gerrit, 239
Corstiaensz, Claes, 55
Council of Troubles (1567), 21
Court, Pieter de la, 296–7, 307
Cramer, Johannes, 309, 320
Crowne, William, diary, 101–2
Cupus, Petrus, 93

Delft
    Guild of St Luke, 82–3, 114, 144, 147, 213
    Mechelen Inn, 88, 89, 99, 127, 146
    Remonstrant Church, 92, 244
    riots (1672), 303
    strategic importance of, 62–3
    'Thunderclap' (1654), 145–7
Devotio Moderna (religious movement), 41
Dissius, Jacob, 7–11, 193, 256, 326–7
Doedijns, Hendrik, 288–9, 324, 356n108
Donteclock, Reinier, 37
Dordt, Synod of (1618–19), 48–9, 65

Dou, Gerard, 166, 190–91, 232, 246
Duarte, Diego, 313
Duck, Jacob, 109
Dürer, Albrecht, 286
Dury, John, 247
Dutch East India Company, 63, 84, 132, 210, 211, 213, 253, 254–5, 274, 277–8
'Dutch Gift', 284, 296
Dutch Reformed Church, 36–9, 47–51, 53
Dutch Republic
    art market, 83
    bread, significance of, 186, 226, 234–6, 238–9, 310
    beterhuizen, 240–42
    Era of True Liberty, 124, 210, 250–51, 263
    formation of, 20, 28–34
    French invasion (1672), 295–7, 300–4
    Golden Age, 96, 341n18
    law and order, strictly maintained, 134
    'little blue books' (pamphlets), 100, 113, 280, 304
    religious divisions in, 34–9
    religious tolerance, 36
    restoration of the Stadtholderate (1672), 303–4
    under siege (1621), 60
    taverns, importance of, 63–4, 100, 340n1
    trade domination, 107–8
    trekschuit network of canals, 99–100, 191, 211, 216, 232, 246, 253, 299, 311
    urbanized nature of Dutch society, 100
    windmills, importance of, 31, 51

INDEX

Dutch Revolt, 20–28
Duyster, Willem, 108, 109

Eighty Years War, 20–28, 60, 62, 95–8
Enlightenment, and religious toleration, 322–4
Episcopius, Simon, 50
  The Remonstrant Confession (1621), 66–7, 201
Erasmians, 112, 247
Erasmus, Desiderio, 110–12, 323, 341n26
Evelyn, John, 315
Everpoel, Tanneke, 239–40
Eyck, Jan van, *Arnolfini Wedding*, 157

Fabritius, Carel, 115, 147–9, 212, 223–4
Fadrique, Don, 23–4, 26
Fell, Margaret, *Women Speaking Justified*, 174, 248, 260
Feltham, Owen, 19
Ferdinand, Cardinal-Infante, 95
Ferdinand II, Emperor, 104
Ficherelli, Felice, 118, 149–53
Fijne, Paschier de, 69–70
Flanders, 32
Fornenburgh, Jan Baptista van, 84
frames *see* boxes, as frames for paintings
Francesca, Piero della, *Senigallia Madonna*, 269
Franck, Sebastian, 37, 67
Frederik Hendrik, Prince, 62, 76, 95, 96–7, 113, 122
Fromantiou, Hendrik, 298, 299

Galen, Christoph Bernhard von, 296

Gentileschi, Artemisia, 292
Gentileschi, Orazio, *Annunication*, 158
Gerrits, Balthasar, 32–3, 51, 60–62, 300
Golden Eagle, The
  Adrian Paets a visitor to, 213
  depicted in *A Little Street*, 200
  possible subject of lost painting, 203
  and the Van Ruijven family, 92–3, 172
  Vermeer's paintings at, 195, 256–7, 262–3
  women's prayer groups at, 183
Gorinchem, peasants' uprising at, 301–2
Gouda, 131
Gowing, Lawrence, 148
Goyen, Jan van, 251
Grimmelshausen, Hans Jakob Christoffel von, *Simplicius Simplicissimus*, 106, 109, 250
Gronewegen, Pieter, 88
Groote, Geert, 41
Grotius, Hugh, 48
guardroom paintings (*kortegarde*), 108–10, 167–8

Haarlem
  Prinsenhof collection, 99–100
  siege of and massacre at (1572–73), 25–7
Haarlem, Cornelis van, *The Massacre of the Innocents*, 99–100
Haller, Albrecht, 134
Hals, Frans, 60, 83, 84
Hals, Reynier, 84
Harrington, James, 296

Hartigvelt, Johan, 211
  The Truly Defenceless Christian, 209
Harvey, William, 273, 283
Hayden, Jan van der, *The Oude Delft Canal and the Oude Kerk* (1675), 199
Hensbeeck, Catharina van, 132
Hensbeeck, Dieuwertje, 311
Hensbeeck, Dirck Cornelis, 131
Heuckelom, Reynier van, 88
Heyden, Jan van der, 251
hidden churches (*schuilkerken*), 92, 93, 128
Hoek, Jacob van, 194
Hooch, Pieter de, 83, *115*, 251
Hooft, Burgomaster, 38–9
Hooft, P.C., 33, 44
Hooghe, Romeyn de, 308
Hoogstraten, François van, 209, 212, 249
Hoogstraten, Samuel van, 148, 212, 287, 347n22
Houbraken, Arnold, 116, 299, 327
Houckgeest, Gerard, *Interior of the Oude Kerk in Delft* (1651), 158
Huguenots, 281
Huisseau, Isaac d,' *The Reunification of Christianity*, 281

Iconoclastic Fury, 20–21

Jansen, Neeltje, 178, 181
Janszoon, Reynier
  birth (1591), 32
  marries Digna Baltens, 51–2
  links to Remonstrant movement, 54–5, 57–60
  accused of assault, 63

innkeeping, 63–4, 81–3
  birth of son Johannes Vermeer, 77–8
  picture dealing business, 117
Jemmingen, Battle of (1568), 21
Jesuits, 129, 131, 221–2, 227, 232–3
Jews, conversion of, 247, 276–8
Jordaens, Johannes, 298

Kempis, Thomas à, *The Imitation of Christ*, 41, 221
Keyser, Hendrik de, 111
Kick, Simon, 109
Knuijt, Maria de
  family background, 7
  friendship with Vermeer's family, 89–95
  patronage of Vermeer, 165–6, 270–71
  charitable causes, 186
  and the Collegiant movement, 194–7
  women's prayer groups, 172–3, 181–3, 259, 262–3
  links to Adrian Paets, 211–14
  bequest to Vermeer, 228–30, 255–6
  death, 325
  disposal of art collection, 254–6
Knuijt, Simon Vincenten de, 88–9
Knuijt, Vincent de, 89
Kodde, Gijsbert van der, 68
Koninck, Phillips de, 251
Kretzer, Maerten, 85

Lairesse, Gerard de, 287–8
Langue, Willem de, 83, 85, *115*, 126, 144
Lansbergen, Samuel, 93

Leeuwenhoek, Anthony van, 319–20
Leiden, 27–8, 41–2, 98, 190–91
Leonardo da Vinci, *Treatise on Painting*, 147, 290
Libertines, 38
Locke, John, 322, 325, 359n37
Lost Tribes of Israel, 247, 276–8
Louis XIV of France, 295, 300–1, 303, 307–8
Luther, Martin, 6
Luxembourg, Duc de, massacres at Bodegraven and Zwammerdam, 308

Maes, Nicolaes, 246
Magdeburg, sack of (1631), 103
Mander, Karel van, *Schilder-boek*, 87
Margaret of Parma, 20
Maurice of Nassau, Prince, 35, 46–8, 60, 61, 76
Maximilian I of Bavaria, 104
Mechelen, Spanish massacre at (1572), 22–3, 99
Melling, Bartolomeus, 125–6
Mennonites, 37, 70, 112–13, 187–8, 195, 260, 347n21
Merode, Bernard van, 22
Mersche, Magdaleentje Willemsdr van der, 89
Metius, Adriaen, *Institutiones Astronomicae & Geographicae*, 276, 283
Metsu, Gabriel, 246
Michelangelo, 257, 290, 291
Mieris, Frans van, 246
  The Charlatan, 154–5
millenarianism, 246–50, 276–8, 354n82

Minne, Ariaentgen Claes van der, 197, 240
Missio Hollandica, 221–2, 232, 234
Monconys, Balthasar de, 230–34, 238, 279, 352–3n75
Montefeltro, Federigo da, 275
Montias, John Michael, 10, 235, 337n30
Moore, Thomas, *Utopia*, 209
Moreelse, Johannes, 292
Muiden, fortress of, 300–2, 302
Münster, 297, 301
  Peace Treaty (1648), 120–21

Naarden, Spanish massacre at (1572), 23, 98
Nederveen, Moijses Jansz van, 218
Netscher, Caspar, 246, 261
Newton, Isaac, 273
Nicodemites, 38, 57
Nieuwenaar, Count, 23

Ochtervelt, Jacob, 246
Oldenbarnevelt, Johan van, 34–6, 46–9, 50
Oldenburg, Henry, 216, 273, 319
Oortman, Jacob, 348n26
Oranj-Appel, Amsterdam (charitable foundation), 179, 193
Ostens, Jacob, 209, 211
Oudaan, Frans Joachimsz, 93–4, 210
Oudaan, Joachim, 209–10, 213, 249, 252, 300, 307
Oudewater, Spanish massacres at, 41, 99

Paciotto of Urbino, Francesco, 21
Paets, Adrian
  influence and circle of friends, 209–17

and the Collegiant movement, 222
aversion to Catholicism, 227
patron to Vermeer, 274, 277–8, 282–3
and religious toleration, 322
diplomatic mission to Madrid (1672), 300, 304, 308
and the Collegiant movement, 209–11
death, 325
Paets, Nicolaes, 212, 229, 254, 347n23
Paets, Vincent, 212
Paets, William, 212
Paets II, Adrian, 213
pamphleteers, 113–14, 304
Parival, Jean de, 134
Parma, Alessandro Farnese, Duke of, 30
Pauw, Adrian, 120, 123
Pauw, Philippus de, 320
Penn, William, 174, 278
Philip II of Spain, 20, 30
Philip IV of Spain, 119
Pijnacker, Arent, 91
plague outbreaks, 43, 63
Poel, Egbert van der, 146–7
Poussin, Nicolas, 147
Prinsenhof collection, Haarlem, 99–100
Proust, Marcel, 204, 251

Quakers, English, 174, 175, 247–8, 260

Ranck, Johannes, 125–6
Raphael, 275
Reformation, 6, 37–8
Rembrandt, 83, 148, 187, 187–8, 260
Remonstrant movement
 in Delft and Rotterdam, 91–5
 and Erasmus, 112
 and Johannes Taurinus, 55–8, 76–7
 origins of, 47–50
 reaction to Thirty Years War, 110
 the *Remonstrant Confession*, 64–7
Renialme, Johannes, 144, 152–3
Requesens, Don Luis de, 27–8
Reynst, Gerard, 284, 297, 299
Ribadineira, Pedro, *Legende der Heylighen*, 287
Ribera, José de, *Beheading of John the Baptist*, 299
Richardot, Jean, 22
Richelieu, Cardinal, 95
Rietwijk, Cornelis Damen, 86–7
Rijinsburg, 179–80, 211, 214–15
Ripa, Cesare, *Iconologia*, 286–7
Roldanus, Joost, 119
Rombouts, Jacob, 53–4
Rombouts, Jacobus, 54, 283, 311–12
Rombouts I, Jacques, 53
Rooleeuw, Isaac, 192–4, 348n27
Rosweyde, Heribert, *Legende der Heylighen*, 287
Rotterdam
 Adrian Paets in, 209
 and the Collegiant movement, 174–8
 and Desiderio Erasmus, 110–12
 and the Remonstrant movement, 93–4
Ruckers I, Andreas, 207
Ruijven, Magdalena Pieters van, 7–10, 189, 195–6, 256, 265–6, 310, 326
Ruijven, Niclaes Pietersz van, 58, 59
Ruijven, Pieter Claesz van
 wealthy background, 7

Ruijven, Pieter Claesz van – *cont'd*
   Remonstrant sympathies, 58–9,
     91–5
   at The Golden Eagle, 92–3, 200
   patronage of Vermeer, 165–6,
     172–3, 228, 270–71, 299
   charitable work, 186
   and the Collegiant movement,
     194–7
   possible depiction in Vermeer's
     The Music Lesson, 209
   and Adrian Paets, 211–14
   sale of The Golden Eagle, 268
   death, 309, 358n15
Ruisdael, Jacob van, 251
Ruisdael family, 83
Ruskin, John, 321
Ruysch, Elizabeth, 212
Ruyter, Admiral Michiel de, 300

Samuels, Maritge, 178
Sarto, Andrea del, 139
Sas van Gent, siege of (1645), 96–7
Sephardic Jews, 36
Servetus, Michael, 43
Silvercroon, Pieter Spierincx, 166, 190
Simons, Menno, 37
Slodtz, Jean-Baptiste, 159
Snellius, Rudolphus, 41
Socinians, 176
Soemans, Maritge, 178, 181
Soetens, Cornelis, 145
Sopingius, Christian, 67
Spanish Netherlands, 29–30
Speenhovius, Johannes, 58–9
Spinola, Ambrogio, 35, 61
Spinoza, Baruch, 194, 214–17, 248,
   250, 273, 289, 306–7, 323–4, 325
Spoor, Matthias, 147
Stevin, Simon, 35

Stol, Barend Joosten, 271
Swanevelt, Herman van, 87
Swartepaert, Adrian, 285
Swartepaert, Isaac, 285
Swieten, P. van, 299
Swoll, Hermann van, 283–9, 299

Taerling, Hermanus, 240–42, 310
Taurinus, Jacobus, 56, 72
Taurinus, Johannes, 55–8, 64, 71,
   78, 92, 202, 337n34, 337n35
   Reflections on the Parable of the
     Samaritan Woman, 75–7, 95, 170
Thins, Cornelia, 125, 133, 135
Thins, Jan Geensz, 129, 233
Thins, Jan Willemsz, 135
Thins, Maria
   daughter Catharina's marriage to
     Vermeer, 124–30
   family, marriage and divorce,
     130–38, 342n34
   and Catholicism, 217–28
   finances, 235, 302–3, 311, 313–15
   commits son to *beterhuis*, 241–2
   account of Vermeer's death,
     313–15
   death, 320
Thins, Willem Jansz, 132, 220
Thirty Years War, 101–7
Thoré, Théophile, 4–5, 11, 204, 324–5
Thorowgood, Thomas, 247
toleration, religious, 321–5
tonal painting, 4, 148

Uchelen, Paulo van, 194
United Provinces of the
   Netherlands, 28, 30, 34–9, 48,
   61, 104, 120, 304, 336n16 *see*
   also Dutch Republic
Utrecht, 301, 303

Uylenburgh, Gerrit, 285, 297–8, 299, 312
Uyttenbogaert, Johannes, 49

Vaccaro, Andrea, 118
The Death of St Joseph, 142, 152–3
Veen, Otto van, *Amorum emblemata*, 87, 160, 171
Velázquez, Diego, 119, 143
Velde, Heijndrick van der, 233
Verburg, Jan Dionyssen, 209, 260
Vermeer, Gertruy, 85, 90–91, 94–5, 182
Vermeer, Johannes
  forebears' arrival in the Dutch Republic, 32–3
  birth and baptism, 77–8
  education, 85–8
  apprenticeship, 114–19, 123–4
  marriage to Catharina Bolnes, 124–30
  watchman in the civil militia, 195, 302
  head of Guild of St Luke, 213, 245, 297
  patronage of Adrian Paets, 211, 213–14
  children of, 217–18, 220, 224–6, 309
  and Catholicism, 217–28
  travels from home, 243–6
  location of studio, 244–5
  testifies against false Italian paintings, 298–9
  finances, 310
  loan from Jacobus Rambouts, 54, 311–12
  art dealer, 312
  death, 313–15
  funeral, 316, 358n26
  death inventory, 85–6, 318
  legacy, 321–5
  auction of his works (1696), 12–15, 327
  and history painting, 138–9
  Italian influence, 152–3
  and religious painting, 203–4
  Works: *Allegory of the Catholic Faith*, 285–8, 356n106; *The Art of Painting*, 155, 289–92, 317–18, 320, 325–6; *The Astronomer*, 213–14, 274–8; *Christ in the House of Martha and Mary* (1654), 142–4; *The Concert*, 205–9; *Diana and Her Companions* (1653), 118, 139–42; *The Geographer*, 213–14, 274–8; *Girl Reading a Letter at an Open Window*, 87, 148, 156–62, 318, 344n59; *Girl with a Pearl Earring*, 196, 264–6, 267; *Girl with a Red Hat*, 267; *The Glass of Wine*, 218–19; *The Guitar Player*, 268, 313; *The Lacemaker*, 268, 269–70, 273; *A Lady Writing*, 257–8; *Lady Writing a Letter with Her Maid*, 316, 352; *The Little Street*, 197–203, 244, 262, 321, 324; *The Love Letter*, 312–13; *A Maid Asleep*, 169–73; *The Milkmaid*, 183–9, 192–4, 262; *Mistress and Maid*, 260–62; *The Music Lesson*, 205–9; *Officer with a Laughing Girl*, 110, 118, 166–9, 172–3, 195, 251; *The Procuress* (1656), 153–6; *The Sleeping Maid*, 265; *St Praxedis*, 149–52, 344n57; *Study of a*

Vermeer, Johannes – *cont'd*
  Young Woman, 267–8; *View of Delft*, 4, 147, 192, 234, 251–4, 255, 256, 324; *The Visit to the Tomb* (lost painting), 144; *Woman in Blue Reading a Letter*, 236, 242–3, 318; *Woman with a Balance*, 183–9, 192–4, 262; *Woman with a Lute*, 317; *Woman with a Pearl Necklace*, 258–60; *Young Woman Seated at a Virginal*, 313; *A Young Woman Standing at a Virginal*, 268–9, 313; *Young Woman with a Water Pitcher*, 236–8; *Young Woman with a Wine Glass*, 218–19
Vermeer, Maria (Vermeer's daughter), 217, 264, 267–8, 309, 317, 320
Vermeer II, Johannes, 225, 226, 320
Veryard, Ellis, 130, 306
Visscher, Nicolaes, 291
Vliet, Christiaen van, 319
Vogelsangh, Goosen Michielsz, 38–9
Voltaire, 322–3
Vondel, Joost van, 33

Wallenstein, Count Albrecht von, 104
Walpot, Jan Pietersz, 75
Warmond, and the Collegiant movement, 67–71
Waterlander Mennonites, 70, 195
Weenix, Jan Baptist, 87
Westminster, Treaty of (1674), 312
Westphalia, Treaty of (1648), 105, 122
Wiel, Antony van der, 85, 90, 195, 302
William I, Prince of Orange, 21–2, 24, 28, 335n5
William II, Prince of Orange, 122–3
William III, Prince of Orange, 301, 303–4
Witt, Johan de, 124, 210, 212, 295, 300, 301, 304–7
Witte, Cornelius de, 305–6
Witte, Emmanuel de, *A Sermon in the Oude Kerk, Delft* (1651–2), 158
Witte, Petrus de, 145–6
women: and prayer groups, 173–83
  status in Collegiant movement, 74, 94, 259–60, 324, 338–9n56

Zutphen, Spanish massacre at (1572), 23

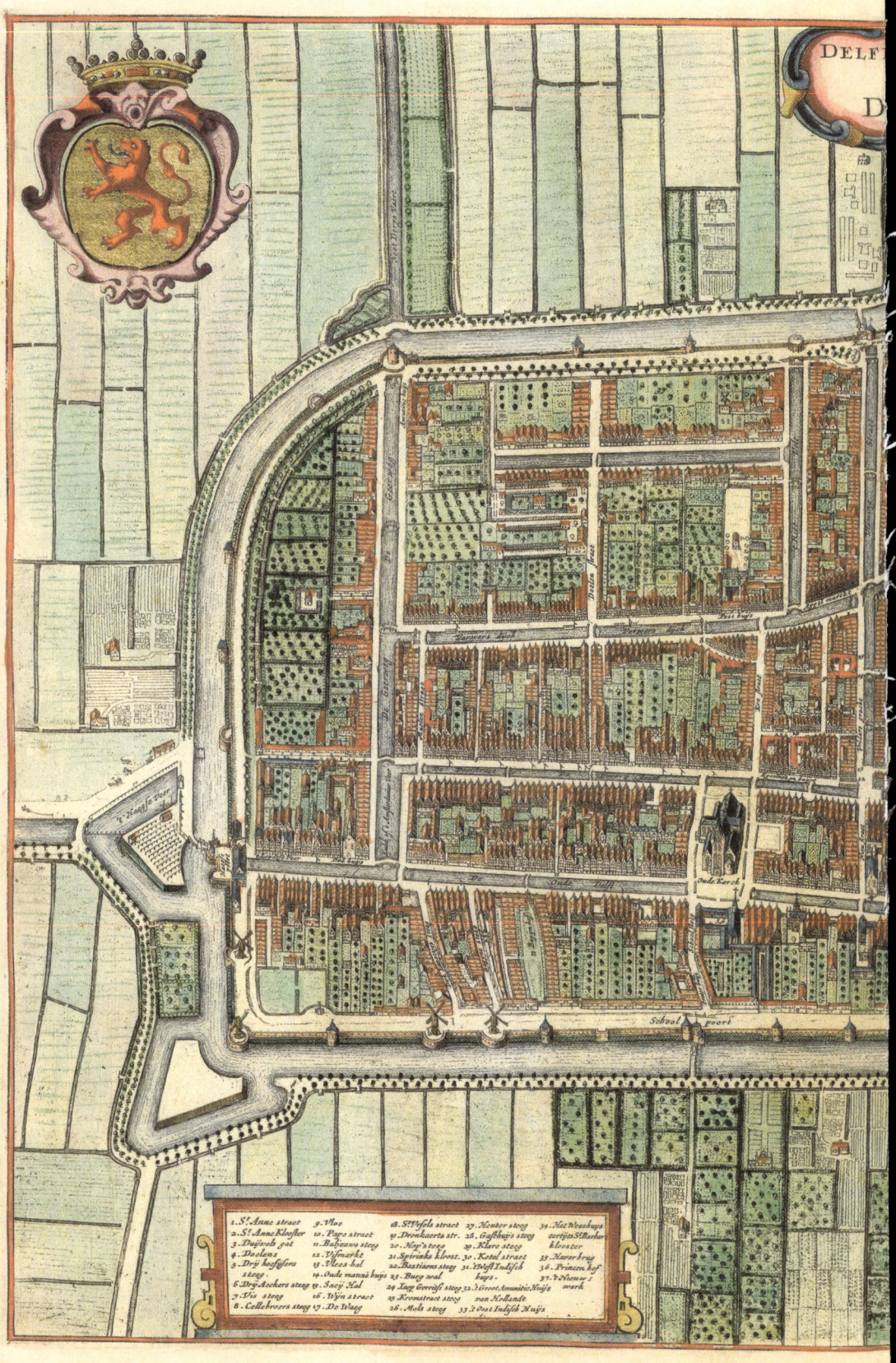